Study Guide

for use with

Principles of
Corporate Finance

Seventh Edition

Richard Brealey
Emeritus Professor of Finance
London Business School

Stewart Myers
Gordon Y Billard Professor of Finance
Sloan School of Management
Massachusetts Institute of Technology

Prepared by
V. Sivarama Krishnan
Professor of Finance
Cameron University

 **McGraw-Hill
Irwin**

Boston   Burr Ridge, IL   Dubuque, IA   Madison, WI   New York   San Francisco   St. Louis
Bangkok   Bogotá   Caracas   Kuala Lumpur   Lisbon   London   Madrid   Mexico City
Milan   Montreal   New Delhi   Santiago   Seoul   Singapore   Sydney   Taipei   Toronto

McGraw-Hill Higher Education

A Division of The McGraw-Hill Companies

Study Guide for use with
PRINCIPLES OF CORPORATE FINANCE
Richard Brealey and Stewart Myers

3 4 5 6 7 8 9 0 VFM/VFM 0 9 8 7 6 5 4

ISBN 0-07-246801-7

www.mhhe.com

Contents

Preface

This Study Guide to *Principles of Corporate Finance* (the text) by Brealey and Myers is designed to help you learn the principles and practice of finance quickly and easily. The Guide has been prepared as an aid to students and will enable you to get the best of out of the text, your finance course work, and this Guide itself. While each student will find her or his own approach and technique to learn from and use this guide, there are at least three ways in which it can help you.

- **As a read-ahead guide to the text and class-work:** The Study Guide can be used as a read-ahead and preparatory guide before you read and work with each chapter of the text. The Guide takes you quickly through the different sections described in the text and can prepare you for the rigors of the detailed discussions found in the text. Each chapter in the Guide sets the scene for the corresponding chapter in the text and explains the concepts and theories contained in the chapter. The Guide explains how each chapter relates to the other chapters in the text.

- **As a study tool and an aid:** The Guide is designed to work with the text and provides you with a number of practice exercises of different types with detailed answers to the exercises given.

- *As an aid to post-class review and for exams:* The Guide summarizes the main points of each chapter in a simple and easily understood language. The exercises and the lists of terms will again come in handy when you are preparing for exams.

THE STRUCTURE OF THE GUIDE

Each chapter of the Study Guide refers to the corresponding chapter of the text and includes the following sections:

INTRODUCTION: The introduction at the beginning of each chapter tells you what the chapter is all about. It sets the scene for the chapter by relating it to the other chapters.

KEY CONCEPTS IN THE CHAPTER: This section contains clear and succinct explanations of the concepts and ideas discussed in the corresponding chapter of the text. The term *concept* is used very broadly and includes ideas, theories, models or a particular perspective used by Professors Brealey and Myers. The section parallels the main descriptive part of the corresponding chapter in the text. This section will be very useful in following the theoretical concepts and ideas discussed in the text. You will find it easier to follow the text if you read this part before you read the text. Then, come back and read the section again to fully digest the concepts and theories.

WORKED EXAMPLES: Nearly all the chapters include a number of worked examples (the exceptions are Chapters 1, 34 and 35). These examples mirror problems you find in the text and problems you are likely to face in exams (and in corporate finance practice, too). The exercises are complete and explain the rationale or models used. Where appropriate, problems are solved through alternate approaches. Chapter 3 includes a sub-section explaining the use of a business calculator to solve time value of money problems. For those who have not used business calculators before, this part should be of help.

SUMMARY:
The summary is a brief overview of what each chapter covered.

LIST OF TERMS: Each chapter includes a list of new terms, which you encounter in the text. Many of these terms are used in the fill-in-questions. You might want to check this section as soon as you read the chapter to see if you can understand the term and its usage. The text has a glossary of all the terms at the back. A complete alphabetical list with reference to the chapter numbers is given at the end of the Guide. The list of terms can be a very useful tool for exams and quizzes.

EXERCISES: The exercises take three forms. A set of fill-in questions includes the new terms you find in each chapter. By completing these questions, you can have a personalized chapter-by-chapter glossary of your own. The second set of exercises consists of problems. These are similar to the types of problems used as worked examples. The third set of exercises is a list of essay questions. Answering these questions require critical thinking, review and analysis of the concepts you learned in each chapter and will be good practice for exams.

ANSWERS: We provide answers to all the exercises other than the essay questions. Complete solutions are given unless a similar problem has been solved earlier in the same chapter. It would be fun to attempt the problems first, before checking the solutions. Again, these are great practice for exams and tests.

Well, I can go on and include tips, suggestions and other great ways to use this guide. But, I am sure that you have seen and heard them all and you would probably like to design your own best approach. I am concluding with one simple advice. Finance is useful because it has great practical value. As you study the different chapters of the text and this Guide, try to put yourself in the position of a manager faced with the issue or problem you are contemplating. See if you can help that manager, because soon you could be that manager! Good luck and have FUN.

V. Sivarama Krishnan
April 2002

1

Finance and the Financial Manager

INTRODUCTION

This chapter provides a brief description of finance and the key role played by a financial manager in the operation of a business. Further, like the customary introductory chapter in most textbooks, the chapter also gives an overview of the book. The chapter is organized in six sections and covers the following topics succinctly.

- Organizational forms for business and the advantages and disadvantages of the corporate form
- The role and the organizational position of the financial manager
- Separation of ownership and management
- Financial markets and financial institutions
- Overview of the book

KEY CONCEPTS IN THE CHAPTER

Corporate and Other Forms of Business Organization: Common organizational forms for businesses include the s*ole proprietorship* – the typical form for a small business owned and managed by a single individual; the *partnerships*, and *corporations*. As the business grows and becomes larger, they tend to be organized as corporations with a large number of stockholders. Most businesses evolve from smaller *privately held* corporations to large *public* corporations. The corporate form enjoys the advantages of limited liability for the owners (stockholders) and the ability to attract large amounts of capital. Professional managers are hired to manage today's typical corporations. This separation of ownership and management gives the firm permanence. Corporations have distinct legal identity and are governed by the *articles of incorporation*. Corporations enjoy considerable flexibility of operation.

The disadvantages of the corporate form include costly legal and accounting set-up and double taxation of earnings.

Financial Manager's Role: Corporations use different *real assets* to run their business and finance the acquisition of these assets partly by raising finances through issue of *financial securities,* which are in the *financial markets* (figure 1.1). The financial manager's primary role is deciding which assets to invest in and how to finance them. Thus the two types of decisions the financial manager is called upon to make are *investing decisions (capital budgeting)* and *financing decisions*. Corporate finance is primarily concerned with these decisions.

Most firms will have other managers in charge of marketing, production, and other functions who work with the financial manager(s) in managing a corporation's operations. Today corporations operate in a global market place with offices and factories located in many countries. Financial markets are also global and companies often raise financing from investors located in many different countries.

Throughout the book, the term financial manager is used in a generic sense meaning anyone who deals with investment and/or financing decisions for a business. Except in very small businesses, the role is typically split into separate positions with the *treasurer* dealing with cash management, raising capital and dealing with investors and financial institutions; and the *controller* entrusted with responsibility for managing the firm's internal accounting, preparation of financial statements, and tax obligations. While small firms typically have a treasurer as the only financial manager, larger firms will have a controller also. As the firm gets larger, the organization of the financial management function becomes more complex and a *chief financial officer (CFO)* oversees the treasurer and the controller with additional responsibility for financial policy and corporate planning. The CFO is part of the top management team for the firm and often is a member of the board of directors. Important financial decisions are often referred to the board of directors and are subject to their approval.

Separation of Ownership and Management: Large corporations have hundreds of thousands of shareholders and it will be impossible to have the "owners" manage the business directly. Thus separation of ownership and management becomes a necessity allowing continuity in management un-affected by changes in ownership. It also paves the way for hiring of professional managers to manage the business. The disadvantage of this separation of ownership and management is that it causes potential *principal-agent problems*. The managers are the agents of the stockholders, who are the principals. The managers may not always act in the best interest of the stockholders. Agency costs are the costs incurred when managers do not act in the interests of the stockholders and their actions need to be monitored. Obviously, owner-managers do not incur any agency costs, as there are no conflicts of interest. Other principal-agent situations in corporate finance include the relationships between the senior managers and the junior managers and that between the lenders and stockholders. The value of a business corporation can be seen as a pie with a number of different claimants such as stockholders, lenders, employees, and even the government vying for a piece of the pie. The different claimants are connected by a web of explicit and implicit contracts. To the extent that the interests of the different claimants differ, conflicts and potential agency problems arise. The principal-agent problem would be easier to solve but for the fact that the parties involved have different information about the value of the business. In other words, agency problems are complicated by *information asymmetry*. Financial managers need to recognize the information asymmetry involved before attempting solutions to the agency problems. The problems of agency costs and information asymmetry receive detailed coverage in later chapters.

Financial Markets and Institutions: Corporations issue stocks and bonds to raise funds for their operations. These are known as *primary issues* and the market in which these issues are sold is known as the primary market. The bonds and stocks later trade in *secondary transactions*, which do not affect the company's cash position or the balance sheet. The daily transactions in the New York Stock Exchange are examples of secondary transactions. Financial markets include physical exchanges such as the New York or Tokyo Stock Exchanges or network of dealers operating through the electronic media. Examples of the latter kind include the over-the-counter exchange and the inter-bank foreign exchange market.

Financial institutions such as banks and insurance companies are also important sources of financing for businesses. These institutions are known as financial intermediaries and they enable flow of capital from the people and institutions, which have savings to the businesses and individuals who need financing. Examples of financial intermediaries include banks, savings and loan companies, mutual funds, and insurance companies. These intermediaries channel and repackage the cash flows they receive from their customers such as depositors, insurance policy holders and investors into loans to individuals and loans to and investments in businesses and other entities. Financial institutions provide *payment mechanism* for the economy and offer *risk pooling,* loans and deposits, and other services to their customers. They are essential to well-functioning market economies.

Overview of the Textbook: The next 34 chapters of the book cover topics, which can be broadly classified into three groups: investment decisions, financing decisions, and decisions where investment and financing interact in such a way that they cannot be separated. The table below provides a summary listing of the different sections, chapters, and topics covered in the book.

Sections	Part	Chapters	Key Topics
Introduction	1	1	Finance and financial managers
The investment decision		2-6	Asset valuation
	2	7-9	Risk
	3	10-12	Capital budgeting practice
Financing decision	4	13-15	Corporate financing and market efficiency
	5	16-19	Theory and practice of dividends and debt policy
	6	20-23	Options and their applications
	7	24-26	Valuing different kinds of debt
	8	27-28	Managing risk
Financial planning	9	29-30	Financial analysis and planning
Short-term financial management		31-32	Managing short-term assets and liabilities
Mergers and governance	10	33-34	Mergers and corporate governance
Conclusion	11	35	What do we know and do not know about finance

SUMMARY

This chapter provides an introduction to the topic of corporate finance and the role of the financial manager. The chapter discusses the corporate form of ownership. Large corporations are typically organized as public corporations and are usually owned by thousands of stockholders. Corporations enjoy distinct identity, the stockholders have limited liability, and the owners are not associated with managing the company. The separation of ownership and management enables businesses to hire professional managers to run the business and allows the business to operate independent of changes in ownership.

The financial manager plays an important role in the management of the company and is concerned with decisions relating to investment and financing. Depending on the size of the company, the finance function may be organized in different ways. Small companies have a treasurer while larger firms may have a treasurer and a controller. While the treasurer is in charge of cash management and obtaining finances for the business, the controller's job is to see that money is used efficiently and well. Very large corporations have a chief financial officer, who oversees the treasurer and the controller and is part of the senior management team of the company.

Shareholders would want the managers to maximize their wealth by maximizing the value of the company's stock. Managers might be interested in objectives other than stockholders' interests. This conflict is one of the several different types of agency problems affecting the management of large corporations. Other principal-agent problems include the stockholder-bondholder conflict. The agency problems are complicated by the fact that the agents often have better information than the principals do.

LIST OF TERMS

Agency problem	Investment
Agent	Limited liability
Bond	Partnership
Capital budgeting	Principals
Chief financial officer	Real asset
Controller	Share
Corporation	Securities
Financial assets	Sole proprietorship
Financial market	Stock
Financing	Tangible asset
Intangible asset	Treasurer

EXERCISES

Fill-in Questions

1. Most large businesses are organized as _____.

2. The financial manager is concerned with _____ and _____ decisions.

3. A _____ is responsible for managing cash and raising finances for the business.

4. The _____ oversees the treasurer and the _____ and is part of the senior management team.

5. A company's _____ include machinery, buildings, and patents.

6. Many accounting firms are organized as _____.

7. A one-person business is organized as a _____.

8. Trademarks, patents, and technical expertise are examples of _____ assets.

9. Stocks and bonds are examples of _____ assets.

10. Shareholders of a corporation have _____.

11. Debt securities issued by corporations are called _____.

12. Purchasing new machinery for expanding production capacity is _____.

13. Managers are _____ of shareholders, who are the _____.

14. _____ is the process of investment decision making.

15. _____ are complicated by the information asymmetry between managers and stockholders.

16. A _____ confers part ownership of a corporation.

17. Corporations issue _____ in capital markets to raise money.

Problems

1. Identify the investment and financing decisions from the following list:

a. Buying new machinery
b. Issuing bonds
c. Acquiring a company
d. Borrowing from the local bank
e. Receiving credit from a supplier
f. Buying new computers to replace the old machines affected by the year 2000 problem
g. Building a new warehouse

2. Separate the real assets from the financial assets:
   a. Shares of IBM
   b. Patents for a new process to manufacture microprocessors
   c. Roads
   d. Brand names
   e. Treasury bonds
   f. An IOU from Bill Gates

Essay Questions

1. Why are most large businesses organized as corporations?

2. "Separation of ownership and management is necessary and desirable." Discuss.

3. "Agency problems will not exist if there was no information asymmetry." Discuss.

4. Describe the differences between each of the following:
   a. A tangible asset and intangible asset
   b. Investment and financing
   c. The treasurer and the controller
   d. A corporation and a partnership

ANSWERS TO EXERCISES

Fill-in Questions

1. Corporations
2. Investment, financing
3. Treasurer
4. Chief financial officer, controller
5. Real assets
6. Partnerships
7. Sole proprietorship
8. Intangible
9. Financial
10. Limited liability
11. Bonds
12. Investment
13. Agents, principals
14. Capital budgeting
15. Agency problems
16. Share
17. Securities

Problems

1. a. Investment   b. Financing   c. Investment
   d. Financing   e. Financing   f. Investment
   g. Investment

2. a. Financial assets   b. Real assets   c. Real assets
   d. Real assets   e. Financial assets   f. Financial assets

2
Present Value and the Opportunity Cost of Capital

INTRODUCTION

This chapter introduces the three basic and related concepts that form the very foundation of modern day finance: *present value* (PV), *net present value* (NPV) and *opportunity cost*. Present value gives the current value of a cash flow received at a future point in time. NPV gives the effective net benefit or value of an investment, and is obtained by subtracting the costs of the investment from the present value of the cash flows generated by the investment. Opportunity cost represents the rate of return on investments of comparable risk. Application of these concepts enables you to value different kinds of assets, especially those, which are not commonly traded in well-functioning markets. The chapter also presents the economic theory behind the concepts.

KEY CONCEPTS IN THE CHAPTER

Present Value: One dollar of cash received next year is worth less than one dollar received today. If you have one dollar today and you can invest it at an interest rate of r, this investment will be worth $1(1+r) next year. Therefore, how much is $1 to be received next year worth today? This value is its *present value* and you can see that it will be $1/(1+r). In general:

$$\text{PV of any cash flow } (C_1) \text{ received next year} = \frac{C_1}{1+r} = C_1\left(\frac{1}{1+r}\right)$$

The present value of any future cash flow is its current equivalent. This process of computing present value is called *discounting* and can be extended to future cash flows beyond next year. Chapter 3 deals with the mechanics of computing the PV for cash flows received at different points in time. The rate of interest or return used in computing the PV is called the *discount rate*.

Opportunity Cost: What rate should be used to discount a future cash flow generated by an asset? This rate is the *opportunity cost of capital* and determined as the rate of return expected to be received from alternate investments forgone. The rate should reflect the investment's risk. In simple terms, it is the rate of return on investments of comparable risk. One typically looks to the capital market to identify an investment of comparable risk. We deal with explicit models for measurement of risk and estimation of rates of returns in later chapters. The terms discount rate, opportunity cost, and hurdle rate are often used synonymously.

Net Present Value: NPV of an asset or investment is the present value of its cash flows less the cost of acquiring the asset. Smart investors will only acquire assets that have positive NPVs and will attempt to maximize the NPV of their investments. Presence of well functioning capital markets enable us to extend this rule to the managers of corporations, which have a number of shareholders with different consumption preferences. The *rate of return* received from an investment is the profit divided by the cost of the investment. Positive NPV investments will have rates of return higher than the opportunity cost. This gives an alternate investment decision rule. Good investments are those that have rates of return higher than the opportunity cost. The opportunity cost is a function of the risk characteristics of the investment. The capital market can provide information, which will help us determine the appropriate opportunity cost for different investments.

Separation of Ownership and Management: Section 2-2 explains the theoretical foundation for the NPV rule for investment decisions and the role of capital markets in enabling the individuals to satisfy their individual consumption preferences. As long as the capital market is perfectly competitive, managers of corporations can use the universal rule of choosing only investments that have positive NPVs. This will maximize the stockholders' wealth and this wealth can be traded in the capital market freely. Individual investors can choose their patterns of consumption preferences by appropriate lending or borrowing choices. Thus, corporate investment decisions can be separated from individual stockholders' preferences for consumption, allowing a clear separation of ownership and management. This is a necessary condition for the operation of large capitalist economies.

Shareholders and the Role of Managers: Shareholders own the corporation and would like to maximize their wealth. Individual shareholders will have different preferences with respect to consumption and saving. However, managers need not worry about individual stockholders' preferences as long as the capital market is competitive. Managers should act to maximize the stockholders' wealth. They can do this by investing only in positive NPV projects. Profit maximization is not a satisfactory goal as the definition or timing of profits can be vague and ambiguous. Further, profit by itself does not capture the risk involved in the investment. Assuming that firms operate in competitive markets, a manager maximizing stockholders' wealth also maximizes the society's wealth because the increased wealth comes from value created by the business.

What makes managers act in the interest of stockholders and not in their own narrow self-interests? Three major factors cause the managers to be efficient and act in the best interests of shareholders. These are: i) managers are monitored by different specialists such as board of directors and investment bankers, ii) poorly performing managers are likely to lose their jobs when the companies run by them get taken over, and iii) compensation packages for managers typically include incentives based on stock performance.

The Capital Market and its Role: The existence of the capital market enables efficient exchange of capital between lenders and borrowers. Lenders save and postpone consumption and borrowers can consume now based on expected future income[1]. Existence of a well-functioning capital market enables us to separate the individual stockholders consumption preferences from the corporate management decisions. The capital market is considered perfectly competitive if the following assumptions are satisfied:

- No individual can influence prices
- Free access to market, cost-free trading, and free availability of information
- No distorting taxes

With perfectly competitive markets, the separation of owners' individual interests from the corporation's investment decisions is complete. While the perfect market assumptions may appear to be too good to be true, it is generally accepted that market satisfies these assumptions to a very high degree of approximation. The effects of some of the capital market imperfections will be discussed in later chapters.

Explanation of Formulas and Mathematical Expressions

Notations:
C_0 = Investment (or Cost of) in the project = Cash flow at time 0
C_1 = Cash flow at time 1
r = Discount rate or opportunity cost of capital

Formulas:
$$PV = \frac{1}{1+r} \times C_1 = \text{Discount factor} \times \text{Cash flow}$$

$$\text{Discount Factor} = \frac{1}{1+r}$$

$$NPV = C_0 + \frac{1}{1+r} \times C_1$$

$$\text{Rate of return} = \frac{\text{Profit}}{\text{Investment}}$$

Investment Decision Rules:
    i) Accept positive NPV investments
    ii) Accept investments with rates of return higher than the opportunity cost or the hurdle rate

---

[1] It is important to note that both lenders and borrowers can be individuals, corporations, and governments (city, state, and national). Also, borrowing as described in this chapter is generic and we will see in later chapters that there are different forms of exchange of capital.

Points to keep in mind:
   i) For most projects, C_0 will usually be negative.
   ii) Discount factor will be less than 1.
   iii) The discount rate should be a function of the riskiness of the cash flow.
   iv) The higher the discount rate, lower the discount factor and lower the PV.

WORKED EXAMPLE

Mary Baines, a software engineer has the opportunity to invest in two projects. Details are given in the table below.

Project	Description	Investment	Payback
A	Developing a simple software package for a local bank.	$12,000	$14,400
B	Developing a complex software package for an online travel services company. The payment for the project will be received in the form of stocks in the company.	$12,000	$20,000

1. Calculate the rate of return on each investment.
2. If the opportunity cost or the hurdle rate for the projects is 15 percent, calculate the NPV for the projects.
3. Calculate the NPV if the opportunity cost is 25 percent.
4. Do you think it is correct to discount the two project cash flows with the same hurdle rate? Why or why not?
5. How would you determine the right hurdle rate or opportunity cost for each project?
6. Ms. Baines does not have all the money needed to buy the resources needed for the projects. Does that change her decision on the projects?

SOLUTION

1. Rate of Return on Project A   = ($14,400 - $12,000)/$12,000   = 20 percent
   Rate of Return on Project B   = ($20,000 - $12,000)/$12,000   = 66.7 percent

2. NPV of project A   = -$12,000 + ($14,400/1.15) = $521.74
   NPV of project B   = -$12,000 + ($20,000/1.15) = $5,391.30

3. NPV of project A   = -$12,000 + ($14,400/1.25) = - $480
   NPV of project B   = -$12,000 + ($20,000/1.25) = $4,000

4. The two projects have very different risk characteristics. Project B is more risky and should have a higher hurdle rate.

5. For project A, the risk is nearly identical to the local bank's debt. For project B, the risk is similar to that of investing in the stocks of companies in online travel services business.

6. Ms. Baines should be able to raise the money needed to invest in the project through the capital market.

SUMMARY

The chapter introduces the key concepts relating to valuation of corporate assets. Corporate assets are typically not traded in markets, and therefore need to be valued using present values of cash flows generated by these assets. Present value of an asset is a function of the cash flow produced by the asset and the riskiness of the cash flow. The chapter also introduces two equivalent rules for investment decisions - the NPV and the rate of return rules. The chapter explains the role of capital market and presents the theoretical basis for the NPV rule. The capital market also forms the basis for the widely practiced separation of ownership from the management of corporations. This allows managers to focus on maximizing the corporation's value without worrying about individual stockholders' consumption preferences.

LIST OF TERMS

Capital market	Opportunity cost
Discount factor	Present value
Discount rate	Rate of return
Hurdle rate	Separation of ownership and management
Net present value	

EXERCISES

Fill-in-Questions

1. Present value of a cash flow to be received one year from now will _____ when the discount rate increases.

2. Discount factor will generally be _____ than one.

3. If the discount rate is 12 percent, the discount factor for a cash flow received one year from now will be _____.

4. The NPV rule for investment requires managers to invest only in projects that have _____ NPV.

5. Managers should invest in projects with rates of return _____ than the opportunity cost of capital.

6. A future cash flow is multiplied by the _____ to give its present value.

7. The _____ of an asset is the difference between the PV of its cash flows and its cost.

8. Financial managers will benefit the stockholders if they _____ the individual stockholders consumption preferences and focus only on the NPV of the projects on hand.

9. The expected return from comparable investments in the securities markets gives the _____ _____ for the project.

10. Opportunity cost of capital for a project is _____ of _____ on alternate investments of comparable risk.

11. Higher risk projects will have _____ opportunity cost of capital.

12. We need a theory of valuation for corporate assets because they _____ _____ traded in well-functioning markets.

Problems

1. You can buy a 1-year T-bill for $976 now. The bill will pay $1,000 one year from now. What is your rate of return on this investment?

2. Jose Mercado, a professional baseball player will be paid $15,000,000 by his major league team. He will be paid $5,000,000 now and $10,000,000 1 year from now. Using a discount rate of 12 percent, calculate the PV of Mercado's pay.

3. Calculate the discount factors for the following discount rates: (a) 20 percent, (b) 30 percent, and (c) 100 percent.

4. June Wayne is planning to buy an old apartment building and modernize it into a new condo complex of six condominiums. She can buy the building for $400,000 and the cost of modernizing is estimated to be $350,000. The project will be completed in one year and each condominium is expected to sell for $200,000. Calculate: (a) the expected rate of return on the project, (b) PV of the cash flows from the sale of the condos, and (c) the NPV of the project. Assume the opportunity cost for the project to be 20 percent.

5. John Miser has $20,000 to invest. He is considering two projects. Project A requires an investment of $10,000 and will pay $11,000 after one year. Project B also requires $10,000 but will pay only $10,700 after one year. What should Mr. Miser do if his opportunity cost of capital is: (a) 6 percent, (b) 9 percent, or (c) 12 percent.

14

6. One ounce of gold sells for $280 now. You can also sell a contract to sell gold one year from now at $296 per ounce. (a) If you buy gold now and sell the contract for future sale of gold (with cash flow to come one year from now) at the above prices, what will be your expected rate of return? Assume zero storage cost. (b) If the rate of return on safe 1-year bonds is 3.5 percent, what is the likely cost of storing gold for one year?

7. Imagine an economy in which there are just three individuals: A, B, and C. Each has money to invest and a number of possible investment projects, each of which would require $1,000. A has $2,000 to invest and two projects, each with 11 percent return. B has $1,000 to invest and has projects yielding 11 percent and 7 percent. C has $1,000 to invest and projects offering 15 percent and 12 percent returns. (a) What projects will be undertaken if there is no lending or borrowing? (b) If they do borrow from and lend to each other, what projects will be undertaken and what will the interest rates be?

8. ABC Corp. has opportunities to invest in three projects with potential payoffs next year linked to the state of the economy. Each project requires an investment of $3 million. The payoffs for different states of the economy are given below:

Project	State of the Economy and Project Payoffs			Hurdle Rate
	Recession	Normal	Boom	
A	$2 million	$4 million	$6 million	20 percent
B	$3 million	$3.5 million	$4 million	10 percent
C	$1.5 million	$4 million	$6.5 million	35 percent

Assume that each state of the economy has equal chances of occurring. Calculate the expected cash flows next year, the rate of return, and the NPV for each project. Which project(s) should be accepted by the company?

9. a. Calculate the NPV and rate of return for each of the investments given in the table below. Assume that the opportunity cost of capital to be 15 percent for all the investments.

   b. It is learned that all four projects require the use of a team of engineers who are very busy and will be available to work on only one of the four projects. In other words, you can choose only one of the four projects. Which one will you choose?

Table for problem 9

Project	Initial Cash Flow	Cash Flow in Year 1
A	-$6,000	$12,000
B	-$8,000	$12,000
C	-$16,000	$24,000
D	-$21,000	$30,000

Essay Questions

1. "Corporate managers will generally act in the interests of their stockholders." Discuss.

2. Explain why corporate managers need not be concerned with the stockholders' individual consumption preferences, even though they are managing the firm on behalf of the stockholders.

3. Explain the NPV and rate of return rules for investment decisions.

4. Explain how the existence of capital market benefits consumers and businesses.

ANSWERS TO EXERCISES

Fill-in Questions

1. Decrease
2. Less
3. $1/1.12 = 0.893$
4. Positive
5. Greater
6. Discount factor
7. NPV
8. Ignore
9. Opportunity cost
10. Rate of return
11. Higher
12. Are not

Problems

1. ($1,000-$976)/$976 = 2.46 percent

2. $5,000,000 + PV of $10,000,000 received 1 year from now =
   $5,000,000 + $10,000,000/1.12 = $13,928,571.43

3. (a) $1/1.2 = 0.833$ (b) $1/1.3 = 0.769$ (c) $1/2 = 0.5$

4. (a) Revenue from the sale of condos = 6 x $200,000 = $1,200,000
   Rate of return = Profit/Cost; Profit = $1,200,000 - $750,000 = $450,000

Cost = $750,000; Rate of return = $450,000/$750,000 = 60 percent

(b) PV of cash flows = $1,200,000/1.20 = $1,000,000

(c) NPV = $1,000,000 - $750,000 = $250,000

5. Calculate the NPVs at each cost of capital for both projects.
   a. NPV of project A at 6%   = ($11,000/1.06) - $10,000 = $377.36
      NPV of project B at 6%   = ($10,700/1.06) - $10,000 = $94.34
      Accept both projects.

   b. NPV of project A at 9%   = ($11,000/1.09) - $10,000 = $91.74
      NPV of project B at 9%   = ($10,700/1.09) - $10,000 = -$183.49
      Accept A, reject B.

   c. NPV of project A at 12%   = ($11,000/1.12) - $10,000 = -$178.57
      NPV of project B at 12%   = ($10,700/1.12) - $10,000 = -$446.43
      Reject both projects.

6. a. Expected rate of return = ($296 - $280)/$280 = 5.71 percent

   b. To get 3.5 percent return on the gold transaction, the sale price should be
      $280 x 1.035 = $289.80; therefore the likely storage costs will be $296 - $289.80 = $6.20

7. a. In the absence of lending and borrowing, A will undertake the two projects with 11
      percent return, B will undertake the project with 11 percent return and C will undertake the
      15 percent project.

   b. C will borrow from either A or B to undertake the 12 percent project in addition to the 15
      percent project. One of the 11 percent projects will be dropped. The rate of interest will
      be 11 percent.

8. Project A: Expected cash flow next year = ($2 m + $4 m + $6 m)/3 = $4 m
                 Rate of return = ($4 m - $3 m)/$3 m = 33.33 percent
                 PV of cash flow = $4 m/1.20 = $3.333; NPV = $0.333 m

   Project B: Expected cash flow next year = ($3 m + $3.5 m + $4 m)/3 = $3.5 m
                 Rate of return = ($3.5 m - $3 m)/$3 m = 16.67 percent
                 PV of cash flow = $3.5 m/1.10 = $3.182; NPV = $0.182 m

   Project C: Expected cash flow next year = ($1.5 m + $4 m + $6.5 m)/3 = $4 m
                 Rate of return = ($4 m - $3 m)/$3 m = 33.33 percent
                 PV of cash flow = $4 m/1.35 = $2.963; NPV = -$0.037 m

Accept projects A and B. Reject C.

9. a. Project A:
   NPV = $12,000/1.15 - $6,000 = $4,434.78,
   Rate of return = ($12,000-$6,000)/$6,000 = 100 percent

   Project B:
   NPV = $12,000/1.15 - $8,000 = $2,434.78,
   Rate of return = ($12,000-$8,000)/$8,000 = 50 percent

   Project C:
   NPV = $24,000/1.15 - $16,000 = $4,869.57
   Rate of return = ($24,000-$16,000)/$16,000 = 50 percent

   Project D:
   NPV = $30,000/1.15 - $21,000 = $5,086.96
   Rate of return = ($30,000-$21,000)/$21,000 = 42.9 percent

   All four projects are good investments.

b. Since only one of the four projects can be chosen, the right decision will be to choose the project with the highest NPV. Choose Project D. This is an example where the NPV rule and the rate of return rule give different decisions.

3

How to Calculate Present Values

INTRODUCTION

This chapter helps you build expertise in calculating present values. The lessons learned in Chapter 2 form the foundation for the chapter. We start with the cash flow one year from now and extend the basic approach to the computation of present value of any stream of cash flows. It is very useful to learn short cuts to calculate the present values of three special types of cash-flow streams, which occur often in real life finance problems. These are:

- Perpetuity: a fixed payment each year forever
- Cash flows growing at a constant rate: payments increasing at a constant rate each year forever
- Annuity: a fixed payment each year for a limited number of years

The chapter also explains the difference between compound interest and simple interest and the effect of different compounding intervals.

Present value calculations can be done in several ways: using the basic formulas, using the tables given in the text, using business calculators or using computer spreadsheet software like Excel. We provide solutions using both the tables and a popular business calculator (BA II Plus).

KEY CONCEPTS IN THE CHAPTER

Present Value of a Stream of Cash Flows: We learned in the last chapter that the present value (PV) of a cash flow received one year from now is:

$$PV = \frac{C_1}{1+r} ; \text{ where } C_1 \text{ is the cash flow and r is the discount rate.}$$

Alternately, $PV = DF_1 \times C$, where DF_1 is known as the discount factor and $= \dfrac{1}{1+r}$

We can extend this approach and calculate the PV of any future cash flow.

> PV of C_2 received two years from now $\quad = C_2/(1+r)^2 = DF_2 \times C_2$
> PV of a cash flow received t years from now $\quad = C_t/(1+r)^t = DFt \times C_t$;
> where $DF_t = 1/(1+r)^t$.

For a stream of cash flows C_1, C_2,... C_t received at 1, 2,...t years from now, the present value is the sum of present values of the individual cash flows.

$$PV = \frac{C_1}{(1+r)} + \frac{C_2}{(1+r)^2} + \ldots + \frac{C_t}{(1+r)^t} = DF_1 x C_1 + DF_2 x C_2 + \ldots + DF_t x C_t$$

Appendix 1 in the text gives values of the discount factors for different rates of return. The general formula for the present value of a stream of cash flows, known as the discounted cash flow formula, is given below:

$$PV = \sum_{t=1}^{n} \frac{C_t}{(1+r)^t}$$

All time value of money (TVM) problems use this basic relationship. Here is an example of a present value problem. Mary just signed up with a women's professional basketball team and has been offered a contract, which pays her $3 million next year, $4 million the year after and $5 million in three years. If the discount rate is 12 percent, what is the present value of the total payments to Mary?

Present value = $3/1.12 + 4/(1.12)^2 + 5/(1.12)^3 = 2.6786 + 3.1888 + 3.5589 = \$9.4263$ million

Alternately we can use the discount factors given in Appendix 1.

Year	Cash flow	Discount factor (12%)	Present value
1	$3 million	0.893	3x0.893 = 2.679
2	$4 million	0.797	4x0.797 = 3.188
3	$5 million	0.712	5x0.712 = 3.560
Total			$9.427 million

The steps involved in this approach to computing present values of a stream of cash flows are:

1. Write the column showing cash flows in each year.
2. Write next to it the discount factors (from Appendix Table 1).
3. Multiply across.
4. Add to get the total present value.

We can use a business calculator to directly calculate the present values. This is shown in the worked examples given later in this chapter.

Future Value: $1 invested at an annual rate of r will grow to $1(1 + r) at the end of 1 year. This is the future value of $1 when compounded at a rate of r for 1 year. If the amount is invested for 2 years the future value will be $1(1 + r)^2$. In general, future values can be expressed as:

$$FV = PV (1+r)^t = FVF \times PV; \text{ where } FVF = (1+r)^t, \text{ is the future value factor and is given in Appendix 2 in the text.}$$

20

Example: Joe Jones has invested $246,000 in mutual funds as part of his pension plan. How much will this amount accumulate to in 15 years if the mutual funds earn an annual return of 8 percent?

Future value = $246,000 $(1.08)^{15}$ = 246,000 x 3.172 = $780,312
(3.172 is the future value factor for 8 percent and 15 years given in Appendix 2)

Special Streams of Cash Flows: There are three special types of cash flow streams commonly encountered in business and everyday life. Short cuts are available to compute the present values (and future values) of these special cases. The special cases are discussed next.

Perpetuity: A perpetuity is an unending stream of equal payments received or paid at equal intervals of time. Imagine you have $5,000 invested in a bank account and the bank promises to pay you $250 every year as long as you have the money with the bank. The rate of return on this investment is $250/$5,000 = 5%. This can go on forever if you keep the deposit with the bank.

The rate of return on a perpetuity = Payment/Present value.
Or, $r = \dfrac{C}{PV}$, or $PV = \dfrac{C}{r}$

It follows that the present value of a stream of equal payments received each year forever will simply be the payment divided by the rate of return.

Alternately, you might prefer to remember that the annual payment is just the principal value times the interest rate ($250 = $5,000 x 0.05, or C = PV x r). Now you can rearrange the expression to get PV = C/r.

Example: Jane Rushton wants to endow a Chair in the English Department at Haights State University. The University suggests an endowment with an annual income of $75,000. If the endowment investments can earn 8 percent annually, how much should Ms. Rushton donate now?

Donation = Annual Payment/Rate of return = $75,000/0.08 = $937,500

Cash flows growing at a constant rate: The present value of a stream of cash flows growing at a constant rate, g, is given by the following formula:

$$PV = \dfrac{C_1}{r - g}$$, where C_1 is the cash flow to be received one year from now.

The formula works as long as r is greater than g.

Example: Haights State University (refer to the previous example) suggests that the endowment income should be annually adjusted for expected salary growth of 5 percent. How much should the initial endowment be if the first year's income is $75,000 and the estimated rate of return on the investments is 8 percent?

Donation = $75,000/(0.08-0.05) = $2,500,000

21

<u>Annuity</u>: Annuities are "truncated" perpetuities. The present value of an annuity for 15 years is the difference in the present values of a perpetuity now (first payment at the end of this year) and the present value of another perpetuity with first payment at the end of 16 years. You can generalize this approach and get the present value for a t year annuity as PV (perpetuity A) – PV (Perpetuity B), where the payments for A starts next year and payments for B starts at the end of t+1 years.

$$PV(PerpetuityA) = \frac{C}{r}$$

$$PV(PerpetuityB) = \frac{C}{r} \, x \, \frac{1}{(1+r)^t}$$

PV(Annuity t years) = PV(Perpetuity A) – PV(Perpetuity B)

$$= C(\frac{1}{r} - \frac{1}{r(1+r)^t})$$

$$= C(\text{Annuity Factor}).$$

The annuity factors for a range of values of r and t are given in Appendix 3. This annuity assumes that payments will come at the end of each year and is called *ordinary annuity*. A stream of cash flows with payments at the beginning of each year is called an *annuity due*. Since each payment in the annuity due begins one year earlier, the present value of the annuity due will be higher than the present value of an ordinary annuity by a factor of (1+r) or:

PV (Annuity due) = PV (Ordinary annuity) x (1+r).

Typical examples of annuities include mortgage loans and car loans. Please note that these loans are usually structured as monthly annuities.

Example: Joe Buck bought a car for $21,000 and financed 90 percent of the purchase price with a loan at an annual interest of 6 percent. Joe will repay the loan with 48 monthly payments starting next month. What is his monthly payment?

The loan amount = $21,000 x 0.9 = $18,900 = PV (Annuity) = PV = C x (Annuity factor), where C is the monthly payment.
C = Loan amount/Annuity factor

$$\text{Annuity factor} = \frac{1}{r} - \frac{1}{r(1+r)^t}$$

r = monthly interest rate = 6/12 = 0.5%
Annuity factor = (1/0.005) – [1/(0.005x1.005^{48})] = 42.580
Payment = $18,900/42.580 = $443.87

Simple Interest, Compound Interest, and Present Values: When interest is computed only on the original principal, year after year, the interest is said to accrue as simple interest. When the interest computed for each year or period is based on the original principal plus the accumulated interest for the previous periods, you are getting compound interest. A deposit of $100 earning simple interest of 10 percent annually for 5 years earns only $100 x 0.10 x 5 = $50. If the deposit is earning compound interest, you will earn $100x1.10^5 - $100 = $61.10. The difference gets

22

larger and larger as the number of periods increase. For example, $100 deposited for 30 years at an annual rate of 10 percent accumulates to $400 on simple interest. The same deposit will become $1,744.94 (= $100x1.10^{30}) if the interest were to accrue on compound basis. It is obvious that deposits earning compound interest will earn significantly more compared to those earning only simple interest.

Most finance problems involve compound interest and unless otherwise stated, it is reasonable to assume compound interest.

Compounding intervals: Computation of interest requires specifying the frequency of accounting for interest. A 12 percent annual rate of interest can mean different things depending on how frequently the interest is credited (or debited) to the account. If the interest is credited semi-annually, you have compounding twice a year. This gives you an effective interest rate of $(1 + r/2)^2 - 1$. In general, compounding m times a year gives $(1 + r/m)^m$ after 1 year. As m approaches infinity, $(1 + r/m)^m$ approaches $(2.71828)^r$, which is e^r. This is called continuous compounding. $1 invested at a continuously compounded rate of r grows to $\$e^r$ in 1 year and to $\$e^{rt}$ in t years. Appendix Table 4 gives values of e^{rt}.

Nominal and Real Interest Rates: Nominal interest rates and cash flows measure what happens in ordinary or current dollar units. Real rates and cash flows measure what happens in units of purchasing power. The relationship between real and nominal cash flows are given by the equation:

Real cash flow = Nominal cash flow/(1+inflation rate)

The relationship between nominal interest rate and real interest rate are given by the following equation:

$1+r_{nominal} = (1+r_{real})(1+$inflation rate$)$

An approximate form of this relationship is written as $r_{nominal} = r_{real} +$ inflation rate

For example, if the nominal interest rate is 7 percent and inflation rate is 2 percent, the real rate is $(1.07/1.02) - 1 = 4.9\%$. Using the approximate relationship, the answer is 5 percent.

Bonds: Bonds are debt instruments issued by corporations and governments. They usually carry regular interest payments, called coupons, and have a stated term or maturity. When you invest in a bond, you receive yearly (or more commonly, half-yearly) coupon payments. At the end of the term of the bond, you will receive the principal or face value of the bond. If we know the required rate of return for the investment in the bond, we can calculate the present value of these payments. The price of the bond should equal the total present value of all the coupon payments and the face value payment. For example, if a 10 percent return is required on a 3-year 6 percent coupon bond with a face value of $1000, the price will equal:

$$PV = \frac{60}{1.10} + \frac{60}{1.10^2} + \frac{1060}{1.10^3} = \$900.53$$

Conversely, if we know the price, we can compute the return earned on the bond investment. This return is the yield to maturity for the bond or the internal rate of return (discussed in Chapter

10) for the investment in the bond. Most bonds have semi-annual coupons and the yield and price calculations will have to be adjusted for this fact.

Summary of Formulas and Mathematical Expressions

Formulas: $PV = \dfrac{1}{(1+r)^t} \, x C_t =$ Discount factor x Cash flow

$$\text{Discount Factor} = \dfrac{1}{(1+r)^t}$$

$$\text{Future value} = C_0(1+r)^t$$

Present value of a stream of cash flows =

$$PV = \sum_{t=1}^{n} \dfrac{C_t}{(1+r)^t}$$

PV of special types of cash flows:

$$\text{PV of a perpetuity} \ = \dfrac{C}{r}$$

$$\text{PV of an annuity} \ = C\left(\dfrac{1}{r} - \dfrac{1}{r(1+r)^t} \right)$$

$$= C[\text{Annuity Factor}]$$

$$\text{Annuity factor} \ = \dfrac{1}{r} - \dfrac{1}{r(1+r)^t}$$

PV of a growing perpetuity = $C_1/(r-g)$

Relationship between nominal and real interest rates: $1 + r_{nominal} = (1 + r_{real})(1 + \text{inflation rate})$
This expression approximates to: $r_{nominal} = r_{real} + \text{inflation rate}$

Using a Business Calculator: The business calculator has become a common tool of the business student and is very useful for solving all types of present value problems. While the details of operations differ for the different models, all business calculators share common features, which enable you to solve for the different parameters in typical TVM problems. In this guide, we provide calculator solutions using Texas Instruments' BA II Plus model in addition to solutions using formulas or the present value tables given in the text.

Most business calculators are designed to solve TVM problems in one of two formats: i) the annuity and a single future value format and ii) net present value of uneven cash flows format. The annuity format allows you to calculate any one of five parameters given the other four. The parameters are: present value (PV), future value (FV), payment (PMT), the number of years (periods), and the rate of return or interest rate (I). The NPV format allows direct calculation of NPV or the internal rate of return (IRR) for any stream of cash flows.

Example: What is the future value of $1,600 invested for 5 years in an account earning 6 percent

24

annually?

Before you start work on the problem, please note that this is an annual compounding problem and therefore you have to set your calculator for annual compounding. This can be done as follows: Press 2nd, and P/Y. Enter 1 and hit the Enter key. Your calculator should now read P/Y = 1. Use the down arrow key (second key from the right on the top row) to see C/Y = 1. You have now set the calculator to do discounting and compounding for annual cash flows for which interest is compounded at annual intervals.

Solution: PV = $1,600, FV = Solve, PMT = 0, N = 5, I = 6; Answer: FV = -$2,141.16.

The calculator shows the answer as a negative number to indicate that the direction of cash flow will be the opposite of the initial flow; i.e. you deposit $1,600 now and you receive $2,141.16 five years later. In order to avoid any confusion, from now on, we will follow the convention of using positive numbers for cash inflows and negative numbers for outflows.

Example: What is the annual payment, which will repay a 3-year, $21,000 loan at an interest rate of 9 percent? Assume equal payments.

Solution: This is an annuity problem.
PV = $21,000, FV = 0, N=3, I = 9; PMT = Solve = -$8,296.15

Example: You have invested $72,000 in a mutual fund earning 8 percent annual return. What will be the accumulated value of your account at the end of 12 years?

Solution: PV = -$72,000, PMT = 0, N= 12, I = 8, FV = Solve = +$181,308.25

Example: You have invested $72,000 in a mutual fund earning 8 percent annual return. How many years will it take to accumulate $500,000?

Solution: PV = -$72,000, FV = +500,000, PMT = 0, I = 8, N = Solve = 25.18 years.

Example: You have invested $72,000 in a mutual fund. If you want to accumulate $500,000 in 20 years, what annual rate of return should you earn?

Solution: PV = -$72,000, FV = +500,000, PMT = 0, N = 20, I = solve = 10.17 %

WORKED EXAMPLES

Problem 1: Rose Perez invests $6,500 in a mutual fund that is expected to earn an annual return of 9 percent. How much will Rose have in the account at the end of 5 years?

Solution using the appendix tables: FV factor from Table 2 for 9 percent, 5 years = 1.539; FV at the end of 5 years = 1.539 x $6,500 = $10,003.50

Using calculator: PV = -$6,500, PMT = 0, N = 5, I = 9, FV = solve = +$10,001.06
Note: The difference between the two solutions is caused by the rounded value for the FV factor in the table. The calculator solution is more accurate.
Problem 2: Jane Duck wants to create an endowment income of $12,000 a year for her alma mater, but proposes that the first payment be made 3 years from now. If she can earn a return of

25

6 percent on her investments, how much should she invest now?

Solution using the appendix tables: The present value of the perpetuity will be $12,000/0.06 = $200,000. This amount has to be invested by the end of 2 years so that the first payment of $12,000 will be received at the end of 3 years. PV of this today = PV factor for 6 percent for 2 years x $200,000 = 0.890 x $200,000 = $178,000.

Solution using calculator: FV = +$200,000, PMT = 0, N = 2, I = 6, PV = solve = $177,999.29

Problem 3: Josh Hyman borrows $125,000 to buy his home. The loan carries an annual interest of 9 percent and requires 180 equal monthly payments. Calculate the monthly payment. What will be the balance on the loan when she has made 90 payments?

Solution using calculator:
PV = Loan amount = +$125,000; FV=0, N=180, I = 9/12 = 0.75, PMT = Solve = -$1,267.83

To calculate the outstanding balance after 90 payments, calculate the PV for 90 payments (180-90). FV = 0, PMT = -$1,267.83, N = 90, I = 0.75, PV = Solve = $82,757.11.

Note that the interest rate was set the monthly rate. Alternately, you can do monthly compounding and monthly payment problems by setting the P/Y = 12, C/Y = 12 and entering the annual interest value for I. The calculator set-up would be as follows:
2nd, P/Y; P/Y =12, 2nd, QUIT; PV = +$125,000; FV=0, N=180, I = 9, PMT = Solve = -$1,267.83.

(This problem cannot be solved using the appendix tables as the table does include values for the range of interest rate and number of periods needed for the problem. You can calculate the annuity factor for the interest rate of 0.75 percent and 180 periods or 90 periods using the formula: Annuity factor = $[(1/r) - (1/r(1+r)^t)]$. The value for 180 periods = 98.593, Payment = $125,000/98.593 = $1,267.84. The factor for 90 periods = 65.275, Loan balance = 65.275x$1,267.84 = $82,758.26)

Problem 4: What is the price of a 10-year, 10 percent coupon bond with a $1,000 face value if investors require a 12 percent return? What is its yield to maturity if its price is $1,100? Assume annual coupon payments.

Solution using calculator: PMT = Coupon payment = $100, FV = Face value = $1,000, N = 10, I = 12, PV = Price = Solve = $887.

Yield to maturity for a price of $1,100: PV = -$1,100, FV = +$1,000, PMT = +$100, N = 10, I = Yield to maturity = solve = 8.48 %

Using Appendix Tables:
Price of the bond = Coupon payment x annuity factor + Face value x PV factor
Annuity factor for 10 years, 12 % interest rate = 5.650, PV factor = 0.322
Price of the bond = 5.650 x $100 + 0.322 x $1,000 = $887
To find the yield to maturity, you have to find the price at different interest rates and by trial and

error get the value closest to $1,100. Price at 9 % = 6.418 x $100 + 0.422 x $1,000 = $1,063.80. Price at 8 % = 6.710 x $100 + 0.463 x $1,000 = $1,134. The yield to maturity will be about 8.5%.

SUMMARY

This chapter completes what was started in chapter 2 and describes several techniques for calculation of present values of different streams of cash flows. Shortcuts and formulas are developed for special streams of cash flows such as perpetuity, annuity and growing perpetuity. These have wide applications in finance. The chapter also discusses simple and compound interest and compounding frequencies. The present value technique is applied to valuation of bonds. Present value computations are made easier by the tables that give the values for the discount, future value or annuity factors for a range of returns and periods. The text has the following tables in Appendix A:

Table 1.	Present value of $1 (discount factors)
Table 2.	Future value of $1 (future value factors)
Table 3.	Present value of an annuity $1 at the end of each year for t years)
Table 4.	Future values with continuous compounding
Table 5.	Present value of an annuity received as a continuous stream.

LIST OF TERMS

Annuity

Compound interest

Continuously compounded rate of interest

Coupon rate

Discounted-cash-flow (DCF) formula

Discount rate

Face value

Internal rate of return

Nominal interest rate

Perpetuity

Real interest rate

Simple interest

Yield to maturity

EXERCISES

Fill-in Questions

1. _____ interest is calculated on initial investment only, without reinvestment of interest.

2. The formula for present value is also called the _____ formula.

3. The present value of a future cash flow is calculated by discounting it at the appropriate _____.

4. _____ interest is calculated on the accumulated amount of the investment, with interest reinvested.

5. A constant stream of cash flows for a limited number of years coming at regular intervals is called a (an) _____ .

6. A constant stream of cash flows that go on forever is called a _____.

7. The interest rate, which is the stated rate in loan and other transactions, is the _____ interest rate.

8. Nominal interest rate less the rate of inflation is the approximate _____ interest rate.

9. The amount of money repaid at the maturity of a bond is the _____.

10. Most bonds usually pay regular interest payments called the _____.

11. The principal amount owed on a bond is repaid on its _____.

12. The rate of return on a bond investment when it is held to maturity is called its

_____.

Problems

1. Here are some investments earning different interest rates and invested for different periods. Calculate the accumulated values at the investment period for each one.

   a. $1,000 invested for 4 years at 8 percent interest.
   b. $1,000 invested for 8 years at 9 percent.
   c. $250 invested for 5 years at 7 percent
   d. $250 invested for 10 years at 7 percent.
   e. $800 invested for 5 years at an annual rate of 12 percent.
   f. $800 invested for 5 years at an interest rate of 3 percent every quarter.
   g. $800 invested for 5 years at an interest rate of 1 percent every month.

2. How long will it take to double $1,000 invested at (a) 3 percent, (b) 5 percent, (c) 10 percent, (d) 12 percent, or (e) 15 percent?

3. An investment of $10,000 will produce income of $2,500 a year for 5 years. Calculate its NPV if the discount rate is 9 percent.

4. An investment costing $4,000 will produce cash flows of $1,500 in year 1, $1,200 in year 2, and $2,000 in year 3. Calculate its net present value at (a) 0 percent, (b) 6 percent, and (c) 12 percent.

5. Mary Jane has already saved $10,000 in a mutual fund account and expects to save an additional $9,000 for each of the next 2 years. She expects to pay $12,000 each at the end of 2 years and 3 years for her son's college education. How much can she afford to spend now on a vacation if she expects to earn (a) 7 percent and (b) 10 percent?

6. I will receive from my late uncle's estate $4,000 in 1 year's time and annually thereafter in perpetuity. What is the value of this perpetuity at an interest rate of (a) 8 percent and (b) 10 percent?

7. How much is the previous perpetuity worth if it begins in 5 years' time instead of one year?

8. I now discover that my uncle's will provides that I receive $4,000 in 1 year's time and that this amount is to be increased annually at a rate of 6 percent. What is the present value of this growing stream of income at an interest rate of (a) 8 percent and (b) 10 percent?

9. Bollywood Inc. is expected to pay a dividend of $4 next year. The dividends are expected to grow at a constant rate of 8 percent. If the shareholders require a return of 12 percent, what will be the likely price of the stock?

10. Reenbee Construction is expected to pay a dividend of $2 next year. The company's shareholders require a return of 14 percent. If the current share price is $40, what rate of dividend growth must they be expecting?

11. I took a car loan of $20,000 from my credit union. The loan carries an annual interest rate of 6 percent and has to be repaid in 30 equal monthly payments. Calculate the monthly payment.

12. I am saving for the down payment needed to buy a house. I have just invested $1,000 and I expect to save a further $1,000 at the end of each of the next six years. If I invest my savings at 12 percent interest, how much will I have after 6 years?

13. A store offers the following credit terms on a color television set "slashed" to a price of only $320: only $20 down and 18 monthly payments of $20. (a) Is this an attractive proposition if I can borrow at 1 percent per month? (b) What monthly interest rate is being charged? (c) What annual rate is being charged?

14. How much does $1,000 grow to at continuously compounded interest when invested for (a) 9 years at 6 percent and (b) 6 years at 9 percent?

15. I can get a nominal interest rate of 4 percent on my money market account. If the expected inflation rate is 2 percent, what is the real interest rate I am getting?

16. Jane wants to save for her 3-year-old daughter's college education. She believes she has 15 years to accumulate the needed $65,000. What is the annual amount she needs to invest in a mutual fund that would give her an annual return of 12 percent?

17. What annually compounded rate is equivalent to an interest rate of 12 percent compounded: (a) semi-annually, (b) quarterly, (c) monthly, (d) weekly (or 52 times a year), (e) daily (365 times a year), and (f) continuously?

18. Value a bond which pays 8 percent coupon, has a face value of $1,000, 10 years till maturity, and the investors require a rate of return of 10 percent. Assume annual coupon payments.

19. If the above bond is selling at a price of $1,070, what is the yield to maturity?

20. An U.S. Treasury bond of 12 years maturity and 9 percent coupon is quoted at a yield to maturity of 8 percent. (a) Calculate its correct price, given that it makes semi-annual coupon payments and the quoted yield is semi-annually compounded. (b) Calculate the (incorrect) price that would have been obtained by assuming annual payments and compounding.

ANSWERS TO EXERCISES

Fill-in Questions

1. Simple
2. Discounted-cash-flow
3. Discount rate
4. Compound
5. Annuity
6. Perpetuity

7. Nominal
8. Real
9. Face value
10. Coupons
11. Maturity date
12. Yield to maturity (or internal rate of return)

Problems

1.

	N	I	PV	PMT	FV = Solve	FV Factors	Solution
			Calculator solutions			Using Appendix Table 1 factors	
a	4 years	8 percent	-1000	0	1360.49	1.360	$1360
b	8 years	9 percent	-1000	0	1992.56	1.993	$1993
c	5 years	7 percent	-250	0	350.64	1.403	$350.75
d	10 years	7 percent	-250	0	491.79	1.967	$$491.75
e	5 years	12 percent	-800	0	1409.87	1.762	$1409.60
f	20 quarters	3 percent	-800	0	1444.89	1.806	$1444.80
g	60 months	1 percent	-800	0	1453.36	1.817	$1453.60

2. Using the calculator: PV = $1,000, FV = -$2,000, PMT = 0, (a) I = 3, N = solve = 23.45 years; (b) I = 5, N = solve = 14.21 years; (c) I = 10, N = solve = 7.27 years; (d) I = 12, N = solve = 6.12 years; and (e) I = 15, N = solve = 4.96 years. You can get the approximate answers using Table 1 and looking for the number of years for which the FV factor is close to 2 for each interest rate.

3. You can find the present value of the cash inflows, which are in the form of an annuity. Then, subtract the initial investment of $10,000.
Using calculator: N = 5, I = 9, PMT = -$2,500, FV = 0, PV = solve = $9,724.13
NPV = -$10,000 + $9,724.13 = -$275.87
From Table 3, the PV factor for 5 years, 9 percent = 3.890, PV = $2,500 x 3.890 = $9,725
NPV = -$10,000 + $9,725 = -$275

4. This problem can be most easily solved using the calculator's cash flow work sheet and the NPV function. Enter the cash flows as follows:
   CF_0 = -$4,000 (Initial cash flow),
   CO_1 = $1,500, FO_1 = 1 (This indicates that this cash flow occurs only once)
   CO_2 = $1,200, FO_2 = 1; CO_3 = $2,000, FO_3 = 1
Once the cash flow data are entered, you proceed to the NPV function work sheet by pressing the NPV key. Entering the appropriate values for I (discount rate), and going down the work sheet using the down arrow key, you can compute the NPVs.

(a) I = 0, NPV = $700; (b) I = 6, NPV = $162.33; and (c) I = 12, NPV = -$280.52

5. The amount she can afford to spend on her vacation is the difference between the present values of her savings and the college education costs. First calculate the present value of Mary Jane's savings for the next two years (an annuity with two payments) and add this to her current savings of $10,000.

   a. PV of the 2 year annuity; N = 2, I = 7, PMT = -$9,000, FV = 0, PV = Solve = $16,272.16
      Total PV of savings = $16,272.16 + $10,000 = $26,272.16.
      PV of education costs:
      $12,000 at the end of 2 years: N = 2, I = 7, PMT = 0, FV = -$12,000, PV = Solve = $10,481.26
      $12,000 at the end of 3 years: N = 3, I = 7, PMT = 0, FV = -$12,000, PV = Solve = $9,795.57
      Total PV of education costs = $10,481.26 + $9,795.57 = $20,276.83
      Amount she can spend on vacation = $26,272.16 - $20,276.83 = $5,995.33

   b. PV of the 2 year annuity; N = 2, I = 10, PMT = -$9,000, FV = 0, PV = Solve = $15,619.83
      Total PV of savings = $15,619.83 + $10,000 = $25,619.83
      PV of education costs:
      $12,000 at the end of 2 years - N = 2, I = 10, PMT = 0, FV = -$12,000, PV = Solve = $9,917.36
      $12,000 at the end of 3 years - N = 3, I = 10, PMT = 0, FV = -$12,000, PV = Solve = $9,015.78
      Total PV of education costs = $9,917.36 + $9,015.78 = $18,933.13
      Amount she can spend on vacation = $25,619.83 - $18,933.13 = $6,686.70

6. a. PV of perpetuity = C/r = $4,000/0.08 = $50,000
   b. PV of perpetuity = $4,000/0.10 = $40,000

7. Using Table 1, PV factor for 5 years, 8 percent = 0.681
   Present value of the perpetuity = 0.681 x $50,000 = $34,050

8. a. This is a growing perpetuity. PC = C/(r-g) = $4,000/(0.08 - 0.06) = $200,000
   b. If r = 10 percent, PV = $4,000/(0.1 - 0.06) = $100,000

9. The stock can be valued as a growing perpetuity. Price = $4/(0.12 - 0.08) = $100

10. Price = Dividend/(r-g) = $40, Dividend = $2, r = 0.14
   Solving for g, g = 0.14 - $2/40 = 9 percent

11. Calculator solution: N = 30, I = 0.5, PV = $20,000, FV = 0, PMT = solve = -$719.58.

12. See this as a six-year annuity plus an initial $1,000. Using the table you can calculate the PV

of the annuity plus the initial $1,000. Then calculate the FV of this amount for six years.
Factor from Table 3 for six years, 12 percent = 4.111, PV of annuity = $1,000 x 4.111 = $4,111
PV of total amount available = $4,111 + $1,000 = $5,111
FV factor from Table 2 for 6 years and 12 percent = 1.974
FV in six years = $5,111 x 1.974 = $10,089.11
Calculator solution: N = 6, I = 12, PV = -$1,000, PMT = -$1,000, FV = solve = $10,089.01

13. a. You are taking a loan of $320-$20 = $300. If your interest rate is 1 percent per month, your payment will be $300 divided by the annuity factor for 18 periods, 1 percent (Table 3). Annuity factor for 18 periods, 1 percent = 16.40; Monthly payment = $300/16.40 = $18.29. Since you are required to pay more than this amount, this is not an attractive proposition.

   b. For payment of $20/month, the annuity factor has to be = $300/$20 = 15. This is very close to the factor for 18 periods and 2 percent (14.99). So the effective interest being charged is 2 percent/month. Effective annual rate = $(1.02)^{12} - 1$ = 26.82 percent.

14. a. and b. The answers for both parts are the same because the product of interest rate (r) and number of years (t) is the same and the future value factor for continuous compounding is given by the formula e^{rt}. The value for the factor from Table 4 = 1.716, FV = $1,000 x 1.716 = $1,716

15. The approximate real interest rate = 4 – 2 = 2 percent.
The exact real rate = (1.04/1.02) – 1 = 0.0196 = 1.96 percent

16. This can be solved easily with the calculator as follows:
N = 15, I = 12, PV = 0, FV = $65,000, PMT = solve = -$1,743.58
Alternately, you can use the Appendix tables to solve this problem in 2 steps. First calculate the PV of $65,000 needed in 15 years. Then find the annual payments that will give you this PV.
PV factor for 15 years, 12 percent (Table 1) = 0.183
PV of $65,000 needed in 15 years = $65,000 x 0.183 = $11,895
Annuity Factor from Table 3 for 15 years and 12 percent = 6.811
Annual investments required = $11,895/6.811 = $1,746.44

17. The equivalent annually compounded rate or the effective annual rate (EAR) is given by the formula $(1+i/m)^m - 1$, where i is the nominal annual rate or the annual percentage rate (APR) and m is the frequency of compounding. The EAR for the different compounding frequencies is:

(a) m = 2, EAR = 12.36%; (b) m = 4, EAR = 12.5509%; (c) m = 12, EAR = 12.6825%; (d) m = 52, EAR = 12.7341%; (e) m = 365, EAR = 12.7475%; and (f) EAR = $e^{0.12}$ = 12.7497%.

18. Calculator solution: N = 10, I = 10, PMT = $80, FV = $1,000, PV = solve = -$877.11
    Using Tables: Value = Coupon Payments x Annuity factor + Face value x PV factor
    $$= \$80 \times 6.145 + \$1,000 \times 0.386 = \$877.60$$

19. Calculator solution: N = 10, PV = -$1,070, PMT = $80, FV = $1,000, I = YTM = 7 percent.
    Using the factors from Tables 1 and 3, you can, by trial and error, get the same result.

20. (a) Calculator solution: N = 2x12=24, I = 4, PMT = $45, FV = $1,000,
    PV = solve = -$1,076.23;
    (b) Incorrect price: N = 12, I = 8, PMT = $90, FV = $1,000, PV = solve = -$1,075.36

4

The Value of Common Stocks

INTRODUCTION

This chapter applies the lessons learned from the last two chapters to valuing stocks and businesses. The chapter begins with a description of market activities related to stock trading and follows this with an explanation of stock valuation. Unlike bonds, stocks do not have specified cash flows; however, the value of a share can be seen as the present value of the dividends paid by the stock. This principle of stock valuation, with some modifications, can be applied to valuing businesses in general. The value of any asset is the present value of the free cash flows generated by the asset. The discount rate for computation of the present value should be the required rate of return demanded by the investors for investing in the asset.

The chapter describes three equivalent ways of looking at the value of a stock: i) as the present value of future dividends, ii) as the present value of free cash flow, and iii) as present value of current earnings plus the present value of growth opportunities. The current market price of a stock can be used to estimate the market capitalization rate or the investors' expected rate of return on the stock. This rate is of practical application in setting rates for regulated utilities and other industries.

KEY CONCEPTS IN THE CHAPTER

How Stocks are Traded: Corporations issue new shares in the *primary market*, which is essentially a distribution network of investment bankers, and brokerage firms, who sell these initial issues to individual investors, mutual funds, and other buyers. Once issued, the stocks trade in the *secondary markets*. Well-known secondary markets include the New York Stock Exchange (NYSE), the "over-the-counter market" which is a network of dealers displaying prices through the National Association of Security Dealers' Automated Quotation system (NASDAQ). The Wall Street Journal and other newspapers publish price, dividend, P/E ratio, and other information on stock market transactions.

Valuation of Common Stocks: The value of a share can be derived by evaluating the cash flows generated by the investment. If the stock is expected to pay a dividend of DIV_1 at the end of the year and the expected price of the stock at the end of the year is P_1, then for an investor requiring a return of r, the price of a stock today is:

$$P_0 = \frac{DIV_1 + P_1}{(1+r)}$$

This can be extended to future years, so that the price next year can be written as:

$$P_1 = \frac{DIV_2 + P_2}{(1+r)}$$

Substituting this into the previous equation for P_0 gives:

$$P_0 = \frac{DIV_1}{(1+r)} + \frac{DIV_2 + P_2}{(1+r)^2}$$

You can substitute the value for P_2 in terms of D_3 and P_3 and so on. This gives you the value of P_0 as the present value of dividends expected to be paid on that stock.

$$P_0 = \sum_{t=1}^{\infty} \frac{DIV_t}{(1+r)^t}$$

The value of a firm will be the present value of all future dividends paid on its current outstanding shares. Future dividends on new stocks issued in later years should not be included.

Estimation of Market Capitalization Rate: The expected return, r is often called the *market capitalization rate*. All securities in the same risk class are priced to offer the same expected return. If one stock offered a higher return, everyone would rush to buy it, pushing its price up and the expected return down. We can use the valuation of a growing perpetuity learned in Chapter 3 to value a stock for which the dividend is expected to grow at a constant rate. If the expected dividend growth rate is g, then

$$P_0 = \frac{D_1}{r - g}$$

Note that this formula requires that $r > g$.

For a stock with constant growth dividends, the market capitalization rate r is given by:

$$r = \frac{D_1}{P_0} + g$$

This is a useful formula to estimate the capitalization rate or the required rate of return on a company's stock. This is the *cost of equity* for the company. Care has to be taken to ensure that the estimated growth rate is realistic and closely approximates the market expectations for the stock. Regulators use the above model to estimate the fair rate of return on gas and electric utilities. For companies which have a regular pay out of dividends and reinvestment of remaining earnings, the growth rate can be approximated as: g = return on equity x plow back ratio, where the plow back (or retention) ratio is the fraction of earnings reinvested in the business.

Some cautionary notes on the estimation of the capitalization rate are in order. Estimates for a single stock may be unreliable and it is better to look at the average of estimates for a number of companies. Remember that the estimated growth rate should reflect long-term average growth rate rather that the current high or low rate.

The Relationship Between Price and Earnings: The valuation model derived earlier shows the relationship between dividends and stock price. Investors often classify stocks as *growth* or *income* stocks depending on the relative growth of earnings and the earnings-price ratio. A growth stock typically has low earnings price ratio and provides most of the return to investors in the form of capital gains. It is important to note that growth, per se, does not add value; only growth opportunities which have positive net present value are valuable and worth pursuing. Depending on the type of growth opportunities, we consider three cases.

a. Zero growth case: In this case, all earnings will be distributed as dividends, therefore $DIV_1 = EPS_1$, where EPS_1 is the earnings per share. $r = DIV_1 /P_0 = EPS_1 /P_0$ or the expected return equals dividend yield and earnings price ratio.

b. Growth rate is positive but the projects have zero NPV: Part of the earnings are reinvested and $(EPS_1 /P_0) > (DIV_1 /P_0)$. The investors exchange reduction in current dividends for gain in long-term dividends; however, the return earned is exactly equal to the opportunity cost of capital and there is no gain in value. Again, $EPS_1 /P_0 = r$.

c. A company with positive NPV growth opportunities: In this case, the company's growth adds value and the price of the stock is increased by the investment in the growth opportunities. A dollar of current dividend is traded off for more than one dollar equivalent in future dividends. This growth adds to the value of the company. The relationship among the stock price, earnings and the present value of growth opportunities (PVGO) can be expressed by the following equations:

$$P_0 = \frac{EPS_1}{r} + PVGO$$

$$\frac{EPS_1}{P_0} = r(1 - \frac{PVGO}{P_0})$$

The earnings price ratio will be less than the capitalization rate if the PVGO is positive. The larger the PVGO as a percentage of the stock price, the more the earnings price ratio will understate the capitalization rate. PVGO is rarely negative, as firms are not required to invest in projects with negative NPVs. Typically, the growth stocks will have a higher percentage of their value represented by PVGO and will thus have low earnings price ratios.

Price-earnings (P/E) ratios are the inverse of earnings price ratios and are published along with stock price quotations in the newspaper. They are based on the most recent earnings announcements rather than next year's earnings. Stocks of companies with high PVGO will show high P/E ratios. This implies higher expected future earnings. Of course, stocks whose current earnings are low may also show high P/E ratios. It should be remembered that high P/E ratios do not mean low cost of capital. It should also be remembered that earnings numbers are influenced by the company's choice of accounting procedures and are unlikely to reflect the amount of money, which could be paid out without affecting its capital value. The P/E ratio can therefore be very misleading even for comparisons of similar companies.

Valuation of a Business Using Discounted Cash Flow: Valuing a business is similar to valuing a stock. Instead of looking at dividends, one has to look at the *free cash flow* produced by the business. The free cash flow is the cash flow that can be withdrawn from the business each year after meeting all its investment needs. Growing firms typically invest more than the depreciation amount and investments made might exceed their earnings. During these years their free cash flow will be negative. When the investment needs are less than their earnings, the business generates free cash flow, which is similar to dividends. The value of the business is the present value of the free cash flows generated by the business. The procedure for valuation includes estimating free cash flows to a time *horizon* at which point the cash flows follow a constant growth pattern. The steps involved in valuation of a business are given below:

1. Estimate the free cash flows generated by the business. The free cash flows will be negative for the years when the investment needs of the business exceed its earnings.

2. Choose the horizon date. Free cash flows are estimated to the horizon date from which point the cash flows follow a simple growth pattern. The horizon value can be estimated using one of the short cut valuation formulas.

3. Estimate the horizon value. This will require knowledge of the required rate of return, r. The value of the business can be written as:

$$V = \frac{FCF_1}{1+r} + \frac{FCF_2}{(1+r)^2} + ... \frac{FCF_H + PV_H}{(1+r)^H}$$

The value of the business and the horizon value, PV_H, will be very sensitive to the assumptions used. Therefore, it is always prudent to cross check the value using other valuation measures or benchmarks such as P/E ratios, market to book ratios of other similar companies.

WORKED EXAMPLES

1. Estimation of PVGO: LSB Corp. is expected to earn $6 per share next year. The company is expected to distribute dividends of $3 and reinvest the remaining earnings on projects with an average ROE of 12 percent. Its capitalization rate is estimated to be 9 percent. Calculate the stock price, the P/E ratio, and the PVGO. What percentage of the stock price is represented by the PVGO?

   Dividends next year = DIV_1 = $3
   Plowback ratio = ($6-$3)/$6 = 0.50
   Growth rate = Plow back ratio x ROE = 0.50 x 0.12 = 0.06

Price = $3/(0.09-0.06) = $100
P/E ratio = $100/$6 = 16.67
PVGO = P − (EPS$_1$/r) = $100 − ($6/0.09) = $33.33
Thus, PVGO reflect 33.33 percent of the value of the stock.
An alternate way of estimating the PVGO is to look at the investment made in the first year and its NPV. The $3 invested in the first year earns $3 x 0.12 = $0.36 in perpetuity. PV of this cash flow is $0.36/0.09 = $4, NPV = $4 - $3 = $1. Each year the company is making similar investments, which are growing at 6 percent. Thus, the PVGO is a growing perpetuity = $1/(0.09 - 0.06) = $33.33.

2. Bunny Corp. is an established movie producer that specializes in cartoons and animation movies. The projected earnings and cash flow for the company are given below. Jake Candy wants to buy the business and requires a rate of return of 20 percent on his investment. Estimate the value of the business.

Dollars million

Years	1	2	3	4	5	6
Assets	50	75	100	125	140	151.2
Earnings	12	18	24	30	33.6	36.29
Net Investment	25	25	25	15	11.2	12.10
Free cash flow	-13	-7	-1	15	22.4	24.19
Earnings growth from previous period (%)		50	33.3	25	12	8

The cash flows start growing at a constant rate of 8 percent from the end of 5 years. At this stage, the business is reinvesting one-third of each year's earnings and is earning a ROE of 24 percent. Therefore, the growth rate = 24 x 1/3 = 8 percent. We can choose 5 years as the horizon. The value of the business at this point is that of a growing perpetuity growing at 8 percent.
Horizon Value = Value at the end of five years = 22.4x1.08/(0.20-0.08) = $201.6 million

Value of the business = Present value of free cash flows

$$PV(FreeCashflows) = \frac{-13}{1.2} + \frac{-7}{(1.2)^2} + \frac{-1}{(1.2)^3} + \frac{15}{(1.2)^4} + \frac{22.4 + 201.6}{(1.2)^5} = \$80.98 \; million$$

Note: Present value computations like the above can be easily solved using the Cash Flow and NPV worksheets in the BA II Plus calculator. The calculator entries are as follows:
CF$_0$ = 0, CO1 = -13, FO1 = 1, CO$_2$ = -7, FO2 = 1, CO$_3$ = -1, FO3 = 1, CO$_4$ = 15, FO4 = 1, CO$_5$ = -224, FO5 = 1. Once you complete the cash flow worksheet, use the NPV worksheet: I = 20, NPV (CPT) = $80.98 million.

SUMMARY

This chapter applies the principles of discounted cash flow to valuing stocks and businesses. The cash flows generated by a stock are the dividends and therefore the value of a stock will be the present value of all future dividends paid by it. This does not imply that the return on a stock investment is only in the form of dividends. The value of stock held for one year is the present value of the dividends expected to be received and the expected price at the end of the year. Thus, the return received on a stock investment is the dividend yield and the expected capital gain from the price appreciation. Extending this logic for longer periods will lead to the result that the current price is the present value of all future dividends.

Using the simplifying assumption of constant dividend growth, current price of a stock can be derived as the value of a growing perpetuity: $P_0 = D_1/(r-g)$. The assumption of constant growth should be seen as an approximation rather than an exact condition. The formula also gives one a simple approach to estimating market capitalization rate or cost of equity capital from current market price of the stock: $r = (D_1/P_0) + g$.

The stock valuation model can be used to derive the relationship between earnings, growth opportunities, and the current stock price. The current price of a stock is the sum of the present value of the current earnings in perpetuity and the present value of growth opportunities or PVGO. This relationship also leads to the result that the earnings price ratio will understate the capitalization rate for companies with significant growth opportunities.

The approach used to value stocks is extended to value businesses. In general, the value of a business will be the present value of the free cash flows generated by the business. Free cash flows are similar to dividends and are the earnings less net investments needed to be made in the business to generate the earnings.

LIST OF TERMS

Cost of equity capital	Payout ratio
Dividend yield	Plowback ratio (Retention ratio)
Free cash flow	Price-earnings ratio (P/E ratio)
Growth stock	Primary market
Income stock	Return on equity (ROE)
Market capitalization rate	Secondary market

EXERCISES

Fill-in Questions

1. New York Stock Exchange is an example of a _____.

2. The market capitalization rate for a firm's common stock is also known as its _____.

3. The _____ is the return that investors require from investment in a stock or bond.

4. Annual dividend per share/share price = _____.

5. The proportion of earnings retained in the business is called _____.

6. New issues of stocks are issued through the _____, which is a network of investment bankers and brokerage firms.

7. The proportion of earnings paid out as dividends is called _____.

8. A firm with significant opportunities to invest in positive net present value projects will have a high _____ ratio.

9. Stocks, which give a high proportion of their return in the form of dividends, are usually called _____.

10. Stocks, which are expected to have high price appreciation, are known as _____.

11. The cash generated by a company net of its investment needs is the _____.

12. The ratio of the net profit earned by a company to the book value of stockholders' equity is _____.

Problems

1. Doreme Corp. is expected to pay dividends of $2, $3, and $5 for the next three years. Thereafter, the dividends are expected to grow at a constant rate of 8 percent. If the required rate of return is 16 percent, what will be the current stock price? What will be the stock price next year and at the end of three years?

2. BMK Corp. is expected to pay a dividend of $6 a share next year. The dividends are expected to grow at the rate of 6 percent annually. If the current stock price is $60, what is the implied market capitalization rate?

3. You forecast that ITT will pay a dividend of $2.40 next year and that dividends will grow at a rate of 9 percent a year. What price would you expect to see for ITT stock if the market capitalization rate is 15 percent?

4. If the price of ITT is $30, what market capitalization rate is implied by your forecasts of problem 3?

5. Great Leaps Corp. stock is currently selling at $45. Next year's earnings are expected to be $3. Assuming that the current level of earnings can be maintained without any new investment, calculate the PVGO if the investors require a return of: (a) 10 percent (b) 15 percent.

6. Jack Corp. retains 60 percent of its earnings and invests them at an average return on equity (ROE) of 15 percent. Jill Inc. retains only 30 percent of its earnings but invests them at an average ROE of 25 percent. Which company has the higher P/E ratio?

7. Bear Corp. shares are expected to pay a dividend of $4 next year. The dividends are expected to decrease (because the company's sales are declining on account of an industry wide decline) at the rate of 15 percent annually. If the market capitalization rate is 15 percent, what will be the current stock price?

8. The current earnings of M & M Corp. are $5 a share, and it has just paid an annual dividend of $2. The company is expected to continue to retain 60 percent of its earnings for the next 3 years and that both earnings and dividends will grow at 20 percent a year over that period. From year 4 on, the payout ratio is expected to increase to 70 percent and the growth rate to fall to 10 percent. If the capitalization rate for this stock is 15 percent, calculate (a) its price, (b) its price-earnings ratio, and (c) the present value of its growth opportunities.

9. Big Enchilada Corp. (BEC) has the following estimated earnings and net investments.

Dollar millions

Years	1	2	3	4	5	6
Assets	24.00	40.00	52.00	60.00	68.00	73.44
Earnings	4.80	8.00	10.40	10.80	10.88	11.75
Investments	16	12.00	8.00	8.00	5.44	5.88

The company will continue a payout ratio of 50 percent beyond year 6 and earn 16 percent on the assets. If the market capitalization rate is 15 percent, estimate the value of the business as the present value of free cash flows.

10. Refer to problem 9. What is the horizon value at the end of year 5? If the industry values for mature companies similar to BEC in year 5 are: P/E ratio = 16 and Market-to-book ratio = 1.5. Compare alternate valuation methods to the horizon value estimated using the constant growth model.

11. Big Bull Corp. is expected to pay dividends of $3, $5, and $7 for the next three years. Thereafter, the dividend is expected to grow at the rate 8 percent. If the market capitalization rate is 16 percent, calculate the current stock price and the stock price for each of the next three years.

12. Calculate the dividend yield and capital gains for each of the next three years for the Big Bull Corp. of problem 11.

Essay Questions

1. "High P/E ratios imply high growth." Discuss.

2. What is the relationship between earnings price ratio and market capitalization rate?

3. A company's earnings figure represents money, which in principle may be distributed to shareholders. Explain why the stock price represents the present value of dividends rather than earnings.

4. Some companies have a policy of retaining all earnings and never paying a dividend. Does this invalidate the principle that the stock price equals the present value of future dividends? Discuss.

ANSWERS TO EXERCISES

Fill-in Questions

1. Secondary market	7. Payout ratio
2. Cost of equity	8. P/E ratio
3. Market capitalization rate	9. Income stocks
4. Dividend yield	10. Growth stocks
5. Plowback (retention) ratio	11. Free cash flow
6. Primary market	12. Return on equity

Problems

1. $P_0 = DIV_1/(1+r) + DIV_2/(1+r)^2 + DIV_3/(1+r)^3 + P_3/(1+r)^3$;
   where $P_3 = DIV_4/(r-g) = 5 \times 1.08/(0.16 - 0.08) = \$67.50$;
   $P_0 = (2/1.16) + (3/1.16^2) + (5 + 67.5)/1.16^3 = 50.40$; $P_1 = (3/1.16) + (5 + 67.5)/1.16^2 = \$56.47$

2. $r = DIV_1/P + g = \$6/\$60 + 0.06 = 0.16 = 16\%$

3. $P_0 = DIV_1/(r-g) = \$2.4/(0.15 - 0.09) = \$40$

4. $r = DIV_1/P + g = \$2.40/\$30 + 0.09 = 0.17 = 17\%$

5. (a) PVGO $= P - EPS_1/r = \$45 - \$3/0.10 = \$15$; (b) PVGO $= \$45 - \$3/0.15 = \$25$

6. $P_0 = EPS_0 (1+g) (payout)/(r-g)$; $g = ROE \times plowback$; PE ratio $= (1+g) (payout)/(r-g)$
   For Jack Corp., P/E ratio $= 1.09 \times 0.4/(r - 0.09)$.
   For Jill Inc., P/E ratio $= 1.075 \times 0.7/(r - 0.075)$.
   P/E ratios for Jack Corp. and Jill Inc. are shown for different values of r:

r	10%	12%	14%
Jack Corp.	43.6	14.5	8.72
Jill Inc.	30.1	16.72	11.58

We can solve for the value of r at which the P/E will be same for both companies. The value turns out to be 11.06% and the P/E is 21.1.

7. $P_0 = \$4/[0.15-(-0.15)] = \$13.33$

8. $DIV_0 = \$2$, $DIV_1 = \$2 \times 1.2 = \$2.40$, $DIV_2 = \$2.40 \times 1.2 = \$2.88$, $DIV_3 = \$2.88 \times 1.2 = 3.46$
   $EPS_4 = \$5 \times 1.2^3 \times 1.1 = \$9.50$, $DIV_4 = \$9.50 \times 0.7 = \$6.65$, $P_3 = \$6.65/(0.15 - 0.1) = \$133$
   $P_0 = (2.4/1.15) + (\$2.88/1.15^3) + [(\$3.46 + \$133)/1.15^3] = \$93.99$, P/E $= \$93.99/2 = 47$
   $PVGO = P_0 - (EPS_1/r) = \$93.99 - (\$6/0.15) = \$53.99$.

9. The earnings, investments, and free cash flows (in $ millions) for the first 5 years are given in the table below. From year six, the free cash flows are growing at 8 percent. We can calculate the horizon value at the end of year 5 and then discount all cash flows and the horizon value to the present at the market capitalization rate of 15 percent.

Years	1	2	3	4	5
Earnings	4.80	8.00	10.40	10.80	10.88
Investments	16.00	12.00	8.00	8.00	5.44
Free cash flow	-11.20	-4.00	2.40	2.80	5.44

Value of cash flows from year 6 onwards = Free cash flow$_6$/(r-g) = (5.44x1.08)/(0.15-0.08)
$$= 5.88/0.07 = \$84 \text{ million}$$
Value of the business = PV(Free cash flows)

$$= \frac{-11.20}{1.15} + \frac{-4}{(1.15)^2} + \frac{2.40}{(1.15)^3} + \frac{2.80}{(1.15)^4} + \frac{5.44 + 84}{(1.15)^5}$$

$$= \$34.88 \text{ million}$$

10. Horizon value using free cash flow approach = $84 million
    Horizon value using the PE ratio = 16 x $5.44 = $87.04 million.
    Using market-to-book = 1.5 x 68 = $102 million.

11. $DIV_4 = \$7 \times 1.08 = \$7.56$, $P_3 = \$7.56/(0.16 - 0.08) = \$94.50$, $P_0 = \$3/1.16 + (\$5/1.16^2) +$
    $[(\$7 + \$94.50)/1.16^3] = \$71.33$, $P_1 = \$5/1.16 + (\$101.5/1.16^2) = \$79.74$, $P_2 = \$101.5/1.16 = \$87.50$.

12. Dividend yield for year 1 = $3/71.33 = 4.21%, Capital gains = $(P_2 - P_1)/P_1 = 11.79\%$.

Dividend yield for year 2 = $5/79.74 = 6.27%, Capital gains = 9.73%. From year 3 onwards, the dividend yield will be 8% and the capital gains will also be 8%. The capital gains for a stock with constant growth dividends will equal the growth rate in dividends.

5

Why Net Present Value Leads to Better Investment Decisions than Other Criteria

INTRODUCTION

Chapters 2 and 3 introduced the concept of net present value (NPV) and its use for making investment or capital budgeting decisions. This chapter starts with a review of the NPV approach to investment decision making and then presents three other widely used measures. These are:

- the book rate of return,
- the payback period, and
- the internal rate of return (IRR).

The chapter describes these methods and their major drawbacks. The measures are inferior to the NPV and should not, with the qualified exception of the IRR, normally be relied upon to provide sound corporate investment decisions. The IRR can provide correct and sound decisions if used properly. The primary reason why a chapter is devoted to these measures is that these are commonly used in corporate practice and are often popular. Hence, you should understand the methods and the pitfalls in their use.

The chapter also describes how to take capital budgeting decisions when one is faced with the so-called capital rationing problem. This introduces a fourth method called the profitability index. More complex constraints can be dealt with using a technique called linear programming.

KEY CONCEPTS IN THE CHAPTER

NPV Basics: The first section gives a review of the net present value method. The NPV represents the value added to the business by the project or the investment. It represents the increase in the market value of the stockholders' wealth. Accepting a project with positive NPV will make the stockholders better off by the amount of its NPV. The NPV is the theoretically correct method to use in most situations. Other measures are inferior because they often give decisions different from those given by following the NPV rule. They will not serve the best interests of the stockholders.

Here is a review of the steps involved in calculating NPV, the decision rule for using NPV, and the advantages of NPV. This is followed by similar discussion of each of the other measures.

Calculating NPV:

Forecast the incremental cash flows generated by the project. Determine the appropriate discount rate, which should be the opportunity cost of capital. Calculate the sum of the present values (PV) of all the cash flows generated by the investment.

NPV = PV of cash inflows - initial investment.

Decision rule and interpretation:

Accept projects with NPV greater than zero. For mutually exclusive projects, accept the project with the highest NPV, if the NPV is positive. The NPV represents the value added to the by the project stockholders' wealth. The discount rate should reflect the opportunity cost of capital or what the stockholders can expect to earn on other investments of equivalent risk.

Advantages:

The NPV approach correctly accounts for the time value of money and adjusts for the project's risk by using the opportunity cost of capital as the discount rate. Thus, it clearly measures the increase in market value or wealth created by the project. The NPV of a project is not affected by "packaging" it with another project. In other words, NPV (A+B) = NPV (A) + NPV (B). The NPV is the only measure that provides the theoretically correct measure of a project's value.

Book Rate of Return (BRR): This is a rate of return measure based on accounting earnings and is defined as the ratio of book income to book assets.

Decision rule and interpretation:

Accept projects with returns greater than the average return on the book value of the firm, or some benchmark return. The book rate of return depends on the accounting rules followed by the company and not on the cash flows generated by the project. This is extremely unlikely to maximize the stockholders wealth.

Advantages and disadvantages:

Accounting earnings are reported by firms to the stockholders and the book return measure fits in with the reported earnings and the accounting procedures used by firms. However, the measure suffers from the serious drawback that it does not measure the cash flows or economic profitability of the project. It does not consider the time value of money and gives too much weight to distant earnings. The measure depends on the choice of depreciation method and on other accounting conventions. The BRR can give inconsistent ranking of projects and rankings may be altered by packaging. There is very little relationship between the book return and the IRR. Chapter 12 discusses some of the problems of using book returns.

Payback Period: The payback period is simply the time taken by the project to return your initial investment. The measure is very popular and is widely used; it is also a flawed and unreliable measure.

Calculation:

The cash flows from each year are added to find out the point in time at which the cumulative cash flows equal the initial investment.

Decision rule and interpretation:

Accept projects with payback less than some specified period. E.g. accept projects with payback of 4 years or less. Payback represents the number of years required for the original cash investment to be returned, but the time value of money is ignored. Therefore, it will be misleading to think that all cash flows after payback represent profit.

Advantages and disadvantages:

It is simple to calculate and easy to comprehend. However, payback period has very limited economic meaning because it ignores the time value of money and the cash flows after the payback period. It can be inconsistent and the ranking of projects may be changed by packaging with other projects.

Discounted payback is a modified version of the payback measure and uses the discounted cash flows to compute payback. This is an improvement over the traditional payback in that the time value of money is recognized. A project, which has a measurable discounted payback, will have a positive NPV. However, the other disadvantages of payback still apply. It is also not simple anymore.

Internal (or Discounted-Cash-Flow) Rate of Return (IRR): IRR is defined as the discount rate at which the NPV equals zero.

Calculation:

Follow the steps for calculating the NPV and calculate the NPV for several discount rates. Start with a low discount rate and then calculate the NPV at progressively higher rates till the NPV calculated has a negative value. In general, the NPV will decrease as the discount rate is increased. Plot the NPVs (y-axis) against the discount rate (x-axis). The IRR is that discount rate at which the line crosses the X-axis (NPV=0). Some business calculators are programmed to compute IRR directly.

Decision rule and Interpretation:

Accept projects that have IRR greater than the opportunity cost of capital. IRR is often interpreted as the effective rate of return for the investment made in the project. Strictly, this interpretation is true only for a one-period project.

Advantages and Disadvantages:

Used properly, the IRR will give the same result as the NPV for independent projects and for projects with normal cash flows.[1] As long as the cost of capital is less than the IRR, the NPV for the project will be positive. IRR can rank projects incorrectly, and the rankings may be changed by the packaging of the projects. For mutually exclusive projects, IRR can give incorrect decisions and should not be used to rank projects. If one must use IRR for selection between two

---

1 Normal projects are projects with initial investment (negative cash flows) followed by a number of positive cash flows.

mutually exclusive projects, it should be done by calculating the IRR of the differences between the cash flows of the projects.

The IRR can also be misleading in cases where the project cash flow patterns are the opposite of the normal project. These projects give cash inflows first, followed by outflows. Thus, it is like borrowing and in such cases, the IRR decision rule should be reversed. The project should be accepted only if the IRR is *less than* the hurdle rate.

Another problem with the IRR is that projects whose cash flows change sign more than once may have more than one IRR. In such cases, it may not be obvious whether a high IRR is good or bad. One will need to look into the "NPV profile" (the NPV-discount rate graph) to identify the discount rate range for which the NPV is positive. *Modified IRR* is an improvement over the IRR and is used to overcome the problem of multiple IRRs. The cash flows that change signs during the project's life are discounted using the opportunity cost of capital and added to the cash flows of other years. This removes the multiple changes of sign. IRR does not allow different discount rates to be used for different time periods', i.e., no account can be taken of the term structure of interest rates.

Capital Rationing and the Profitability Index: Occasionally, companies face resource constraint or capital rationing. The amount available for investment is limited so that all positive NPV projects cannot be accepted. In such cases, stockholder wealth is maximized by taking up projects with the highest NPV per dollar of initial investment. This approach is facilitated by the *profitability index* (PI) measure. The profitability index is defined as: NPV/Investment. The decision rule for profitability index is to accept all projects with a PI greater than zero. This rule is equivalent to the NPV rule. The modified rule applied in the case of capital rationing is to accept projects with the highest profitability index first, followed by the one with next highest, and so on till the investment dollars are exhausted. This rule will maximize the NPV and stockholder wealth. If the resource constraint is on some other resources, the profitability index needs to be modified to measure the NPV per unit of the resource that is rationed. When more than one resource is rationed, a more complicated (linear programming) analysis is needed. The profitability index cannot cope with mutually exclusive projects or where one project is contingent on another.

Capital constraints are often self-imposed by companies to force divisions to focus on priorities and to weed out projects that stem from over-optimism. Such cases are termed *soft rationing*. The more serious case of capital rationing is when a firm cannot raise capital to finance all its positive NPV projects. This implies capital market imperfections and is termed *hard rationing*. The use of NPV is still justified in such cases as long as the firm's stockholders have opportunities to invest in capital markets in projects comparable to the ones taken up by the firm.

NPV and Other Criteria: The NPV is superior to other criteria because: i) it is the only measure which considers the time value of money, properly adjusting for the opportunity cost of capital, ii) gives consistent measures of the project's value (i.e. not affected by packaging with other projects), and iii) it clearly measures the value added to the stockholders' wealth. However, the

50

other three criteria for the evaluation of projects are found to be popular in corporate practice. If you have to use them, make sure you use them in the best possible way and understand the limitations of them. For example, always compare mutually exclusive projects on the basis of the difference between their cash flows. Remember that it is the cash flows that determine the value of a project. Inadequate forecast of the cash flows can be far more disastrous than using the wrong appraisal technique. Cash flow forecasts are difficult to make and can be expensive. It does not make sense to waste the forecasts by using an inferior method of evaluation.

WORKED EXAMPLE

Skeleton Rides Inc. is considering an expansion project with an estimated investment of $1,500,000. The equipment will be depreciated to zero salvage value on a straight-line basis over 5 years. The expansion will produce incremental operating revenue of $600,000 and incremental operating costs, excluding depreciation, of $200,000 annually for 5 years. The company's opportunity cost of capital is 12 percent. Ignore taxes. Calculate: (a) payback period, (b) book rate of return, (c) NPV, (d) IRR, and (e) profitability index.

SOLUTION

First calculate the annual earnings and cash flows:

Operating revenues	= $600,000
Less:	
Operating costs	= $200,000
Depreciation	= $300,000

Book Income	= $100,000
Add back:	
Depreciation	= $300,000
Cash flow	= $400,000

a. Payback = $1,500,000/$400,000 = 3.75 years

b. Average book income = $100,000,
    Average book value of investment = ($1,500,000+0)/2 = $750,000
    Book rate of return = $100,000/$750,000 = 13.33%

c. NPV calculation:

	Amount	Discount factor	Present value
Year 0 Initial investment	-$1,500,000	1	-$1,500,00
Years 1 through 5 Cash flow	$400,000	3.605	$1,442,000
Net Present Value			-$58,000

d. IRR is calculated by trial and error. Calculate the NPV at different discount rates:
    NPV at 10 percent = $400,000(discount factor for 10%, 5 years) - $1,500,000

$$= \$400,000 \times 3.791 - \$1,500,000 = \$16,400$$

NPV at 11 percent $= \$400,000 \times 3.696 - \$1,500,000 = -\$21,600$

IRR lies between 10 percent and 11 percent. IRR $= 10 + [16,400/(16,400+21,600)] = 10.43\%$

Note: You can obtain the solution directly by using the calculator.

PV $= -\$1,500,000$, FV $= 0$, PMT $= \$400,000$, N $= 5$, I $=$ IRR $=$ solve $= 10.42\%$

e. Profitability Index $=$ NPV/Investment $= -\$58,000/\$1,500,000 = -0.04$

SUMMARY

This chapter reviews the different decision tools used to evaluate projects. The chapter begins with a review of the NPV, which has already been introduced in the earlier chapters. This is followed by a detailed discussion of three commonly used, but inferior, tools for evaluation of capital budgeting projects. The book rate of return is an accounting measure and suffers from all the weaknesses inherent in accounting earnings being subject to the relatively arbitrary nature of accounting assumptions. The book return does not use cash flows in its computation and can lead to poor investment decisions. The payback period is simply the number of years required to recoup the project's initial investment. Aside from its simplicity, there is not much to be said for the payback; it ignores the time value of money, ignores all cash flows after the payback period, and leads to inconsistent ranking of projects.

The internal rate of return or IRR is based on discounted cash flows and can give correct decisions for independent projects. The decision rule is to accept projects with an IRR greater than the cost of capital. Any project that satisfies this rule will have a positive NPV. However, the measure should not be used for selection of the best among mutually exclusive projects. A modified approach is needed to get the correct decision using IRR when selecting among mutually exclusive projects. The approach involves calculating the IRR for the differences in cash flows of the two mutually exclusive projects.

The NPV is superior to the other decision tools because it gives the correct decision and is a direct measure of the value added to the stockholders' wealth. The only exception occurs when a firm is constrained by capital rationing. This implies that the firm cannot finance all positive NPV projects and should therefore choose projects that give the highest NPV for each dollar of investment. The profitability index can be used to make the correct choice for this situation.

LIST OF TERMS

Book rate of return

Capital rationing

Discounted-cash-flow rate of return

Discounted payback

Internal rate of return

Linear programming

Mutually exclusive projects

Payback period

Profitability index

EXERCISES

Fill-in Questions

1. The _____ is the time it takes an investment to repay its initial investment.

2. The _____ is the time beyond which cash flows could disappear and still leave the project with a positive net present value.

3. The _____ is defined as the book income/book investment.

4. The _____ is the discount rate for which the NPV equals zero.

5. _____ is needed to deal with capital rationing or resource constraint problem spread over more than one year.

6. _____ are competing projects among which only one can be selected.

7. The NPV of the project divided by the investment is called _____.

8. _____ is another name for the IRR.

9. _____ exists when a firm is constrained by limited availability of funds to invest.

Multiple Choice Questions

Choose from among the five criteria to which the statement applies. Net present value (NPV), payback (P), book rate of return (BRR), internal rate of return (IRR), or profitability index (PI):

	NPV	P	BRR	IRR	PI	None
1. Could be misleading if the project cash flow patterns are reversed.						
2. Affected by the depreciation method used.						
3. Puts too much weight on distant cash flows.						
4. May have several values.						
5. Gives the same accept-reject decisions as NPV on single projects.						
6. Works well for single period capital rationing.						
7. Ignores cash flows beyond some point.						
8. Can use multiple discount rates.						
9. Gives consistent rankings even if the projects are packaged together differently.						
10. Gives the same decisions as the NPV for independent projects.						

ite and Company is considering an investment in a new plant, which will entail an immediate capital expenditure of $4,000,000. The plant is to be depreciated on a straight-line basis over 10 years to zero salvage value. Operating income (before depreciation and taxes) is expected to be $800,000 per year over the 10-year life of the plant. The opportunity cost of capital is 14 percent. Calculate (a) the book rate of return, (b) the payback and discounted payback periods, (c) NPV, (d) IRR, and (e) the profitability index. There are no taxes.

.   Jenny Burgess owns a computer reselling business and is expanding her business. The estimated investment for the expansion project is $85,000 and it is expected to produce cash flows after taxes of $25,000 for each of the next 6 years. An alternate proposal involves an investment of $32,000 and after-tax cash flows of $10,000 for each of the next 6 years. The opportunity cost of capital is 13 percent. Calculate (a) payback, (b) book rate of return, (c) IRR, and (d) NPV and advise Jenny.

3. Refer to problem 2. Is there an opportunity cost of capital that would make Mary indifferent between the two projects?

4. For each of the following projects, calculate the IRR, NPV, and the profitability index. Assume the cost of capital to be 10 percent. Rank the projects using each criterion.

Projects	Cash flow in $ (1,000)			
	Year 0	Year 1	Year 2	Year 3
Project A	-100			145
Project B	-100	115		
Project C	-100	230	-120	
Project D	-45	20	20	20

5. An investment of $100 will produce a level stream of cash flows for T years. Find what level of cash flows will give an IRR of: (a) 12 percent and (b) 14 percent for T = 6 years and T = 10 years.

6. Plymouth and Company is considering the following mutually exclusive investments. Calculate the payback, IRR, and the NPV for the two projects. Assume a cost of capital of 13 percent. Which project would you choose? Why do the ranking by the different methods differ?

Projects	Project cash flows – ($1,000s)			
	Year 0	Year 1	Year 2	Year 3
Project A	-400	220	310	0
Project B	-400	130	190	260

7. Ruckhouser Corp. has an opportunity cost of capital of 10 percent and the following projects. Assuming theses to be independent projects, select the best project(s) for the company. Explain why all the projects will not be selected.

Projects	Cash flow in $ (1,000)				
	Year 0	Year 1	Year 2	Year 3	IRR -%
Project A	-112	40	50	60	15
Project B	45	60	-70	-70	16
Project C	-100	-26	80	80	11
Project D	146	-70	-60	-50	12
Project E	-100	450	-550	175	29

8. Refer to question 7. How would your decision change if the projects were not independent projects?

9. Fingerhaus Inc. is considering a project with an investment of $300,000. The project is expected to generate annual cash flows of $85,000 in the first two years and $100,000 from years 3 to 7. At the end of year 8, the company will have to incur a cash flow of $250,00 to clean up the plant facility. Calculate the NPV and IRR for the project. Assume a cost of capital of 12 percent.

10. M & M Corp. has existing operations that will generate cash flows of $150,000 in year 1 and $200,000 in year 2. If the company makes an investment of $40,000 now, it can expect to receive $230,000 in year 1 and $180,000 in year 2. M & M's cost of capital is 12 percent. Calculate the NPV and IRR of the project. Why is the IRR a poor measure of the project's profitability in this case?

11. Please refer to problem 10 above. M & M Corp. finds that the investment needed for the project is $50,000 instead of $40,000. Evaluate the project.

12. Mickey Minn Corp. is considering the following projects. The company is facing resource constraints and can invest only $800,000 this year. Advice the company.

Projects	Investment ($1,000s)	NPV ($1,000s)	IRR (%)
A	100	8	13.9
B	400	43	14.4
C	300	25	16.0
D	200	23	14.1
E	200	21	16.1
F	200	19	15.7

Essay Questions

1. IRR should never be used to evaluate mutually exclusive projects. Discuss.

2. Why is NPV superior to the other measures of project profitability?

3. IRR, used properly, will give correct decisions. Discuss.

4. How can the problem of capital rationing be handled? Discuss the role and limitations of profitability index as the criterion to be used for projects under capital rationing.

5. Why is the measures payback and book rate of return used in capital budgeting?

ANSWERS TO EXERCISES

Fill-in Questions

1. Payback period
2. Discounted payback
3. Book rate of return
4. Internal rate of return
5. Linear programming

6. Mutually exclusive projects
7. Profitability index
8. Discounted-cash-flow rate of return
9. Capital rationing

Multiple Choice Questions

1. IRR
2. None
3. BRR
4. IRR
5. IRR

6. PI
7. P
8. NPV
9. NPV
10. IRR

Problems

1. (a) Operating revenues   = $800,000
       Less depreciation   = $400,000
       Book Income   = $400,000
       Cash flow   = $800,000

       Average book income = $400,000
       Average book value of investment = ($4,000,000+0)/2 = $2,000,000
       Book rate of return = $400,000/$2,000,000 = 20 %

    (b) Payback period = $4,000,000/$800,000 = 5 years
       Discounted payback is the number of years needed to get the PV of the cash flows to equal
       the initial investment.
       Using the calculator: PV = -$4,000,000, PMT =$800,000, FV = 0,
       I = 14%, N = solve = Discounted payback = 9.2 years.

    (c) NPV: Present value of cash flows = $800,000 x 5.216 = $4,172,800
       NPV = $4,172,800 - $4,000,000 = $172,800
       Alternately, using the calculator you can find the present value of the cash flows to equal
       $4,172,892. NPV = $172,892
       (N = 10, I = 14, FV = 0, PMT = $800,000, PV = solve = $4,172,892)

    (d) IRR can be directly obtained by using the calculator:
       PV = -$4,000,000, PMT = $800,000, FV = 0, N = 10, I = solve =
       IRR = 15.1%

2. Proposal 1: Payback = $85,000/$25,000 = 3.4 years
    Book income = $25,000 – Depreciation = $25,000 – ($85,000/6) = $10,833
    Book rate of return = $10,833/$42,500 = 25.5%
    IRR = 19.1% (PV = -$85,000,FV = 0, PMT = $25,000, N = 6, I = IRR)
    NPV = present value of cash flows - $85,000 = $99,939 - $85,000 = $14,939
    (PMT = $25,000, FV =0, N = 6, I = 13, PV = solve = $99,939)

    Proposal 2: Payback = $32,000/$10,000 = 3.2 years
    Book rate of return = $4,667/$16,000 = 29.2%
    IRR = 21.6 %
    NPV = $7,975

    Mary should choose proposal 1 as it has a higher NPV. IRR, BRR, or the payback should not
    be used to choose among mutually exclusive projects.

3. The cost of capital at which the two projects will produce the same NPV can be found by
    calculating the IRR of the difference in cash flows between the two projects. Proposal 1

requires an additional investment of $53,000 and generates extra cash flows of $22,000 for six years. The IRR for this set of cash flows is 17.6 % (PV = -53,000, PMT = 15,000, N = 6, I = IRR). This also means that for any cost of capital below 17.6%, proposal 1 will have a higher NPV.

4. Project A:
   IRR = 13.2% (PV = -100, FV = 145, PMT = 0, N = 3, I = IRR)
   NPV = $8,940 (PV of $145 received 3 years from now is $108.94)
   Profitability index = 8.94/100 = 0.0894

   Project B:
   IRR = 15%; NPV = $4,545; Profitability index = 0.0455

   Project C:
   IRR = -20% and 50%. The project has two IRRs because of the pattern of cash flows (two sign changes).
   NPV = -100 + 230/1.1 – 120/1.21 = 9.917 = $9,917
   Profitability index = 0.0992

   Project D:
   IRR = 15.9%; NPV = $4,737; Profitability index = 4.737/45 = 0.1053

   Ranking of projects:
IRR:	1. C	2. D	3. B	4. A (also C)
NPV:	1. C	2. A	3. D	4. B
PI:	1. D	2. C	3. A	4. B

5. (a) Using the Appendix table 3, the annuity factor for 12% and six years is 4.111. Cash flow = $100/4.111 = $24.32. The factor for 10 years is 5.650. The cash flow = $100/5.650 = $17.70.

   (b) Using the calculator: PV = -100, FV = 0, I = 14%, N =6 years, PMT = solve = $25.72. For 10 years, N = 10, PMT = $19.17

6. Payback for A = 1 + 180/310 = 1.58 years.
   Payback for B = 2 + 80/260 = 2.31
   NPV for A = $37,466; NPV for B = $44,035
   IRR for A = 19.7%; IRR for B = 18.7%

   Based on NPV, the company should choose project B. Payback and IRR rank project A better because of the difference in cash flow patterns. Project A has more of its cash flow in the earlier years.

7. The NPVs for the projects are as follows:

Project A = $10,765
Project B = -$10,898
Project C = $2,585
Project D = -$4,789
Project E = -$13,974

Only projects A and C have positive NPVs. The others are really "borrowing" projects and should not be selected as the cost of borrowing (IRR) is higher than the opportunity cost of capital.

8. If the projects were mutually exclusive, one would select project A as it has the highest NPV.

9. Using the calculator:
CF_0 = -300,000, CO_1 = 85,000, FO_1 = 2, CO_2 = 100,000, FO_2 = 5
CO_3 = -250,000, FO_3 = 1, IRR = solve = 16.6%; NPV: I = 12%,
NPV = 30,054

10. Incremental cash flows are: CF_0 = -40,000, CO_1 = 80,000,
CO_2 = -30,000; NPV: I = 12, NPV = $7,512; IRR = 50 %

11. With an increase of $10,000 in the initial investment, the project's NPV will become negative.   NPV = -$2,488; IRR = 0.

12. The profitability index and ranking based on PI for the different projects are:

Project	Investment	PI	Ranking
Project A	$100,000	0.080	6
Project B	$400,000	0.108	2
Project C	$300,000	0.083	5
Project D	$200,000	0.115	1
Project E	$200,000	0.105	3
Project F	$200,000	0.095	4

Projects D, B, and E should be selected to invest the $800,000.

6

Making Investment Decisions with the Net Present Value Rule

INTRODUCTION

This chapter discusses the details and nuts and bolts issues of making investment decisions and applying the NPV rule in practice. Specifically, the chapter focuses on three tasks faced in practical capital budgeting. The first issue is to determine what should be discounted to compute the NPV. The answer, of course, is cash flows relevant to the project. The second task is the compilation of the "bottom-line" cash flow forecast. The chapter describes the items to be included and also excluded and gives a detailed example.

The third problem in the application of the NPV rule arises when one has to modify the NPV rule to suit special situations relating to mutually exclusive project choices. This often requires converting the NPV into equivalent annual costs or benefits for the project choice. A typical example might involve alternative proposals, with different project lives, for the replacement of existing machinery. The proper evaluation in this case will be to compare the alternatives in terms of the equivalent annual costs rather than the total costs for each alternative. This technique finds extensive application in a number of different situations. The chapter also presents situations where the NPV rule has to be modified because of the interactions between investment projects and other activities or decisions of the firm. These project interactions have to be carefully sorted out and included in the project analysis and decision.

KEY CONCEPTS IN THE CHAPTER

Focus on Cash Flow: Capital budgeting decisions should be based on analysis of cash flows and not accounting earnings. It is important to understand that accounting earnings can differ from cash flows because of the set of rules followed by accountants in classifying income and expenditures. Care has to be taken to ensure that cash flows are counted at the point of time they are received or paid out. This might require more than simple manipulation of accounting numbers.

Incremental, After-tax Cash Flow: Project evaluation should be based on after-tax cash flows caused by or incidental to the project. All the cash flows that are caused by or are due to the project or are changed by the acceptance of the project should be considered. The following are some useful pointers in identifying the relevant cash flows:

Incremental, not average: It is easy to confuse between the average cost and incremental cost. What is relevant to the project analysis is the portion of the cost or revenue in cash flow terms

61

that will change because of the project. Expenses incurred regardless of what happens to the project should not be considered, as they are not affected by the project.

All incidental effects: All cash flows flowing out of the decision on the project should be included in the project analysis. If the project causes a sales increase in another division's business or an increase in administrative expenses, these should be included in project evaluation.

Working capital changes: Changes in working capital (accounts receivable plus inventory minus accounts payable) needs caused by the project are part of the cash flows that should be included. It is easy to ignore these and one has to be careful to account for the changes in inventory, receivables, and accounts payables. The investment in working capital is usually recovered at the end of the project.

Sunk costs: Sunk costs are costs that have already been incurred and will not be affected by the decision on the project. These should be ignored, as they are not incremental to the project.

Opportunity costs: Opportunity costs of all resources, including managers and other personnel, should be included even if there may not be an explicit cash flow relating to that item. When a project uses a resource already owned by the company, the resource is not available for any alternate use. Thus, the execution of the project precludes alternate use of the resource and the project should be charged for the use of the resource.

Allocated overheads: Accounting rules followed by companies often included allocated charges for use of services. These are typically based on the company's historic costs and experiences and do not bear any direct relationship to the project's actual usage of services or other resources. Thus allocated overheads should be ignored and be counted only to the extent they are actual incremental costs.

Financing charges: Interest payments and other financing charges are normally not included in project cash flows. Throughout this chapter, we assume that the project is financed through all equity funds. This enables us to separate investment and financing decisions. The effect of financing mix will be built into project evaluation in later chapters through appropriate adjustments to the cost of capital.

Depreciation: Depreciation is not a cash flow but has cash flow consequences because it is a deductible expense for tax purposes. Most corporations keep two sets of books – one for reporting earnings to stockholders and another for tax returns filed with the Internal Revenue Service (IRS). Our tax laws permit accelerated depreciation for most assets used in business. These are based on notional lives assigned to classes of assets. Table 6.4 in the text gives the depreciation schedules for different classes of assets. The effect of depreciation is to provide a reduction in taxes or *tax shield* equal to the dollar amount of depreciation multiplied by the marginal tax rate of the company.

Consistent Treatment of Inflation: Inflation affects both the project cash flows and the opportunity cost of capital used to discount the cash flow. One has to be careful to treat inflation effects consistently and correctly. The opportunity cost of capital estimated from current market costs are *nominal* costs with inflation effects already built into them. Thus, it is easiest to discount *nominal* (money) cash flows at a *nominal* discount rate. Some companies prefer to project cash flows in *real* terms and discount them at a real rate of interest. The relationship between nominal rates, real rates, and inflation is given by the equation:

$$1 + r_{nomial} = (1 + r_{real})(1 + \text{inflation rate}).$$

It is important to be consistent in the treatment of inflation. Either discount nominal cash flows with a nominal rate or discount real cash flows with a real rate; do not mix them.

NPV in Other Currencies: The general principles of finance you learn in this book have universal relevance and applicability. Thus, while an American company will compute its cash flows and NPVs in US dollars, a Japanese firm will do the same using the same principles we discuss in this and other chapters, but in Japanese yen. A German or French firm will have its cash flows in the Euro, the new common European currency. Some details will differ, though. For example, nominal interest rates, inflation rates, and the opportunity cost of capital may be different from country to country. The tax rates and depreciation rules are decided by the local governments in each country and can be substantially different.

Equivalent Annual Costs: The NPV is the current equivalent of cash flows during the life of a project. For certain situations, the NPV will have to be converted to equivalent annual cost (EAC) or benefit. Converting the present value (or NPV) into equivalent annual costs is easy; you simply divide the present value by the appropriate annuity factor. The EAC is particularly useful for deciding among similar facilities (such as machines) with different lives and for deciding on when an existing facility should be replaced. Some typical cases where the EAC approach is appropriate are discussed below.

Projects with different lives: The basic NPV rule will not provide correct decisions in the evaluation of mutually exclusive projects with different lives. We can convert the project's costs or benefits into annual equivalents and choose the better alternative.

The replacement decision: The capital cost of a new machine can be restated in terms of the equivalent annual cost (EAC). Its optimal life is the one that minimizes its EAC. We can decide whether to replace an existing machine by comparing its cost for the next year (including the loss of salvage value over the year) against the EAC of the new machine.

EAC is simple to compute and use in a world of certainty. Inflation can be factored in or do the analysis in real terms. Other important considerations, such as technological changes or other uncertainties, could complicate the problem.

The cost of excess capacity: Currently available excess capacity of any resource (plant, computers, or a warehouse) may not be free as increased utilization of the resource (such as a computer) may bring forward the date of future replacement of the facility. It is, therefore, essential to consider the cost (an opportunity cost, really) of the use of this excess capacity and factor that into the project's cash flows.

Project Interactions: Most investment decisions involve more than one choice or affect other activities of the business. At the least you can always decide to invest or not to invest, invest now or invest later. Other choices might involve replacing old machinery which still has some useful life left, or choosing between machines with different project lives. Often when one investment proposal is accepted, it means that other alternative proposals must be rejected. These are all choices that are mutually exclusive. While the NPV rule is still useful, it is essential to take a sufficiently broad view of net present value and to remember that the goal is to maximize the present value of the whole company. A new project may affect the value of other investments and sometimes it might be necessary to work out detailed scenarios to unravel these effects.

Optimal timing of investment: The fact that a project has a positive NPV does not mean that it is best undertaken now. It may be even more valuable if undertaken at a later date. The optimal choice of timing is the one that maximizes the NPV. Imagine you have some vintage whiskey for which you can get $1,000 now or $2,000 if you sell it five years from now. If the present value of $2,000 received 5 years from now is higher than $1,000, it makes sense to wait. It is quite likely that you will get even more than $2,000 if you sell six years later or seven years later. The optimal choice will be the one that gives the highest present value.

Fluctuating load factors: A large plant may have positive NPV but is justified only if the NPV is higher than a smaller size plant, which might be able to do the job as well. In other words, you have to consider different sizes of investment and choose the size, which has the highest, positive NPV.

WORKED EXAMPLES

1. Gino's Trattoria is considering a new project, which requires an investment of $2 million. The project is expected to generate sales revenue of $1 million in the first year, $2 million in the second year and $3 million for years 3, 4, and 5. The cost of goods sold is expected to be 75 percent of sales revenue. Other costs are expected to be 7 percent of sales in the first year and 5 percent of sales thereafter. The project will need working capital investment of $200,000 in the first year and an additional $100,000 in the second year. The investment in plant ($2 million) will be depreciated using the MACRS schedule for the 5-year class. If the company's opportunity cost of capital is 10 percent, calculate the NPV for the project. Assume that the plant will operate for 6 years, and at the end of 6 years, the plant can be sold for a salvage value of $300,000. The tax rate for the company is 36 percent.

SOLUTION

Cash flows ($1000s)

Years	0	1	2	3	4	5	6
1. Investment and salvage	-2,000						192[1]
2. Sales		1,000	2,000	3,000	3,000	3,000	3,000
3. Cost of goods sold		750	1,500	2,250	2,250	2,250	2,250
4. Other costs		70	100	150	150	150	150
5. Depreciation		400	640	384	230	230	116
6. Pre-tax profit [2-3-4-5]		-220	-240	216	370	370	484
7. Tax at 36% of 6		-79	-86	78	133	133	174
8. Profit after tax [6-7]		-141	-154	138	237	237	310
9. Operating cash flow [8+5]		259	486	522	467	467	426
10. Change in working capital		-200	-100				300
11. Total cash flows [1+9+10]	-2,000	59	386	522	467	467	918
12. Present value at 10%	-2,000	54	319	392	319	290	518
13. Net present value	-2,000+54+319+392+319+290+518 = -108						

Notes: 1. Salvage value $300,000 less tax of $108,000 = $192,000

2. Marie's Nuts is considering replacing their roaster oven with a new one. They have received two offers. Oven A has an initial cost of $34,000, annual operating costs of $6,000, and an operating life of 4 years. Oven B has an initial cost of $24,000, annual operating costs of $8,000, and operating life of 3 years. Which oven is the better choice? Assume an opportunity cost of capital of 12 percent.

SOLUTION

Present value of costs for oven A = $34,000 + $6,000 x 3.037 = $52,222
Equivalent annual cost = $52,222/3.037 = $17,195
Present value of costs for oven B = $24,000 + $8,000 x 2.402 = $43,216
Equivalent annual cost = $43,216/2.402 = $17,992
A is the better choice as it has lower EAC.
(3.037 and 2.402 are the annuity factors for 4 years and 3 years for discount rate of 12 percent.)

3. Joe Vino inherited a cellar of wines from his aunt. The local wine dealer offered Joe $70,000 for all the entire collection. A sommelier (wine expert) friend of Joe suggested that if he kept the wines for another five years he could sell them for $150,000. If Joe's opportunity cost is 14 percent, what is the best course of action for Joe?

SOLUTION

Present value of $150,000 received 5 years from now = $150,000/1.14^5 = $77,905
Joe will be better off waiting 5 years.

SUMMARY

This chapter describes the application of the NPV rule to practical project evaluation. The focus is on three key tasks faced by financial managers engaged in capital budgeting decisions: i) what to discount, ii) how to compile the overall cash flow forecast from the various details relating to the project, and ii) how to deal with special situations where the simple NPV rule would have to be modified to give the value maximizing decision. Project evaluation should use incremental after-tax cash flows. Specifically, the evaluator should consider all cash flows incidental to and caused by the project. Care has to be taken to ensure that items like working capital increases are considered and sunk costs are ignored.

The treatment of inflation in project evaluation should be consistent and avoid confusion between real and nominal cash flows. If nominal cash flows are used, they should be discounted with a nominal cost of capital. By the same token, real cash flows should be discounted by a real cost of capital.

The NPV rule has to be modified in some cases involving projects with unequal lives, replacement decision for old machinery with some useful life, and the cost of excess capacity. These problems can be evaluated using the technique of EAC. It is also necessary, in the case of excess capacity, to explicitly recognize the opportunity cost of using the capacity, the cost being early replacement of the resource being used.

Project interactions can be of several different types. Some typical cases include optimal timing of investment and fluctuating load factors. For optimal timing, one has to look at the choice, which will maximize the NPV. Evaluation of projects with fluctuating load factors should include explicit consideration of alternatives with different capacities and choosing the one with the highest NPV. The essential point to note in the evaluation of all mutually exclusive projects is the definition of alternative projects available and possible. Also, remember that many projects have interactions that will result in mutually exclusive choices.

LIST OF TERMS

Accelerated depreciation	Recovery period class
Equivalent annual cost	Straight-line depreciation
Net working capital	Sunk costs
Nominal interest rate	Tax depreciation
Opportunity cost	Tax shield
Real interest rate	

EXERCISES

Fill-in Questions

1. Costs that occurred in the past and are irrecoverable are called _____.

2. The cost of a resource for its best alternate use is its _____.

3. Current assets minus current liabilities equal _____.

4. An interest rate adjusted for inflation, so that it represents an increase in purchasing power, is called the _____ rate.

5. The stated interest rates in most transactions have no adjustment for inflation and is the _____ rate.

6. Under_____, the amount of depreciation is the same each year.

7. _____ is the general term for any depreciation method that provides larger deductions in the early years of the asset's life.

8. To work out the after-tax cash flows from an investment, we need to know what_____ is allowed, rather than how it is depreciated for accounting purposes.

9. The tax depreciation allowed for a particular asset depends on which_____it belongs to.

10. The tax depreciation amount multiplied by the tax rate is called the depreciation _____.

11. The _____of equipment is the constant annual charge, which, over the life of the equipment, has the same present-value cost as the equipment.

Problems

1. Ohno Hardware Inc. (OHI) is considering an investment of $5 million in plant and machinery. This is expected to produce sales of $2 million in year 1, $4 million in year 2, and $6 million in year 3. Subsequent sales will increase at the expected inflation rate of 10 percent. The plant is expected to be scrapped after 6 years with a salvage value of $1 million. It is depreciated for tax purposes on a straight-line basis of $1 million per year. Operating costs are expected to be 70 percent of the sales. Working capital requirements are negligible. OHI pays tax at 35 percent. Calculate the expected cash flows in each year and the NPV of the investment when the required rate of return is 16 percent.

2. Repeat the calculation of problem 1, doing the analysis in *real* instead of nominal terms. Discount the cash flows using the approximate real rate of 5.45 percent.

3. How does your analysis of problem 1 change if the new plant qualifies for tax depreciation under the 5-year recovery period class?

4. Kats Corp. is evaluating an investment project, which will cost $40 million and generate taxable revenues of $11 million per year for 7 years. There will be no salvage value at the end of this period. Kats is currently unsure whether the investment will belong to the 3-year, 5-year, or 7-year recovery period class. Calculate the NPV of the project for each of these three possibilities. Kats' tax rate is 35 percent and its required return is 15 percent.

5. An investment of $200,000 in a computer is expected to reduce costs by $40,000 a year in perpetuity. However, the prices of computers are predicted to fall at 10 percent a year for the next 5 years. When should the computer be purchased if the cost of capital is 13 percent?

6. The Bluebird Company must choose between machines A and B, which perform exactly the same operations but have different lives of 2 and 3 years, respectively. Machine A costs $30,000 initially and has annual costs of $5,000. Machine B has an initial cost of $40,000 and annual costs of $7,000. If Bluebird's cost of capital is 10 percent, which machine should it choose?

7. A machine costs $100,000. At the end of the first year, $5,000 must be spent on maintenance. Each year, the cost of maintenance rises by 15 percent. How long should the machine be kept before it is scrapped if the opportunity cost of capital is 10 percent? (Assume the machine has a zero salvage value.)

8. CME Company is considering whether to replace an existing machine or to spend money on overhauling it. The replacement machine would cost $18,000 and would require maintenance of $1,500 at the end of every year. At the end of 10 years, it would have a scrap value of $2,000 and would not be maintained. The existing machine requires increasing amounts of maintenance each year, and its salvage value is falling as shown below:

Year	Maintenance Cost	Salvage Value
0	$2,000	$2,500
1	$3,000	$2,000
2	$4,000	$1,500
3	$5,000	$1,000
4	$5,000	0

If CME faces an opportunity cost of capital of 15 percent, when should it replace the machine?

9. The acceptance of a particular capital budgeting proposal will mean that a new computer costing $200,000 will be purchased in 1 year's time instead of in 3 years' time. This also implies that an extra computer programmer costing $30,000 a year must be hired in year 1 instead of year 3. Work out the present-value cost of these two items when the opportunity cost of capital is 14 percent.

10. Tacoma Timber has vast tracts of timberland. One tract in the northwest region has timber ready for harvest and at current market prices will fetch net revenue of $12 million. If the

company waited for 1 year, 2 years, 3 years, and 4 years, the values would be $15 million, $17 million, $18 million, and $19 million respectively. What is the optimal harvesting point for the company if the cost of capital is 15 percent?

11. How will your answer change if you are told that the above estimates for the timber values are real dollars and not nominal dollars and the cost of capital is nominal value with an inflation component of 5 percent?

12. Redo problem 3 in the worked examples by assuming a cost of capital of 16 percent.

Essay Questions

1. Project evaluation should consider only incremental after-tax cash flows. What are incremental, after-tax cash flows?

2. Depreciation is not a cash flow and therefore should not be considered in project evaluation. Discuss.

3. "We always allocate a proportion of company overhead to a new project in relation to its payroll requirements. After all, in the long run, there's no difference between average and marginal cost." Discuss.

4. Describe how to work out the economic life of a piece of machinery and how to decide when to replace an existing machine, which performs the same function.

ANSWERS TO EXERCISES

Fill-in Questions

1. Sunk costs
2. Opportunity cost
3. Net working capital
4. Real interest
5. Nominal interest
6. Straight line depreciation
7. Accelerated depreciation
8. Tax depreciation
9. Recovery period class
10. Tax shield
11. Equivalent annual cost

Problems

1. The cash flows and the present values are given in the table below.

Cash flows ($1000s)

Years	0	1	2	3	4	5	6
1. Investment and salvage	-5,000						650[1]
2. Sales		2,000	4,000	6,000	6,600	7,260	7,986
3. Cost of goods sold		1,400	2,800	4,200	4,620	5,082	5,590
4. Depreciation		1,000	1,000	1,000	1,000	1,000	0
5. Pre-tax profit [2-3-4]		-400	200	800	980	1,178	2,396
6. Tax at 35% of 5		-140	70	280	343	412	839
7. Profit after tax [5-6]		-260	130	520	637	766	1,557
8. Operating cash flow [7+4]		740	1,130	1,520	1,637	1,766	1,557
9. Total cash flows [1+8]	-5,000	740	1,130	1,520	1,637	1,766	2,207
10. Present value at 16%	-5,000	638	840	974	904	841	906
11. Net present value	-5,000+638+840+974+841+906 = 103						

Notes: 1. Salvage value $1,000,000 less tax of $35,000 = $650,000

2. The real cash flows and the present values are given in the table below.

Cash flows ($1000s)

Years	0	1	2	3	4	5	6
1.Nomianl cash flows (same as in problem 1)	-5,000	740	1,130	1,520	1,637	1,766	2,207
2. Real cash flows[1]	-5,000	673	934	1,142	1,118	1,097	1,246
3. Present value at 5.45%	-5,000	638	840	974	904	841	906
4. Net present value	-5,000+638+840+974+841+906 = 103						

Notes: 1. The real cash flows are calculated by the following formula = $C_t/1.1^t$

3. See the table below.

Cash flows ($1000s)

Years	0	1	2	3	4	5	6
1. Investment and salvage	-5,000						650[1]
2. Sales		2,000	4,000	6,000	6,600	7,260	7,986
3. Cost of goods sold		1,400	2,800	4,200	4,620	5,082	5,590
4. Depreciation		1,000	1,600	960	576	576	288
5. Pre-tax profit [2-3-4]		-400	-400	840	1,404	1,602	2,108
6. Tax at 35% of 5		-140	-140	294	491	561	738
7. Profit after tax [5-6]		-260	-260	546	913	1,041	1,370
8. Operating cash flow [7+4]		740	1,340	1,506	1,489	1,617	1,658
9. Total cash flows [1+8]	-5,000	740	1,340	1,506	1,489	1,617	2,308
10. Present value at 16%	-5,000	638	996	965	822	770	947
11. Net present value	-5,000+638+996+965+822+770+947 = 138						

4. The tables below give the cash flows and the NPV for the 3 different scenarios.

Cash flows ($1000s)

	3- Year class	5 year class	7 year class
Investment	-40,000	-40,000	-40,000
PV of depreciation tax shield	10,719	9,662	8,778
Net revenues	29,747	29,747	29,747
Net present value	466	-591	-1,475

5. The NPV of purchasing the computer after t years is $(-200{,}000 \times 0.90^t + 40{,}000/0.13)/1.13^t$. This expression takes its maximum value of $114,098 (over integer t) for t = 2 years.

6. Present value of costs for A = $38,678, EAC = $22,286
Present value of costs for B = $57,408, EAC = $23,085
A is cheaper.

7. The maintenance cost at the end of year 1 is $5,000, year 2 is $5,000 x 1.15 = $5,750, and so on. You can calculate the PV of the maintenance costs and the initial investment of $100,000 and convert them into EACs for 5 years, 10 years, and so on. The lowest EAC is for 12 years as shown in the table below.

Years kept	PV of cost	Annuity factor	EAC (PV/Ann. Factor)
5	119,459	3.791	$31,512
10	149,192	6.145	$24,279
11	155,974	6.495	$24,014
12	163,063	6.814	$23,931
13	170,475	7.103	$24,000

8. The present value of total costs of the new machine is $24,663. This converts to an EAC of $4914.20. The costs of each year's operation of the old machine (adjusted to the end of each year) are given below.

Years	Cost of operation	How calculated
1	$3,175	(2000+2500)x1.15-2000
2	$4,250	(3000+2000)x1.15-1500
3	$5,325	(4000+1500)x1.15-1000
4	$6,900	(5000+1000)x1.15

The old machine should be replaced after 2 years.

9. Present-value cost of change in computer timing = $40,444. Present-value cost of extra programmer = $49,400.

10. The table below gives the present values of harvesting at different years.

Dollars in 1000s

Years	0	1	2	3	4
Net revenue	12,000	15,000	17,000	18,000	19,000
Present value at 15 %	12,000	13,040	12,854	11,835	10,863

The optimal timing will be to harvest at the end of year 1.

11. The real values will have to be discounted at the real rate of $(1.15/1.05) - 1 = 9.5\%$. The table below gives the present values of harvesting at the end of different years.

Dollars in 1000s

Years	0	1	2	3	4
Net revenue	12,000	15,000	17,000	18,000	19,000
Present value at 9.5%	12,000	13,699	14,178	13,710	13,216

The optimal harvesting will be at the end of 2 years.

12. Present value of $150,000 received 5 years from now $= \$150,000/1.16^5 = \$71,417$
    Joe will be better off waiting 5 years.

7

Introduction to Risk, Return, and the Opportunity Cost of Capital

INTRODUCTION

Investors generally dislike uncertainty or risk and agree that a safe dollar is worth more than a risky one. Therefore, investors will have to be persuaded to take higher risk by the offer of higher returns. This chapter is the first of three chapters dealing with the risk and return trade-off, and its implications to corporate finance. The chapter defines risk faced by individual investors holding portfolios of securities. The next two chapters will connect this to the opportunity cost of capital for corporations.

The chapter starts with a detailed description of the historic performance of different securities in the U. S. capital markets. This lesson is used to provide basic benchmarks for risk and return. The chapter also describes how we can measure the risk of securities and the role of diversification in reducing risk. The statistical measures of variance and standard deviation are used to measure the risk of individual securities and portfolios. Individual stocks are more risky than portfolios. As the number of the stocks in a portfolio increases, the risk of the portfolio is reduced. The reduction in risk however levels off once the number of stocks in the portfolio reaches a certain number. Thus, there is a certain level of risk that you can never diversify away. This undiversifiable risk stems from economy-wide perils that affect all businesses; it is called market risk. The risk a security adds to a well-diversified portfolio depends on its market risk. This risk is called beta and finds extensive applications in later chapters.

Statistics: This chapter uses some basic statistical concepts and will be easy to follow if you already know some elementary statistics. The text gives all the necessary definitions, but you may want to refresh your memory from a statistics textbook. It will help if you are familiar with the terms such as variance, standard deviation, and covariance, and normal distribution.

KEY CONCEPTS IN THE CHAPTER

Capital Market History: The chapter begins with a description of the market performance of five different classes of securities over the 75-year period from 1926 to 2000. The five portfolios are: the U. S. treasury bills, the long-term U. S. government bonds, long-term corporate bonds, common stocks of large companies represented by the Standard & Poor's 500 (popularly known as the S&P 500), and a portfolio of small firm common stocks. The five portfolios represent different risk classes. Treasury bills are considered risk-less and the benchmark for the safest investment possible. On the other extreme the portfolio of small-company stocks has provided the highest historic returns, but has also carried the highest level of risk. The S&P 500 portfolio

73

is considered representative of the stock market as a whole. The portfolio, while comprising only 500 stocks from around 7,000 shares traded in the market, accounts for seventy percent of the market value. The historic returns for the Treasury bill portfolio have averaged 3.9 percent in nominal terms compared to the S&P 500 portfolio return of 13 percent and the small-firm portfolio's return of 17.3 percent. These historic averages are often used to estimate required rates of returns or opportunity cost of capital.

Use of historic returns: The historic data are often used for valuation or cost of capital estimation. Two types of average measures are calculated from the historic data: the arithmetic average and the geometric mean. The arithmetic average will be higher than the geometric mean and is the appropriate yardstick to use for valuation or cost of capital estimation.

Interest rates change frequently, and the expected return on the market will change with them. However, the risk premium on the market (the difference between the market return and the return on the risk-free investment (T-bill) is fairly stable. Therefore, when we wish to estimate today's expected return on the market portfolio, we should take the current treasury-bill yield and add to it the normal risk premium (the long-term average) equities have earned above treasury bills. As an example, the current T-bill yield (as of February 2002) is about 1.7 percent. The long-term average risk premium is 9.1 percent. Therefore, the expected market return can be estimated as $1.7 + 9.1 = 10.8$ percent. Note that not everyone agrees that the long-term average from the historic data is the right risk premium for the market. It is possible that for a number of reasons, the long-term average may be overestimating the expected risk premium.

Risk: The idea of risk is a familiar one and implies uncertain outcomes. It also means that there are a number of possible outcomes and some of the outcomes are not desirable. The return from an investment in a stock or a portfolio of common stocks cannot be predicted with any accuracy. It is risky. The use of statistics helps us to analyze this type of risk in a precise way. The spread of past returns gives a good indication of the range of uncertainty about future returns. The spread, or the uncertainty of outcomes, is measured by the standard deviation or the variance.

The standard deviation of the annual returns on the Standard & Poor's 500 Index over the 75-year period is 20.2 percent compared to only 3.2 percent for the portfolios of treasury bills. The higher risk of the stock portfolio explains its high return, which is 9.1 percent over that of the t-bills.

Diversification and Risk: Diversification is an important concept with powerful implications. When stocks are combined into portfolios, it is observed that the risk of the portfolio decreases as the number of stocks in the portfolio increases. The risk in a diversified portfolio is lower than for a single security because the returns of different stocks do not move perfectly together. Statistically, individual stock returns are less than perfectly correlated. When we hold many stocks, the risks, which are unique to each one, tend to cancel, as they are largely unconnected. Some risks, though, stem from uncertainty about factors, which affect the whole of the market. This market risk cannot be eliminated by diversification and must be borne by investors, and investors can expect to earn a higher return for bearing it.

Calculation of Portfolio Returns and Risk Measures: The chapter describes how the expected return and standard deviation of a portfolio may be calculated from the characteristics of the individual stocks. It also describes how we can calculate the risk that a particular stock adds to an incompletely diversified portfolio. The section on formulas and computations describe the methods. If these seem too complicated to you, the chapter also gives the following useful rule of thumb to the benefits of diversification. The variance of a portfolio consisting of equal holdings of N stocks is equal to:

Average covariance + (1/N) (average variance – average covariance)

The average variance of annual returns on individual stocks is about 1,500, and the average covariance between pairs of stocks is about 400. As N becomes larger, 1/N becomes very small and the significance of the individual variances becomes less and less. Thus, the variance of the portfolio returns gets closer to the average covariance of 400. The standard deviation of the returns from a portfolio is simply the square root of their variance, and would approach 20 percent.

Beta: The contribution each security makes to the risk of a well-diversified portfolio depends on the security's covariance with other securities in the portfolio. This will depend on how sensitive it is to the changes in the market portfolio. Beta measures this sensitivity. The average stock return will tend to move up and down nearly in tandem with the market. It will move up 5 percent when the market moves up 5 percent. Of course, sometimes it will go up (or down) more or less than the market. However, on average, it moves one for one with the market. This means that its beta is 1. A stock that is more sensitive to market movements might tend to move twice as far (10 percent) in response to a market rise of 5 percent. Conversely, it would tend to fall 10 percent if the market fell 5 percent. This stock is twice as sensitive as the average, and its beta is 2.

The beta of a portfolio is the weighted average of the betas of the stocks included in it. In other words, if a portfolio consists of 30 percent of stocks with betas of 1.5 and 70 percent of stocks with betas of 0.8, the beta of the portfolio is (0.3 x 1.5) + (0.7 x 0.8) = 1.01. When a portfolio is well diversified, the amount of unique risk it contains is negligible. In this case, the standard deviation of the portfolio will be its beta multiplied by the standard deviation of the return on the market portfolio. This makes beta an important number. Beta measures how much a stock contributes to the risk of a well-diversified portfolio.

Diversification and Value Additivity: Diversification is good for individual investors. Since it would be relatively easy for investors to diversify directly by holding a variety of stocks, they have no reason to pay more for the stocks of companies, which are already diversified. This has implications for corporate attempts at diversification for the purpose of risk reduction. The implication is that the value of a project does not depend on how its returns mesh with the returns from other activities of the company, which undertakes it. If the capital market establishes a value of PV (A) for asset A and PV (B) for asset B, the market value of a firm that holds only

75

these two assets is:

$$PV(AB) = PV(A) + PV(B)$$

This is known as the value-additivity principle.

Explanation of Formulas and Mathematical Expressions: The chapter describes a number of formulas for calculating expected returns, standard deviations, variances, and betas of securities and portfolios.

Expected return of portfolios: The expected return of a portfolio of stocks is the weighted average of the expected returns on the individual stocks. Expected portfolio return, r_p, i.e. given by:

$$r_p = x_1 r_1 + x_2 r_2 + \ldots\ldots + x_n r_n$$

where x_1 = proportion of portfolio in stock 1, r_1 = expected return on stock 1, etc.
Example: Stocks A, B and C have returns of 12 percent, 16 percent, and 11 percent respectively. What is the expected return of a portfolio, which includes 40 percent of its value invested in A, 40 percent in B, and 20 percent in C?

$$\text{Expected return} = (0.4 \times 12) + (0.4 \times 16) + (0.2 \times 11) = 13.4\%$$

Portfolio variance: Portfolio variance is not the simple weighted average of the individual standard deviations (unless they are perfectly correlated). The portfolio variance is a function of the individual variances of the different stocks and the covariance of all the pairs of stocks in the portfolio.

$$
\begin{aligned}
\text{Portfolio variance } &= x_1^2 \sigma_1^2 + x_1 x_2 \sigma_{12} + \cdots + x_1 x_N \sigma_{1N} \\
&+ x_2 x_1 \sigma_{21} + x_2^2 \sigma_2^2 + \cdots + x_2 x_N \sigma_{2N} \\
&+ \cdots + \cdots + \cdots \\
&+ x_N x_1 \sigma_{N1} + x_N x_2 \sigma_{N2} + \cdots + x_N^2 \sigma_N^2
\end{aligned}
$$

where, σ_1^2 = variance of stock 1 (σ_1 is its standard deviation)
σ_{12} = covariance between stock 1 and stock 2, = $\sigma_1 \sigma_2 \rho_{12}$, where ρ_{12} is the correlation between stock 1 and stock 2.

If there are N equal-size holdings (i.e. $x_i = 1/N$),
portfolio variance = $(1/N)^2 [N \times \text{average variance} + (N^2 - N) \times \text{average covariance}]$
= average covariance + $(1/N) \times$ (average variance - covariance)

A security's contribution to portfolio risk: From the top row of the portfolio variance calculation:

Stock 1's contribution to risk = $x_1 (x_1 \sigma_1^2 + x_2 \sigma_{12} + \cdots + x_N \sigma_{1N})$
Proportionate contribution to risk = $x_1 \sigma_{1P}/\sigma_P^2$

where σ_{1P} is its covariance with the portfolio and σ_P^2 is the variance of the portfolio.

Here σ_{1P}/σ_P^2 is the sensitivity of stock 1 to changes in portfolio value.
Since $\sigma_{iM}/\sigma_M^2 =$ beta, beta measures a stock's contribution to the risk of the market portfolio.

$$\text{Beta of stock i} = \frac{\sigma_{im}}{\sigma_m^2} = \frac{\rho_{im}\sigma_i}{\sigma_m}$$

The effect of individual stocks on portfolio risk: The risk of a well-diversified portfolio depends on the market risk of the securities included in the portfolio. Beta (β) measures the market risk of a stock as its sensitivity to market movements. Stocks with betas greater than one are usually more sensitive (than the average stock) to market movements. Stocks with betas less than one are less sensitive to market movements. The beta of a portfolio is the weighted average of the beta of the securities included in it. That is,

$$\beta_P = x_1\beta_1 + x_2\beta_2 + \cdots\cdots + x_N\beta_N$$

The standard deviation of a well-diversified portfolio is its beta times the standard deviation of the market portfolio. A diversified portfolio of high-beta stocks is therefore more risky than a diversified portfolio of low-beta stocks. Beta is important because it measures how much a stock contributes to the risk of a well-diversified portfolio.

WORKED EXAMPLES

1. Calculate the standard deviation and expected return for the portfolio given below, and work out how each stock contributes to the portfolio's risk.

Stock	Percentage held	Expected return	Standard deviation	Correlation among stocks		
				Stock 1	Stock 2	Stock 3
Stock 1	40	15	18	1	0.1	0.4
Stock 2	30	16	24	0.1	1	0.5
Stock 3	30	20	36	0.4	0.5	1

SOLUTION

To work out the standard deviation of a portfolio, we need to first calculate the covariance between stocks.

Covariance $\sigma_{ij} = \sigma_i\sigma_j\rho_{ij}$
Given below is a table of all the covariances. All values are rounded off to whole numbers.

Stocks	Stock 1	Stock 2	Stock 3
Stock 1	18x18x1 = 324	18x24x0.1 = 43	18x36x0.4 = 259
Stock 2	24x18x0.1 = 43	24x24x1 = 576	24x36x0.5 = 432
Stock 3	36x18x0.4 = 259	36x24x0.5 = 432	36x36x1 = 1296

Notice that this table is symmetric about the diagonal (that is, $\sigma_{12}, = \sigma_{21}, \sigma_{13} = \sigma_{31}$, etc.). To get the portfolio covariance, each covariance (σ_{ij}) is multiplied by the percentages held in each of the stocks ($x_i x_j$). The table below gives the values for covariance multiplied by the corresponding $x_i x_j$.

Stocks	Stock 1	Stock 2	Stock 3
Stock 1	0.4x0.4x324 = 51.8	0.4x0.3x43 = 5.2	0.4x0.3x259 = 31.1
Stock 2	0.3x0.4x43 = 5.2	0.3x0.3x576 = 51.8	0.3x0.3x432 = 38.9
Stock 3	0.3x0.4x259 = 31.1	0.3x0.3x432 = 38.9	0.3x0.3x1296 = 116.6

The portfolio variance is the sum of the values all the cells.

Portfolio variance = 51.8 + 51.8 + 116.6 + 2(5.2 + 31.1+38.9) = 370.6

Portfolio standard deviation = $\sqrt{370.6}$ = 19.25 %

Portfolio return = (0.4 x 15) + (0.3 x 16) + (0.3 x 20) = 16.8 %

The sum of each row in the variance calculation shows how much each stock contributes to the total variance.
Contribution by stock 1 = σ_{1P}/σ_P^2 = (51.8 + 5.2 + 31.1)/370.9 = 0.24
Contribution by stock 2 = σ_{2P}/σ_P^2 = (5.2 + 52.1 + 38.9)/370.9 = 0.26
Contribution by stock 3 = σ_{3P}/σ_P^2 = (31.1 + 38.9 + 116.6)/370.9 = 0.50

To get the sensitivity of each stock to changes in the portfolio value or beta of the stock with respect to this portfolio, we need to divide the proportionate contribution by the percentage of each stock in the portfolio.

β_1 = 0.24/0.4 = 0.6, β_2 = 0.26/0.3 = 0.87, β_1 = 0.50/0.3 = 1.67
(Note that these are betas with respect to this portfolio and not the market.)

2. Marquis Fund has four stocks in its portfolio. The percentage of each stock held and the beta for each stock are: Stock A – 15%, beta = 1.2; Stock B – 25%, beta = 0.9; Stock C – 30%, beta = 1.8; and Stock D – 30%, beta = 0.6. Calculate the portfolio beta.

SOLUTION
Portfolio beta = (0.15 x 1.2) + (0.25 x 0.9) + (0.3 x 1.8) + (0.3x0.6) = 1.13

SUMMARY

This chapter provides the first formal introduction to risk and the measurement of risk. The chapter starts with a detailed description of the history of the U. S. capital market from 1926 to 2000. This history lesson is a useful way to understand the risk-return trade off faced by an investor in the capital market. The market performance provides useful benchmarks of risk and return with the U. S. Treasury bills as the risk-free investment and the market portfolio of common stocks as the risky investment with significantly higher expected return. Later chapters use these benchmarks for modeling the risk and expected return of an investment.

The chapter also introduces you to the effects of diversification. Shareholders can, and do, reduce their risk very significantly by diversification. The risk that matters to them is, therefore, the market risk that each security adds to a diversified portfolio. This leads to the risk measure, beta, which is the sensitivity of a security's return to the return on the market portfolio. It is the beta of a security that determines how much risk that security contributes to a diversified portfolio. Later chapters will revisit beta and it will be a very useful tool in estimating the opportunity cost of capital for investment projects.

The value of diversification does not imply that corporations can create shareholder value by diversifying their business assets. The value of a project depends only on its cash flows and its market risk and not on how well its returns relate to the other activities of the company. This implies value additivity: the value of project A and the value of project B combined is simply the sum of value of A and the value of B.

LIST OF TERMS

Beta (β)
Correlation
Covariance
Diversification
Expected market return (r_m)
Expected return
Market portfolio
Market return

Market risk
Market risk premium (r_m - r_f)
Risk-free rate of return (r_f)
Standard deviation (σ)
Unique risk
Value additivity
Variability
Variance (σ^2)

EXERCISES

Fill-in Questions

1. Combining stocks into a portfolio provides an investor _____ and risk reduction.

2. The difference between the risk free rate and the _____ is called the _____.

3. Standard & Poor's Composite Index is often regarded as the_____.

4. Diversification cannot eliminate all risk because all stocks are subject to _____.

5. The average annual _____ between 1926 and 1997 was 13 percent.

6. Diversification reduces _____.

7. The principle of _____ means that $PV(AB) = PV(A) + PV(B)$.

8. The _____ of the market as a whole is one.

9. The _____ of the S&P 500 portfolio has averaged about 20 percent over the 72-year period of 1926 to 1997.

10. Projects, which have the same risk as the market portfolio, can be evaluated by a discount rate equal to the _____ plus the normal risk premium for the market portfolio.

11. The contribution a stock makes to the portfolio risk is measured by its _____.

12. _____ is the square of standard deviation.

13. The covariance between two stocks is the product of their standard deviations and the _____ coefficient between them.

14. The variability of a well-diversified portfolio depends almost entirely on the average _____ between individual stocks.

Problems

1. May & June Company is considering investing in a project, which has risk similar to the market risk. The current risk free rate as measured by the rate on treasury bills is 1.7% and the average for the last three years was 3.7 percent. The returns on the S&P 500 portfolio for the last three years were -12 percent, -7 percent, and 22 percent. Suggest an appropriate discount rate for the project.

2. Stock A has an expected return of 16 percent and standard deviation of 28 percent. Stock B has an expected return of 21 percent and standard deviation of 36 percent. Calculate the expected return and standard deviation of a portfolio which is invested equally in the two stocks if the correlation coefficient between the stock returns is: (a) 1, (b) 0.5, and (c) –0.5.

3. Refer to the problem 2 above. If the correlation coefficients of stock returns of A and B to the market portfolio were 0.7 and 0.3 respectively and the standard deviation of market returns is 14 percent, what will be the betas for A and B?

80

4. A portfolio of stocks has risk similar to a portfolio consisting of 40 percent of Treasury bills and 60 percent of Standard & Poor's index. The Treasury bill rate is 1.8 percent, and you expect a normal risk premium of 9.1 percent on Standard & Poor's index. What return would you expect from the portfolio of stocks?

5. Refer to problem 4. What will be the beta of the portfolio?

6. Your investment will give a return of either -10 or +30 percent. (a) Calculate the expected return and the standard deviation of return if these outcomes are equally likely. (b) Calculate the expected return and the standard deviation of return if there is a 0.6 probability of the -10 percent return and a 0.4 probability of the +30 percent return.

7. A portfolio consists of the three stocks with betas of 0.8, 1.4, and 1.6. If the portfolio is equally invested in each stock, what is the portfolio beta?

8. The diagram below shows the effect of diversification. Label the diagram with appropriate words for the different letters.

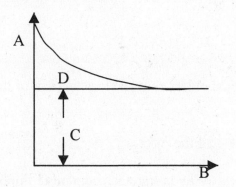

9. Details of the stocks held in a portfolio are given below.

Stocks	Beta	Expected return	Percentage held
Stock A	1.1	14	25
Stock B	0.8	10	18
Stock C	1.4	17	23
Stock D	1.5	19	34

Calculate the expected return and the beta of this portfolio.

10. Calculate the betas of the following stocks if the standard deviation of the market returns is 14 percent.

Stocks	Standard deviation	Correlation coefficient with the market portfolio
Stock P	18%	0.7
Stock Q	24%	0.3
Stock R	38%	0.5
Stock S	42%	0.2

11. The average variance of the annual returns from a typical stock is about 1,500, and its average covariance with other stocks is about 400. Work out what this implies for the standard deviation of returns from: (a) a fully diversified portfolio, (b) a portfolio of 64 stocks, (c) a portfolio of 16 stocks, and (d) a portfolio of 4 stocks. Assume equal-size holdings of each stock.

12. You hold a portfolio of 16 Stocks, each of which has a variance of 1,500 and a covariance of 400 with the other stocks. One stock comprises 25 percent of your portfolio, and the other stocks are held in equal amounts of 5 percent each. (a) What is the standard deviation of your portfolio? (b) How many stocks held in equal amounts would give approximately the same standard deviation?

Essay Questions

1. Corporate diversification is good for the stockholders as it reduces the risk of the firm. Discuss.

2. Why is it that diversification cannot eliminate all the risk?

3. Describe what is meant by the beta of a stock. Why is a stock's beta more important than its standard deviation?

4. Is it possible for a company's stocks to have a high standard deviation but a low beta? What kind of industries will this stock belong to?

5. Stockholders of publicly quoted companies do not benefit from corporate diversification since they can diversify for themselves. Discuss under what conditions (if any) this principle extends to the case of a privately held company, which is 100 percent, owned by a single individual.

ANSWERS TO EXERCISES

Fill-in Questions

1. Diversification
2. Expected market return, market risk premium

3. Market portfolio
4. Market risk
5. Market return
6. Unique risk
7. Value additivity
8. Beta

9. Standard deviation
10. Risk free rate
11. Beta
12. Variance
13. Correlation
14. Covariance

Problems

1. Use the current risk-free rate and the long-term average risk premium.
   Discount rate   = risk-free rate + risk premium
                    = 1.7 percent + 9.1 percent
                    = 10.8 percent

2. Expected return = $(0.5 \times 16) + (0.5 \times 21) = 18.5$ percent

   a. Variance of the portfolio = $0.5 \times 0.5 \times 28^2 + 2 \times 0.5 \times 0.5 \times 28 \times 36 \times 1 + 0.5 \times 0.5 \times 36^2$
      = 1024, standard deviation = 32 [Since the correlation coefficient is 1, the standard deviation will be the weighted average of the standard deviations of the two stocks.
   b. Variance = 772, Standard deviation = 27.8 percent.
   c. Variance = 268, Standard deviation = 16.4 percent.

3. $\beta_A = (28/14) \times 0.7 = 1.4$, $\beta_B = (36/14) \times 0.3 = 0.8$

4. Expected return = $(0.4 \times 1.8) + 0.6 \times (1.8 + 9.1) = 7.26$ percent

5. Beta of the portfolio = $(0.4 \times 0) + (0.6 \times 1) = 0.6$ (The T-bill being risk-free will have beta of zero.)

6. a. Expected return = 10 percent, Standard deviation = 20 percent.
   b. Expected return = 6 percent, Standard deviation = 19.6 percent.

7. Portfolio beta = $(0.8 + 1.4 + 1.6)/3 = 1.27$

8. A = Portfolio standard deviation, B = Number of stocks, C = Market risk, D = Unique risk

9. Expected return = $(0.25 \times 14) + (0.18 \times 10) + (0.23 \times 17) + (0.34 \times 19) = 15.67$ percent
   Portfolio beta = $(0.25 \times 1.1) + (0.18 \times 0.8) + (0.23 \times 1.4) + (0.34 \times 1.5) = 1.25$

10. $\beta_P = (18/14) \times 0.7 = 0.9$, $\beta_Q = 0.51$, $\beta_R = 1.36$, $\beta_S = 0.6$

11. Portfolio variance = Average covariance + (1/N) (Average variance −Average covariance).
    For fully diversified portfolio, N is very large and Portfolio variance = Average covariance.
    For others substitute the value of N = 64, 16, and 4 to get the answers.

a. Standard deviation = Square root of 400 = 20 percent; b. 20.43 percent;
c. 21.65 percent; d. 25.98

12. a. Variance = 510, Standard deviation = 22.58 percent.
   b. Variance = 400 + (1/N)(1500-400) = 510, Solving for N, N = 10

8
Risk and Return

INTRODUCTION

Chapter 7 introduced risk and risk measurement and showed us how diversification enables an investor to reduce risk. Of course, there is a limit to risk reduction and only risk unique to individual securities can be diversified away. The risk that a security bears as part of the overall economic system remains in the portfolio. This risk was termed market risk. A fully diversified portfolio will have only market risk. This chapter builds on the lessons of chapter 7 and presents formal models linking risk and expected return. The chapter begins with a discussion on portfolio theory pioneered by Harry Markowitz. This theory formed the basis for the most popular and widely used model of risk-return relationship: the Capital Asset Pricing Model or CAPM. The CAPM has some empirical evidence to support the basic conclusions derived from the model. Recently, it has been challenged by other theories that purport to rely on assumptions less restrictive than the ones used by CAPM. The chapter presents three alternate theories to CAPM. While CAPM is far from perfect, it remains the most widely accepted model, primarily because of its relative simplicity and ease of application.

KEY CONCEPTS IN THE CHAPTER

Portfolio Theory: Stock market returns of individual stocks covering relatively short periods closely approximate the normal distribution. This enables one to describe the entire distribution of the returns in terms of two parameters- the mean and standard deviation. Individual investors are assumed to be risk-averse, meaning that they would like to be compensated for bearing more risk. This also means that they like higher returns and lower risk. The standard deviation of returns measures risk.

The portfolio theory gives the basic principles of selecting the optimal portfolio in terms of risk and return. We learned in the last chapter that when two stocks are combined into a portfolio, the risk (standard deviation of the portfolio) is less than the average of the two individual standard deviations. Of course, when combining securities into a portfolio, an infinite number of combinations are possible. But investors would choose only those that are *efficient portfolios*. Portfolios are considered efficient if, for a given standard deviation, they give the highest return, or for a given return they have the lowest standard deviation. Investors need only consider efficient portfolios, for all other portfolios give them a poor deal.

Investors have more than two stocks to choose from and we can extend the idea of efficient portfolio to the universe of available securities. All the efficient portfolios can be identified and depending on one's own risk-return preference, an investor can choose the best portfolio of his liking. The technique of *quadratic programming* can be used to choose the efficient portfolio of one's preference. If one were to graph the set of all efficient portfolios selected from all the stocks available it will look like the curve shown in Figure 1. The part BC of the curve represents all the available efficient portfolios. Any choice not on the efficient set will be dominated by a portfolio on the efficient set. Every investor will only choose a portfolio on this curve.

Figure 1

Investors' choices can be expanded by introducing the possibility of lending or borrowing at the risk-free rate. This will allow the investors to combine investing in the stock portfolios given by the efficient set with lending or borrowing (borrowing can be seen as negative lending). The possibilities are shown in Figure 2.

Figure 2

Investors can choose along the line starting from the risk-free rate to the portfolio S. If the investor chooses to invest all her money in risk-free lending, she will have the risk-free rate at zero standard deviation. Any point between r_f and S will mean that part of the money is invested in the stock portfolio S and the remaining lent at the risk-free rate. An investor is also free to choose points to the right of S. This would mean that the investor is borrowing money at the risk free rate and investing that along with his own money in portfolio S. You can clearly see that regardless of where the investor wants to be, the stock portfolio will be the same, namely the portfolio S. In other words, S is the best of all the efficient portfolios and every investor will be invested in this portfolio. This will also mean that every stock will be held as part of this portfolio.

An investor's job can be separated into two parts: first, to choose the best (risky) portfolio of stocks S and, second, to combine it with the right amount of lending or borrowing to adjust to the preferred level of risk. This is known as the separation theorem: the job of selecting individual stocks in one's portfolio can be independently of one's risk preference. In a competitive market, there is no reason to concentrate portfolios in any particular stock, and we can identify S as the market portfolio. Everyone holds S. Risk preference only decides what fraction of one's investment goes to S.

Capital Asset Pricing Model: Capital Asset Pricing Model (CAPM) is an extension of what we saw in Figure 2. Investing in risky assets such as the market portfolio, S should carry a premium compared to the risk-free rate. Otherwise, investors will not take the risk. The market portfolio is the basic benchmark of risk in the CAPM. The risk premium on the market portfolio, measured as the difference between the market return and the risk-free rate is called the market risk premium. The beta for the market portfolio is 1. The CAPM postulates a linear relationship between risk and return as shown in Figure 3. Figure 3 shows the *security market line* (SML).

Figure 3

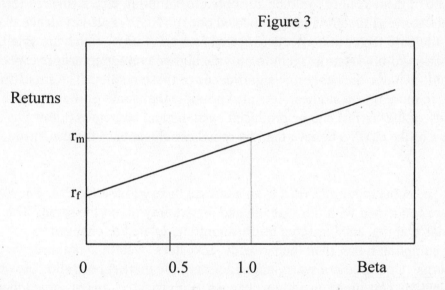

The risk of each stock is measured by its beta and the risk premium varies in direct proportion to beta. All stocks will lie along the SML and the expected return on a stock can be calculated by adding the risk premium to the risk-free rate.

Expected risk premium = $r - r_f = \beta(r_m - r_f)$

A key implication of the CAPM is that the risk of a stock that matters is its contribution to portfolio risk. This is what is measured by beta and depends on the stock's sensitivity to changes in the value of the market portfolio.

Validity of CAPM: Over the years, a lot of research has been done to test the validity of CAPM. The CAPM is a theory about expected returns. We can only measure actual returns. This makes

87

it difficult to test the theory as it is conceived. Another problem in testing CAPM is that the market portfolio should include all assets, not just stocks traded in stock exchanges. In practice, most of the tests use stock market indexes such as the S & P 500 as proxies for the market portfolio.

One of the best known tests of the validity of CAPM involved analyzing portfolio returns over the period 1931 to 1991. The study, conducted by Fischer Black, grouped all New York Stock Exchange stocks into 10 portfolios selected according to the ranking of the betas of their stocks. Every year these portfolios were readjusted, using monthly data from the previous 5 years, so that portfolio 1 always contained the 10 percent of stocks with the lowest betas, portfolio 2 the next 10 percent, and so on up to portfolio 10 with the highest beta stocks. The performance of these portfolios was assessed over the 60-year period. The results showed a strong positive relationship between beta and returns and thus broad support for the CAPM. However, it was found that the security market line was flatter than the theory predicted and it was above the risk-free rate.

In recent years, the relationship between beta and the risk premium has been particularly flat. It has been argued that some of these results could be attributed to sampling errors (the realized average returns are not the same as the previously expected ones). There is also evidence that suggests that beta is not the only factor that affects expected returns. Firms, which are small, and ones, which have low market-to-book ratios, seem to provide higher average returns irrespective of their betas. It is difficult to judge the economic significance of these results. The small-firm effect is found to be less in more recent studies. It is also possible that some of the results that cast doubts on the validity of the CAPM can be produced by statistical strategies (known as "data mining"). The supporters of the CAPM believe that the broad conclusions of the theory are valid.

Consumption CAPM: The consumption CAPM is an alternate theory to the CAPM. The CAPM assumes that investors are concerned with their wealth and uncertainty about the same. The consumption CAPM holds that risk and expected return should be related to changes in investors' aggregate consumption rather than their wealth. Investors' wealth is not directly relevant to the stock returns. One need not worry about defining the market portfolio. However, you have to estimate aggregate consumption and its changes. Empirically, it is observed that estimated aggregate consumption changes rather gradually through time. This does not give a good explanation of past average rates of return. In short, the model has not caught on and its practical appeal seems limited.

Arbitrage Pricing Theory: The arbitrage pricing theory (APT) was the first serious challenger to CAPM. It does not involve many of the restrictive assumptions of CAPM. It postulates that each stock's return depends on several pervasive macroeconomic factors and the risk premium depends on the factor weights. The general model can be written as:

$$\text{Return} = a + b_1 (\text{factor 1}) + b_2 (\text{factor 2}) + \cdots$$

Alternately, the risk premium: $r - r_f = b_1 (premium_1) + b_2 (premium_2) + \cdots$

The APT is general and has appealing features. The market portfolio has a role in the model and thus we need not be concerned with measuring the same. The model is general and is dependent on the absence of arbitrage opportunities. The model does not specify either the number of factors or identity of these factors. The major problem is that there is little agreement on what the factors are. There have been many empirical attempts at identifying the factors. These have been met with limited success. The APT is still a long way from replacing the CAPM as the primary theory for risk-return relationship.

The Three-Factor Model: Eugene Fama and Kenneth French incorporate the small-firm effect and the book-to-market ratio effect seen in empirical studies into a formal risk-return relationship model. The model can be represented as:

$$r - r_f = b_{market} (r_{1market-factor}) + b_{size} (r_{size\ factor}) + b_{book-to-market} (r_{book-to-market})$$

The model is a practical extension of CAPM.

WORKED EXAMPLES

1. Daisy Chang wants to invest $100,000. She has the choice of a risky portfolio of stocks, M, with an expected return of 13 percent and a standard deviation of 16 percent. She can also lend and borrow at the risk-free rate of 3 percent. Show how Daisy can construct a portfolio with standard deviations of (a) 8 percent, (b) 24 percent, and (c) 32 percent. Calculate the expected return for each of these portfolios.

SOLUTION

Since the standard deviation of lending or borrowing at the risk free rate is zero, the portfolio standard deviation is the fraction invested in M multiplied by its standard deviation. If she invests half of her money ($50,000) in M, the portfolio standard deviation will be: 0.5 x 16 = 8 percent. If she borrows $50,000 and invests $150,000 ($100,000 of her own plus the borrowed $50,000) in M, the standard deviation of her investment portfolio will be 1.5 x 16 = 24 percent. Similarly, to get a portfolio with standard deviation of 32 percent, she will have to borrow $100,000 and invest $200,000 in M. The expected return for each portfolio will be:

a. (0.5 x 3) + (0.5 x 13) = 8%
b. (1.5 x 13) – (0.5 x 3) = 18%
c. (2 x 13) – (1 x 3) = 23%

2. The Treasury bill rate is 3 percent and the market portfolio return is expected to be 12.5 percent.
   a. What is the market risk premium?
   b. What is required rate of return on an investment, which has a beta of 1.8?
   c. If the required return on Grey Puppet Corp. stock is 12 percent, what is its beta?

d.   If an investment with a beta of 1.2 were expected to give a return of 14 percent, would you accept it?

SOLUTION

a.   Market risk premium = 12.5 – 3 = 9.5%
b.   Required rate of return for an investment of beta of 1.8 = 3 + 1.8(9.5) = 20.1%
c.   Return = 3 + β (9.5) = 12, β = $\dfrac{12-3}{9.5}$ = 0.95
d.   Required rate of return = 3 + 1.2(9.5) = 14.4%. The investment return is less than the required rate of return. Hence, its NPV will be negative and not an acceptable investment.

3.   Gemini Inc. wishes to use the Fama-French 3-factor model to estimate its cost of equity capital. The company has estimated the following factor sensitivities and factor risk premiums:

Factors	Factor Sensitivity	Factor risk premium
Market factor	1.2	6.2 percent
Size factor	-0.5	2.6
Book-to-market factor	0.2	5.2

If the risk free rate is 3 percent, estimate the cost of equity capital for the firm.

SOLUTION

Risk premium = 1.2x6.2 - 0.5x2.6 + 0.2x5.2 = 7.18 percent
Cost of equity capital = 3 + 7.18 = 10.18 percent.

SUMMARY

The chapter describes the basic principles of portfolio selection and the theories of which provide formal models of the relationship between risk and return. Risk averse investors choose portfolios based on risk and return. It makes sense to choose only efficient portfolios--portfolios, which provide the highest return for a given level of risk. In the presence of the possibility of risk-free lending and borrowing, investors will end up choosing the one portfolio that, in combination with risk-free lending/borrowing, gives the best choices regardless of one's own risk preferences. This forms the basis for the widely accepted theory, Capital Asset Pricing Model. The CAPM uses the market portfolio as the basic benchmark for risky investments and the risk of any stock or investment is measured relative to the market portfolio. The risk measure is beta and it reflects the stock's sensitivity to changes in the value of the market portfolio. The risk-return relationship is captured by the security market line and the risk premium on any stock is proportional to its beta.

The CAPM theory finds some empirical support, though questions have been raised about the strict validity of the security market line. Alternate theories of risk-return relationship include the consumption CAPM, the arbitrage pricing theory, and the three-factor model. Each of these theories has some intellectual appeal and might someday prove to be a replacement to the CAPM; however for the present the CAPM still rules. The primary attraction of the CAPM is its relative simplicity and ease of practical application. The CAPM should be seen as an approximate and partial explanation of the risk-return trade off faced by the investor. We will find many applications of the CAPM in the later chapters.

LIST OF TERMS

Arbitrage pricing theory
Capital Asset Pricing Model
Consumption beta
Consumption CAPM
Efficient portfolios
Expected risk premium

Market risk premium
Normal distribution
Quadratic programming
Security market line
Three-factor model

EXERCISES

Fill-in Questions

1. The _____ uses less restrictive assumptions than the CAPM does and postulates that returns are dependent on pervasive macroeconomic factors.

2. The distribution of stock returns when considered over fairly short periods, closely follow _____.

3. A(n) _____ is a portfolio that gives the highest expected return for a given standard deviation or the lowest standard deviation for a given return.

4. Fama and French proposed the _____.

5. Optimal portfolio selection can be done using the_____ technique.

6. The _____ relates the risk premium to the sensitivity of the investment to changes in consumption, and this sensitivity measure is called the _____.

7. The _____ relates the risk premium to sensitivity of the asset's returns to changes in the value of the market portfolio.

8. The expected return on a stock investment, according to CAPM, equals the risk free rate plus _____.

9. The difference between the expected market return and the risk-free rate is _____.

10. According to the CAPM, the expected returns from all investments must plot along the
    _____.

Problems

1. Pick the better investment from each of the following pairs of portfolios.
   a. Portfolio A: expected return 14 percent, variance 400.
      Portfolio B: expected return 13 percent, variance 441.
   b. Portfolio J: expected return 20 percent, variance 529.
      Portfolio K: expected return 20 percent, variance 400.
   c. Portfolio R: expected return 8 percent, variance 225.
      Portfolio S: expected return 9 percent, variance 225.
   d. Portfolio X: expected return 12 percent, variance 380.
      Portfolio Y: expected return 15 percent, variance 460.

2. Calculate the expected return for the following portfolios:
   a. beta = 1.2
   b. beta = 1.8
   c. beta = 0.5
   d. beta = 0
   Assume the risk free rate to be 3 percent and the expected market risk premium to equal 9 percent.

3. Your broker is urging you to invest in one of three portfolios on which the returns are expected to be as follows: portfolio A, 12 percent; portfolio B, 16 percent; portfolio C, 20 percent. You believe these estimates, but you also have sufficient data to calculate the betas of the portfolios with confidence. You find the betas are 0.5 for A, 1.1 for B, and 2.0 for C. Which portfolio is best and why? (Hint: See if you can duplicate portfolio B by some combination of A and C.)

4. Stock J has a beta of 1.2 and an expected return of 16 percent, and stock K has a beta of 0.8 and an expected return of 12.4 percent. What must be (a) the expected return on the market and (b) the risk-free rate of return, to be consistent with the capital asset pricing model?

5. Stock A has an expected return of 14 percent and a beta of 1.1. Stock B has an expected return of 18. The risk free rate is 5.2 percent. Assume that stock A is correctly priced (i.e. it is on the security market line). If stock B has a beta of 1.4, is it correctly priced?

6. An alternate form of the CAPM is written as: $r = \alpha + \beta r_m$. Write a general expression for α and find the value for α for each of the following cases: (a) beta = 1, (b) beta = 2, and (c) beta = 0. What is the value of beta if α = zero?

7. The return on a proposed investment is expected to be 24 percent. The standard deviation is estimated at 30 percent. The risk free rate is 4 percent. Assume the expected market risk

premium to be 9 percent. Assume that the standard deviation of market returns to be 15 percent. If the project correlates fairly highly with the economy, comment on the attractiveness of the project.

8. You are told that Burgess Corp. stock has a beta of 1.2. Estimate its cost of equity capital.

9. A three factor APT model has the following factors and risk premiums:

Factors	Risk premiums
Change in GNP	4 %
Change in dollar exchange rates	-2
Change in energy prices	-1

Calculate the expected rates of return on the following stocks, assuming the risk-free rate to be 5.5 percent.
   a. Company A: $b_1 = 0.5$, $b_2 = -1.5$, $b_3 = 0.3$
   b. Company B: $b_1 = 1.2$, $b_2 = 0$, $b_3 = -0.5$
   c. Company C: $b_1 = 2$, $b_2 = 0.5$, $b_3 = -2$

10. Use the information on factor risk premiums from the worked example three-factor model problem to calculate the required rate of return on the following stocks with factor sensitivities to market, size, and book-to-market as follows:
   a. Factor sensitivities: 1.2, 2, and 0
   b. Factor sensitivities: 1.5, 0.3, and 1
   c. Factor sensitivities: 0.5, 0, and 1.5

Essay Questions

1. Explain the basic principles of portfolio theory. What is an efficient portfolio?

2. Explain the separation theorem and how it leads to all investors choosing the same portfolio of common stocks.

3. Compare and contrast the CAPM, consumption CAPM, and the APT.

4. The CAPM can be considered a special case of the APT. Discuss.

ANSWERS TO EXRECISES

Fill-in Questions

1. Arbitrage pricing theory
2. Normal distribution
3. Efficient portfolio
4. The three-factor model
5. Quadratic programming

6. Consumption CAPM, consumption beta
7. Capital asset pricing model
8. Risk premium
9. Market risk premium
10. Security market line

Problems

1. The efficient portfolios are:
   a. Portfolio A - higher return, lower variance
   b. Portfolio K - same return, lower variance
   c. Portfolio S - higher return, same variance
   d. Cannot decide between the two without knowing the investor's risk preference

2. The expected returns can be calculated by the formula: $r = r_f + \square (r_m - r_f)$
   a. $r = 3 + 1.2(9) = 13.8\%$
   b. $r = 29.2\%$
   c. $r = 7.5\%$
   d. $r = 3\%$

3. A portfolio containing 60 percent A and 40 percent C will have the same beta as that of B but has lower return (15.2 %) than that of B. Thus, B is a better choice.

4. $r_f + 1.2(r_m - r_f) = 16$, $r_f + 0.8(r_m - r_f) = 12.4$ Solving for r_f and r_m, gives you: $r_f = 5.2$ percent, $r_m = 14.2$ percent.

5. Stock A return $= 5.2 + 1.1(r_m - 5.2) = 14$, $r_m = 13.2$ percent.
   Expected return for B, as per CAPM $= 5.2 + 1.4(13.2 - 5.2) = 16.4$ percent.
   This is lower than the expected return given. Stock B will not be on the SML.

6. $\alpha = (1 - \beta) rf$
   a. If $\beta = 1$, $\alpha = 0$.
   b. If $\beta = 2$, $\alpha = - r_f$
   c. If $\beta = 0$, $\alpha = r_f$
   If $\alpha = 0$, $\beta = 1$

7. Beta for the project $= \dfrac{\rho_{mp} \sigma_p}{\sigma_m}$, where ρ_{mp} is the correlation coefficient for the project returns

   with the market returns and σ_p and σ_m the standard deviation of the project returns and the market returns respectively. If the correlation coefficient is positive 1 (the highest possible value), the beta for the project will be $= 30/15 = 2$. Substituting the values in the CAPM formula for required rate of return, you get required return $= 4 + 2(9) = 22$ percent. The project's return is higher than this and it appears to be a good project.

8. Based on historic market risk premium of about 9.1 percent, the risk premium for this stock will be 1.2x9.1 = 10.92 percent. Add this to the current risk-free rate to get an estimate of the cost of equity capital.

9. The returns for the different stocks are:
   a. $r = 5.5 + 0.5(4) - 1.5(-2) + 0.3 (-1) = 10.2\%$
   b. $r = 5.5 + 1.2(4) + 0 -0.5(-1) = 10.8\%$

c. $r = 5.5 + 2.0(4) + 0.5(-2) -2(-1) = 14.5\,\%$

10. The returns are:
   a. $r = 3 + 1.2(6.2) + 2(2.6) + 0 = 15.64\,\%$
   b. $r = 3 + 1.5(6.2) + 0.3(2.6) + 1(5.2) = 18.28\,\%$
   c. $r = 3 + 0.5(6.2) + 0 + 1.5(5.2) = 13.9\%$

9

Capital Budgeting and Risk

INTRODUCTION

Investment decisions require evaluation of cash flows produced by the proposed projects using appropriate, risk-adjusted discount rates. This takes us to one of the most common and important applications of the CAPM. Chapter 9 describes this application and explains how to estimate the required rate of return or discount rate for projects using the CAPM. It is important to remember that the required rate of return on a project is a function of the risk of the project and does not depend on whom or which company undertakes it. The relevant risk of the project is, of course, its market risk or beta and not the total risk. A company's stock beta and its cost of capital reflect the nature of all its assets as well as the financial leverage or the debt it carries in its balance sheet. Using the company cost of capital as the discount rate for all its new projects would be a serious error. We would still want to know what return is expected from the securities of a company and the cost of capital for the company as a whole, because this provides us with a benchmark return. From this, we can work out what return is required from projects whose risks are similar to those of the company's existing business. Riskier projects should have a higher hurdle rate and safer projects a lower cutoff rate.

The chapter describes how one can estimate betas for companies using market information. We can estimate the beta of a stock by comparing the stock's returns over time against the market returns. Individual company beta estimates tend to be unstable and it is often better to calculate the beta for the industry group to which the company belongs. The chapter also has a detailed discussion of the relationship between beta, financial leverage, and operating leverage.

Other related topics covered in the chapter include the risk and betas for foreign projects, basic determinants of beta, and the common, but often erroneous, practice of using arbitrary risk premiums (fudge factors) to adjust for projects considered risky. The concept of certainty equivalent, an alternate approach to adjust for the risk of cash flows, is also explained in this chapter.

Most of the discussions on risk-adjusted returns in the chapter use the CAPM as the theoretical risk-return model. The basic principles covered apply to other models like the APT or the three-factor model as well.

KEY CONCEPTS IN THE CHAPTER

Company and Project Cost of Capital: *Cost of capital* for a company is the required rate of return demanded by the investors on the securities issued by the company. In practice, this is the weighted average of the return on the company's securities, typically debt and equity.

Companies estimate their cost of capital using market data and use this company cost of capital as the discount rate for evaluating new projects. This cost of capital is appropriate and correct only if the project under consideration is exactly like the existing operations of the company, which is unlikely to be the case for any company with more than one type of business. Please remember that required rate of return demanded by investors depends on the use to which the capital is put.

Each project has to be evaluated as a mini-firm and the required rate of return for the project should be a function of only its market risk or beta. It should not make any difference as to which company undertakes the project. This follows directly from the CAPM and the value additivity principle. Thus, the discount rate used to evaluate a project should be estimated using the project's beta.

This does not mean that company cost of capital estimates have no practical value. In fact, they are extremely useful in estimating market's assessment of the required rate of return on the typical mix of the company's assets. Thus, for any project, which is of comparable risk, the company cost of capital might be a very good measure. For projects, which have higher risk, a higher discount rate will need to be used and projects, which have lower risk, should be evaluated with lower rate of return.

Cost of Equity and Beta: The beta of a company's stock measures how its price responds to market movements and is estimated by plotting or regressing the returns on the stock against the returns on the market index. Monthly returns are commonly used and the slope of the fitted line through the scatter of points is the beta of the stock. Typically the estimated beta is used to compute the cost of equity capital using the CAPM formula: $r = r_f + \beta (rm - r_f)$. It is important to note that estimates of individual company betas are highly unstable and it is better to use industry betas with any adjustment for financial leverage as discussed later. A beta, calculated for an industry group, would generally provide a more accurate measure of the beta of a project than that of the estimate for a single company.

One can also use published betas produced by a number of brokerage and advisory services. Standard and Poor and Merrill Lynch, among others, publish information on betas. The *R-squared* (R^2) gives the proportion of the variance of the stock returns explained by market movements. One can also interpret this as the percentage of market risk in the stock's total risk. If a stock's return shows an R^2 of 30 percent, it implies that 30 percent of its risk is market risk. The remaining 70 percent is unique or company specific risk. Note that the betas calculated from regression are estimates and are subject to high degrees of error. The *standard error* of beta estimate measures the probable accuracy of the estimate.

As stated before, the required rate of return for a project depends on its systematic risk and is measured by its beta. The problem of choosing a suitable discount rate for a project therefore amounts to working out what sort of beta it has. We cannot do this directly because individual investment projects are not traded in the New York Stock Exchange. The best approximation is obtained by estimating the betas of companies, which are in the same business as the project. If one can estimate the betas for a number of companies in an industry and then estimate an average beta for the industry, this will be a reliable estimate for the industry represented by the companies.

Capital Structure, Cost of Capital and Beta: Companies generally use financing mix comprising debt and equity. The cost of capital for a company will reflect the mix of financing used. The following relationships have to be kept in mind when using the cost of capital is to value a company's assets.

$$\text{Company cost of capital} = r_{assets} = r_{portfolio} = \frac{debt}{debt + equity} \times r_{debt} + \frac{equity}{debt + equity} \times r_{equity}$$

The change in financial structure should not normally affect the risk of the cash flows produced by the asset and thus should not affect the required return on the assets. Of course, as the company increases its debt, the stockholder's risk increases and this would increase the beta of equity.

The beta of a project in a strict sense should reflect its business risk. The typical beta measured using stock returns reflect not only the business risk, but also the effect of any financial leverage or borrowing of the company. When a company borrows money it increases the risk of the stockholders. Thus, other things equal, financial leverage increases the risk of the company and the beta of a stock with leverage will be higher than the pure asset beta. We can derive the effect of leverage on beta using the relationship:

$$\text{Value of assets} = \text{value of equity} + \text{value of debt}$$

with all the values measured in market values. The beta of a portfolio is the weighted average of the individual security betas. Consider the company's assets as financed by a portfolio of liabilities or sources of funds, i.e. partly by equity and partly by debt. Therefore, the beta of the assets should equal the beta of the weighted average of the betas of the liabilities.

$$\beta_{assets} = \beta_{equity} \times \frac{equity}{V} + \beta_{debt} \times \frac{debt}{V}$$

where V = equity + debt

The beta of debt is often very close to zero. Therefore, we can rewrite the relationship as:

$$\beta_{assets} = \beta_{equity} \times \frac{equity}{V}$$

$$\beta_{equity} = \beta_{assets} \times \frac{V}{equity}$$

These equations can be used to calculate the beta of assets from the market-estimated beta of a leveraged company stock.

Example: CMI Corp. stock has a beta of 1.3. The company has a debt/assets ratio of 30 percent. Assuming the debt beta to be zero,

$$\beta_{assets} = 1.3x0.7 = 0.91$$

What will happen if the company reduces its debt to 20 percent of assets? Again, we can use the relationship above to figure out the beta for the stock.

$$\beta_{equity} = \beta_{assets} x \frac{V}{equity}$$

$$\beta_{equity} = 0.91x \frac{1}{(1-0.2)} = 1.14$$

The impact of leverage on beta and the cost of capital presented in this chapter ignore the effect of taxes. We will deal with that in Chapter 19.

Betas and Discount Rates for International Projects: The conventional wisdom on overseas investments is that they are generally riskier than investments in one's own country. This perception is based on the general feeling that things get more uncertain when one leaves one's home country. However, this ignores the fact that the risk that matters should be the non-diversifiable risk that is measured by beta and that beta is a function of not only the standard deviation of the project's cash flows but also the correlation of the project's cash flows to the domestic market returns. While the standard deviation for foreign projects can be higher than their domestic counterparts, it is also generally true that the correlation of such projects are a lot less than a comparable domestic project will have to the domestic market return. Thus, it does not automatically follow that foreign projects will have higher betas and should be evaluated at higher discount rates. One should analyze both the standard deviation and the correlation of the project to domestic market returns. This will apply to a foreign company undertaking a project in the U.S. as well.

Cost of Capital Across Countries: It is a mistake to compare interest rates and costs of capital across countries without adjusting for the differences in inflation. The nominal interest rates across countries will differ because of the differences in inflation. Thus, the fact that interest rates in Japan are 2 or 3 percentage points lower than the corresponding US interest rate does not mean that it is cheaper to borrow in Japan and Japanese companies enjoy a lower cost of capital advantage. One has to compare the real interest rates before making any judgment. Of course, it is possible that the savings and therefore, the supply of loanable funds could be different and relatively large in one country relative to the demand for loans. In such a case, the country could have a lower real rate. This line of argument assumes that capital does not easily flow across borders; an assumption not too realistic in an increasingly global economy.

Arbitrary Discount Rates: Corporate managers often face the task of setting discount rates for projects, which are different from the typical project handled by them. These projects may be considered riskier than normal and are often evaluated with an arbitrary and higher discount rate than normal. The higher discount rate may be assigned to cover for an imprecise cash flow estimate and/or for the perceived higher uncertainty surrounding the project. One needs to think through the nature of the risk involved and distinguish between systematic and unique risk. The question is not simply what makes an asset's future earnings uncertain. What matters is the extent to which abnormally low earnings are likely to coincide with low earnings in the economy as a whole. It is also better to sort out the cash flow estimation problems by correcting the estimates rather than add an arbitrary risk premium for a vaguely defined risk. High discount rates heavily penalize projects with cash flows in later years of the project's life.

Cyclicality, Operating Leverage, and Beta: High standard deviation of earnings does not necessarily mean high beta. What matters are the earnings variability and its relationship to the market returns. Cyclical firms, whose earnings are strongly dependent on the state of the business cycle, tend to have high betas. Variability of earnings can be due to unique risk. A strong relationship between a firm's earnings and aggregate earnings means high market risk. The *accounting beta* or the *cash-flow beta* can be used to measure this. These betas are estimated using the accounting earnings or cash flows instead of security returns.

Beta is also a function of the operating cost structure. Other things equal, higher fixed costs will mean higher beta. The high level of fixed cost produces a leverage effect, which makes profits particularly vulnerable: a small percentage change in revenues will produce a much larger percentage change in profits. Companies with high fixed costs (often called high *operating leverage*) tend to have high betas. The relationship can be expressed as follows:

$$\beta_{asset} = \beta_{revenue} \left\{ 1 + \frac{PV(fixed\ cost)}{Pv(asset)} \right\}$$

Certainty-Equivalent Cash Flows: The standard approach for calculating present value of a stream of uncertain cash flows is to discount the cash flows using a *risk-adjusted rate* derived from the CAPM or some other risk-return model. That is:

$$NPV = \sum_{t=0}^{n} \frac{C_t}{(1+r)^t}$$

where $r = r_f + \beta(r_m - r_f)$. This procedure would be inappropriate for a project whose beta is expected to vary through time. In such cases, it is better to use the certainty equivalent cash flows (CEQ), which are cash flows fully, adjusted for the risk involved so that they can be discounted using the risk-free rate. Thus, the NPV can be written as:

$$NPV = \sum_{t=0}^{n} \frac{CEQ_t}{(1+r_f)^t}$$

The certainty equivalent CEQ_t is some fraction of the expected cash flow C_t. *The* two methods must give the same present value, so

$$NPV = \sum_{t=0}^{n} \frac{CEQ_t}{(1+r_f)^t} = \sum_{t=0}^{n} \frac{C_t}{(1+r)^t} = \sum_{t=0}^{n} \frac{C_t}{(1+r_f)^t} x \frac{(1+r_f)^t}{(1+r)^t}$$

$$CEQ_t = a_t C_t, \text{ where } a_t = \frac{(1+r_f)^t}{(1+r)^t}$$

The certainty equivalent approach is suited for projects where cash flows have uneven risk through the life of the project, so that using one constant discount rate will lead to incorrect decisions.

WORKED EXAMPLES

1. Drury Inc. is interested in finding the appropriate discount rate for its new project for making colored widgets. The average beta of a group of colored widget manufacturers is 1.2 and their average debt-equity ratio is 0.40. Drury plans to have a debt-equity ratio of 0.30. If the risk-free rate is 3 percent and the expected risk premium on the market portfolio is 9 percent, what is: (a) the required return for the project and (b) the required return on the shares of the company?

SOLUTION

The average beta of the shares of the other widget manufacturers is 1.2. Debt to equity ratio of 0.4 means debt/assets = 0.4/1.4 = 0.29. Equity/asset = 1 - 0.29 = 0.71. Assuming beta for debt is zero,

$$\beta_{asset} = \beta_{equity} x \frac{equity}{V} = 1.2 x 0.71 = 0.85$$

Required rate of return for the project = 3 + (0.85 x 9) = 10.65 percent
Debt/asset ratio for Drury = 0.3 /1.30 = 0.23, Equity/asset = 1 - 0.23 = 0.77

Beta of the shares of Drury = $0.85 x \dfrac{1}{0.77} = 1.10$

Return on McIntosh shares = 3 + (1.10 x 9) = 12.9 percent

2. Hawalska Airlines is considering a project, which requires an investment of $200,000 now to buy the exclusive rights to a new high tech airport security system. The security system is still under trial. The results of the trial will be known next year. The experts associated with

102

the project feel that there is a 50 percent chance that the trials will be successful. If found successful, HA will invest $2,000,000 and install the system in airports around the country. The project will generate a cash flow of $400,000 forever, starting from year 2. The project has a beta of 1.1. The risk free rate is 3 percent and the market risk premium is 9 percent. The cost of capital for the typical project is thus estimated at 12.9 percent. Ms. Lila Mani, the CEO of the company, feels that the project has very high risk and therefore wants to discount the cash flows from the project using a rate of 26 percent (double the normal rate). Calculate the NPV of the project using the 26 percent discount rate. Is there a more appropriate way to evaluate the project?

SOLUTION

$$\text{NPV using 26 percent discount rate} = -200,000 - \frac{2,000,000}{1.26} + \frac{400,000/0.26}{1.26} = -\$566,300$$

A more appropriate approach will be to evaluate the project in steps. The cash flows from the $2,000,000 investment made next year have the same risk as any other airport security system projects or the discount rate for this should be: $r = r_f + \beta(r_m - r_f) = 3 + (1.1 \times 9) = 12.9$ percent.
The NPV of the investment of $2,000,000 will then be:

$$\text{NPV} = -2,000,000 + \frac{400,000}{0.129} = \$1,100,775$$

There is a 50 percent chance of this happening. That is, for the initial investment of $100,000, the company will get either zero (the trial fails) or $1,100,775 (trial succeeds). Thus, the overall project NPV for the initial investment of $100,000 is:

$$\text{NPV} = -200,000 + \frac{0.5 \times 1,100,775}{1.129} = \$287,500$$

SUMMARY

This chapter deals with the application of CAPM to practical capital budgeting problems. These problems include estimation of required rates of returns for projects and cost of capital. The chapter stresses the essential element of the CAPM – the risk that matters is the non-diversifiable risk. Thus, the required return on any investment should be related to this risk component and not the total risk. The chapter also points out the fact that the required rate of return on a project will depend on its market risk and not who undertakes the project. It is a mistake to use the company cost of capital to evaluate all the projects undertaken by a company. The company cost of capital reflects the mix of assets the company has and the only project to which one can apply the company cost of capital are those, which are mirror images of the company's existing operations.

Estimation of a company's stock beta involves determining the relationship between the stock's returns and the market returns. This is easily accomplished by plotting the two sets of returns on a graph and calculating the slope of the fitted line. It is important to note that the estimated beta reflects the business risk of the company's assets and the financial risk of the company. Higher leverage or borrowings lead to a higher beta. The asset beta reflecting the pure business risk of the assets can be derived from the stock beta. The relationship can be used to find betas at different levels of leverage.

The common perception that international projects are riskier ignores the fact that international projects often have lower correlation to the domestic market returns than their domestic counterparts. This results in a lower beta, even though the variance of cash flows might be higher. This assumes that each country's investors have a predominantly domestic bias and their market portfolio essentially comprises their home country stocks.

The chapter also discusses the common but erroneous practice of adding fudge factors to account for perceived risks. The fudge factors are arbitrary risk premiums and in many cases reflect non-systematic risk. They are also often used for the correction of cash flow estimation problems. One should look at the factors causing the risk and try to identify the effect they will have on the project's beta. Remember that beta is a function of not only the project cash flows' variance, but also the correlation of these cash flows to market returns. Other things equal, a non-cyclical project will have a lower beta compared to a cyclical project.

The standard approach to project evaluation uses a risk-adjusted discount rate for discounting all cash flows. This assumes that the project's cumulative risk increases at a constant rate. There may be projects that have cash flows whose risk does not increase steadily. For such projects, the certainty equivalent approach might be preferable. This allows separate risk adjustment for cash flows of different periods.

LIST OF TERMS

Accounting beta
Alpha
Business risk
Cash-flow beta
Certainty equivalent
Company cost of capital
Cyclical

Financial leverage
Financial risk
Industry beta
Operating leverage
Project beta
Risk-adjusted rate

EXERCISES

Fill-in Questions

1. The use of the _____ as a discount rate ignores differences in the risk of projects.

2. The discount rate for evaluating a capital budgeting proposal should be derived from the _____.

3. _____ measures the average rate of price appreciation on a stock in the past, when investors in the market as a whole earned nothing.

4. When a company raises debt finance, it increases the _____ borne by its shareholders.

5. The cost of capital depends on the _____ of the firm's investments.

6. Financial risk is produced by _____ leverage.

7. Companies with high fixed costs have high _____.

8. A firm whose revenues and earnings are strongly dependent on the state of the business cycle is said to be a _____ firm.

9. We can measure the strength of the relationship between a firm's earnings and the aggregate earnings on real assets by estimating either its _____ beta or its _____.

10. Instead of discounting the expected value of a cash flow by its _____, we may discount its _____ at the risk-free rate.

11. The beta of a portfolio of stocks drawn from a single industry is called a (n) _____.

Problems

1. A firm is considering the following projects:

PROJECT	BETA	EXPECTED RETURN, %
A	0.7	11
B	1.4	15
C	1.8	18
D	0.9	12

The firm's cost of capital is 13 percent. The risk-free rate is 3 percent and the expected market risk premium is 9 percent.
   a. Which projects will be accepted if the firm's cost of capital is used?
   b. Which projects should be accepted?

2. Hill Corp. is considering investing in two new projects. Project A is estimated to give a return of about 14%. The estimated standard deviation for the cash flows from the project is 30% and the correlation coefficient of the cash flows to market returns is 0.4. The standard deviation for the market returns is 15%. The expected market return is 14% and the risk free rate is 5%. The CEO of the company has decided that the project is not a good investment because of its "high risk" as measured by the standard deviation. The CEO does like Project

B, which is expected to give a return of 20% with the same standard deviation of cash flows as Project A. The correlation coefficient for this project's cash flow with that of the market is estimated at about 0.9. Is the CEO right? Is Project B a better investment than project A? Explain your answer to the CEO.

3. Flakes Corp. stock has the following characteristics:

   Adjusted beta   1.33
   Alpha   - 0.56% per month

   These parameters represent the relationship: $r = \alpha + \beta r_m$

   a. How much would the stock tend to go up in a month in an unchanged market?
   b. How much would the stock tend to go up in a month when the market went up 10 percent?

4. Mikon Inc. stocks have a total market value of $50 million and debt of $30 million. A plot of the returns on the stock against the market returns shows a scatter of points through which a line can be fitted with a slope of 45°.
   a.   What is the company's financial leverage?
   b.   What is the beta of the stock?
   c.   What is the beta of the company's assets?

5. Mikon Inc., of problem 4, now decides to invest $20 million in additional assets that are similar to its existing assets. It decides to finance this investment by borrowing a further $20 million of debt. The current Treasury bill rate is 3 percent, and the expected market risk premium is 9 percent.
   a.   What is the beta of the additional assets?
   b.   What discount rate should be used for these additional assets?
   c.   What is the beta of the stock after the debt issue?

6. The market value of the shares of SkyCab Corp. is currently $24 million, and their beta is 1.4. SkyCab has a nominal $6 million of 8 percent coupon debentures outstanding, which mature in 7 years. These debentures have a beta of 0.1, and they currently yield 10 percent. What is the beta of SkyCab's assets?

7. Other things being equal, which company (from each of the following pairs) do you think should be using the higher discount rate in its capital budgeting?
   a.   (i) A steel company, (ii) a brewing company
   b.   (i) a manufacturer of recreational vehicles, (ii) a mining company
   c.   (i) a company with high operating leverage, (ii) a company with high financial leverage
   d.   (i) a manufacturer of office equipment, (ii) an electric utility company.

8. A project is expected to generate net cash flows of $1,000 in each of years 1 and 2. Its beta will be 1.5 throughout its life. The risk-free interest rate is 3 percent, and the expected return on the market is 9 percent. Calculate:

a. the present value of the cash flows
b. the certainty equivalents of the cash flows
c. the ratios of the certainty equivalents to the expected cash flow (that is, a_1 and a_2).

9. MBA Inc. is expanding its business in Europe. It is evaluating projects in 3 countries with details as follows:

Country	Project standard deviation	Correlation of project returns to US market returns
Country A	36 percent	0.4
Country B	28 percent	0.6
Country C	42 percent	0.2
Country D	22 percent	0.8
US project	18 percent	0.9

The standard deviation of U.S. market returns is 14 percent. Calculate the beta for evaluation of the projects in each country.

Essay Questions

1. Write a short memorandum describing how you will set discount rates for projects with different risks.

2. Your company uses the DCF rate of return to appraise new investment projects in the following way:
   a. Projects with paybacks less than 3 years are accepted if their DCF rate of return exceeds 12 percent.
   b. Projects with paybacks longer than 3 years are accepted if their DCF rate of return exceeds 16 percent.

   Discuss the advantages and disadvantages of this rule.

3. Describe how you would calculate the cost of capital of a company using the CAPM.

4. Explain why foreign projects need not necessarily have a higher discount rate than their domestic counterparts.

5. Explain the difference between the use of risk-adjusted discount rates and certainty-equivalent cash flows. Give an example of a situation where you think the certainty-equivalent method is preferable.

ANSWER TO EXERCISES

Fill-in Questions

1. Company cost of capital
2. Project beta
3. Alpha
4. Financial risk
5. Business risk
6. Financial

7. Operating leverage
8. Cyclical
9. Accounting, cash-flow beta
10. Risk-adjusted rate, certainty equivalent
11. Industry beta

Problems

1. a. Only B and C will be accepted. A and D will be rejected.

   b. The company should use risk-adjusted rates based on project betas. The risk-adjusted rates based betas for the different projects are: A = 9.3 percent, B = 15.6 percent, C = 19.2 percent, and D = 11.1 percent. B and C have returns less than their required rates of return; so they should be rejected. A and D have returns higher than the required rates and should be accepted.

2. Beta for Project A = $\dfrac{0.4 x 30}{15} = 0.8$; Beta for Project B = $\dfrac{0.9 x 30}{15} = 1.8$

   Based on the betas, the required rates of returns for the projects will be 12.2 percent and 21.2 percent. This shows that project A gives a return higher than its required rate of return, while project B does not clear its hurdle rate.

3. a. -0.56 percent.   b. r = $-0.56 + 1.33 x 10 = 12.74$ percent

4. a. The financial leverage = debt/assets = $\dfrac{30}{30 + 50} = 0.375$;

   b. Beta = 1;

   c. You can calculate the beta of assets using the relationship:

   $\beta_{asset} = \beta_{equity} x \dfrac{equity}{V} = 1 x (1 - 0.375) = 0.63$ (assumes beta of debt = 0)

5. a. Beta = 0.63.

   b. Discount rate = $3 + (0.63 x 9) = 8.67$ percent. c. Beta = $0.63 x \dfrac{100}{50} = 1.26$

6. Market value of bond: N = 7, I = 10% (P/Y = 1), PMT = $80, FV = $1,000, Solve for PV
   PV = - $902.63
   Value of debt = Market price per bond x 6000 bonds = $902.63 x 6,000 = $5.42 million
   Value of equity = $24 million

Total market value of firm = value of debt + value of equity

$$= 5.42 + \$24.00$$
$$= \$29.42 \text{ million}$$

$$\beta_{assets} = \beta_{debt} x \frac{debt}{V} + \beta_{equity} x \frac{equity}{V} = 0.1x \frac{5.42}{29.42} + 1.4x \frac{24}{29.42} = 1.16$$

7. a. i   b. i   c. i   d. i

8. a. Using $r = 3 + 1.5(12 - 3) = 16.5$ percent, PV = \$1,595.17
   b. Certainty - equivalent cash flows are \$884.12 and \$781.67.
   c. $a_1 = 1.03/1.165 = 0.884$ and $a_2 = (1.03/1.165)^2 = 0.782$

9. The betas for the different country projects are: A = 1.03; B = 1.2; C = 0.6; D = 1.26; Beta for the U.S. project = 1.16

10

A Project Is Not a Black Box

INTRODUCTION

The chapters covered till now provided us with the basic tools and techniques needed to evaluate projects. In particular, chapters 2 to 6 showed us how to calculate net present values and how to use them to make capital budgeting decisions. Chapters 7 to 9 explained how the risk of a project affects the discount rate that should be used to evaluate it. However, investment decisions require a lot more than the knowledge of tools and techniques. There are a number of practical issues to be considered. A manager should be able to understand what is going on inside a project. Detailed project analysis enables a manager to understand the vulnerabilities, strengths and weaknesses of a project. Chapters 10, 11, and 12 deal with these issues. These chapters address specific questions such as how to analyze capital investment projects, how to ensure that cash-flow forecasts are realistic, and how to organize and control capital expenditures.

The title: "A Project Is Not a Black Box," clearly brings out the central theme of the chapter. A black box is something that you accept without questioning what is inside. A financial manager should not simply accept a set of cash-flow forecasts, choose a discount rate, and crank out a net present value. She must understand the internal workings of the project and think about where those cash flows came from and what can go wrong with them. Chapter 10 describes five commonly used techniques of project analysis which can help the financial manager understand the project's structural strengths and weaknesses, its dependence on one or more key inputs, and interrelationships the project might have with future decisions. The techniques described are: *sensitivity analysis, scenario analysis, break-even analysis, the Monte Carlo simulation*, and *decision trees.*

The chapter also provides an overview of *real options* associated with projects. Managers and companies are not passive investors in the investment projects undertaken by the company. Managers have the ability, intention and resources to continually monitor projects as they proceed and will modify the projects to adapt to the changing conditions in the market. This ability to modify projects means real options linked to projects and these options need to be evaluated as part of the project evaluation process.

KEY CONCEPTS IN THE CHAPTER

Sensitivity Analysis: Of all the techniques described in this chapter, sensitivity analysis is perhaps the most useful and important one. It is simple to apply and understand and can be particularly effective in identifying the need for additional information. Sensitivity analysis captures the effect of key inputs or variables on the project, one variable at a time. It answers questions such as: what happens to the NPV of the project if the cost of goods sold turns out to be at its pessimistic worst?

The NPV of a project is arrived at by combining a number of different forecasts to estimate the after-tax cash flows and then discounting these cash flows. The forecasts include the size of the total market for the product, the company's share of that total market, the price of the product, etc. All the numbers that go into the analysis are the best estimates or expected values. We cannot, however, be sure what the actual outcome will be for any of these variables. Sensitivity analysis identifies the difference made by the variation from the forecast for any key input. The method for accomplishing this is to identify the key variables that determine the success of the project, such as sales volume, fixed cost, unit variable cost, and selling price. For each variable, the expected value is replaced by both an optimistic and a pessimistic estimate, and the cash flows and NPVs are recalculated. This is done by taking one variable at a time. In this way financial managers can identify those variables, which affect NPV most. Additional information or research to reduce the uncertainty of those variables, as well as other, overlooked factors, may then be in order.

The results of the sensitivity analysis is typically set out in tables such as the one below which represents part of Table 10-2 of the Brealey and Myers text.

NET PRESENT VALUE (Billions of yen)			
Variable	Pessimistic	Expected	Optimistic
Market size	1.1	3.4	5.7
Market share	-10.4	3.4	17.3
Unit price	-4.2	3.4	5.0
Unit variable cost	-15.0	3.4	11.1
Fixed cost	0.4	3.4	6.5

The table clearly shows that the impact of variations in the unit variable cost or the market share is far more significant than the impact of variations in the total market size or of the project's fixed costs. The manager can now consider actions that might reduce or eliminate the uncertainty with respect to these key components. For example, it may be worth investing in a market survey, which will reduce the uncertainty about market share. A survey, which indicates poor prospects for the company, would allow the project to be abandoned before any major expenditure is incurred. Alternately, expenditure on a different advertising campaign might bolster market share and improve the prospects for the project. Thus, sensitivity analysis alerts the management to the importance of keeping a sharp eye on what happens to components key to the success of the project. In the above example, it is alerted to the crucial nature of its variable costs and market share. Steps could be taken to remove uncertainty with respect to key material inputs. These could include hedging in commodity futures markets, negotiating long-term supplier contracts, or commission an additional design study on material efficiency.

The strength of sensitivity analysis lies in its ability to highlight key variable and key assumptions, to expose inconsistencies, and to identify where additional information is worthwhile. Sensitivity analysis is limited in its scope, however, because of the subjectivity of the optimistic and pessimistic forecasts and because it ignores interrelationships among variables.

Scenario Analysis: Scenario analysis can be seen as the logical extension of sensitivity analysis. Altering the variables one at a time, as is done for sensitivity analysis, ignores the fact that the variables are usually interrelated. One way around this problem is to look at how the project would fare under a number of different plausible scenarios of the future. Forecasts are made for all variables so as to be consistent with a particular view of the world. In the text, for example, the forecasters are asked to consider the effects of an immediate 20 percent rise in the price of oil, and the NPV of the project is recalculated on the resulting assumptions.

Scenario analysis can be very useful to evaluate the project's exposure to a combination of changes in key variables. The manager can specify the scenarios he would like to have the project analyzed under.

Break-even Analysis: Break-even analysis calculates the sales level that will give zero NPV for the project. Knowing the break-even level, one can assess the chances of the project's success. The break-even point can be computed by working out the NPV or the present values of cash inflows and outflows at different sales level. Many companies (and textbooks) use the break-even level known as the accounting break-even level. This is computed on a different basis and is the level of sales that gives a zero accounting profit. Zero accounting profit could mean a big economic loss or negative NPV because the accounting profit measure ignores cost of capital.

Break-even analysis enables managers to analyze the impact of *operating leverage* or fixed costs on the project's NPV. A project with high fixed costs will have a NPV, which is more sensitive to the level of sales. At higher sales levels, the project would do very well, but if the sales levels happen to be lower than expected, the project would fare worse than one with lower operating leverage. This technique can be useful to evaluate alternate production technologies that have different fixed-variable cost mix.

Monte Carlo Simulation: Monte Carlo simulation (or simulation, for short) may be regarded as the ultimate extension of the idea of scenario analysis. In scenario analysis, we look at a small number of specially chosen scenarios. In simulation, the analysis is extended to include a very large number of possible combinations of changes in key variables. Simulation analysis uses complex computer programs to generate possible values for all key inputs to the project. The project analyst specifies probability distributions for all these variables and the computer generates random values for the key variables and the project is simulated. The process is repeated a number of times to produce a distribution of project cash flows. This provides you with a picture of the variability of the project's cash flows. All interrelationships among the variables can be taken into account in the simulation model.

Simulation involves three stages:

- Establish equations to model the cash flows of the project. These must reflect any interdependencies among variables.
- Specify the probabilities of forecast errors of different magnitudes for each variable
- Sample outcomes. The computer samples from the distribution of forecast errors, calculates the cash flows, and records them. This is repeated a large number of times until an accurate picture of the distribution of possible outcomes has been built up.

As with all models, Monte Carlo simulation has its good and bad points. On the positive side, simulation forces explicit specification of interdependencies. It can be used also to explore possible modifications to a project. On the negative side, simulation can be time-consuming and expensive. Realism means complexity; building the model may have to be delegated, and this can diminish its credibility to the decision maker. It may replace one "black box" with another.

Beyond these points a common misuse of simulation arises when it is used to obtain distributions of "NPVs," which are calculated by discounting at the risk-free rate. The object is to avoid prejudging the risk of the project, which is reflected in the spread of the distribution. This practice, however, is highly erroneous and misleading because:

- "NPVs" calculated in this way have no real meaning and no longer represent market values of the project.
- The distribution does not give the information that would be needed to work out the market value of the project.
- The method ignores the investor's ability to diversify.
- It offends the value additivity principle.

Real Options: The simple discounted cash flow (DCF) analysis used to compute NPV and evaluate projects does not work very well for all projects. The DCF analysis is designed for analyzing investments, which do not change their nature during the life of the project. It is ideally suited for evaluating passive investments like bonds and stocks. Corporate assets are, on the other hand, actively managed by the manager and the projects can very often change their nature in terms of expansion and abandonment possibilities, timing of the investment and flexibility of input and output. Projects, which can be modified or adapted to varying market conditions, have *real options* in them. These options add value to the project and thus have to be included in the evaluation of the projects with real options. The options are generally worth more when the project faces higher uncertainty. The real options associated with projects can be classified one of the following four types.

The Option to Expand: Capital budgeting projects are rarely finite, clean-cut one of a kind investment with no connections to the future. Many projects have expansion opportunities attached to them. These follow-on investment opportunities add value to the original project. Typical examples include R & D projects and investments in new markets, foreign countries, and new technology. Remember that the uncertainties associated with the project actually make the value of options even more attractive. The value of all the options to expand is included in the present value of growth opportunities (PVGO) discussed in chapter 4.

114

<u>The Option to Abandon:</u> The option to abandon a project, when things are not going as well as one expected, is a very valuable option that can enhance the value of the project. The abandonment option can be analyzed in terms of the possible project outcomes. For simplicity and convenience, we can assume that two mutually exclusive outcomes are possible: one is a success route; the other is a failure route. The option to bail out is worth something, especially if the bail out value exceeds the value of the project at that time. An abandonment option can be seen as an insurance policy.

<u>The Timing Option:</u> Many projects can be started now or some time in the future. The fact that the project has a positive net present value does not necessarily imply that now is the best time to initiate the project. Valuing the timing option is simple when there is no uncertainty. One can calculate the project's NPV at various dates of project commencement and pick the one date with the highest NPV. Of course, this will not work when there is uncertainty. The timing option exists, if the project's commencement can be delayed.

<u>Production Option:</u> The ability to switch production facilities to manufacture different types of products or use different types of raw materials is a very valuable option for manufacturing companies. In general, flexibility is very useful in manufacturing especially, when the nature of the demand for the company's products can change very quickly. The flexibility can be to switch machine set ups, sources of raw material or utility, or location of manufacturing from one country to another.

Decision Trees: Decision trees are very useful for analyzing a sequence of different possible uncertain events and decisions through time. Decision trees can show linkages among decisions spread over different periods and dependent on possible and uncertain future outcomes. Moreover, they force implicit assumptions to be expressed. In particular, they enable us to analyze such things as the option to expand, and the option to abandon a failing project.

To draw a decision tree, branches from points marked with squares are used to denote different possible decisions. Branches from points marked with circles denote different possible outcomes (with their probabilities often indicated in brackets) and the decisions and outcomes are linked in the logical sequence. Present values are calculated starting from the end the most distant branches first. "Roll back" to the immediate decision by accepting the best decision at each of the later stages. (See problem 2 of our worked examples.)

While the basic technique is simple, the trees can get complicated very quickly. Usefulness of decision trees is limited, however, because they become unmanageably complex very quickly. They also fail to tell us how to adjust our discount rates to reflect the differences in risk among alternatives.

WORKED EXAMPLES

1. The following forecasts have been prepared for a new investment of $20 million with an 8-year life:

	PESSIMISTIC	EXPECTED	OITIMISTIC
Market size (Units)	60,000	90,000	140,000
Market share, %	25	30	35
Unit price	$750	$800	$875
Unit variable cost	$500	$400	$350
Fixed cost, millions	$7	$4	$3.5

Use straight-line depreciation and assume a tax rate of 35 percent, and an opportunity cost of capital of 14 percent. Calculate the NPV of this project and conduct a sensitivity analysis. What are the principal uncertainties of the project?

SOLUTION

The first step is to calculate the annual cash flows from the project for the base case (the expected values). These may be calculated as shown:

DESCRIPTION	HOW CALCULATED	VALUE ($ in millions)
1. Revenues	90,000 x 0.30 x $800	21.600
2. Variable cost	90,000 x 0.30 x $400	10.800
3. Fixed cost	$4,000,000	4.000
4. Depreciation	$20,000,000/8	2.500
5. Pretax profit	Item 1 - (items 2 + 3 + 4)	4.300
6. Tax	Item 5 x 0.35	1.505
7. Net profit	Item 5 – item 6	2.795
8. Net cash flow	1tem 7 + item 4	5.295

This level of cash flow occurs for each of the 8 years of the project. The present value of an 8-year, $1 annuity is 4.639 at 14 percent. The NPV of the project is therefore given by:

$$NPV = \$5,295,000 \times 4.639 - \$20,000,000 = \$4,563,505$$

Now that the base case has been completed, the next step is to alter the forecasts one at a time to their optimistic and pessimistic values. The easiest way to do this is to work out how much each change affects the net cash flow and then use the annuity factor as before to work out the NPV. For example, the optimistic value of the market size increases the pretax revenues by 50,000 x 0.30 x ($800 - $400) = $6 million; so it increases the (after-tax) net cash flow by $6 million x 0.65 = 3.90 million, to $9.195 million. The NPV now becomes

$$NPV = \$9,195,000 \times 4.639 - \$20,000,000 = \$22,655,605$$

116

The following table shows the net cash flows and NPVs corresponding to the pessimistic and optimistic forecasts for each variable.

	Net Cash Flow ($m)		NPV ($m)	
	Pessimistic	Optimistic	Pessimistic	Optimistic
Market size	2.96	9.20	-6.27	22.67
Market share, %	4.13	6.47	-0.84	10.01
Unit price	4.42	6.61	0.50	10.66
Unit variable cost	3.54	6.17	-3.58	8.63
Fixed cost	3.35	5.62	-4.46	6.07

The table clearly shows that the most crucial variable is the total market size. Both the fixed and variable costs also need watching, while market share and unit price seems less likely to cause serious problems.

2. MerryGoRound is evaluating a possible investment in a new plant costing $2,000. By the end of a year, it will know whether cash flows will be $300 a year in perpetuity or only $140 a year in perpetuity. In either case, the first cash flow will not occur until year 2. Alternately, the company would be able to sell their plant in year 1 for $1,800 if the demand is low and for $2,000 if the demand is high. There is a 65 percent chance that the project will turn out well and a 35 percent chance it will turn out badly. The opportunity cost of funds is 10 percent. What should the company do?

SOLUTION

The problem can best be analyzed by the decision tree shown below. If things go well, the cash flows of $300 in perpetuity starting in year 2 will be worth $300/0.1 = $3,000 in year 1. If things go badly, the cash flows will be worth $140/0.1 = 1,400 in year 1. To analyze the decision tree, we work backwards from the most distant branches of the tree. At the decision branch points, marked with squares, we make decisions. At the uncertainty ones, marked with circles, we calculate expected values. So, if things go well (high demand), we will decide to continue with the plant at a value of $3,000 in year 1. However, if things go badly (low demand), we will prefer to sell it for $1,800 rather than wait for cash flows worth only $1,400. We can now take the expected value at the uncertainty branch point by weighting each possible outcome by its probability.

Year 0   Year 1

Invest 2,000

High demand (0.65)

PV = $3,000

Sell plant =$2,000

Low demand (0.35)

PV = $1,400

Sell plant = $1,800

Expected value in year 1 = $3,000 x 0.65 + $1,800 x 0.35 = $2,580
Net present value of the investment = $2,580/1.1 - $2,000 = $345.45

The project is worth pursuing.

SUMMARY

Investment decision making involves a lot more than simply cranking out cash flow estimates, discounted cash flows, and NPVs based on these estimates. Investments are always fraught with uncertainties and a project can be vulnerable to a number of factors external and beyond the manager's control. Project analysis enables the manager to identify the project's vulnerabilities and the major threats faced by the project. The chapter describes three approaches to identifying these vulnerabilities and threats – sensitivity analysis, scenario analysis, and the Monte Carlo simulation. Sensitivity analysis is the simplest of these and evaluates the impact on the project's NPV caused by changes in key variables, one variable at a time. This type of analysis enables the manager to identify variables crucial to the project's financial health. The manager might find it prudent to spend resources on getting additional information to reduce the uncertainties related to these crucial variables. An extension of sensitivity analysis is the scenario approach where the impact on the project's NPV under different scenarios, where more than one variable might change, is examined. One can look at all possible combinations of variables and get a complete distribution of possible cash flows from the project by using the Monte Carlo simulation approach. This approach uses a complete model of the project and assigned distribution for the variables to obtain random values for all the variables and simulates many runs of the project.

Simulation can be very useful in understanding the risk and complexities of the project. It forces the project analyst to raise questions that otherwise might not be asked. The process has its limits, though, and can easily be abused. Simulation produces a vast array of data and, in some cases, manager could conceivably get lost in the process.

Very few projects are simple, one time "accept or reject" cases. Projects often involve linkages of decisions over time and can include options to expand, abandon, timing of the investment or otherwise modify the project. These options add value to the project and it is important that they are evaluated properly. Decision tree analysis is ideally suited to evaluate these cases and where one is faced with a sequence of possible decisions.

It is important to remember that none of the techniques discussed in this chapter replaces the NPV analysis; they only facilitate better decision making by enabling more accurate computation of the NPV. These techniques help the manager understand the project better and learn what could go wrong with the project.

LIST OF TERMS

Abandonment value	Production options
Break-even analysis	Project analysis
Decision tree	Real options
Monte Carlo simulation	Scenario analysis
Probability	Sensitivity analysis

EXERCISES

Fill-in-Questions

1. Sensitivity analysis, simulation, and decision trees are three different forms of _____.

2. _____ shows the effect of changes in key variables such as sales, costs, etc., on the value of an investment project.

3. The analysis of a project under different _____ gives us a way to do a kind of sensitivity analysis that takes the interrelationships among variables into account.

4. _____ identifies the level of sales for which the project gives zero NPV.

5. _____ uses a complete model of the project and distribution of all key variables to simulate thousands of project runs and produces a complete distribution of project cash flows.

6. Sequential decisions can be analyzed by constructing a (n)_____.

7. One of the difficulties of using a decision tree or simulation is that it becomes necessary to specify the _____ of different future outcomes.

8. The problem of whether to terminate a project before the end of its normal economic life is called the _____ problem.

9. Many projects can be modified and adapted to meet changing market conditions. These options to modify projects are known as _____ _____.

10. Manufacturing plants included as part of investment projects can be designed to include _____ to meet flexible market and production needs.

Problems

1. Horizontal Drillers Inc. is evaluating a project to produce a high tech deep-sea oil exploration device. The investment required is $80 million for a plant with a capacity of 15,000 units a year. Sales are expected to average 80 percent of capacity. The plant is expected to operate for 5 years. The device will be sold for a price of $12,000 per unit. The variable cost is $7,000/unit and fixed costs, excluding depreciation, are $25 million per year. Use straight-line depreciation and a tax rate of 36 percent. The required rate of return is 12 percent.

    a. Calculate the NPV of the project
    b. Do a sensitivity analysis for the following pessimistic and optimistic assumptions:
        Pessimistic: Sales – 15 percent lower, Unit price – 10 percent lower, Fixed costs – 10 percent higher.
        Optimistic: Sales – 15 percent higher, Unit price – 10 percent higher, Fixed costs – 10 percent lower.

2. Caramel, Custard and Confections Corporation (CCCC) is considering an investment of $500,000 in a new plant for producing a new line of confections. The plant, which has an expected life of 4 years, has a maximum capacity of 700,000 units per year, and sales are expected to be 85 percent of this in each of the 4 successive years of production. Fixed costs are $200,000 per year and variable costs are $1.20 per unit produced. The product will be sold at a unit price of $2. The plant will be depreciated straight-line over 4 years, and it is expected to have a zero salvage value. The required rate of return on the project is 15 percent and the corporation tax rate is 35 percent.

    a. Calculate the NPV of this project under the assumptions given above.
    b. Calculate how sensitive the NPV of the project is to variation in the level of sales, the unit price, the unit variable coot, and the level of fixed costs.
    c. CCCC is uncertain how to price its new product. What price would give a zero NPV?

3. In the investment project of problem 2, calculate what level of sales would give break-even in terms of (a) zero NPV and (b) zero accounting profit.

4. In problem 2, CCCC estimated that the annual sales would be 595,000 units, but there is some chance that the sales level will be inadequate to justify the capital expenditure. By commissioning a market survey, CCCC can hope to reduce this risk. CCCC's marketing department has some experience with such surveys. They estimate that there is a 20 percent chance that the survey will revise the forecast sales to 500,000 or less, in which case the project would not be worth undertaking. If this does not occur (the remaining 80 percent of the time), they would expect the sales forecast to be revised upward to 640,000 units. What is the maximum amount that CCCC should be prepared to pay for a survey of this kind?

5. Emerald and Blue has an investment project with the following characteristics:
   Cost of investment: $800,000
   Expected sales volume: 21,000 units per year for 7 years
   Unit price: $150
   Unit variable cost: $120
   Annual fixed costs: $400,000
   Life of investment: 7 years (zero salvage value)
   Tax rate: 35 percent
   Required rate of return: 12 percent

   Calculate the NPV of this investment and perform a sensitivity analysis (use straight-line depreciation).

6. Analyze the project of problem 2 under the following two scenarios:

	Pessimistic scenario	Optimistic scenario
Sales volume	Expected value -20%	Expected value +10%
Unit price	Expected value -10%	Expected value +20%
Variable cost	Expected value +10%	Expected value -5%
Fixed cost	Expected value +10%	Expected value -5%

7. In problem 4, the first year of operation would give CCCC the same information as their market survey. After that year, if things go badly (with expected sales of 415,000 units), they can abandon the project to obtain a salvage value of $400,000 (less $8,500 tax) by selling the plant to another company. What value does the market survey have in the light of this option to abandon the project after it has been started?

Essay Questions

1. Describe the technique of sensitivity analysis as applied to the appraisal of capital investment projects. What reservations do you have about its usefulness?

2. Describe how to calculate the break-even point for a capital investment project. Why is it misleading to calculate the break-even point in terms of accounting profit?

3. Work out and describe in detail how you would produce and use a Monte Carlo simulation model to represent the purely financial aspects of pursuing an MBA degree in one of the top ten schools. Assume you will be in a business related career for the next 15 years. Some of the things to keep in mind include: the investment in time and money, possible benefits of the MBA, and the pitfalls (things which could go wrong). Make sure to build appropriate interrelationships between variables into the model where necessary.

4. What are the typical real options associated with capital budgeting projects? Do these options always add value to the project?

5. A decision must be made whether to launch a new product immediately or subject it to further market research or abandon the idea altogether. Your boss has heard that decision trees can help with this kind of problem. Write a report on how a decision tree might be used in this situation. Describe what sort of information you would need to apply this in practice and how it would be used.

ANSWERS TO EXERCISES

Fill-in Questions

1. Project analysis	6. Decision tree
2. Sensitivity analysis	7. Probabilities
3. Scenarios	8. Abandonment value
4. Break-even	9. Real options
5. Monte Carlo simulation	10. Production options

Problems

1. a. The following table derives the cash flows and NPV for the base case:

Item	Year 0	Years 1 to 5 ($1000)
Investment	-80,000	
Revenue		144,000
Variable cost		84,000
Fixed cost		25,000
Depreciation		16,000
Pre-tax profit		19,000
Tax @ 36 percent		6,840
Net profit		12,160
Net cash flow		28,160
NPV @ 12 percent		21,510

b. The sensitivity analysis is presented in the table below: ($1,000)

Sensitivity to change of	Effect on annual cash flow	Effect on NPV
Pessimistic:		
15 percent lower sales	-5,760	-20,764
10 percent lower price	-9,216	-33,222
10 % Higher fixed cost	-1,600	-5,768
Optimistic		
15 percent higher sales	5,760	20,764
10 percent higher price	9,216	33,222
10 % lower fixed cost	1,600	5,768

2. a. The following table derives the cash flows and NPV for the base case and for the pessimistic and optimistic scenarios of problem 6. (All cash flows in $1000s)

Item			Years 1 to 4	
	Year 0	Expected	Pessimistic	Optimistic
Investment	-500			
Revenue		1190.0	856.8	1570.8
Variable cost		714.0	628.3	746.1
Fixed cost		200.0	220.0	190.0
Depreciation		125.0	125.0	125.0
Pretax profit		151.0	-116.5	509.7
Tax		52.9	-40.8	178.4
Net Profit		98.1	-75.7	331.3
Net cash flow		223.1	49.3	456.3
NPV at 15 percent		137.0	-359.3	802.7

b. The next table shows how given changes in sales, variable cost, unit price, and fixed cost affect the net cash flows and the NPV. The final column also shows the levels that give break-even points (i.e., zero NPV):

Sensitivity to change of:	Effect on cash flow	Effect on NPV	Break-even level
100,000 sales (units)	52.00	148.46	502,660 units
10-cent variable cost	-38.68	-110.42	$1.32
10-cent unit price	38.68	110.42	$1.88
$10,000 fixed cost	6.50	-18.56	$273,875

c. The final column indicates that a price of $1.88 gives a zero NPV.

3. a. The final column of the previous table also shows that the level of sales required for the break-even point in terms of zero NPV is 502,660 units per year.

b. The base case gave a pretax profit of $151,000 at sales of 595,000. Each unit reduction in sales reduces pretax profits by $0.80, so sales will have to fall by 151,000/0.80 = 188,750 to eliminate profits entirely. That is, break-even sales are 406,250.

4. Without the extra information, the value of the project is its usual NPV of $137,000. With the information, there is a 20 percent chance of a zero NPV and an 80 percent chance of $203,807 (=$137,000 + 148,460 x 45/100). The new NPV is equal to $163,046 (= $203,807 x 0.80) less the cost of the information. The information must be worth $26,046 (= $163,046 - $137,000).

5. Cash flows and NPV for the base case are given below ($ 1,000s):

Item	Year 0	Expected cash flow – Years 1 to 7
Investment	-800	
Revenue		3150.0
Variable cost		2520.0
Fixed cost		400.0
Depreciation		114.3
Profit before tax		115.7
Tax		40.5
Profit after tax		75.2
Cash flow		189.5
Base case NPV at 12 percent		64.8

The sensitivity analysis is given for increase in the value of key inputs.

$1,000s

Sensitivity to	Effect on cash flow	Change in NPV
Sales increase by 1000 units	19.50	+89.0
Variable cost increase by $1	-13.65	-62.3
Unit price increase by $1	13.65	+62.3
Fixed costs increase by $10,000	-6.50	-29.7

6. See the answer to problem 2.

7. Without the abandonment option, we found in problem 4 that the project had an NPV of $163,046 less the cost of the survey, or $137,000 without the survey. This gave the survey a value of $26,046.

With the abandonment option, there is now a 20 percent chance of abandoning at an NPV of -$46,913. This is calculated as follows: the expected first year sales of 415,000 will give a cash flow of $129,550, and there will be $400,000 less $8,500 tax from selling the plant.

124

This makes an expected $521,050/1.15 - $500,000 = -$46,913. There is also an 80 percent chance of $203,807. Combining the two figures, we find that the abandonment option increases the NPV of the project to $153,663 (= -$46,913 x 0.2 + $203,807 x 0.8). This reduces the value of the survey information to $16,663 (= $153,663 - $137,000).

11
Where Positive Net Present Values Come From

INTRODUCTION

This chapter gives some basic and very valuable lessons in the economics of competition. Modern market economies have intense competition in nearly all industries. Very few firms can expect to earn economic profits or have positive NPV investments unless they have a sustainable comparative advantage in the business they are engaged in. No matter how much we know about the theory of making capital budgeting decisions, we will end up making bad decisions if our forecasts of cash flows turn out badly. This chapter shows you how you can ensure that these forecasts are as good as possible.

The first section of the chapter describes how some difficult forecasting problems may be avoided by making use of available market information. The second section focuses on the market in which the firm operates. Firms do not get positive NPV projects without there being some reason for it. A positive NPV can arise only if the firm has some comparative advantage or what the business strategists call competitive advantage. It is important to understand just the nature of such an advantage. What is it that enables the firm and not some other company to exploit the opportunity provided by the project? If you can answer this question satisfactorily, you probably have understood the project and the source of the positive NPV.

These ideas are elaborated using a small case study (Marvin Enterprises). Your company can expect a positive NPV from a project if it has competitive advantage in one or more aspects of the project. However, it is good to remember that other firms are not going to be idle and will whittle away your competitive advantage over time. In other words, competitive advantage is never permanent, so it is reasonable to expect that the source of the positive NPV will disappear over time. You want to keep this in mind when you prepare your cash flow estimates.

KEY CONCEPTS IN THE CHAPTER

Economic Rents: Economic rents are profits in excess of cost of capital. Companies can extract economic rents from its customers if they have an edge over the competition. In competitive markets, all that a firm can expect to get is a fair price covering all its costs. Competition will drive the price down to the point where the price will equal the cost of producing the product or service (cost includes the cost of capital). Whenever you have a positive NPV project, remember that the positive NPV is simply the present value of future economic rents. Look for the source of the economic rent. Economic rent may exist in the short-term when the industry is not in long-run equilibrium. Over the long-term, a company can expect to have economic rents only if it has some kind of monopoly or market power. You should be able to identify the source. Remember the following three points:

- When an industry is in a long-run competitive equilibrium, all assets earn just their opportunity cost of capital, their NPVs are zero, and economic rents are zero.

- Firms can earn temporary (or permanent) economic rents if there is temporary dis-equilibrium, or if they have some degree of monopoly or market power.

- Never accept that a project has a positive NPV unless you understand why your firm has a competitive advantage in doing it.

Market Values as Source of Price Information: Market prices provide extremely useful information about the value of commodities. Since investments in commodities do not provide annual dividends, today's price of a commodity is the present value of the future price of the same. A gold mine can look to the current gold price for the present value of future sales of gold because this is consistent with the equilibrium expected return to investors in gold. You can use market prices to reduce the chance of forecasting errors swamping genuine information. Information that is not generally known can be analyzed separately and added to (or subtracted from) the market value.

Refer to the department store example used in the text. A department store investment involves at least two distinct bets: one on real estate prices and another on whether the real estate is best suited to running a department store. It is helpful to imagine the business as divided into two parts: a real estate subsidiary that buys the building and rents it out and a retailing one that rents and operates it. This forces you to consider whether the department store is the best current use for the real estate, and whether it is likely to remain so. It would be foolish to make a lousy department store investment because of optimism about real estate prices. Instead, it would be better to buy the real estate and rent it out, though a real estate company would have more expertise in this area. Conversely, it would be silly to be deterred from going ahead with a profitable department store because of pessimism about real estate prices. Instead, it is better to sell the real estate and then rent it back for the department store.

Technology, Competition, and Economic Rents: *Marvin Enterprises* is an extended and useful illustration of what happens in an industry when a firm has a technological break-through and is poised to exploit it. While the example is fictitious, the problems it poses are very real and have many parallels in today's world.

The example is about a company that has developed a new technology, but there are other firms hot on its heels and its relative advantage is expected to last for only 5 years. After 5 years, new investments will come in and drive the price of the product (gargle blasters) down to its equilibrium level. The company will therefore earn abnormally high profits (economic rents) only over the first 5 years.

The main argument of the case runs as follows: The price of a product depends on the total amount of it produced. Producers compete with each other and will expand their capacity until the new investment has a zero net present value. From this, it follows that any single producer can expect to find positive NPV projects only if he or she has some kind of relative advantage over the competition. Such advantages certainly exist: a company may have built up a good reputation for its brand name in the marketplace. You can see that these advantages are hard-won and must be protected tenaciously.

The case raises two other important issues. The first is the effect of Marvin Enterprises' new investment on its existing business. Its proposed expansion is sufficiently large to affect the price of the product it is selling. Marvin must worry about the loss of revenue on its existing operations and include this in its calculation of the NPV of the new project. In more extreme situations, this could lead to the company's wishing to suppress its new technology completely.

Second, the less efficient producers play an extremely important role. As the capacity of the industry is increased, the price of the product falls, and it becomes increasingly difficult for these producers to stay in business. If the price falls far enough, some producers may withdraw from the market, and other marginal producers may be on the point of doing so. In this situation, the price of the product will be at the point where it just pays the least efficient remaining producer to stay in business. The size of the economic rent obtained by a more efficient producer will simply reflect the difference between their costs (including the opportunity cost of the capital employed).

Beware of the misleading argument that a fully depreciated plant is cheaper to run than an otherwise identical un-depreciated one. This argument is often made, but it is falsely based on interpreting accounting income as if it were cash flow. Remember, only cash flows matter, not accounting numbers. Since, in this example, there are no taxes; there is absolutely no difference between cash flows of a depreciated plant and those of an un-depreciated one.

Here is a summary of the key points made in the discussion of the Marvin Enterprises case:

- Anticipated and prolonged economic rents are uncommon.
- High economic rents usually attract competitors; try to estimate the timing and extent of new entry.
- Identify your firm's competitive advantages, and try to capitalize on them.
- Successive generations of technology will tend to reduce the value of earlier generation assets. A growth industry has no mercy on laggards.
- The NPV of a project may be reduced by the impact it has on the firm's existing business. This can provide an incentive to slow down the speed of innovation.
- A *marginal producer* is one who will quit if the price goes any lower, i.e., for whom price equals manufacturing cost plus opportunity cost of not selling out. The economic rent to a more efficient producer is simply the difference between its costs and those of a marginal producer.
- A high salvage value increases economic rents. The book value of the old plant is irrelevant.

WORKED EXAMPLE

The Yamaichi Tire & Rubber Company is considering a new investment in a fully automated tire plant. Its existing plant produces 1 million tires a year. It cost $80 million 5 years ago, and it could be scrapped for $30 million at any time. The production costs per tire of the old and new plants can be broken down as follows:

	Old Plant	New Plant
Raw Materials and energy	$15	$17
Labor	10	3
Other direct costs	5	5
Total direct costs	$30	$25

The new plant will be able to produce 500,000 tires a year, and it will cost $35 million. The current price of tires is $38 each. Yamaichi's new investment is not expected to affect this, but the price may fall when other companies complete their modernization programs in 2 years' time. Yamaichi's cost of capital is 10 percent, and there are no corporate taxes.

a. What is the NPV of the new plant?
b. When will the old plant be scrapped, and what is its value today?
c. The costs of raw materials and energy suddenly double. The price of tires changes to $50. What are the answers to (a) and (b) now?

SOLUTION

a. The capital outlay required on the new plant is $70 per annual tire capacity. The break-even price to give a zero NPV is therefore (10 percent x $70) +$25 (direct costs) = $32. This is the price that we should expect to see in 2 years' time. With the price now at $38, Yamaichi can expect economic rents of $6 per tire per year for 2 years. The NPV of the new plant is therefore:

$$500,000x\left(\frac{\$6}{1.1}+\frac{\$6}{1.1^2}\right)=\$5,206,611$$

b. The old plant should be scrapped when it can no longer earn the opportunity cost of its salvage value, that is, 10 percent x $30 million, or $3 on each tire produced. It will be scrapped when the price falls below $33, that is, in 2 years' time. Meanwhile, it will produce cash flows of $8 million for 2 years. Its value today is therefore:

$$\frac{\$8,000,000}{1.1}+\frac{\$8,000,000+\$30,000,00}{1.1^2}=\$38,677,686$$

c. The change in energy and materials costs modifies the direct costs to $45 and $42 for the old and new plants, respectively. This increases the breakeven price on the new plant to $49, just

130

$1 below the current price of $50. The economic rent is now only $1 per tire produced (for 2 years), so the NPV of the new plant is:

$$500,000 \times [(\$1/1.1) + (\$1/1.1^2)] = \$867,769$$

The old plant will now be scrapped only if the price of tires falls below $45 + $3 = $48. It is now sensible for manufacturers to build only sufficient new plants to push the price down to $49. The old plant is no longer expected to be scrapped but will earn $5 per tire for 2 years and $4 per tire after that. In year 2, it will be worth 4/0.1 = $40 million; so today it is worth:

$$\frac{\$5,000,000}{1.1} + \frac{\$5,000,000 + \$40,000,000}{1.1^2} = \$41,735,537$$

SUMMARY

Project evaluations can show positive NPVs either because the cash flow projections are too good (and wrong) or the project is really good and the company can extract economic rents on account of its competitive advantage over its rivals. Managers should ensure that when they accept positive NPV projects, they belong to the latter group. The biggest practical difficulty in applying the NPV criterion is in establishing reliable cash flow forecasts. The chapter illustrates the most important dangers and difficulties in forecasting cash flows, and it provides advice on how best to combat them. Although it is hard to provide rules, which would cover all situations, it is common sense to look for the source of the positive NPV. Throughout, the key idea is that you can expect a positive NPV only if you have some kind of competitive advantage relative to your rivals in the industry.

Market prices provide very useful information on the value of many assets and commodities. Unless you have reason to believe that you know better than the market, you would be well advised to accept the markets values. This applies to real estate or gold or oil, any of the well-traded assets or commodities. If you think an asset is worth more in your possession than its market value, you should be able to explain why.

Technological breakthroughs give companies tremendous advantage and significant economic rents. However, this advantage does not last forever; competitors catch up soon. This economic rent will be a direct function of the cost difference between the technology leader and the surviving marginal producer. Marginal producers will survive as long as the price in the market is above their cost. It should also be noted that technological breakthroughs might not be an unmixed blessing as they affect existing operations of the company negatively just as much as they harm the competitors' business. The impact of new investments on existing operations should be analyzed carefully as part of the new project evaluation.

LIST OF TERMS

Comparative advantage   Competitive advantage
Economic Rent   Marginal producer

EXERCISES

Fill-in Questions

1. A firm needs to have some _____ over its rivals in the same business in order to economic profits.

2. _____ is another term used to denote comparative advantage.

3. A _____ is a producer who will cease production if there is any fall in the price at which the product is sold.

4. _____ is the term used to describe profits, which are in excess of the cost of capital.

Problems

1. Which of the following are true and which are false?

   a. A monopoly can obtain permanent economic rents unless it is regulated in some way.
   b. The average forecasting error for the cash flow of a project is zero.
   c. New capacity decisions must take account of the effect on sunk costs, such as investments in existing plants.
   d. No firm can earn economic rents if it has to buy inputs at a price that reflects their value to the firm.
   e. Marginal producers have assets with zero market value.
   f. Fully depreciated assets always have a present value of zero.
   g. Stock prices reflect the value of growth opportunities only after the firm has announced its plans to invest in new capacity.

2. Nevada Mining Company is considering opening a second gold mine. This mine will cost $15 million to develop, and it will produce 30,000 ounces of refined gold a year for 5 years at a cost of $220 an ounce. The current gold price is $280 an ounce, and the opportunity cost of funds is 10 percent.

   a. What is the NPV of this project if you assume that the gold price will grow at 5 percent per year?
   b. What is the NPV if you assume that the gold price is expected to grow at the cost of funds?

3. Tizzal Corp. makes mobile phones that sell for $80 each and cost $50 each to manufacture. The existing plant produces 30 million units per year, which represents a significant part of the total market. The company is considering investing in a new plant that will increase capacity by 20 million units per year. When the increased volume of production hits the market, the market price of mobile phones is expected to fall to $65 per unit. Tizzal is currently negotiating contracts for the construction of its new plant, which will reduce production costs to $30 per unit. The cost of capital for this project is 15 percent.

   a. What is the maximum price that Tizzal should be prepared to pay for its new plant, assuming that it can expect to retain a monopoly of the more efficient production technology indefinitely?
   b. What would the plant be worth to another company that did not already mobile phones?

4. The manufacture and sale of Bubby Tubbies is highly competitive. The industry is composed of three firms with the following capacities and manufacturing costs:

Firms	Sales (million units)	Unit cost
A	8	8
B	6	9
C	4	10
Total	18	

The demand curve for Bubby Tubbies is given by:

   Price (in dollars) = $24 - 0.5 x (quantity in millions)

The industry opportunity cost of capital is 10 percent, and new plant costs $70 per unit of capacity. All the plants have indefinitely long lives but could be scrapped at salvage values of $30 per unit of capacity. Firm C discovers a way of reducing unit-manufacturing costs to $7, keeping capital costs unchanged. It manages to secure monopoly rights to the technique for an extremely long period, and it decides to challenge firm A's market leadership by immediately adding 5 million units of the new capacity.

   a. What is the present value of firm C's existing plant after the new capacity is added?
   b. What is the maximum addition to capacity before it is worthwhile to scrap firm C's original plant?
   c. What is the NPV of firm C's new investment project?
   d. Can firm C make any profitable investment without first disposing of its old plant?

5. Bay Corp. and Valley Inc. have identical plants that can each manufacture 100,000 chips a year, at a unit cost of $6. These plants could be scrapped at any time with a scrap value of

$1.5 million. Bay Corp. plant has been fully depreciated for tax purposes, whereas Valley Inc. plant has been depreciated only to a book value of $1 million and will give rise to annual $500,000 depreciation allowances for the next 2 years. Since both companies pay tax at 50 percent, Bay Corp. would realize only a net of $750,000 from scrapping its plant immediately; while Valley Inc. would realize $1.25 million net. At what prices for chips will each company find it economical to cease production immediately and scrap its plant? (Assume the opportunity cost of capital is 10 percent.)

6. The market for shipping crude oil can be represented in terms of a number of types of tanker serving a number of different routes. One very simplified representation is given below. It shows, in millions, the available tonnage of each class of tanker, the total tonnage required on each route, and the operating costs of each tanker on each route.

		ANNUAL OPERATING COSTS (PER TON)		
TANKER TYPE	TONNAGE	ROUTE 1	ROUTE 2	ROUTE 3
VLCC	500	$ 30	$ 34	Too large
MLCC	400	35	37	$ 38
Other	300	40	40	40
Tonnage required		300	500	250

All tankers are available for charter in a competitive market, and the price mechanism will allocate them to routes so as to minimize the total costs of transporting crude. All tankers have a useful life of 15 years and can be sold for scrap at any time for $150 per ton. Assume the cost of capital is 10 percent.

a. What type or types of tanker will be used on each route?
b. What will be the annual rental (per ton) for chartering each type of tanker?
c. What will be the market price per ton) for purchasing each type of tanker?
d. What could happen to the usage and the prices of each type of tanker if the tonnage of VLCCs increased to 700?
e. What would happen if (with no increase in the tonnage of VLCCs) an environmental lobby succeeded in banning VLCCs from 50 percent of the required tonnage of route 1?

Essay Questions

1. Describe the different kinds of biases in forecasts that can affect capital budgeting decisions. Give some guidelines for minimizing their effects.

2. Discuss the relationship among competitive advantage, economic rent, and positive NPV projects.

3. Explain clearly why a company may have an economic incentive to suppress an improvement in technology.

4. Explain clearly what is meant by the statement, "The level of economic rents is determined by the costs of the marginal producer."

5. In the Marvin Enterprises example, users of the earlier and more expensive technologies were prepared to continue to produce even at prices that gave negative profits after depreciation. Explain what factors determine their willingness to do so.

6. Describe an industry that has experienced the type of situation and decisions described in Marvin Enterprises. What are the most important similarities and differences between your example and the imaginary gargle blaster industry?

7. Discuss whether a company can still have an incentive to suppress an improvement in technology if all its shareholders hold the market portfolio.

ANSWERS TO EXERCISES

Fill-in Questions

1. Comparative advantage
2. Competitive advantage

3. Marginal producer
4. Economic rent

Problems

1. a. True
   b. False
   c. True
   d. True

   e. False
   f. False
   g. False

2. a. For each ounce of gold mined per year, the present value of the gross revenue stream is:

   280 x (annuity factor: t = 5, r = 1.1/1.05 = 4.76%; 4.358) = $1,220
   PV of costs = $220 x (annuity factor: t = 5, r = 10%; 3.791) = $834
   NPV = -15,000,000 + 30,000 [1,220 - 834] = -$3,420,000

   b. NPV = -15,000,000 + 30,000 [(5 x 280) - ($834)] = $1,980,000

3. a. Tizzal will gain net revenues of $35 on each of its 20 million new units a year, and it will lose $15 each of its existing 30 million units of output. This gives an incremental cash flow of:

   (20,000,0000 x $35) - (30,000,000 x $15) = $250 million

   At a 15 percent discount rate, the present value is $1,667 million, and this is the maximum price Universal should be prepared to pay.

b. Another company would not stand to lose revenues on the existing plant. The new plant would be worth \$700 million/0.15 = \$4,667 million to such a company.

4. a. The extra capacity will drive the price down to \$12.50 [\$24 – (0.5 x 23)], but it is best to scrap C's old plant at any price below \$13 [\$10 + (\$30 x 0.1)]. The existing plant is therefore worth only its salvage value of \$120 million (4 x \$30).

   b. 4 million units, because at a price of \$13 the unit will have to be scrapped. A total capacity of 22 million units will cause the price to fall to \$13 = \$24 – (0.5 x 22).

   c. Assuming the equilibrium price is \$13, the NPV of firm C's project is given as

$$NPV = [5,000,000 \text{ x } (\$6/0.1 - \$70)] - [\$4,000,000 \text{ x } (\$5/0.1 - \$30)]$$
$$= -\$50,000,000 - \$80,000,000$$
$$= -\$130,000,000$$

   If firm C scraps all its old plant and the price goes to \$14.50, the NPV is still negative (-\$55 million).

   d. It is not possible. When the price is \$15, each unit of investment has a NPV of -\$70 +\$8/0.1 = \$10, but unless the old investment has been scrapped, we also reduce the present value of the old plant by

$$4 \text{ x } \$0.5/0.1 = \$20$$

5. The incremental cash flows from Bay Corp. decision to maintain production are as follows:

	YEAR 0	YEAR 1
Net revenues after tax		0.5 x (P - 6) x 0.1
Proceeds on disposal	-0.75	0.75

Where P is the unit price in dollars and the cash flows are expressed in millions of dollars. These cash flows will have a positive NPV if the price is greater than \$7.50.

Similarly, the incremental cash flows from Valley Inc.'s decision to maintain production are:

	YEAR 0	YEAR 1
Net revenues after tax		0.5 x (P - 6) x 0.1
Depreciation tax shield		0.25
Proceeds on disposal	-1.25	1.00

These cash flows will have a positive NPV if the price is greater than \$8.50.

6. a. We can figure out from the structure of operating costs that the total costs of transporting crude are minimized when the demands of each route are satisfied as follows:

> Route 1: 300 VLCC
> Route 2: 200 VLCC, 300 MLCC
> Route 3: 100 MLCC, 150 other

b. Since 150 "other" tankers are in use and the remaining 150 are idle, this category of tanker represents a marginal producer, and its rent must equal the opportunity cost of salvage. Since the cost of capital is 10 percent and the salvage value is $150 per ton, the rental must be $15 per ton.

MLCCs and "other" tankers are both used on route 3, but the MLCCs are cheaper to operate by $2 per ton. They can therefore command a $2-higher rental of $17 per ton.

VLCCs and MLCCs are both used on route 2, with a $3 cost advantage to the VLCCs. This gives them a $3 rental advantage, and the VLCC rental is $20 per ton.

c. Capitalizing the rentals of $20, $17, and $15, we find that the market prices of the VLCC, MLCC, and "other" tankers are $200, $170, and $150.

d. Route 2: 400 VLCC, 100 MLCC; route 3: 250 MLCC. All "other" would be scrapped, MLCC would drop to salvage value of $150 per ton, and VLCC to $180 per ton.

e. Compared with (a), the 150 tons of route 1 VLCCs would switch with 150 tons of route 2 MLCCs. There is no change in tanker prices. Price for shipping oil on route 1 increases by $5 per ton.

12

Making Sure Managers Maximize NPV

INTRODUCTION

This chapter describes the organization of the capital budgeting process. The chapter also discusses the agency problems involved in investment decision making at different levels of management and possible steps needed to ensure that the managers make optimal investment decisions in the best interests of the shareholders. The measurement problems encountered with the commonly used accounting profitability measure are analyzed. Alternate concepts of residual income and economic value added are presented.

KEY CONCEPTS IN THE CHAPTER

The Capital Budgeting Process: Capital budgeting process typically involves the following four stages.

Preparation of capital budget - This is a broad list of projects to be taken up during the year. The list has summary details and is typically generated through a *bottom-up* process with different departments, plants, or divisions coming up with their list of proposed projects.

Project authorization - This step involves formal vetting of the projects by the top management through appropriate analyses and screening. The step ensures that the projects included reflect the firm's strategic direction. Before expenditure on individual projects is committed through *appropriation requests,* project details are prepared and analyses using NPV or other measures of project acceptability are conducted. Typically, managers are delegated authority to approve expenditures up to set ceilings with the projects requiring large investment requiring approval at the highest level or the board of directors.

Implementation and control - Project details are monitored during construction with appropriate information feed back to top management for control and necessary corrective actions. Project cost, time schedule, and any change in key inputs or factors affecting the project viability are among the elements monitored regularly.

Post-audit - Firms do post-audits of completed projects shortly after the project is completed. This enables the management to identify the errors and omissions with respect to project details. The step is part of a continuous learning process for everyone involved in project management and enables the firm to avoid the errors in the future.

Note that there are important and often sizable investments made by firms, which are not part of the capital budgeting process. These include R and D, marketing campaigns, training and development expenditures, and investment in information technology. The control systems and screening procedures in place should take into account the existence of these projects and ensure that proposals for these expenses are evaluated properly.

Information: Timely and accurate information is needed by top management to ensure that right decisions are made and implemented. The structure and organization of the capital budgeting process should guard against the common pitfalls of *inconsistent assumptions* across the firm and at different levels of management and *bias* on the part of project sponsors. *Accuracy and timeliness* of the information are very important. *Conflicts of interest* on the part of the project sponsors and decision makers should be avoided. The managers should be rewarded appropriately and given the right incentives to take NPV maximizing decisions. In short, the structure of the rewards system should be such as to minimize the effect of agency problems.

Agency Problems: Investment decisions are among the most important decisions taken by corporate managers. The right decisions, properly implemented, will result in enhanced shareholder value and wrong decisions will lead to deterioration of shareholder wealth. The stockholders are the principals and the managers are the agents given the responsibility of running the firm on behalf of the stockholders. Corporate managers rarely own significant amounts of the firm's stock; therefore they do not necessarily share the stockholders' enthusiasm for maximizing NPV. This is the essence of the agency problems, which cause sub-optimal behavior on the part of the managers. Some examples of this behavior include - *reduced efforts* (or shirking), use of *perks, empire building* or expanding the business for its own sake, taking up *entrenching investments* which ensures the manager's position, and a tendency to avoid *risk* even when it is in the interest of the stockholder. The empire-building propensity is caused by the fact that the manager's relative importance, authority, and position are a function of the size of the operation she or he commands rather than the value added by it. The reduction in value of the firm caused by the agency problems is the agency cost.

Mitigating Agency Costs: While the agency cost cannot be totally eliminated, the organization of the capital budgeting process and the rewards system for managers should be structured such that the agency cost is reduced to the minimum possible. This is achieved through a mix of *monitoring* of managers' behavior and by designing the managers' rewards and incentives in a way to align the managers' interests with that of the stockholders. Monitoring is done at different levels and is delegated by the stockholders to the board of directors who monitor the top management. The top management in turn takes care of monitoring the managers at lower levels. Accounting firms who perform regular audits of companies' books of accounts and financial statements perform an important role in the overall monitoring of corporations. In general, small stockholders leave it to the larger stockholders to closely watch corporate performance on a regular basis. This might actually lead to the *free-rider problem*, where everyone assumes that someone else will do the job and nobody does it.

Monitoring has its limits and to be effective has to be used in combination with well-designed *compensation* plans for managers. The ideal compensation plans will succeed in aligning the managers' interest with that of the stockholders. A fixed salary will never work, as this does not

140

give any incentive to the manager to do the best she or he can. Part of the problem in rewarding managers is the fact that managerial inputs cannot be measured effectively and the output depends on not only managerial input but also on external factors on which the manager has no control. In practice, more and more firms are designing managerial compensation packages such that they include a fixed component and bonuses or rewards for improved corporate performance. Rewards for the top management can be based on the overall corporate performance or price of the firm's shares. However, compensating managers at divisional and plant levels on the basis of the company's share performance is not fair and will not produce the best efforts from these managers. Here one has to use other measures of performance.

Measuring Performance: If performance based compensation plans for managers are to be effective, the measures of performance have to reflect the performance accurately. The traditional tool used in the past is the accounting measure, *return on investment* (ROI). The ROI and accounting earnings (net income) have two major advantages: i) it measures performance on absolute basis and ii) this can be used to measure performance of managers of departments and divisions. However, the accounting measures also suffer from some major drawbacks: i) it is subject to manager's control, ii) they are often biased and are subject to the type of accounting rules used, and iii) the typical accounting profit does not include any provision for the cost of funds used in the business. This means that positive earnings and earnings growth by themselves do not reflect superior performance. Accounting earnings are also biased against new investments in that they understate a project's profitability in the early years of the project and overstate the same in the later years. Comparison of accounting earnings across firms in different industries can be very misleading. Unless firms earn more than their cost of capital, they are not adding value to the firm or its stockholders.

An alternate measure, which overcomes most of the drawbacks of the accounting earnings, is the residual *income* or the *economic value added* (EVA$^@$).[1] EVA measures the value added after covering the cost of capital for the investment used in the business. It equals the income earned less the cost of funds used. A similar measure is the *economic profit* (EP) used by McKinsey and Company. This is measured as the capital used in the business multiplied by the difference between the return on investment and the cost of capital. EVA explicitly recognizes the cost of capital and focuses on profits earned after meeting the cost of capital. It has become quite popular in recent years and firms use EVA to measure and reward divisional performance. While EVA is a great improvement over the accounting earnings, it retains some of the biases of the accounting profits. Thus for new projects or investments carrying long-term benefits and short-term costs, EVA will understate the value added in the early years. The problem here is that EVA, like accounting earnings, is understating real economic income. This is often because of overstatement of depreciation or inclusion of elements, which are investments rather than current expenses (e.g. R & D). Effective implementation of EVA as a measurement and compensation tool requires changing some of the accounting rules or adjusting for them so that EVA is an accurate reflection of the value added.

---

[1]@ - This is a copyrighted term registered by the consulting firm, Stern and Stewart.

Economic Depreciation: Economic depreciation measures the real decline in the value of the asset and thus is measured by the change in the present value of cash flows generated by the asset. Unlike accounting or book depreciation, economic depreciation can be negative (i.e. the value of the asset increases).

Explanation of Formulas and Mathematical Expressions

Notations:
C_1 = Cash receipts during the period
P_0, P_1 = Price of the asset at the beginning and the end of the period
BV_0, BV_1 = Book value at the beginning and the end of the period
r = Cost of capital
ROI = Return on investment

$$\text{Rate of return} = \frac{C_1 + (P_1 - P_0)}{P_0}$$

EVA = Income earned - Cost of capital x Investment
Economic Income = Cash receipts - Economic depreciation
Economic depreciation = $P_0 - P_1$
EP = (ROI - r) Capital employed
Book income = Cash receipts - Book depreciation = $C_1 + (BV_1 - BV_0)$

$$\text{Book ROI} = \frac{C_1 + (BV_1 - BV_0)}{BV_0}$$

Points to keep in mind:
  i)   EVA = EP
  ii) Book depreciation will always be positive or zero.
  iii) Economic depreciation may be negative or the asset value may increase.

WORKED EXAMPLE

Bugsy Inc. is considering an investment of $120 million on a project with the following expected cash flows. The project generates cash flows for 5 years and will be closed down after that. The cost of capital is estimated at 15%. Assume straight-line depreciation for book income calculations.

Year	0	1	2	3	4	5
Cash flows (millions)	-120	20	30	46.3	46.3	46.3

Calculate the NPV for the project and forecast the book income, the ROI, the economic income and EVA for the project.

SOLUTION

$$NPV = -120 + \frac{20}{1.15} + \frac{30}{(1.15)^2} + \frac{46.3}{(1.15)^3} + \frac{46.3}{(1.15)^4} + \frac{46.3}{1.15^5} = 0$$

Forecast of book income and ROI:

Cash flow in millions

Years	1	2	3	4	5
Cash flow	20	30	46.3	46.3	46.3
Beginning book value	120	96	72	48	24
Ending book value	96	72	48	24	0
Change in book value	-24	-24	-24	-24	-24
Book income	-4	6	22.3	22.3	22.3
Book ROI	-0.033	0.063	0.310	0.465	0.929
Book depreciation	24	24	24	24	24

Book income = cash flow + change in book value
Book ROI   = Book Income/Beginning book value

Forecast of economic income, economic rate of return, and EVA:

Cash flow in millions

Years	1	2	3	4	5
Cash flow	20	30	46.3	46.3	46.3
Beginning present value	120	118	105.7	75.3	40.3
Ending present value	118	105.7	75.3	40.3	0
Change in value	-2	-12.3	-30.4	-35	-40.3
Economic income	18	17.7	15.9	11.3	6
Economic rate of return	0.15	0.15	0.15	0.15	0.15
Economic depreciation	2	12.3	30.4	35	40
Economic value added	0	0	0	0	0

Economic income = cash flow + change in present value
Economic return = Economic income/Beginning present value

143

Economic value added = Economic income - cost of capital x beginning value

SUMMARY

This chapter describes the capital budgeting process, which typically includes the four stages of *budget preparation, project authorization*, procedures for *control of projects,* and *post-audits* conducted soon after project completion. Ideally, the capital budgeting process should combine bottom-up projects generation and top down strategic planning. It is to be noted that many important investments do not necessarily go through formal capital budgeting procedures. These include R & D expenditure, major marketing campaigns, and training and development expenses. The finance manager should be aware of these and proper control and evaluation procedures should be in place to ensure that these projects add value.

The chapter also discusses the need for and significance of accurate information and forecasts on projects. The senior management can make the right decisions only if the information is accurate and timely. The financial manager should be aware of the typical problems involved in information gathering: bias on the part of project sponsors, inconsistent assumptions, and conflict of interests. Monitoring and appropriate rewards and incentives for managers are essential to ensure that managers maximize NPV.

Structuring rewards and incentives for managers require accurate measurement of performance. The chapter analyzes the drawbacks of the widely used accounting measures of performance. The accounting earnings and ROI understate the profitability of new projects and overstate the earnings and ROI of older projects. Alternate measures like EVA based on economic income and economic depreciation are better in measuring performance.

LIST OF TERMS

Appropriation request
Capital budget
Economic depreciation
Economic income
Economic profit

Economic value added
Post-audit
Project authorization
Return on investment

EXERCISES

Fill-in Questions

1. The initial step in the investment process is the preparation of the list of projects proposed to be undertaken during the year called _____.

2. The accounting ROI generally _____ the profitability of new projects and

_____ that of older projects.

3. Most companies require that a formal _____ be prepared before funds are released for a project.

4. Economic income is measured by the cash flow plus the change in the _____ of the assets.

5. Project sponsors generally tend to _____ the benefits of the project and _____ the costs of the project.

6. _____ of projects are usually undertaken soon after the projects are completed.

7. Senior management can be considered as the _____ of the _____.

8. Senior managers are monitored by _____.

9. Auditing firms also provide _____ of the firm's performance.

10. Managers sometimes sponsor projects, which have a _____ for their skills.

Problems

1. True or False?
   a. Fixed salaries rarely provide the right incentives for managers.

   b. Accounting ROI provides an absolute measure of performance.

   c. Inflation has little effect on the ROI as it affects both the revenues and costs.

   d. All important expenditures pass through the capital budgeting process.

   e. Economic value added as usually calculated reflects the NPV of the project.

   f. Book depreciation cannot be negative.

   g. Economic depreciation can be negative.

   h. Changing project hurdle rates has little effect on the number of projects proposed.

2. Web Café is considering an expansion project, which requires an investment of $200,000 and is expected to produce after-tax annual cash flows of $60,000 for each of the next five years. The cash flows beyond five years are ignored. Calculate the NPV, IRR, pay back, and the average accounting ROI for the project. Assume a cost of capital of 15 percent and straight-

line depreciation.

3. A project has the following cash flows: $C_0 = -168$, $C_1 = 60$, $C_2 = 75$, $C_3 = 90$.
   a. Calculate the IRR.
   b. Find the accounting rate of return for each year using straight-line depreciation.
   c. Calculate the weighted average accounting rate of return using the beginning period book value discounted at the IRR as the weight for each year.

4. An asset costs $740,000 and is expected to produce a cash flow of $180,000 each year for the next 6 years. The cost of capital is 12 percent.
   a. Calculate the accounting income using straight-line depreciation.
   b. Calculate the economic income for each year.
   c. What are the cash flows required to make the economic depreciation straight-line and provide the same present value?

5. Division X of ABC Inc. has an accounting income of $145,000. The division uses assets of $800,000 and has a cost of capital of 15%. Calculate the ROI and the EVA.

6. Given below are the income and asset values for three divisions of Gujarat Corp. Calculate the ROI and the EVA. Between accounting income and EVA, which measures the performance of the divisions better?

	Division 1	Division 2	Division 3
Net Income	$215 million	$400 million	$125 million
Assets employed	$2,100 million	$2,600 million	$750 million
Cost of capital	14%	11%	12%

Essay Questions

1. Describe the various stages of the capital budgeting process.

2. Discuss the relative merits of using EVA and ROI for measuring the operating performance of divisions and departments.

3. Explain the importance of timely and accurate information in the capital budgeting process.

4. "It is not possible or even desirable to eliminate all agency costs." Discuss.

5. Describe some of the problems involved in managing and controlling the capital budgeting process and ensuring that managers maximize the shareholders' wealth.

6. Compare and contrast economic and book income. Do you agree with the view that

accountants should not try to measure economic income?

ANSWERS TO EXERCISES

Fill-in-Questions

1. Capital budget
2. Understates, overstates
3. Appropriation request
4. Price
5. Overestimate, underestimate

6. Post-audit
7. Agents, shareholders
8. Board of directors
9. Monitoring
10. Need

Problems

1. True or False?
   a. True   b. True   c. False   d. False
   e. False   f. True   g. True   h. True

2. NPV = \$1,129   IRR = 15.24%   Pay back period = 3.33 years

$$\text{Average accounting ROI} = \frac{Average Accounting Income}{Average Investment}$$
$$= \$20,000/\$100,000 = 20\%$$

Average accounting income = cash flow - book depreciation = \$60,000 - \$40,000 = \$20,000

3. a. IRR = 15 %

    b. Accounting rates of return are given in the table below:

	Year 1	Year 2	Year 3
Cash flow	60	75	90
Beginning book value	168	112	56
Depreciation	56	56	56
Book income	4	19	34
Accounting ROI (%)	2.38	16.96	60.71

    c. Weighted average accounting ROI:

147

Year	Discounted book value	Weight	Accounting ROI	Weighted ROI
1	168/1 = 168	168/307.73 = 0.5459	2.38	1.30
2	112/1.15 = 97.39	97.39/307.73 = 0.3165	16.96	5.37
3	$56/(1.15)^2$ = 42.34	42.34/307.73 = 0.1376	60.71	8.35
Total	307.73	1.00		15. 02

The weighted average ROI is the same (except for rounding error) as the IRR.

4. a. Accounting income = cash flow - depreciation = \$180,000 - (\$740,000/6) = \$56,667

b.

Year	0	1	2	3	4	5	6
Cash flow		180	180	180	180	180	180
Present value	740	649	547	432	304	161	0
Economic depreciation		91	102	115	128	143	161
Economic income		89	78	65	52	37	19

c. Each year the present value should decrease by (740,000/6) = \$123,333. Each year's cash flow will be the depreciation amount + 12 percent of the previous year's present value. The present value and cash flows are given in the table below:

Year	Present value	Cash flow
0	\$740,000	
1	\$616,667	\$212,133
2	\$493,333	\$197,333
3	\$370,000	\$182,533
4	\$246,667	\$167,733
5	\$123,333	\$152,933
6	0	\$138,133

5. ROI = \$145,000/\$800,000 = 18.13%
   EVA = \$145,000 - 0.15x\$800,000 = \$25,000

6.

	Division 1	Division 2	Division 3
Net income	$215 million	$400 million	$125 million
ROI	215/2100 = 10.24%	400/2,600 = 15.38%	125/750 = 16.67%
EVA	215 - 0.14 x 2100 = -$79 million	400 - 0.11 x 2600 = $114 million	125 - 0.12 x 750 = $35 million

The EVA is a better measure of performance as it adjusts for the capital employed and the business risk through the cost of capital. Division 1 has not earned enough income to cover its cost of capital.

13

Corporate Financing and the Six Lessons of Market Efficiency

INTRODUCTION

The chapters covered so far have focused on the asset side of the balance sheet. This chapter is the first of many chapters dealing with corporate financing decisions. The focus now shifts to raising funds to finance corporate investments. While both financing and investment decisions can add or destroy value; it is much harder to find positive NPV financing decisions. Financial markets are efficient and fiercely competitive. It is unlikely to find opportunities in these markets to make easy gains through financing decisions. While analyzing investment decisions, we have assumed away the financing question or taken the financing as given. The same approach, in reverse, is used for evaluating the financing decisions. With the investment decisions as given, what will be the best financing decision? The primary goal of maximizing the NPV remains the same.

Understanding market efficiency and its implications is key to understanding all financing decisions. The chapter explains the concept of market efficiency in detail and reviews the evidence supporting and contradicting market efficiency. The chapter concludes with the six lessons or the key implications of market efficiency for the corporate finance manager. The fundamental point made in this chapter is that owing to the extremely competitive nature of the financial markets, it will be very hard to find positive NPV financing opportunities.

KEY CONCEPTS IN THE CHAPTER

NPV of Financing Decisions: When corporations raise money in the capital market through a bond or stock issue, they receive funds in exchange for explicit or implied promise of future payments to the investors who buy these bonds or stocks. The NPV for a financing decision can be calculated just like it was done for the investment decisions, though the pattern of cash flows will be somewhat different, with cash inflows at the beginning and outflows in later years. The discount rate used for computing present values should reflect the normal cost of the type of financing used. In general, financing decisions differ from investment decisions in the following ways: i) financing decisions are more complex because of the variety of financing forms used - debt, equity, long-term and short term debt, convertible debt, debt with adjustable interest rates, to name some typical forms used, ii) it is harder to find positive NPV financing decisions because of intense competition in the capital market, and iii) financing decisions can often be reversed more easily than most investment decisions. Another important difference between financing and investment is that firms rarely have a competitive advantage in financing unlike in real product markets where they have often built up competitive advantage in terms of brand loyalty

151

and reputation for quality and service. It is also true that financial markets are far less segmented than some might imagine. Capital flows freely across borders and different types of markets.

Market Efficiency: A market is considered efficient when prices in the market fully reflect information about the securities. Since new information about securities, by definition, will be random, price changes also must be random. In other words, day-to-day price changes cannot be predicted and will be totally random. Way back in 1953, Maurice Kendall, a British statistician found that actual price changes were as random as the results of a serial coin tossing game with a slightly higher pay-off for heads. A direct implication of market efficiency is that it will not be easy to find positive NPV financing or investment opportunities. In other words, it will not be possible to find under-priced or overpriced securities. Economists have classified market efficiency into three forms based on the type of information that is reflected in security prices. These are briefly described below.

Weak form efficiency: The market is said to be weak form efficient if prices fully reflect all information about past prices. In other words, market prices will not follow any predictable patterns. Any forecast based on past price patterns will be useless as investment tools and will not help an investor make superior returns. Competition for profits will destroy any useful patterns or cycles.

Semi-strong form efficiency: The market is said to be semi-strong form efficient if security prices fully reflect all publicly available information such as announcement of earnings, issues of stocks or bonds, stock splits, mergers, etc. A semi-strong form efficient market will react quickly and instantaneously to new information and it will be impossible to trade on the news and make money.

Strong form efficiency: The most rigorous form of efficiency implies that security prices will fully reflect all information including that, which is not publicly available. It implies that even information, which is unearthed by careful and expensive research by analysts and investment managers, will not give you superior returns, as the prices will reflect even this information.

Semi-strong form efficiency implies weak form efficiency and strong form efficiency implies weak and semi-strong form efficiencies. Market efficiency is the result of competition among investment analysts, portfolio managers, and professional traders who attempt to exploit any mis-pricing observed in the market. The analysts and portfolio managers spend enormous amounts of resources to uncover the latest and most useful information about any stock they are interested in. The market competition these professionals will ensure that market prices reflect all available information.

Empirical Evidence: Market efficiency is one of the most researched topics in financial economics and empirical evidence generally finds market to be efficient. Different types of tests were used to test the different forms of market efficiency. Weak form efficiency was tested by using trading rules suggested by technical analysts who claimed to have discovered patterns in price movements. It was invariably found that these trading rules did not generate superior profits. Other tests for weak form efficiency included tests for significant relationships between successive daily or weekly returns. Tests have found little serial correlation in daily or weekly returns for markets in many different countries.

The tests for semi-strong form efficiency have included analyzing market reactions to earnings announcements; stock splits, accounting changes, and mergers or other significant corporate events. In general, these tests attempt to isolate the effect of the news or event on the stock price. The tests estimate the *abnormal stock return* as the measure of the impact of the news or event. The abnormal return is defined as actual return - *expected return.* The expected return is estimated using the simple market model: $\alpha + \beta$(actual market return). The abnormal return computed this way excludes the effect of market-wide influences. These tests for semi-strong efficiency have generally shown that market reaction to events and news items of significance is swift and nearly instantaneous leaving very little time to make profitable trades once the news is announced.

Performance of mutual fund managers and stock analysts has been used to test the strong form efficiency. If these professionals show superior performance, it can be interpreted as market inefficiency. While some fund managers appear to have shown consistently better performance, most studies have failed to find superior performance by fund managers and analysts. In general, few mutual funds consistently do better than the market averages or comparable benchmarks. When the mutual fund performance is adjusted for expenses, the returns on average are lower than comparable market benchmarks. This is fairly strong support of the efficient market hypothesis.

Evidence Against Market Efficiency: While the evidence for market efficiency is very convincing, researchers have also discovered a number of *anomalies* or *puzzles*, which seem to indicate some market inefficiencies. These anomalies include: significantly higher returns for smaller stocks, persistent patterns of higher returns for the month of January compared to other months, lower returns for Mondays compared to Fridays, and patterns indicating differing returns for different times of the trading day. Researchers have offered different explanations for these puzzles and anomalies. The small firm effect, for example, may be explained as one of three possible cases: i) higher risk premium required by investors that is not fully captured by the CAPM, ii) result of the specific time period used for the study - the effect would disappear if one looked at the returns for the nineties, and iii) a possible exception to the efficient market theory. Recent years seem to show somewhat of a reversal in the small firm performance, as large firms appear to have done better.

Two other anomalies appear to have persisted. The *earnings announcement* puzzle shows that market under-reacts to earnings announcements such that firms with best earnings news outperform those with worst earnings news. The *new issue puzzle* is the sharp price rise for new stock issues immediately following their issue and the below market long-term (five-year) performance for these stocks. For the period 1970-1998, portfolio of new issue stocks, bought right after the issue, showed returns 33 percent lower than comparable portfolios.

153

Behavioral Finance: It is important to note that few of the anomalies and puzzles have actually yielded opportunities for making money in the market. Behavioral finance is an alternate theoretical attempt to explain market anomalies and investor behavior. Essentially, the behavioralists suggest that investor behavior is less than perfectly rational. Investors often overreact or under-react based on short-term memory. These behavioral traits manifest in the investors' *attitude to risk;* they become are more risk-averse than justified. Most investors are also prone to make systematic errors in assessing probable likelihood of different events and seem to be guided more by their recent experience than by the totality of lessons covering all the information from the past. Investors also seem to suffer from overconfidence. These behavioral inadequacies and less than rational behavior on the part of many investors are offered as explanation for market inefficiencies and anomalies. However, the behavioral approach falls short of a full explanation and seems to work only selectively. Further, professional investors should be able to exploit the opportunities provided by irrational behavior of others. The fact that they have not been able to do so, suggests that the anomalies are not quite predictable or easy to exploit.

The 1990s witnessed another market phenomenon, which cannot be easily explained in the efficient market framework. This is the so called dot-com bubble. Between 1995 and early 2000 the NASDAQ Composite Index, dominated by technology stocks, rose by 580 percent. Then in the next 18 months the Index lost about 70 percent of its value. This could be a classic example of irrational exuberance on the part of investors, but it appears that professional investors and analysts failed to see what was coming.

Relative vs. Absolute Efficiency: An implication of market efficiency is that securities are fairly priced and the prices reflect the intrinsic value of the securities. The stock market crash of October 19, 1987 - prices dropped 23 percent in a single day - raised serious doubts about the market's ability to value securities correctly. If the prices were fair the day before the crash, it is hard to argue that they remained fair the day after. While one can justify large price changes as the result of changes in expectations of earnings growth, it will be hard to argue that the market or the investors can always correctly price securities on an absolute basis. The pricing or valuation can be correct only in a relative sense. It is impossible to test absolute intrinsic valuation and thus absolute efficiency. We can price the stock of General Motors and be reasonably sure about its valuation, only if we assume that Ford or some other automobile manufacturer comparable to GM is priced reasonably correct. In the absence of such a benchmark for comparison, we cannot be sure of our valuation. Thus, while we are reasonably certain about the market being relatively efficient, one cannot make any claim about absolute market efficiency. Note that the above explanation can be applied to the dot-com bubble also.

Implications of Market Anomalies: Market anomalies may lead to under-pricing or overpricing of the firm's stock. It is important to note that overpricing of your firm's stock does not mean that it is good to issue stocks and invest in negative NPV projects; you are better off in investing in the capital markets in other securities. Under-pricing of your stock precludes you from issuing stocks.

The Six Lessons of Market Efficiency: While the anomalies and puzzles raise serious questions about market efficiency, the finance manager will do well to heed some basic lessons about market behavior. These are summarized below.

<u>Lesson 1 - Markets have no memory</u>: This stresses weak form efficiency and clearly implies that attempts at timing the market for bond or stock issue are unlikely to result in value maximizing decisions. Historic prices and recent trends are not much help in forecasting the market trend. It is unfortunately true that many managers try to time the market by picking the best time to issue securities.

<u>Lesson 2 - Trust market prices</u>: It is not possible for most investors to consistently find bargains or under-priced securities in the market. Market prices reflect the collective wisdom of all the investors and analysts and therefore will be the best estimates of the value of the securities. In other words, it is unreasonable and unwise to assume that one can predict the prices better than the market itself.

<u>Lesson 3 - Read the entrails</u>: Market prices tell us a lot about the future. Security prices typically reflect what investors expect to happen in the future. For example, the difference between short-term and long-term interest indicates the expected changes in interest rates. The return offered by a company's bonds and the variability of its common stock prices are good indicators of the probability of its going bankrupt. Market reactions to corporate announcements such as mergers, acquisitions, and restructuring give managers fair indication of the valuation effect of these actions.

<u>Lesson 4 - There are no financial illusions</u>: Investors are concerned with the firm's cash flows and are unlikely to be impressed by accounting gimmicks or other cosmetic changes, which do not enhance the cash flows. Therefore, a firm cannot expect to increase its value by merely cosmetic changes such as stock splits or by manipulating the earnings reported to shareholders.

<u>Lesson 5 - The do-it-yourself alternative</u>: Investors will not pay others for anything that they can create or do themselves at a lower cost. An implication of this lesson is that corporate combinations pursuing diversification for risk reduction is unlikely to be valued highly in the market as investors can duplicate this strategy at lower costs by buying shares of companies in different industries.

<u>Lesson 6 - Seen one stock, seen all</u>: Unlike branded products, stocks do not have unique qualities; investors buy a stock if the expected return it offers is fair compensation for the risk it entails. This means that stocks, which offer similar return-risk trade off, are near perfect substitutes for each other and the demand for any given stock is highly elastic. The implication is that large blocks of a stock can be sold at close to the market price as the market is convinced that you have no private information.

Explanation of Terms and Mathematical Expressions

NPV of financing = Present value of amount raised - Present value of all future payments

NPV of a loan (or bond issue) = Amount borrowed - PV (interest payments) - PV (principal payments)

Abnormal return = Actual return - Expected return

Expected return = $\alpha + \beta\ r_m$, where α is the return on the stock when the market return is zero and β is the beta of the stock.

Abnormal return measures the extra return on a stock as a reaction to a specific announcement by the company and is used to measure the impact of an action taken by the company using the event study method.

WORKED EXAMPLE

a. Merkur GmbH, a German machine tool manufacturer, is planning to expand its manufacturing base in the US and has been offered a special loan of $25 million by the state of Alabama. The loan is for a term of 5 years and carries an interest of 4% to be paid annually. Mekur's normal borrowing rate for 5 year borrowing is 6%. What is the value of this special loan to Merkur?

b. Myro Labs, a biotech firm, is trying to decide on an issue of new shares. The company already has 6 million shares outstanding and it is authorized to issue up to an additional 2 million shares. The company's shares are currently selling at $50.

   i. What proportion of the firm will have to be sold in order to raise $15 million if shares can be sold: at $50 each and at $30 each?

   ii. What is the loss to the existing shareholders if the shares are actually sold to new investors at $30?

   iii. If the market is efficient, what is the likely price at which the company can sell the shares?

SOLUTION

a. The special loan offer is obviously a good one and the value of the special loan can be calculated by computing the NPV of the loan using Merkur's normal borrowing rate of 6%.
   NPV = + 25 - PV (interest payments) - PV (principal) = 25 - 4.212 - 18.682 = $2.106 m

b. i) Number of shares to be issued to raise $15 m:
   @ $50/share = 15,000,000/50 = 300,000; total shares after the issue = 6,300,000

Proportion sold to new investors = 300,000/6,300,000 = 4.76%
@ $30/share = 15,000,000/30 = 500,000; total shares after the issue = 6,500,000
Proportion sold to new investors = 500,000/6,500,000 = 7.69%
ii) Value of the firm before the new issue = $50 x 6,000,000 = $300 m

New capital raised	= $30 x 500,000 = $15 m
Total value of the firm after issue	= $315 m
Value per share	= $315/6.5 = $48.46/share
Loss to existing stockholders	= 6,000,000 ($50-$48.46) = $9.24 m

iii) If the market is efficient, the stocks could be sold at a price closer to $50 than at $30.

SUMMARY

This chapter covered one of the most important ideas of modern financial economics - the efficient market hypothesis. The financial markets are characterized by intense competition among investors trying to exploit all the information they have and thus causing prices to be fair and competitive. It is not easy to make money in the financial markets; one can only get fair returns for the risk born. Market prices fully reflect information available about the securities. The efficiency is termed weak form, semi-strong form, or strong form depending on the type of information, which is reflected in the security prices (historic prices for weak form, public information for semi-strong form, and all information for strong form). The three forms are nested; strong form efficiency implies the other two forms and semi-strong form implies weak form efficiency.

Empirical evidence strongly supports weak form and semi-strong form and offers qualified support for the strong form. Researchers have discovered several anomalies and puzzles. This has led to some serious challenges to the efficient market hypothesis. Market efficiency implies fair valuation of assets; however, valuation can only be relative. There is no way we can be sure about intrinsic valuation of assets in an absolute sense. We can only be certain of market efficiency in a relative sense. Efficient market provides six important lessons to the finance manager. A smart manager will heed these lessons, as ignoring them is unlikely to lead to value enhancing decisions.

LIST OF TERMS

Abnormal return
Efficient market
Elasticity of demand
Random walk
Semi-strong form efficiency

Stock dividend
Stock split
Strong-form efficiency
Weak form efficiency

EXERCISES

Fill-in-Questions

1. In an efficient market, security prices fully reflect _____ about the securities.

2. The three forms of market efficiency are _____, _____, and _____.

3. A strong form efficient market implies _____ and _____ also.

4. The prices of securities appear to follow a _____ in which each successive price change is independent of all previous price changes.

5. A strong form efficient market implies that investors can only earn a _____ return on their investment.

6. If prices reflect all published information, the market satisfies the conditions for _____.

7. If prices fully reflect historic information on prices, the market is said to be _____.

8. The _____ of an article is the percentage change in the quantity demanded for one-percent change in its price.

9. The abnormal return on a firm's stock is the difference between its actual return and its _____ return.

10. A _____ increases the number of outstanding shares and reduces the unit price.

Problems

1. True or False?

   a. A market which is weak form efficient will also be semi-strong form efficient.

   b. A strong form efficient market will also be weak form efficient.

   c. In an efficient market, investors can only earn the risk free rate of return.

   d. The demand elasticity for stocks is fairly low.

   e. A stock split by itself will enhance shareholder value.

f. If short-term interest rates were lower than long-term rates, it would be better to borrow short-term.

g. In an efficient market investors cannot expect to earn high abnormal returns.

2. Patel Electronics Corp. (PEC) is planning to invest in a new microprocessor plant in Ireland and the Irish government has offered them a low interest loan for $15 million. The loan has a term of 3 years and an interest rate of 3%. The cost of a comparable bank loan for PEC is 5%. What is the value of the special loan to PEC?

3. Hick Bill Inc. has 72 million shares outstanding and the stock is currently selling at $96. The company announced a 2 for 1 stock split. What will be the stock price after the split becomes effective? How many outstanding shares will there be after the split?

4. Krytech believes that its stock is currently overvalued by the market. Its shares are selling at $60 although management believes they are worth only $40. There are currently 10 million shares outstanding, and the company plans to raise $50 million by issuing 1 million shares at $50 each. The existing shareholders can sell their rights to subscribe to this issue for $9,090,900. Assume that the existing stockholders sell their rights and all the new shares are taken up by new investors. How much will the original shareholders have gained if: (a) the shares were worth only $40 before and (b) they were worth $60?

5. You can buy a 12 percent coupon, 15-year bond at $1,000 (face value). It is expected that one year from now, the bond will yield 10 percent. (a) If this forecast is correct, what will be your return on this investment? (b) What implications does this have for forecasting interest rates in terms of (i) its usefulness and (ii) its difficulty? Assume interest is paid annually.

6. The highly respected economic forecasting department of a major United States bank announces that its latest forecast predicts a significant upturn in economic activity and corporate profits starting in 2 years and lasting for 3 or 4 years. What effect on share prices do you expect this to have (a) immediately, (b) in 2 years, and (c) in 6 years?

7. Identify for which two of the following items demand is least elastic with respect to price and for which two it is most elastic: (a) steak, (b) tobacco, (c) a financial security, (d) gasoline, (e) tuxedos, and (f) shortening.

8. Davy Technology Inc. has a market value of $724 million. Pampaq Inc. has a market value of $376 million. A proposed merger between them seems likely to reduce the standard deviation of their equity returns from 40 percent individually to 25 percent combined. What would you expect the market value of the combined company to be after the merger, if risk reduction is the only benefit from the merger?

9. Which of the following is most likely to result in an increase in the value of a company's shares? (a) It announces that its long-awaited contract with the federal government has now been finalized, and production will begin as soon as a satisfactory specification can be agreed

159

upon. (b) As a result of a change in its depreciation policy, the earnings figure in its newly released annual report is almost double the figure for the previous year. (c) It announces a 50 percent increase in its dividend. (d) Its main competitor announces a price cut.

10. In 1998, Daimler Benz, the German automobile manufacturer, and Chrysler Corporation agreed to merge. Each Chrysler share was to be exchanged for 0.625 shares of Daimler. Shortly after the announcement, Chrysler shares were selling for $52 and the Daimler shares were selling at $96. (The basic share traded in German marks, but its equivalent American Depository Receipts (ADR) traded in the New York stock exchange.). Some saw this as an opportunity to make money with no risk and an example of market inefficiency. What do you think?

Essay Questions

1. "Financing decisions are easier to make, but it is harder to increase shareholder value through financing decisions." Discuss.

2. "There are so many anomalies and puzzles that efficient market is an exception rather than the rule." Discuss.

3. Double-Bull mutual fund has earned high annual returns for each of the last three years beating the market handily. Can this be seen as clear evidence against the strong form efficiency?

4. "Performance of some very successful mutual funds is proof that the market is inefficient." Discuss.

ANSWERS TO EXERCISES

Fill-in Questions

1. Information
2. Weak form, semi-strong form, strong form
3. Semi-strong form and weak form
4. Random walk
5. Fair
6. Semi-strong form
7. Weak form
8. Demand elasticity
9. Expected
10. Stock split (or stock dividend)

Problems

1. a. False b. True c. False d. False
  e. False f. False g. True

2. Value of the special loan to PEC = NPV of the loan financing at 5 percent
$$= +15 - PV \text{ (interest payments)} - PV \text{ (principal)}$$
$$= +15 - (2.7232 \times 0.45) - (0.8638 \times 15)$$
$$= \$0.817 \text{ million}$$

160

3. Stock price after the split $= \$96 \times 1/2 = \$48$

   Number of shares after the split $= 72 \times 2/1 = 144$ million shares

4. a. If the shares were worth \$40:

   Value before issue $= \$40 \times 10 = \$400$ million

   After the issue, the existing stockholders receive \$9.0909 million and $10/11^{th}$ of the value of the firm before the issue plus the \$50 million raised by the issue.

   Value after the issue $= \$9.0909 + 10/11(400+50) = \$418.182$ million

   The existing shareholders have benefited by \$18.182 million.

   b. If the shares were worth \$60:

   Value before issue $= \$60 \times 10 = \$600$ million

   After the issue, the existing stockholders receive \$9.0909 million and $10/11^{th}$ of the value of the firm before the issue plus the \$50 million raised by the issue.

   Value after the issue $= \$9.0909 + 10/11(600+50) = \$600$ million

5. a. The value of the value of the bond one-year from now will rise to \$1,147.33 [N=14, I=10, PV=solve, PMT=\$120, FV=\$1,000]. An investor buying the bond today will receive the coupon of \$120 plus \$1,147.33 earning a total return of 26.73 per cent.

   b. Any one who can forecast interest rates accurately can make a lot of money. It will be extremely difficult to make accurate forecasts.

6. There will be an immediate effect on the stock price to the extent that the forecast represents an improvement for the company's prospects. There will be no effect in later years.

7. The tobacco and tuxedos will have the lowest elasticity and the financial security and shortening will have the highest.

8. There will be no gain from the merger and value of the combined company will be about \$1,100 million. The market price for each company already reflects its market risk as measured by its beta and the merged firm's beta will be the weighted average of the two betas.

9. The award of the contract is likely to result in an increase in its stock price to the extent this is not already expected and reflected in the price. Announcements c and d may affect the stock price to the extent they were unexpected.

10. If Chrysler shares were to fully reflect the value of the impending merger, they should be selling at $\$96 \times 0.625 = \$60$. Thus, it appears that they are undervalued. However, an arbitrage transaction involving buying Chrysler shares and selling Daimler shares in equivalent quantities is unlikely to be risk free. Two factors to be considered are: i) potential foreign exchange risk (Daimler shares are priced in German marks), and ii) possible breakdown in the merger talks. Thus, the market price is probably a reflection of the risks involved rather than an opportunity to make money in a risk free transaction.

161

14

An Overview of Corporate Financing

INTRODUCTION

This chapter provides a descriptive overview of corporate financing and the three main types of securities companies issue: common stock, preferred stock, and debt. The chapter also includes a broad introduction to financial markets and institutions. While companies finance a large part of their new investments from internally generated funds, they also use large amounts of externally raised money. Most of this external funding comes from the issuance of either debt or equity.

The simple classification of external financing sources as debt and equity takes away all the details in which these can be different. The debt securities issued by a company can differ in so many little details, with some important consequences for the firm. Even equity issues can have different classifications based on voting rights. All these have given rise to a number of technical terms used in the world of corporate finance. The chapter explains these terms and the context of the use for them. Students of finance are expected to have at least a passing familiarity with this language of investment banking. The list of the main new terms and the set of fill-in questions should prove to be very useful in learning these terms.

The first section of the chapter provides a description of the changing patterns of corporate financing in the U.S. The section also includes a very interesting comparison of the financing patterns across countries. It is important to realize that comparisons of this type have to take into account the differences in accounting rules and conventions followed in different countries. Each of the next three sections covers common stock, debt, and preferred stock. This is followed by a short introduction to financial markets and institutions and their role in the economy.

KEY CONCEPTS IN THE CHAPTER

There are few new concepts in this chapter. The chapter essentially provides a descriptive overview of corporate financing. We will give here key terms and substantive material included in the text.

Patterns of Corporate Financing: The table below summarizes the uses and sources of funds by the U.S. non-financial corporations. The pattern during the period 1990 to 1999 was similar though year-to-year variations were there. For seven of the ten years, companies bought back stock or there was net negative stock issue. These large net repurchases of this decade are atypical. More commonly, you will find a small percentage of stock issue. What is also common is the high percentage of funds provided by internally generated cash.

Uses	Percent	Sources	Percent
Capital Expenditure	86.6	Internally generated	76.7
Net working capital	13.4	External financing	
		Net stock issue - -14.3	
		Net debt issue - 37.6	
			23.3
Total	100.0	Total	100.0

Companies have to make two basic financing decisions: what percentage of profits to be paid out as dividends (the remaining to be reinvested in business) and what mix of debt and external equity should be used to finance the deficit. These questions take you directly to dividend and debt policies and are discussed in chapters 16, 17, and 18. Overall, financing decisions can be regarded as the marketing of a package of securities with rights to the company profits and cash flows.

In general, during the last five decades, companies' balance sheets have shown a marked increase in the proportion of debt to total assets (from a little over 30 percent in the fifties to over 60 percent in the nineties). At least part of the reason is the progressive inflation that increased the market values of assets relative to their book values. It is also observed that debt ratios of the nineties are similar to the ratios of the 1920s and 1930s. The proportion of debt in U.S. balance sheets does not seem too out of line when international comparisons are made. One has to be careful to correct for accounting differences before drawing conclusions about differences across countries. The U.S. companies are in the middle of the international pack compared.

Common Stock: Common stock represents ownership of the company and common stockholders, as owners of the company, have general preemptive right to anything of value that the company may wish to distribute after satisfying claims of lenders and preferred stockholders. They receive distribution of profits usually in the form of dividends. While most companies have only one form of common stock, some companies have issued stocks of different classes with different voting rights.

A company is allowed to issue shares up to the amount specified by its *authorized* share capital, which can only be increased with the permission of the shareholders. *Outstanding shares* are those held by investors. Shares that have been issued but subsequently repurchased and held by the company are called *treasury shares*. They are said to be issued but not outstanding. All issued shares are entered in the company's accounts at their par value. Because some states do not allow companies to sell shares below par value, par value is generally set at a low figure, which has no economic significance.

The stockholders, as owners of the company, have the ultimate control of the company. Their control over the company's affairs is manifested by their right to vote on appointments to the board of directors and on some other issues such as a merger of the company with another. The stockholders have to vote approval of major changes in the articles of incorporation of the company. Voting may be on a *majority* basis or on a *cumulative* basis. Cumulative voting makes it more likely for minority groups to obtain representation on the board. Under this system shareholders may, if they wish, allot all their votes to one candidate. For example, if six directors are to be elected, a shareholder can allocate all six votes from each share to a single candidate and does not have to choose six candidates to vote for. Where there are different classes of stocks with different voting rights, the classes with more voting rights will generally command a premium in the market. The premium will be a function of the extra benefits the stockholders can get because of their superior voting rights.

Ownership interests in businesses may be held in forms other than common stock. While common stocks are issued by corporations, comparable ownership securities for other organization forms of business are called different names such as units in *master limited partnerships* and *real estate investment trusts*.

Preferred Stock: Preferred stock is legally considered as equity but generally has only limited voting rights. Unlike common stock, though, most preferred stock is issued with a stipulated dividend and this dividend has to be paid before any dividend to common stockholders can be paid. Preferred stockholders' claims take precedence over that of the common stockholders if the company ever goes out of business. In general, only a small portion of corporate financing needs is met through the issue of preferred stock. It can be very useful means of financing in certain special situations.

There are some interesting tax implications with preferred stock dividends. Preferred stock dividends are not tax-deductible expenses for the company paying them. However, corporations receiving preferred stock dividends have to pay tax only on 30 percent of the dividends. Most of the preferred stocks is held by corporations (favorable treatment of dividend income), and most is issued by regulated utility companies (who would be made to lower their rates if they used subsidized debt instead).

Corporate Debt: There are a great variety of ways in which companies can borrow money. The common feature is that the company promises to make regular interest payments and to repay the principal amount according to an agreed schedule. The shareholders' liability is limited, so lenders can only look to the earnings and assets of the company for their payment. Lenders cannot look beyond those assets to the shareholders for repayment. Some of the choices available to firms considering debt issue are summarized below.

- *Maturity or the term of debt*: Companies can borrow short-term or long-term. Short-term debt is typically used for seasonal needs related to working capital, while long-term debt is usually chosen for financing long-term assets. Debt issued may have provisions for repayment on a steady basis or at the end of maturity. The borrower may have a right to prepay the debt and occasionally the lender may demand prepayment.
- *Fixed rate or floating rate*: The interest rate may be *fixed* for the whole term of the loan when the debt is issued. Alternatively, it may be a *floating rate*, determined from time to time during the term according to an agreed formula such as "1 percent above *prime*" or "1/2

percent above *LIBOR*." Floating rate debt may be issued using a number of different benchmark interest rates.

- *Country and currency*: Although most borrowing by United States corporations is done in the United States and in United States dollars, firms may also borrow in foreign countries or in foreign currencies. When a company issues debt in a currency outside the currency's home country (e.g. yen bonds outside Japan), these are called *eurobonds*.
- *Seniority*: Debt may be junior or senior. If the company goes bankrupt, its junior (or *subordinated*) debt is not eligible to receive payment until all senior debt has been paid in full.
- *Security*: Debt may be secured by some or all of the assets of the company. A lot of corporate debt is issued as unsecured debt without explicit collateral. Secured debt has first claim, in the event of default, on the assets specified as collateral. A *mortgage* is an example of this, while long-term bonds, which are unsecured, are called debentures.
- *Public versus privately placed debt*: Bonds sold as a public issue are offered to anyone who wants to buy them and can be freely traded afterwards. Bonds sold in a private placement are sold directly to a small number of qualified institutional investors, and subsequently can only be resold among these investors.
- *Warrants:* companies often issue Warrants as part of a package to sell other securities. Most commonly they are used to sell bonds. Warrants give their owner the right to purchase one share of common stock at a specified price on or before a specified future date. Thus, they are essentially call options issued by the company.
- *Convertible Bonds*: These are bonds issued by the company that can be exchanged for (or converted to) a specified number of shares on specific future dates if the holder wishes. The holder will, of course, wish to convert if the stock price goes up well above the level when conversion makes sense. If the stock price does not go up, the holder has no obligation to convert. Essentially, a convertible bond is like a package of a bond plus a warrant. One difference is that when the convertible bondholder converts, she exchanges the bond for a certain number of shares, but pays no cash. The warrant holder has to pay cash to get his shares.

Financial Markets: Financial markets and intuitions are essential and very important parts of the market economy. Financial markets facilitate exchange of capital between savers or surplus units and borrowers or deficit units. Corporations and other borrowers sell financial assets such as stocks and bonds in the *primary market* to raise cash for the business. The stocks and bonds issued in the primary market are then traded in the *secondary markets* (e.g. the New York Stock Exchange), which provide liquidity and convenience for the stockholders and bondholders. The secondary markets include not only the organized exchanges such as the NYSE, but also the *over-the-counter* (OTC) markets, which are essentially network of dealers and traders brought together often through the electronic medium. Foreign exchange markets and the NASDAQ are examples of OTC markets.

Financial Institutions: Financial institutions are key players in financial markets and own a large proportion of securities issued by corporations. Commercial banks, saving and loan companies, mutual funds and insurance companies are among the major institutions. These institutions act as *financial intermediaries* between lenders or savers and borrowers. Commercial banks collect deposits from individuals and corporations and provide loans, mostly short-term, to commercial and other borrowers. Insurance companies provide long-term financing and own both long-term debt and common stock.

Financial institutions differ from manufacturing corporations in both the assets they own and the ways they raise financing. While most of the assets owned by manufacturing corporations would be real assets, the assets owned by financial institutions comprise mostly financial assets such as bonds, stocks and various kinds of loans to individuals and businesses. Similarly, the sources of funds available to financial institutions are unique to the nature of their business and include deposits of various kinds, insurance policies, and other investments. Essentially, these institutions sell one kind of claims and then repackage them into a different type of financial assets. They add value by providing risk and term intermediation as well as savings in transaction costs.

Financial institutions play a very important role in the smooth functioning of the economic system. They provide *payment mechanism* for most of the commercial and personal transactions in the economy. This is facilitated through a variety of means including checking accounts, credit and debit cards, and electronic and other means of transfer of funds. Financial institutions also facilitate transfer of funds between saving units (those who want to invest) and deficit units (those who want to borrow). Different institutions do these in many different ways. Banks provide opportunities for investing simple deposit instruments, while mutual funds offer virtually unlimited ways of investing money for different terms and at different risk levels. Financial institutions also provide *risk pooling* and risk management services. Again, insurance companies and mutual funds have a number of products to meet the needs of individuals and businesses.

While financial markets and institutions serve the same basic functions around the world and since the dawn of market economy, market forces and changing regulatory structure have caused the role of the institutions to change over time. Two trends are note worthy. First, there has been a significant shift and change in the role of commercial banks as providers of commercial credit. Larger corporations depend a lot less on commercial banks for their financing needs as they find it cheaper and more convenient to borrow from the market directly or from other institutions like insurance companies and mutual funds. The second trend is *globalization* of markets. This has resulted in extensive cross-border lending and borrowing on the part of companies from different countries and investors.

SUMMARY

This chapter provided an overview of the different types of securities issued and used by corporations. The chapter also gave a historic perspective on the changing patterns of corporate financing in the U.S. and provided international comparisons with other industrialized countries. The chapter also gave you a glimpse of financial markets and institutions and their role in the economy. The primary objective of the chapter is to familiarize you with the broad features of corporate securities and the terminology used in corporate finance.

Corporations use three types of securities to raise the financing they need. The simplest of these is common stock. Common stockholders are owners of the corporation and are entitled to its profits, vote on the composition of the company's board of directors, and other important matters.

Companies occasionally use preferred stock, though its use is far less common than debt and is used in special situations. Preferred stock has features of both debt and common stock – it has a fixed payment, but it is legally considered equity, and payments to preferred stockholders are not tax-deductible.

Debt is widely used by companies to meet part of their external funding needs. Debt comes in many different varieties and the chapter lists the many features taken on modern day corporate debt. Debt can be classified in terms of its maturity, repayment provisions, seniority of the debt, security, interest payment, issue procedures, and currency of the debt.

LIST OF TERMS

Authorized share capital	Outstanding shares
Convertible bond	Par value
Cumulative voting	Preferred stock
Eurobond	Secured
Eurodollar	Senior
Floating rate	Subordinated
Line of credit	Treasury shares
Majority voting	Warrant

EXERCISES

Fill-in Questions

1. The maximum number of shares that a company can issue is known as its
    _____.

2. Shares that have already been issued and are held by investors are called
    _____.

3. _____ are shares that have been repurchased by the company.

4. The _____ of a security is the value at which it is entered in the company's books.

5. _____ is the name for the voting system under which each director is voted on separately.

168

6. The voting system under which a stockholder may cast all of her or his votes for one candidate is known as _____.

7. In the event of bankruptcy, _____ debt must be repaid before subordinated debt receives any payment.

8. _____ debt represents a junior claim, which, in the event of default, is paid only after all senior creditors are satisfied.

9. In the event of default, _____ debt has first claim on specified assets.

10. The interest on a(n) _____ loan varies with the short-term interest rate.

11. A(n) _____ is a dollar that has been deposited with a bank outside the United States.

12. A(n) _____ is an issue of debt that is sold simultaneously in several countries.

13. _____ stock is an equity security, which offers a fixed dividend that must be paid before any dividend can be paid on the common stock.

14. A(n) _____ is a long-term security issued by a company, which gives the holder the right to purchase one share of common stock at a set price on or before a set date.

15. A bond that may be converted to the company's common stock at the discretion of the holder is called a(n) _____.

Problems

1. The authorized share capital of Grayson Corp. is 8 million. The equity is currently shown in the company's accounts as follows:

	Dollars
Common stock ($0.10 par value)	500,000
Additional paid-in capital	4,500,000
Retained earnings	23,000,000
Common equity	28,000,000
Treasury stock (1,000,000 shares)	4,000,000
Net common equity	24,000,000

a. How many shares are issued?
b. How many are outstanding?

c. How many more shares can be issued without the approval of the shareholders?

d. What is the share price if it is twice its book value?

2. Grayson Corp. of problem 1 issues a further 1 million shares at an issue price of $4 a share. How will the equity be shown in the company's books after the issue?

3. There are nine directors to be elected, and I own a round lot of 100 shares. What is the maximum number of votes I can cast for my favorite candidate under: (a) majority voting and (b) cumulative voting?

4. The shareholders of Bounty Corp. need to elect five directors. There are 4 million shares outstanding. How many shares do you need to own to ensure that you can elect at least one director (a) under majority voting and (b) under cumulative voting?

5. The Clear Mustard Company has the following income for the year:

Taxable income from operations	$253,000
Interest income	42,000
Dividends from preferred stock	20,000
Dividends from common stock	10,000
Total income	$325,000

It has paid interest charges amounting to $59,000 and dividends on its preferred and common stock of $35,000 and $50,000 respectively. If it pays tax at 35 percent, what is its tax bill for the year?

6. The Clear Mustard Company of the last problem had the following income and payments in the previous year:

Income from:	
Operations	$224,000
Interest	32,000
Preferred dividends	40,000
Common dividends	40,000
	$336,000

Payments:	
Interest	$44,000
Preferred dividends	$35,000
Common dividends	$45,000

How much tax should it have paid?

7. Which of the following are true and which are false?

a. Commercial banks provide over 50 percent of all corporate financing needs.

b. The assets owned by financial institutions differ significantly from those owned by manufacturing corporations.

c. All partners in a master limited partnership have unlimited liability.

d. U.S. leverage ratios have risen steadily over the last 40 years.

Essay Questions

1. Explain how issued share capital is shown in a company's accounts, and describe what rights and privileges shareholders enjoy.

2. Describe the variety of different types of debt that a company can issue.

3. What is preferred stock, who issues it, who buys it, and why?

4. Describe the main sources and uses of companies' funds.

5. Describe the role and functions of financial markets and institutions in the economic system.

ANSWERS TO EXERCISES

Fill-in Questions

1. Authorized share capital
2. Outstanding shares
3. Treasury shares
4. Par value
5. Majority voting
6. Cumulative voting
7. Senior
8. Subordinated
9. Secured
10. Floating-rate
11. Eurodollar
12. Eurobond
13. Preferred
14. Warrant
15. Convertible bond

Problems

1. a. 5 million shares   b. 4 million shares   c. 3 million shares
   d. The book value =$24,000,000/4,000,000 =$6; Market price = 2 x $6 = $12

2. The books will show the equity account as follows:

	Dollars
Common stock ($0.10 par value)	600,000
Additional paid-in capital	8,400,000
Retained earnings	23,000,000
Common equity	32,000,000
Treasury stock (1,000,000 shares)	4,000,000
Net common equity	28,000,000

3. a. 100 votes   b. 900 votes

171

4. a. More than half the outstanding shares are needed, that is, 2,000,001 shares.
   b. As long as your candidate comes out in the top of a field of six or more candidates she will get elected. This means that she needs one more than one-sixth, that is, 666,667 is sufficient.

5. The taxable income is calculated as follows:

Income from operations	$253,000
Interest income	42,000
30 percent of dividends	9,000
	$304,000
Less interest expense	59,000
	245,000

   Its tax bill is 35 percent of $245,000, which is $85,750.

6. Taxable income is given by:

Income from operations	$224,000
Interest income	32,000
30 percent of dividends	24,000
	$280,000
Less interest expense	44,000
Taxable income	$236,000

   Tax is 35 percent of $236,000, which is $82,600.

7. a. False
   b. True
   c. False
   d. True

15

How Corporations Issue Securities

INTRODUCTION

This chapter describes the procedures used by companies for raising long-term funds in the capital market. It provides a wealth of institutional details and guidance to managers on decisions about long-term capital. It describes the *venture capital* financing of a young company and then takes you through to the company's *initial public offering* (IPO). The subsequent sections describe the *general cash offer* used for most public issues of debt or equity securities in the United States. Equity issues made directly to existing shareholders are called *privileged subscription issues* or *rights issues* and are covered in Appendix A. The chapter also discusses the role of the *underwriter* and the costs of different types of issues. An overview of *private* placements is also included in the chapter.

Financial managers concerned with raising finance need to decide the method of issue, the size of the issue, the pricing of the security, the use of an underwriter, and the type of underwriting arrangement. The manager should also be concerned with the effect the issue will have on the firm's market value. All these are closely related to market efficiency. The manager will do well to remember the lessons of market efficiency learned in Chapter 13. Here are some important implications of market efficiency relevant to this chapter.

Financing Decisions and Stockholder Wealth: In general, it is very unlikely that financing decisions will enhance the market value of the firm as a whole. It is reasonable to assume that most financing decisions have a net present value of zero. This is because a positive NPV financing decision is one where the money raised exceeds the value of the liability created. In the highly competitive capital market, it is not possible for any firm to consistently fool investors in this way.

Financing Decisions and the Distribution of Wealth: Financing decisions can, however, affect the distribution of wealth between security holders and that there may be wealth transfer between one group of security holders and another. If new securities are under-priced, new holders will obtain a bargain at the expense of existing holders. This is not a problem, however, in the case of rights issues, where existing holders are given the rights to subscribe in proportion to the size of their holdings.

The Importance of Market Prices: When a company is deciding on the issue price for new securities, the best guide to what a company can hope to obtain is the price of closely comparable securities, which are already traded.

KEY CONCEPTS IN THE CHAPTER

Venture Capital: Equity investment in the early stages of a business can be very risky and is often called venture capital. Venture capital is key to the success of any growing new business as the original investors and founders of the business are unlikely to have the needed capital. The investment is risky, but is rewarded by the high returns of the successful ventures. Specialist investors who are often organized as partnerships typically provide this type of financing. Wealthy individuals and financial institutions are also important players in the venture capital business. In order to monitor the progress of the business and to limit the risk of the investment, venture capital financing is provided in stages with each additional stage of funding contingent on successful completion of some set targets or milestones. *First-stage financing* generally is based on a *business plan*. The business plan describes the exact nature of the proposed business: the product, the market, the resources it will use, and the income it will generate. In obtaining an injection of equity capital, the *after-the-money valuation* is important in putting an implicit valuation on the entrepreneurs' existing equity. Successful completion of the first stage will lead to the *second-stage financing* and possibly further stages before the company is ready to go public with an initial public offering.

Venture capital market: The United States has a well-developed venture capital market. Most of venture capital funding is provided by specialist partnerships, which pool funds from a variety of investors and seek out fledgling companies to invest in. Some large technology companies are also active in providing venture capital to firms in the areas of their interest. Occasionally, start-up firms obtain funding from wealthy individuals or *angel investors*. Venture capital firms provide more than capital and often help the young start-up companies with advice and management expertise. Venture capital firms get their returns either the sale of the funded firm or when a successful start-up decides to go public. Note that venture capital investments are very risky. Generally, for every ten first-stage venture capital investments, only two or three may survive as successful businesses. However, if one funded firm becomes very successful, it will make up for all the others.

The Initial Public Offering: The initial public offering or IPO is the first issue of shares to the general public. Generally, IPOs are done when the business has made considerable progress and is on its way to successfully establishing itself in the market. The IPO establishes a market value of the investment made by the founding entrepreneurs and the venture capitalists. A *primary offering* is one where shares are sold to raise additional cash for the company. Often a primary offering is combined with a *secondary offering* where existing shareholders (the venture capitalists and sometimes the founding entrepreneurs) sell some of their shares.

The Underwriters: An *underwriter* is used to sell the offered shares to the general investor. The underwriters provide valuable advice on all matters related to the stock issue. They also buy the stock from the company and then resell it to investors. The underwriters establish the price of the stock set for IPO and gauge the demand for the issue through discussions and survey of potential investors such as mutual fund managers and other clients. This process of compiling a list of potential orders is known as *bookbuilding*. The underwriters are compensated through the spread between the *issue price* (or *offering price*) and the price at which they buy the securities from the company. Where a new issue of common stock is unusually risky, the underwriter may handle the issue on a *best-efforts* basis (not guaranteeing to sell the entire issue) or on an *all-or-none* basis (where the deal is called off completely if the entire issue is not sold).

A syndicate of underwriters usually handles large issues. In this case, the syndicate manager keeps about 20 percent of the spread, a further 20 to 30 percent goes to pay the members of the group who buy the issue, and the remainder goes to the firms who actually sell the issue. Members of the underwriting syndicate are not allowed to sell securities at below the issue price, although they may be allowed to "support" the market by buying them at the market price. This helps stabilize the market for the stock in its early trading days. Underwriters often get an option (called *greenshoe option)* to buy additional shares from the company. This provision enables them to sell more than the committed number of shares in case they find that the demand for the stock is high. It also nets them extra profit if the stock offering has high demand and the stock price rises on trading on the opening day.

Issue Procedures: The formal procedures for an IPO starts with the appointment of the managing and co-managing underwriters. The managing underwriter maintains the *book* for the issue which tracks the potential demand for the issue and helps in estimating the likely issue price. The bookbuilding approach to gauging demand and arriving at the issue price is popular in the US. An alternate approach to selling the securities uses auctions. The auctions can be *discriminatory auctions* or *uniform price auctions*. In the former method, each successful bidder pays the price he or she bid, whereas in the uniform price auction everyone pays the same price, namely the lowest winning bid price.

The company enters into a formal agreement with the underwriters specifying details of the underwriting commitment, the spread and any greenshoe option agreed. Following these steps a *registration statement* is prepared for submission to the Securities and Exchange Commission (SEC). This statement presents information about the proposed financing, the firm's history, existing business, and plans for the future. The first part of the registration statement is usually distributed as a preliminary *prospectus*, also called a *red herring*. It contains a statement printed in red ink, which draws attention to its preliminary status and that securities are not permitted to be sold until the registration becomes effective. A marketing campaign for the issue is launched through road shows arranged by the underwriters. Meanwhile, the SEC studies the documentation and sometimes requests changes to it. Finally, an amended statement is filed with the SEC. After registration, the final prospectus is issued, giving the issue price, which is fixed at this stage. A *registrar* is appointed to record any issues of stock and to prevent unauthorized issues' taking place. A *transfer agent* is also appointed to look after the transfer of the newly issued securities. These steps are followed by the formal issue, allotment of stock by the underwriters and trading of the stock in the secondary market. Typically, the lead underwriter makes market in the stock providing liquidity and also initiates research coverage on the stock.

Costs of new issue: Public issue can be expensive. The costs include the administrative and transaction costs as well as the cost due to underpricing of the shares. The administrative costs

175

include preparation of all the documentation by management, legal counsel, and accountants, besides other fees, printing and mailing costs. Underpricing of the issue is the hidden cost and can be very high in many cases. The company and its underwriters discuss and agree on the issue price. The company would, of course, like to secure the highest possible price. But if the price is set too high and the issue fails, the underwriter could suffer heavy financial losses and a loss of reputation. If the stock is underpriced the existing stockholders have given away part of the firm. A study of nearly 15,000 new issues from 1960 to 2000 indicated average under-pricing of 18.4 percent. It is sometimes argued that underpricing of an issue leads to successful IPO, because it pushes up the demand for the shares and leads to higher stock prices after the stock has started trading in the market. This helps the firm in raising capital in the future. One can also see the incentive the underwriter has for underpricing because that lowers the risk of loss from the issue.

Winners curse may be part of the explanation for underpricing found in many IPOs. This means that a successful bidder in an auction is likely to have overvalued the asset. Thus, investors, being unaware of other investors` valuation of the stock, can end up paying a high price.

Sale of Security by Public Companies: Public issue of securities can be either *general cash offers* or *rights issues*. General cash offers are made to the public. This is the most commonly used mode for all debt and most equity issues in the United States. In some other countries it is common to find rights issues (also known as *privileged subscription issues)* where the issue is offered to the existing shareholders as a right. The shareholders can sell their rights to subscribe to the issue in the market.

Companies can file a single *shelf registration* statement covering financing plans for up to 2 years into the future. This provides prior approval to issue a stated amount of securities during this period and without being tied to particular underwriters. The company is then able to issue securities at its convenience and it can do it at very short notice. Large, well-established companies often issue securities in more than one country and these are known as *International issues.* Both debt and equity securities are issued in international markets and the regulatory procedures depend on the countries included. SEC approval is not required if the securities are not issued to investors in the United States.

There is considerable economy of scale in issue costs. The percentage cost is smaller for large issues than for small ones. We also have to consider the effects of under-pricing and price pressure. The announcement of new issues of common stock on average results in a decline in the stock price of about 3 percent for industrial issues in the United States. This is probably an information effect: managers are more likely to issue stock when they think it is overvalued.

Private Placements: A private placement is an alternative to public issue and has certain advantages compared to a public offering. Private placements do not involve registration and is limited to a few buyers. Transaction costs will be lower. The placement can be made very quickly. There are disadvantages too. The securities issued in this way are very illiquid and are held for long-term investment rather than resale. This is a greater disadvantage for issues of common stock than for debt issues, so private placements of common stock (called *letter stock*) are rare. Bond issues, particularly of small- and medium-sized firms, account for the bulk of private placements. Since 1990, large financial institutions (known as *qualified institutional buyers*) have been allowed by the SEC to trade unregistered securities among themselves, and this has provided a further boost to this market.

Rights Issue (The Privileged Subscription): A rights issue can be a very effective and inexpensive way of raising additional funding. The issue is offered to the firm's existing stockholders in proportion to their current holding in the company. The stockholders can transfer or sell their rights in the market. Rights issue effectively avoids wealth transfer between existing stockholders and new stockholders, since they are one and the same. Therefore, the actual pricing of the issue is of little consequence.

WORKED EXAMPLES

1. Cory Leone and Maurice Greenberg are biotechnologists who pioneered new applications of DNA. They founded LeoGreen Biotech Corp (LBC) to commercialize these applications. The entrepreneurs' original investment in LBC amounted to $30,000. Six months after the launch of LBC, the friends were able to obtain first-stage financing of $500,000 and the after-the-money valuation on the firm was placed at $1 million. A year later at the next stage of financing LBC the enterprise was valued at $5 million before financing.

   a. What (paper) return and increase in value did the entrepreneurs get in each of these two stages?

   b. How would your answer to the previous question change if they had agreed on a first-stage after-the-money valuation of $800,000 million instead of $1 million and a second stage valuation of $4 million?

SOLUTION

   a. Cory and Maurice have a paper value of $500,000 for their stock at the first stage. With the additional $500,000 external financing, they now have 50 percent of the firm's stock. At the second stage, when the company is valued at $5 million their stocks are worth $2.5 million. These valuations represent 16.67 fold and 5-fold increases in the two stages, representing returns of 1567 percent and 400 percent respectively.

   b. At $800,000 firm valuation, Cory and Maurice have a paper value to their stock of $300,000 at the first stage. This gives them 37.5 percent of the stock in the firm ($300,000/$800,000). This is worth $1.5 million at the second stage ($4 m x 0.375). These valuations represent 10-fold and 5-fold increases in the two stages giving them returns of 900 percent and 500 percent respectively.

2. Jackrabbits Corporation is making a rights issue to raise $6 million. Baby Rabbit owns 20,000 shares. Just before the issue, Jackrabbits' stock price was $20, and the terms of the issue are 1 new share for every 4 shares held at a subscription price of $15. Calculate (a) the

expected price of the stock after the rights issue, (b) the value of the right to buy one new share and (c) the rights Baby will have to sell to maintain the same ($400,000) investment in the company?

SOLUTION

a. For every 4 shares worth $20 before the issue, there will be 5 shares worth $20 x 4 + $15 (= $95) after the issue. Each share will, therefore, be worth $95/5, so the ex-rights price is $19.

b. The value of right to buy one new share = $19 - $15 = $4.

c. Baby Rabbit will get 5,000 rights and if he were to keep all his rights, he would end up with 25,000 shares valued at a total of 25,000 x $19 = $475,000. In order to retain his original investment, he should have $400,000/$19 = 21,053 shares. Therefore, he needs to keep only 1,053 rights and sell the remaining 3,947 rights. This will give him $3,947.

SUMMARY

This chapter provided a summary description of the procedures used by corporations for raising long-term finance through the issue of securities. Companies raise finances through a variety of ways. Young start-up companies get much of their early funding through venture capital financing. Established and mature companies are able to raise money through seasoned issues. The chapter highlighted some very important implications for the financial manager. These can be summarized as below:

- Larger is cheaper. This suggests that there is economy of scale in raising money and the manager can take advantage of this by avoiding small issues.

- Beware of under-pricing. Perhaps the most significant of the hidden costs of financing is under-pricing of the security. This is especially true for the IPOs. Underwriters may be tempted to go too far to reduce the fear of winners' curse make an impression on the investor, but this comes at the expense of the issuing firm's existing stockholders.

- Winners' curse may need to be addressed in IPOs and careful design of issue procedures is needed.

- New stock issues cause lowering of stock price. This may be due to information the market might be reading into the company's actions. Managers would do well to keep the market fully informed.

- Take advantage of shelf-registration, which is particularly useful for debt issues of established, financially strong firms.

LIST OF TERMS

After-the-money valuation
All-or-none
Best efforts
Bookbuilding
Business plan
Discriminatory auction
First-stage financing
General cash offer
Initial public offering
Issue price
Offering price
Preemptive rights
Primary offering
Private placement
Privileged subscription
Prospectus

Red herring
Registrar
Registration statement
Rights issue
Road show
Seasoned stock issue
Secondary offering
Shelf registration
Spread
Transfer agent
Underpricing
Underwriting
Uniform price auction
Unseasoned issue
Venture capital

EXERCISES

Fill-in Questions

1. Equity investment in young private companies is generally known as _____.

2. In order to obtain capital, the young company must first prepare a detailed _____.

3. The first injection of equity capital from the venture capital market is known as _____.

4. The proportion of the company, which the original owners will have to give up, depends on the _____ of the company.

5. The first issue of a security by a company is known as a(n) _____ or a(n) _____.

6. Before a general cash offer or a large public issue, companies often put on a _____ to familiarize the investors with the company.

7. When new shares are sold to raise additional cash for the company, it is called _____.

8. When shares of existing shareholders are offered to the public, it is called _____.

179

9. An issue of securities that is offered to the general public or investors is called a(n) _____.

10. An issue of securities that is offered to current stockholders is usually called a(n) _____.

11. Rights issues are also known as _____ issues.

12. For most public issues, a(n) _____ must be submitted to the Securities and Exchange Commission.

13. Information about an issue is provided in its _____, which must be sent to all purchasers and to all those who are offered securities through the mail.

14. The preliminary prospectus is called a(n) _____.

15. _____ is the process through which the managing underwriter collects information, gauges the demand for the issue and compiles a list of potential orders for the IPO.

16. A financial institution is usually appointed as _____ to record the issue and ownership of the company's securities.

17. A(n) _____ may be appointed to look after the transfer of newly issued securities.

18. The sale of a public issue is normally handled by a(n) _____, who provides financial and procedural advice and usually buys the security for less than the offering price and accepts the risk of not being able to resell it.

19. The underwriter's _____ is the difference between the price at which the underwriter buys an issue from a company and the _____ or _____.

20. Occasionally, the underwriter does not guarantee the sale of an entire issue but handles the issue on a(n) _____ basis, promising only to sell as much of the issue as possible.

21. _____ underwriting is where the entire issue is cancelled if the underwriter is unable to resell it all at the offer price.

22. _____ occurs in a general cash offer when securities are sold at an offer price, which is below their market price.

23. When _____ is used to sell securities, each winner is required to pay the price he or she bid for the issue.

24. Stock for which there is an existing market goes by the spicy name of _____ stock.

25. The _____ rights of common stockholders (to anything of value distributed by the firm) include the right to subscribe to new offerings.

26. The _____ provides an alternative to making a public offering.

27. When _____ is used to sell securities, everyone pays the same price.

28. _____ allows large companies to obtain prior approval for their financing plans for up to 2 years into the future.

Problems

1. Windsors is a young company started by two sisters, Ann and Wendy, with their savings amounting to $200,000. The firm received venture capital financing two years after its start-up. The venture capitalists provided first-stage financing of $2.5 million and valued the firm after-the-money at $5 million. Two years later, the firm received second-stage financing from the same venture capital company. Windsors received $6 million and was valued at $20 million after-the-money. A year later, Windsors was ready for its IPO and the underwriters valued the company (before the IPO) at $60 million. Calculate the returns for the sisters and the venture capital firm at each stage of financing.

2. The entrepreneurs' original investment in Marvin Enterprises amounted to $100,000. First-stage financing raised $1 million and placed a $2 million after-the-money valuation on the firm. At the next stage, the enterprise was valued at $10 million.

   a. What (paper) return and increase in value had the entrepreneurs enjoyed by each of these two stages?
   b. How would your answer to the previous question change if they had agreed on a first-stage after-the-money valuation of $1.50 million instead of $2 million and a second stage valuation of $9 million?

3. AZB Corp. decides to issue the stock via a general cash offer. The board believes it can raise the $18 million the company requires by issuing shares at $36. The company has 5 million shares outstanding and the current stock price is $40. Ignoring the underwriter's spread, calculate the following:

   a. The number of new shares that AZB will have to offer.
   b. The expected price of the shares after the issue.

181

c. The loss per share to existing holders.
d. The percentage reduction in value of an existing stockholder's investment in the company
e. The net present value of purchasing 100 shares via the general cash offer.

4. AZB is considering the alternative of a privileged subscription stock issue to raise $18 million. The terms of the issue are 1 for 10 at $36, and the corporation's current stock price is $40. Calculate the following:

   a. The market value of the corporation's equity prior to the issue.
   b. The percentage increase in market value due to the issue.
   c. The expected price of the stock after the issue.
   d. The expected price of the right to buy one share.

5. Vanessa's Attic is issuing a 20-year bond to raise $10 million. The corporation can choose one of the following alternatives:

   a. Issue the bond publicly, in which case it will be sold at par and will carry a 9 percent coupon. The underwriter's spread would be 0.5 percent, and there are no other issue costs.

   b. Issue the bond through a private placement, in which case it will be sold at par and carry a 9 1/8 percent coupon. The total cost of the private placement will be $20,000.

   Assume annual coupon payments. Which option should the firm choose?

Essay Questions

1. Discuss the following statement: Venture capital is essential for a young, growing company, but it is also an expensive way of raising money.

2. Describe the main features of the process by which a young company might raise venture capital.

3. Discuss the following statement: Rights issue is the best way to raise new equity for an established company, as one does not have to worry about underpricing.

4. Discuss the relative merits of a public issue versus a private placement for a company wishing to raise new debt finance. What factors should be taken into account in pricing the bond issue?

5. Compare and contrast the role of the investment banker (or underwriter) in (a) general cash offers of either stock or bonds and (b) private placements of bonds

6. Describe how the costs of raising new capital depend on the type and amount of financing raised.

ANSWERS TO EXERCISES

Fill-in Questions

1. Venture capital
2. Business plan
3. First-stage financing
4. After-the-money valuation
5. Initial public offering, unseasoned issue
6. Road show
7. Primary offering
8. Secondary offering
9. General cash offer
10. Rights issue
11. Privileged subscription
12. Registration statement
13. Prospectus
14. Red herring
15. Bookbuilding
16. Registrar
17. Transfer agent
18. Underwriter
19. Spread; issue price; offering price
20. Best efforts
21. All-or-none
22. Under-pricing
23. Discriminatory auction
24. Seasoned
25. Preemptive
26. Private placement
27. Uniform price auction
28. Shelf registration

Problems

1. The sisters' initial investment of $200,000 became $2.5 million in the first stage financing providing 12.5 fold increase or 1,150 percent return. During the next phase, the $2.5 million became $7 million (half of $20 million - $6 million). This is now 35 percent of the value of the firm. The return during this phase is 180 percent. At the time of IPO, the sisters' stake is valued at $21 million ($60 million x 0.35) and the return during this phase is 200 percent. The venture capitalists' initial investment of $2.5 million became $7 million at the time of second financing providing a return of 180 percent. During the next phase their investment of $13 million became $39 million to give a return of 200 percent.

2. The original stockholders' investment in the firm has a paper value of $1 million at the first stage. With an additional $1 million raised, they own 50 percent of the firm. At the second stage, when the company is value at $10 million, their stake is worth $5 million. These valuations represent 10-fold and 5-fold increases in the two stages, representing returns of 900 percent and 400 percent respectively.

b) At a $1.5 million firm valuation, the original stockholders' investment would have a paper value of $0.5 million at the first stage. With an additional $1 million raised, they have only one-third of the company's stock. At the second stage, when company is valued at $9 million their stake is worth $3 million. These valuations represent 5-fold and 6-fold increases in the two stages (returns of 400 percent and 500 percent respectively).

3. a. Number of new shares = $18,000,000/$36 = 500,000 shares

    b. Value of company after issue = $200,000,000 + $18,000,000 = $218,000,000
        Share price after issue $218,000,000/5,500,000 = $39.64

    c. Loss per share to existing holders = $40 - $39.64 = $0.36

    d. Percentage reduction in value = ($0.36/$40) x 100 percent = 0.90 percent

    e. NPV of purchasing 100 shares via offer = 100x($39.64 - $36) = $364

4. a. Value of equity before issue = 5,000,000 x $40 = $200,000,000.
    b. Increase in value = $18 m/$200 m x 100 percent = 9%.
    c. Share price after issue = $218 m/5.5 = $39.64.
    d. Value of the right to buy one share = $39.64 - $36.00 = $3.64

5. a. Cost of public issue = $10,000,000 x 0.5 percent = $50,000

    b. Cost of private placement = $20,000 + additional interest cost
        Additional interest = $10,000,000 x 1/8 percent = $12,500 per year for 20 years

        If we discount these interest payments at 9 percent, i.e., the market rate for identical cash
        flows which are traded in the capital market, we obtain, PV = $114,107
        [N = 20, I = 9%, (P/Y = 1), PV = SOLVE, PMT = $12,500, FV = 0]
        Total cost of private placement = $20,000 + $114,107 = $134,107

        That is, shareholders will be better off if the firm chooses the public issue alternative.

16

The Dividend Controversy

INTRODUCTION

This chapter addresses the issue of dividend policy. Dividend policy is among one of the most controversial issues of corporate finance. The controversy surrounds the question - do dividends increase the value of a firm? Three broad and divergent views have emerged in response to this question. The prevailing wisdom before the seminal work by Modigliani and Miller (MM) was that increased dividend payouts increase firm value. MM argued that a firm's value is decided by the success of its investments and not by how it pays dividends. A more radical view suggests that in view of the differential taxation of dividends and capital gains, dividends will reduce the firm's value as they are taxed at a higher rate. The dividend irrelevancy argument of MM assumes a world of perfect capital markets. MM's position was a direct challenge to the traditional view, which held that high payout ratios tend to increase the value of the firm. While there is still debate on the issue, it appears that the traditional position has weakened considerably and there is more acceptance of the general wisdom of MM's argument.

Part of the controversy and confusion about dividends arises from the way the issue is framed. In order to decide whether dividends add value to the firm, one has to keep other variables like investment policy and debt policy constant. One has to isolate he dividend policy effects from those of capital budgeting and borrowing decisions. This means that the dividend policy trade-off is between retaining earnings for reinvestment on the one hand and paying dividends and financing the investments with newly issued stocks on the other. In other words, dividend policy issue is not about paying off any excess funds the company has; but whether a company should pay out earnings as dividends when it can profitably reinvest the same.

A financial manager needs to understand the issue and trade-off involved in order to be able to make the right decisions. It is also essential that she be familiar with the terms and terminology of dividends and the current practice of corporations in establishing dividends. The chapter helps you do this with descriptive material on the mechanics of dividend payments and corporate dividend practice. The chapter also includes a description of alternative tax systems and their implications for dividends.

KEY CONCEPTS IN THE CHAPTER

Mechanics and Terminology of Dividends: Dividends have been around for a long time. In order to familiarize yourself with the way dividends are paid out and handled by companies, you should know terms and phrases commonly used by corporations. Here is a summary description of the mechanics and an explanation of the terms used.

The mechanics: The board of directors decides the amount of dividends and how they are to be paid, on the recommendation of the management of the company. Corporations in the U.S. generally pay their dividends quarterly, although any other schedule is possible. There are legal restrictions in most states on what can be paid out as dividends. Generally, dividends cannot be paid out of legal capital, usually defined as the par value of all outstanding shares. When there is no par value, the legal capital is usually defined as the receipts from the stock issue. Some exceptions to this rule may be permitted for mining companies.

The company makes an announcement of the dividend decision on the *announcement date*. The announcement gives the details of when the dividend will be paid to shareholders who are registered in the company's books.

The practice of regular cash dividends is less common than it used to be. The percentage of American companies paying regular cash dividends has declined from about 67 percent in 1978 to about 20 percent now. Companies, which do pay dividends, typically have regular quarterly dividends. Occasionally companies pay an extra dividend when further cash is available. A stock dividend affects the stock price as the number of shares increases without any change in the value of the company's assets. Stock repurchase is another way of returning cash to the stockholders. Stock repurchases permit the investors to choose whether to receive the cash or not. It also enjoys favorable tax treatment.

Dividend reinvestment plans (DRIP) have become popular with stockholders and many companies have instituted these plans. This allows the shareholder to automatically reinvest the dividends in the company's shares often at a discount from the current market price.

Terminology: A number of terms are commonly used to describe the various dates and events associated with dividend payments. Here is a list:

Announcement date: This is the date on which the dividend is formally announced by the company and starts the dividend process for that specific dividend. The announcement carries details of different dates important for the payment of the announced dividend.

Ex-dividend date: This is the first day on which the stock trades without the right to receive the announced dividend. This will be a few days before the record date. A person who sells the stock before the ex-dividend date will still receive the dividend when it is paid out, even though he will not be holding the stock on that date.

Record date: This is the date on which the list of shareholders eligible to receive the dividend is made. This follows the ex-dividend date.

Payment date: This is the date on which checks are sent to shareholders of record. Normally, it takes about 2 weeks after the record date.

With-dividend: This denotes that shares are selling with the cash dividend attached. All the stocks traded before the ex-dividend date will carry the right of dividends.

Share repurchase: Share repurchase can be an attractive alternative to cash dividends. It is attractive for two reasons: i) it lets the stockholder choose whether to receive the cash or retain his level of ownership and ii) gains from stocks sold are treated as capital gains (assuming the stockholder has held the stock for more than one year). Companies use three different ways to repurchase stocks: open market purchase; tender offer, which is an offer to buy back a certain number of shares, often at a premium; and negotiated repurchase from individual stockholders. Open market repurchases are the most common. Share repurchases are generally not seen as a substitute for cash dividends; many companies do both repurchases and have cash dividends. Repurchases are used to return extra cash back to investors and are more volatile than cash dividends. Some countries do not permit companies to buy back their own shares, though many countries are changing the laws to allow stock repurchases.

Corporate Practice: A survey of corporate managers conducted by John Lintner in the mid-1950s provided very useful information on how companies decide on dividend payments. Most of Lintner's findings are still relevant. The findings can be summarized as follows:

- Firms generally set long-run *target payout ratios*. The payout ratio is a function of the company's growth prospects and earnings variability. Companies with stable earnings generally have high payouts and those that are growth companies have low payouts.

- The changes in dividends are considered more important than the level of dividends.

- Dividends follow changes in the long run, sustainable earnings. In other words, major changes are not made unless the managers are sure that changes in earnings are long-term and not transient. Managers also practice short-term smoothing of dividends.

- Managers are reluctant to make any major changes in dividends unless they are sure that the changes will not be reversed.

Lintner developed a simple model, which can be expressed as below:

$$DIV_1 - DIV_0 = \text{adjustment rate} \times (\text{target ratio} \times EPS_1 - DIV_0)$$

The implication of the model is that current dividends depend in part on current earnings and in part on the dividends of previous years, with more distant years being given less weight than more current years.

Information Content of Dividends and Stock Repurchases: Dividends and stock repurchases may signal important information to shareholders because they may indicate management's assessment of future sustainable earnings. Dividend increases are viewed as a signal of increased future earnings. Dividend cuts signal bad news about the future. Empirical evidence supports this view.

Share repurchases are different from dividends in that they are, usually, one-time events. A company may resort to share repurchase when it has more cash than it can profitably invest. Alternately, a share repurchase may be financed by additional borrowing. In either case, the manager is clearly indicating that stockholders' money is not being retained for making unprofitable investments. Yet, another reason for share repurchase may be the manager's confidence in the future prospects of the company and feeling that the stock is currently undervalued. Empirical evidence shows that share repurchases in general are greeted positively by the investors. The positive reaction is even greater when the stock repurchase is at a significant premium to the current price.

The Dividend Controversy: The essence of the dividend controversy centers on the extent to which dividend policy affects the value of the enterprise. There is little dispute as to the relevance and importance of dividends as signals of future prospects of the company. What is to be settled is whether the dividend decision itself contributes to a change in the value of the company. We review the three main views in this controversy.

The MM irrelevance view: MM started the whole controversy by challenging the prevailing view on dividend policy. They showed that under perfect market conditions, a firm's value is decided by its investments and not its dividends. MM's argument begins with these assumptions:

- No taxes, transactions costs, or other market imperfections.
- A fixed investment policy or capital budgeting program.
- A financing policy in which borrowing is set.
- Remaining needed funds come from retained earnings, and extra cash is paid as dividends.
- Capital markets are efficient and transactions take place at fair prices.

Given the assumptions, it is very hard to reject MM's basic conclusion that dividend policy is irrelevant. Essentially, a firm's original shareholders can raise cash in two ways. They can collect dividends or they can sell a part of their holdings in the market to receive the same amount of cash (see figure 16-2 and 16-3). In each case, the cash received is offset by a decline in the value of the old stockholders' claim on the firm. If the firm pays a dividend, each share is worth less because more shares have to be issued against the firm's assets. If the old stockholders sell some of their shares, each share is worth the same but the old stockholders have fewer shares. It follows that:

- If dividends are increased, the firm must issue more shares (because investments and borrowing are fixed).
- No one will buy the shares at more or less than their true value.
- The total market value of the firm is unchanged, and the sale of new shares only results in a transfer of part ownership of the firm from the old shareholders to the new.

- The new purchasers receive shares at a price less than that on the old shares, and it is less by the amount of the dividend paid.
- In efficient capital markets, shareholders that need cash can either sell shares or receive cash dividends and the path they choose will not make any difference to the value of the firm.

Thus, dividend policy is irrelevant and depends on the firm's investment and financing decisions. Note that share repurchases are the reverse of the above process: Dividend reductions are accompanied by an equivalent reduction in shares, and total wealth of shareholders is unaffected.

The MM position can be challenged using evidence of market imperfections or inefficiencies. Taxes and transaction costs, however, might drive one to the conclusion that dividends may actually decrease value (See the "leftists" view below). Other imperfections such as the existence of a special clientele who prefer high-payout stocks or dividends as purveyor of valuable information about future prospects do make a case for the relevance of dividends. We will come back to this after summarizing the other views on dividend policy.

The MM irrelevance proposition applies to share repurchases decisions also. That is, keeping investment and debt policy constant, a firm's value is unaffected by any decisions to repurchase stock. Again, this assumes away any signaling effect from share repurchases.

The Rightists: The traditional finance literature before MM favored liberal dividends. This belief was supported by many in business and investment communities because they believed increased dividends made shareholders better off. The main arguments made in support of dividends centered on: i) dividends are less risky than capital gains and ii) capital market imperfections give rise to investors who prefer high dividends for personal and institutional reasons. Analysis of these arguments shows that they have limited validity in refuting MM's irrelevance conclusions. While it is true that dividends are more stable than capital gains, it is also true that the risk of the cash flows of the firm is determined by the firm's investment and debt policies. The dividend payout should not have any effect. As for the clientele argument, it is conceded that there are groups of investors who like regular and high dividends and therefore high payout firms. However, the demand for high payout firms by this clientele would be fully satisfied by now and it is very hard to imagine that a company can gain value by simply changing its payout policies.

The empirical evidence supporting the traditional view is limited and untenable. A better argument could be that investors lack complete trust in managers to spend retained earnings wisely. The dividend decision forces the managers to raise additional finances from capital markets to finance any new investment. This keeps them on a tight leash and possibly more efficient in spending.

Taxes and the Radical Left: The radical left position in the dividend controversy focuses primarily on the tax effects, which influence the preference for cash dividends. When dividends are taxed more heavily than capital gains, paying higher dividends will actually lead to a loss in

189

value. The firm is better off paying any excess cash through stock repurchases rather than dividends. Thus, radical left view is that dividends are bad for the stockholders as they cause avoidable taxes. Of course, this extreme view will run afoul of the IRS and therefore few managers ever declare a policy on the lines suggested by the leftists' view.

The tax law changes affect the relative advantage of capital gains over dividends. The Tax Reform Act of 1987 reduced this advantage by essentially taxing both capital gains and dividends at the same rates. This was reversed by the tax law changes of 1998 bring back some of the advantages with the reduction of maximum capital gains tax rate to 20 percent on any investment held for more than one year. The maximum tax rate on dividend income is 39.6 percent.

Empirical studies give some support to the leftists' view in that investors in low marginal tax brackets appear to prefer high-payout stocks, and vice versa. However, note that there are serious measurement and other problems in some of these studies. It is very hard to measure expected return and tax effects caused by dividends. Further, tax effects on dividends are not uniform across different investors.

The Middle-of-the-Roaders: This position essentially holds that a company's value is not affected by its dividend policy. While conceding the effect of market imperfections on MM's theoretical arguments, this group views that the impact of market imperfections is not significant. If low or high payouts increased the value of the firm, financial managers would do so. The fact that we do not see a rush to change dividend policies one way or the other suggests that it is not terribly important. While the 1986 Tax Reform Act changed the balance between capital gains and dividends somewhat (by making taxes on dividends close to those on capital gains), the changes in the tax laws made in 1998 reversed the scale again. Since capital gains enjoy lower rates once again, it is unlikely that there will be any great increase in corporate payout ratios.

Alternative Tax Systems: The chapter includes a brief discussion of alternative tax systems employed in different countries. These can be summarized as below:

- *The two-tier system:* Dividends are taxed at both corporate and individual levels. This is the approach followed in the U.S.

- *Split-rate system:* Investors are taxed at higher rates on dividends than on capital gains, but the firm is taxed more heavily on retained profits than on distributed profits. This is the system followed in Germany.

- *Imputation system:* Dividends are taxed at the individual level, but the corporate share of taxes is deductible from their tax bill. This approach is used in Australia.

WORKED EXAMPLES

1. Match the following dates from the left and the right columns.

(A) Friday, November 2   (a) record date
(B) Tuesday, November 13   (b) announcement date
(C) Friday, November 16   (c) ex-dividend date
(D) Tuesday, December 8   (d) payment date

SOLUTION

(A) Friday, November 2   -   (b) Announcement date
(B) Tuesday, November 13   -   (c) Ex-dividend date
(C) Friday, November 16   -   (a) Record date
(D) Tuesday, December 8   -   (d) Payment date

2. Texas Power paid $0.75 per quarter in 2001. Calculate the stock's dividend yield based on its recent market price of $40.00.

SOLUTION

Dividend yield = yearly cash dividends/current market price per share
          = (4 x $0.75)/40.00 = $3.00/$40.00 = 7.5 percent

3. If Texas Power's 2001 earnings per share were $5.50 and per share and the annual cash dividends were $3, what was the company's dividend payout?

SOLUTION
          Payout ratio = estimated cash dividends per share/estimated earnings per share
                    = $3.00/$5.80 = 51.72 percent

4. Texas Power declared a stock dividend of 25 percent and its market price was $40. Assuming nothing else changed, what would you expect the price of the shares to be after the stock dividends are distributed?

SOLUTION

The stock dividend, by itself, has no expected effect on the value of the firm.
Thus, 1.25 x Price per share after stock dividend = $40
Price per share after stock dividend = $40/1.25 = $32

5. Lentle Corporation's financial numbers are as follows:

Net income	$45 million
Earnings per share	$3
Number of shares outstanding	15 million
Price-earnings ratio	10

The management plans to repurchase 5 percent of the company's outstanding shares at the going market price. What effect does the stock repurchase have on the above numbers? What effect does it have on the value of the firm? Explain.

SOLUTION

The earnings per share is $3 and with a P/E of 10, the stock price will be $30. The company's market value is $450 million ($30 x 15 million). The company needs $22.5 million in cash to buy 0.75 million shares at $30 each. If it does not have the cash, it must sell assets. If it sells typical assets, its net income will shrink to $42.75 million. Second, the number of shares outstanding decreases to 14.25 million. Third, earnings per share remain at $3 ($42.75 million/14.25 million shares). And fourth, because the price-earnings ratio stays the same, the value of the shares also stays at $30 each.

Prior to the repurchase the value per share was $30 with 15 million shares outstanding and the firm's value at $450 million. After the repurchase, the value of the shares remains at $30 each, which, when multiplied by the 14.25 million then outstanding, results in a total value of $427.5 million, which equals, not coincidentally, the value before repurchase less the value of assets used to repurchase the shares. The size of the firm contracts with and no gain or loss to its shareholders.

LIST OF TERMS

Announcement date	Regular cash dividend
Dividend policy	Repurchase
Ex-dividend	Special dividend
Legal capital	Stock dividend
Payment date	Target payout ratio
Payout ratio	With-dividend
Record date	

EXERCISES

Fill-in Questions

1. The date on which dividend checks are actually mailed out is the _____.

2. _____ is concerned with the trade-off between retaining earnings on the one hand and paying out cash and issuing new shares on the other.

3. The _____ is the date on which the list of registered shareholders that are to receive cash dividends is made.

4. Shares bought and sold before the record date are said to be transacted _____ whereas those bought and sold after the record date are said to be transacted _____.

5. A firm's _____ consists of the par value of all its outstanding shares.

6. The date on which the company makes a formal announcement of its dividends is the _____.

7. _____ are cash dividends, which a company usually expects to be able to maintain in the future.

8. _____ are cash dividends paid irregularly and are not necessarily expected to be maintained in the future.

9. _____ are similar to stock splits in that no cash is paid to stockholders.

10. The percentage ratio of cash dividends to earnings is called the _____.

11. Lintner's empirical study showed that companies tend to adjust their payout ratios towards a _____.

12. Companies sometimes buy back or _____ their own shares.

13. The United States has a(n) _____ system in which dividends are taxed at both corporate and investor levels.

Problems

1. Arrange the following dates into order of occurrence: Payment date, announcement date, ex-dividend date, and record date.

2. On June 1, 2001 Mundy Corporation split its stock 2 for 1. The cash dividend is at $0.125 a quarter. The closing stock price on the record date was $29.875.

   a. What would you expect the price of the stock to be before the split, assuming nothing else changed?
   b. Could the adjustments in per share price and cash dividends have been accomplished by a stock dividend?
   c. If so, what size would the stock dividend have to be to accomplish this goal?
   d. What was the annual dividend yield before and after the split?
   e. What was the payout ratio, given expected annual 2001 earnings of $1.95 a share?
   f. During the past 10 years the company's payout ratio averaged about 16 percent. Are you willing to say that this particular payout contained valuable information? Why or why not?

3. On Friday, August 10, 2001, Rise Corp. announced a quarterly dividend of 12.5 cents and a stock dividend of 10 percent payable on Monday, September 10, 2001 to shareholders of record on Friday, August 24, 2001.

   a. If the August 10 market price of $16.50 remains the same, at what price would you expect the stock to sell for after the cash and stock dividends?
   b. When would you expect the stock to go ex-dividend?
   c. Assuming that the quarterly cash dividend of 12.5 cents per share will continue after the stock dividend, what is the effective percentage increase in the cash dividend?
   d. What is the expected annual dividend yield, using your estimate of the ex-dividend price and the 12.5 cents quarterly cash dividend?
   e. If expected annual earnings per share are $3, what is the annual expected dividend payout?

4. On Thursday, August 17, 2000, City First Bank declared a 20 percent common stock dividend payable on September 15 to stockholders of record on August 28. It was also announced that the cash dividend payment of $0.25 a share per quarter, payable on October 6 to stockholders of record on September 18, would remain the same.

   a. By how much did the quarterly dividend increase?
   b. What would you expect the price of shares to be after the stock dividend, given that on the date of the announcement they were selling at 24 ¼?
   c. Are the shareholders necessarily any better off? That is, does their wealth increase as a result of the stock dividend?

5. On August 15, 2001, Murray Corp. announced a 1-for-10 reverse split, the event to occur on September 6, subject to shareholder approval. The stock's closing price on August 14 was 1 3/8. If nothing changes, at what price would you expect the stock to sell after the stock split is made effective on September 6?

6. Regression analysis reveals that the changes in MTY's annual dividend can be explained by the equation: $D_t - D_{t-1} = 0.18 E_t - 0.30 D_{t-1}$. What does this reveal about MTYs target payout ratio, and how far each year does the current dividend adjust towards it?

Essay Questions

1. Explain the mechanics of paying dividends.

2. "Stock repurchases can add value to the firm, even though dividends do not." Discuss.

3. Compare and contrast the middle-of-the-roaders' view and the MM irrelevance proposition.

4. How can it be said that cash dividends are financially equivalent to stock issues, once investment and financing policies are fixed? Explain fully.

ANSWERS TO EXERCISES

Fill-in Questions

1. Payment date
2. Dividend policy
3. Record date
4. With dividend; ex-dividend
5. Legal capital
6. Announcement date
7. Regular cash dividends

8. Special dividends
9. Stock dividends
10. Payout ratio
11. Target payout ratio
12. Repurchase
13. Two-tier system

Problems

1. Announcement date, ex-dividend date, record date, and payment date.

2. a. $30.00 \times 2 = \$60.00$.
   b. Yes.
   c. 100%, so that two additional shares are outstanding for every old share.
   d. Before: $[(\$0.125 \times 4)/\$59.75] \times 100 = 0.84\%$;
      After: $[(\$0.125 \times 4)/\$29.875] \times 100 = 1.67\%$.
   e. $[(\$0.125 \times 4)/\$1.95] \times 100 = 25.6\%$.
   f. No, this is not an unusual event. Invariably, large deviations from the usual contain valuable information.

3. a. $(\$16.50 - \$.125)/1.10 = \$14.89$, or $14.875 to the nearest eighth of a dollar.
   b. Tuesday, August 21, 2001.
   c. 10 percent.
   d. $(\$0.125 \times 4)/\$14.875 = 3.36\%$.
   e. $\$0.50/\$3.00 = 16.7$ percent.

4. a. The cash dividend increase was also 20%. Think of it this way: if you had one share before the split, you received $1.00 a year in cash dividends; afterward, you have 1.2 shares, on which you receive $0.25 a share for a total of $1.2 \times \$0.25 \times 4 = \$1.20$; an increase of 20%.
   b. One would expect the stock to decline to: $\$24.25/1.2 = \$20.21$.
   c. The shareholders, all else the same, are not necessarily better off. If the dividend increase were expected, that would be built into the dividend discount model and reflected in share prices. If the dividend increase were unexpected, there might well be positive wealth effects for shareholders because the unexpected increase in dividends may signal from management sustainable earning power to cover not only the increase in dividends but also all other corporate needs. The share price closed down one-eighth on the day of the announcement, suggesting that the dividend increase was expected.

5. 10 x $1.375 = $13.75.

6. The equation can be rearranged as: $D_t - D_{t-1} = 0.30 (0.60 E_t - D_{t-1})$; so, we see that the target payout ratio is 60% and the dividend adjusts 30% of the way towards this each year.

17

Does Debt Policy Matter?

INTRODUCTION

This chapter describes the classic Modigliani and Miller (MM) propositions concerning the capital structure of business firms. MM's proposition I states that under perfect market conditions the value of a firm is unaffected by the financing mix of debt and equity used by the firm. Proposition II, which is the corollary of the first proposition, states that the required rate of return on the equity increases with an increase in proportion to debt such that the weighted-average cost of capital does not change. The implication of these two propositions is that the choice of debt-equity mix or capital structure is irrelevant and has no effect on the value of the firm. Debt policy does not matter and investment and financing decisions can be separated.

The chapter focuses on MM's propositions, the conditions under which their case is made, and the counter argument put forth by the traditional view that financial leverage has some intrinsic advantage. MM views are clearly difficult to challenge, once the perfect market conditions are accepted. The primary logic of the MM propositions is that a firm's value is based only on the stream of cash flows produced by its assets. The claims to this cash flow can be packaged in different ways, but unless there are market imperfections, arbitrage across these claims will ensure that the value of the firm is unaffected by the capital structure changes.

In practice, capital structure matters because deviations from perfect market conditions are present in the real world. These deviations are discussed in Chapter 18. The significance of the MM propositions is not that they depict a realistic picture of the world, but a clear understanding of the propositions enables you to understand why capital structure decisions are important and why one capital structure may be better than another.

KEY CONCEPTS IN THE CHAPTER

Leverage and its Effects in Perfect Markets: Under perfect market conditions, financial leverage has no effect on the value of the firm. MM presents simple arguments to prove this point. Imagine two firms, U (unleveraged) and L (for leveraged), with identical operating cash flows but with different capital structures. Owning one percent of firm U will be equivalent in terms of claims to cash flows to owning one percent of both the debt and equity of firm, L. Ownership of one percent of each firm gives claims to identical cash flows. Therefore, the values of these claims should be identical. Hence, $V_U = V_L$. An alternate approach is to compare ownership of one percent of the equity of the leveraged firm to ownership of one percent of the unleveraged firm and finance it by borrowing an amount equal to one percent of the leveraged firm's debt. Again, the claims are identical and it leads to the result, $VU = V_L$. It follows that under these conditions, debt policy is irrelevant. This is proposition I.

Proposition I is essentially a restatement of the *value additivity principle* (see chapter 7): PV(A+B) = PV(A) + PV(B). Proposition I applies this in reverse. It can be called the *law of conservation of value*. The value of an asset is based on the cash flows produced by the asset and is not affected by the nature of claims against it.

MM's arguments supporting proposition I assume that both firms and individuals can borrow at the same interest rate. This assumption is not crucial to the proposition. A fact, which might appear to give corporate debt some advantage, is that corporate stockholders have limited liability and thus can borrow with limited liability. Individuals cannot, on their own, have limited liability. Thus, corporate debt might have some advantage over personal debt. However, the advantage is unlikely to be of any significant value now since there are any number of corporations that can and have issued limited liability debt. In other words, any demand for limited liability debt would have been fully met by now.

Leverage and Returns: Proposition I leads to proposition II, which gives the relationship of returns on the debt, equity, and the asset return. If proposition I is to hold, the asset return, r_A is unaffected by leverage. This means that when the firm borrows, the required rate of return demanded by the shareholders increases as their risk increases. Proposition II states that the expected return on equity increases in proportion to the debt-equity ratio, expressed in market value. The rate of increase in return depends on the difference between the return on assets and the return on debt. The relationship can be expressed as follows:

$$r_A = [D/(D + E) \times r_D] + [E/(D + E) \times r_E].$$

Rearranging, r_E is given by:

$$r_E = r_A + (D/E)(r_A - r_D)$$

The essential implication of proposition II is that the increased return given by the equity in a leveraged firm reflects the increased risk. Therefore, the shareholders will demand a higher *required* rate of return. Or, the higher expected rate of return for the equity is simply the reflection of the higher risk involved and will be exactly matched by the higher required rate of return by the stockholders. Thus, the higher return is not going to result in a higher value of the stock.

Leverage and Beta: The effect of leverage on beta is similar to the effect on expected return. The relationship can be stated as follows:

Beta of the firm's assets:

$$\beta_A = [D/(D+E) \times \beta_D] + [E/(D+E) \times \beta_E]$$

Rearrange to obtain the beta of the equity of a leveraged firm.

$$\beta_E = \beta_A + D/E(\beta_A - \beta_D)$$

This is an alternative explanation of why equity investors require higher returns as debt increases. Proposition II is consistent with CAPM.

The Traditional View: Prior to MM's work, the traditional wisdom was that some leverage was beneficial and by leveraging, a firm increased the return on equity. The traditional position used the *weighted-average cost of capital,* which is the expected return on the portfolio of all the company's securities. Weighted-average cost of capital is used to compute net present values of project cash flows when the project being evaluated does not differ from the firm's business risk. If leverage lowers the weighted-average cost of capital, then (assuming that the leverage *does not lower* cash flows correspondingly) the value of the firm will increase.

$$r_A = (D/V \times r_D) + (E/V \times r_E)$$

The traditional position held that increasing leverage resulted in lower weighted-average cost of capital because an increase in the cost of equity, if at all, is not proportionate to the increase in leverage. The traditional view, if correct, has the following implications:

- Proposition II does not hold or the expected return on equity does not increase as a firm borrows more.

- The weighted-average cost of capital declines at first as the debt-equity ratio increases and then rises.

- There is an optimal D/E ratio for which the cost of capital is lowest.

A word of caution is in order. The firm should try to *maximize* the value of the firm. This is not always equivalent to having the *lowest cost of capital.* The two goals will be equivalent *only* if the operating income is not affected by the change in leverage.

Beware of the managers who make the simplistic argument that they can enhance the firm's value by lowering the cost of capital, by borrowing more, as the cost of debt is lower than the cost of equity. This argument ignores proposition II.

The traditional view made two arguments to support its claim. The first one essentially said that the shareholders did not increase their *required* rate of return in exact proportion to the rise in leverage. This argument implied some irrationality on the part of the shareholders. If some debt is good, more debt must be even better, and the optimal leverage would be one hundred percent debt. The second argument used possible imperfections in the market and the advantage for corporate debt over personal debt suggesting that individuals could not borrow at the same rate as corporations. It is true that some individuals face higher borrowing cost on account of transaction costs (lack of economies of scale). Such individuals might find it advantageous to borrow through a corporation. However, any such demand for corporate debt must be fully satisfied now. In other words, trying to make money by leveraging now is like trying to make money selling automobiles or personal computers. You are late by a few decades.

Essentially, borrowing costs should be a function of the risk of the borrower or more specifically, the use to which the borrowed money is put (or to be more exact, how the loan is backed or secured). Most individuals can get mortgage loans or margin loans from their broker at very competitive rates.

To sum up, the traditional view lacks support and it is not backed by valid arguments. One has to look elsewhere for weaknesses in MM's position. If you can find deviations from the perfect market framework used by MM, you can find situations where their propositions will not hold. Many of these deviations are created by government regulations. Chapter 18 focuses on the practical implications of the market imperfections for corporate debt policy.

It is possible that there may be unsatisfied clienteles demanding specially designed securities with unique features. If a firm can design and structure a package of securities that exploits these needs, it can profit from it and you will find an exception to MM's proposition I. Of course, investment bankers are trying to do this all the time and it is very unlikely that there is any unsatisfied demand for the garden-variety or plain vanilla debt security. The next several chapters describe different type of securities invented by investment bankers and companies. It is however, hard to see that a firm's value can be increased greatly by these innovations in the absence of some government created imperfection.

WORKED EXAMPLES

1. Black Bird Corp. operates in perfect capital markets with no corporate or personal taxes. The company has 30 percent debt and 70 percent equity in its capital structure. The expected return on debt is 10 percent and the rate of return on equity is 14 percent. Calculate its expected return on assets.

SOLUTION

$$r_A = \frac{ExpectedOperatingIncome}{MarketValueofAllSecurities}$$

= (proportion in debt X expected return on debt) + (proportion in equity X expected return on equity)
= (weight of debt X cost of debt) + (weight of equity X cost of equity)
= $W_D r_D + W_E r_E = [D/(D + E) \times r_D] + [E/(D + E) \times r_E]$
= (0.30 X 0.10) + (0.70 X 0.14) = 12.8 percent

2. Wise Aaron Corp. has an operating income is $12,000, and the market value of all its all-equity-financed securities is $60,000. If the company decides to sell $20,000 of debt and

retire an equal amount of equity, how will the rate of return for equity change? Assume that it operates in perfect capital markets with no corporate or personal taxes, and that the expected return on debt is 12 percent.

SOLUTION

r_A = expected operating income/market value of all securities
= $12,000/$60,000 = 20 percent

In an all-equity-financed firm, the return on equity r_E is equal to the return on assets; so

$r_E = r_A$ = 20 percent

While borrowing changes the return on equity, it will not change the return on assets. This will remain the same because the value of the firm does not change and the expected operating income does not change. Therefore, the return on equity is:

$r_E = r_A + (D/E)(r_A - r_D)$
= 0.20 + ($20,000/$40,000)(0.20 - 0.12) = 0.20 + 0.5(0.08) = 24 percent

3. Use the information given in problem 2 and assume that the beta of the firm is 1.2 before the debt financing and the beta of the debt is 0.5. What is the beta of the equity with the debt financing given in problem 2? What will the beta of the equity be if the debt-equity ratio were 30, 60, and 70 percent?

SOLUTION

The beta of the equity without any debt financing is the same as the beta of the assets because no other securities are outstanding. After the financing, the beta of the equity changes as follows:

$\beta_E = \beta_A + (D/E)(\beta_A - \beta_D) = 1.2 + 0.5(1.2 - 0.5) = 1.55$

For the other debt proportions, β_E is given in the table below.

D/E (%)	β_E
30	1.41
60	1.62
70	1.69

4. Beta of equity with no debt is 1.2. Calculate the equity betas for different debt levels for the following values of beta for debt: 0, 1.2 and 0.5. Compare these results with those of problem 3.

SOLUTION

The values for β_E for different debt/equity ratios and different β_D are given in the table below.

D/E (%)	β_E for different value of β_D		
	$\beta_D = 0$	$\beta_D = 1.2$	$\beta_D = 0.5$
0	1.20	1.20	1.20
5	1.26	1.20	1.24
10	1.32	1.20	1.27
20	1.44	1.20	1.34
40	1.68	1.20	1.48
60	1.92	1.20	1.62
80	2.16	1.20	1.76
100	2.40	1.20	1.90

While the data above are somewhat contrived, several interesting results emerge. You can clearly see that the increase in the risk or beta of the equity with increased debt levels is a function of the beta or risk of the debt itself. First, when the beta of the debt is equal to the beta of the firm, when it is all-equity-financed, for all practical purposes, the company has issued another dose of equity and not debt. Consequently, the beta of the equity does not change. If the company were able to issue debt at the zero-beta level, the risk-free rate, the betas of the equity would tend to increase substantially with additional debt. In practice and in most cases, the beta of corporate debt is greater than zero but less than the beta of the all-equity-financed firm.

5. May Burke, the financial manager of Leverage Unlimited thinks she can increase shareholder value by increasing the leverage of the company. The company is currently all equity financed and is earning 20 percent. The company can borrow at 10 percent and the beta of the debt is at 0.4. The beta of equity before borrowing is 1.2. There are 10,000 shares outstanding and the price-earnings ratio of the common shares is 5 on an operating income of $25,000. The company can be expected to continue to generate that amount of operating income after the debt financing. Ms. Burke feels that the leverage will substantially raise the value of the firm and wants to buy back half the shares of the company. Formulate a response to Ms. Burke assuming operation in perfect capital markets with no corporate or personal taxes.

SOLUTION

Value of the firm before the debt financing = $25,000/0.20 = $125,000
Value per share is = $125,000/10,000 = $12.50
Earnings per share = $25,000/10,000 = $2.50
Price-earnings ratio =$12.50/$2.50 = 5

Next, determine the earnings per share after the debt financing. The company must sell $62,500 of debt at the going market rate of 10 percent in order to repurchase an equivalent amount of equity ($125,000x0.5).

Operating income	$25,000
less interest	6,250
Equity earnings	$18,750

With 5,000 shares now outstanding, earnings per share increase to $3.75 ($18,750/5000 shares). Ms. Burke assumes that she can still get the same price-earnings ratio of 5. Then, the shares have a market price of $18.75 (5 x $3.75). But going into debt entails additional risk to the shareholders. The beta will increase substantially. Using the formula:

$$\beta_E = \beta_A + D/E(\beta_A - \beta_D)$$

Before borrowing:

$$\beta = 1.2 + 0.0(1.2 - 0) = 1.2$$

After borrowing:

$$\beta = 1.2 + 1.0(1.2 - 0.4) = 1.2 + 0.8 = 2.0$$

Risk increases by two-thirds. With increased risk, the required rate of return on equity increases too. Assuming that the return on asset stays same, we can calculate the required return as follows:

$$r_E = r_A + (D/E)(r_A - r_D)$$
$$= 0.20 + 1.0(0.20 - 0.10) = 0.20 + 0.10 = 30 \text{ percent}$$

$$\text{Value per shares} = \$3.75/0.30 = \$12.50$$

Thus, there is no change in the value of the stock and leverage does not increase the value of the stock. Any increase in earnings is fully neutralized by the corresponding increase in risk and required rate of return. The price-earnings ratio will go down and the market price of the shares will remain the same.

SUMMARY

This chapter presents the well-known Modigliani-Miller propositions on debt policy under perfect market conditions. Proposition I states that a firm's value is unaffected by changes in leverage. Proposition II states that the risk of equity and therefore the required return increase in proportion to the debt-equity ratio. Thus, under perfect market conditions, debt policy is irrelevant and the firm's value is not affected by changes in financial leverage. The value of a firm depends only on the cash flows produced by its assets. While financial leverage tends to magnify returns to common stockholders, their risk is increased too. Therefore, they require higher returns on their shares; thus, the value of a share remains unchanged.

Proposition I is very general and applies to all types of securities (short-term debt vs. long term debt, equity vs. preferred stock, etc.) and one can say that no combination of securities is better than any other. The MM propositions have replaced the traditional view that the cost of capital will tend to decrease initially as debt is added to the capital structure but that it will increase only after a market-determined intolerable-threshold level of risk is passed. At that point, the cost of equity and the cost of debt increase significantly. The traditional view cannot be supported unless one is willing to accept irrational behavior on the part of investors or the presence of market imperfections.

MM's propositions cannot be refuted once the perfect market conditions are accepted. Any violation of MM's propositions can only be caused by market imperfections. These market imperfections are often created by government regulations (differential tax treatment of income streams, for example) and can create profitable opportunities for firms. It is also possible that there are clienteles for specific types of securities such as money market mutual funds and floating-rate notes. However, demand for by any such security is often quickly met by an adequate supply of the security in demand and a firm getting into these markets now is unlikely to benefit.

LIST OF TERMS

Capital structure
Financial leverage
Gearing
Law of conservation of value
Proposition I

Proposition II
Separation of investment and financing
Value additivity
Weighted-average cost of capital

EXERCISES

Fill-in Questions

1. _____ is another term used to describe financial leverage.

2. _____ is the term used to describe the mix of debt and equity used by a firm.

3. _____ states that the value of the firm is not changed by the mix of debt and equity.

4. A firm that borrows is said to engage in _____.

5. The _____ states that the value of an asset is preserved regardless of the nature of the claim on it.

6. The _____ is the sum of the returns on debt and equity each weighted by its percentage in the capital structure.

7. _____ states that the expected return on the common stock of a financially leveraged firm increases in proportion to the debt ratio.

8. Proposition I of Modigliani and Miller permits _____ decisions.

9. Proposition I is a restatement of the _____ principle learned in Chapter 7.

Problems

1. Pier Morganty Corp. is operating in perfect market conditions with no corporate or personal taxes. The company's debt has an expected return of 12 percent and the return on equity is 16 percent. The debt to assets ratio is 40 percent. Calculate the return on assets.

2. Use the information given in problem 1. How will the return on equity change if the debt is increased to 60 percent?

3. What is the expected return on assets for a firm that is 60 percent debt-financed and pays an expected return on debt of 9 percent and has a required return on equity of 20 percent? Assume the firm operates in perfect capital markets with no corporate or personal income taxes.

4. Your firm's expected operating income is $5,000, and the market value of its outstanding securities is $25,000 when it is all-equity-financed. Assuming that the firm operates in perfect capital markets with no corporate or personal taxes, calculate the required return on equity when the firm sells enough debt to repurchase half of the outstanding equity for each of the following rates of return on debt: (a) 8 percent, (b) 10 percent, and (c) 12 percent.

5. Using the data in problem 4 above, beta for the firm at 1.5, and the beta for the debt of 0.6, what is the beta of the equity after the financing?

6. The financial manager of Moon Bucks, Inc. estimates that she will increase the earnings per share of her presently all-equity-financed firm if she borrows at the going market rate of 8 percent. She estimates the debt's beta to be 0.3 and the beta of the all-equity firm is 0.8. A return of 12.5 percent is expected on the all-equity firm, the price-earnings ratio of 8 is expected to persist, expected operating income is $300,000, and 100,000 shares are outstanding. She plans to replace 40 percent of her equity with debt. How will the values of the shares change?

Essay Questions

1. Explain the Modigliani and Miller's propositions I and II and their implications for financial managers.

2. Discuss the following argument often heard in defense of leverage. "Cost of debt is definitely less than the cost of equity. By using the cheaper source of funds, a firm can increase the return available to its equity holders and thereby increase their value."

3. "Modigliani and Miller propositions I and II have very little practical appeal as they assume the so called perfect market conditions, which do not exist." Give a detailed response to that statement.

4. How may individual investors augment or undo the debt policy of firms in which they wish to invest? Explain fully. Also explain why this concept is important to the Modigliani-Miller position regarding debt policy.

5. Demonstrate how the beta of a firm is dependent on the beta of the capital structure components.

ANSWERS TO EXERCISES

Fill-in Questions

1. Gearing
2. Capital structure
3. Proposition I
4. Financial leverage
5. Law of conservation of value

6. Weighted-average cost of capital
7. Proposition II
8. Separation of financing and investment
9. Value additivity

Problems

1. $(0.4 \times 0.12) + (0.6 \times 0.16) = 14.4$ percent

2. $r_E = r_A + D/E\,(r_A - r_D) = 0.14 + 1.5(0.14 - 0.11) = 18.5$ percent

3. $(0.6 \times 0.09) + (0.4 \times 0.2) = 13.4$ percent

4. $r_A = \$5,000/\$25,000 = 20$ percent. $r_E = r_A + D/E(r_A - r_D)$.
   a. When $r_D = 8$ percent, $r_E = 0.20 + [(0.5/0.5)(0.20 - 0.08)] = 32$
   b. When $r_D = 10$ percent, $r_E = 30$ percent
   c. When $r_D = 12$ percent, $r_E = 28$ percent.

5. $\beta_E = \beta_A + D/E(\beta_A - \beta_D) = 1.5 + 1.0(1.5 - 0.6) = 2.40$

6. The analysis is the same as that for problem 5 of the Worked Examples.

First, calculate the value of the all-equity firm:

Value = $300,000/12.5 percent = $2,400,000
Value per share = $2,400,000/100,000 shares = $24
Earnings per share = $300,000/100,000 = $3

Then, compute the effect of debt financing on earnings per share:

Amount of required debt: 0.4($2,400,000) = $960,000

Operating income	= $300,000
less interest (0.08 X $960,000)	= 76,800
Equity earnings	= $223,200

Earnings per share: $223,200/60,000= $3.72

Now, calculate the beta of equity after debt financing:

Before-debt financing: 0.8; after:

$$\beta_E = \beta_A + D/E(\beta_A - \beta_D)$$
$$= 0.8 + 0.4/0.6(0.8 - 0.3)$$
$$= 1.133$$

Now, we can calculate the return on equity, after debt financing:

$$r_E = r_A + (D/E)(r_A - r_D)$$
$$= 0.125 + (0.4/0.6)(0.125 - 0.08)$$
$$= 15.5 \text{ percent}$$

Market price of equity after debt financing can be calculated as below:

Market price per share = $3.72/0.155 = $24

Value of equity = market price per share X number of shares
= $24 X 60,000 = $1,440,000

Value of firm after debt financing = Debt + Equity
= $960,000 + 1,440,000
= $2,400,000

The value of the firm is unaffected by the leverage.

18

How Much Should a Firm Borrow?

INTRODUCTION

This chapter provides the practical world's view of debt policy. Chapter 17 presented the view that debt policy did not matter under perfect market conditions. We know, however, that in the real world debt policy matters because there are a number of deviations from the perfect market conditions assumed in MM's theoretical framework. While capital markets work reasonably well, there are the following to consider: corporate and personal income taxes, the probability of bankruptcy and the costs associated with it, costs of other forms of financial distress, and differing goals and conflicts of interests among lenders and shareholders. These factors cause the debt policy to assume practical relevance and importance. The MM analysis enables us to understand the significance of these deviations from the perfect market conditions and their impact on corporate debt policy.

The chapter presents two broad theories to explain capital structures of corporations. The first theory, known as the *trade-off theory*, suggests that corporations can arrive at an optimal debt ratio by comparing the positive and negative aspects of borrowing. The primary positive side or benefit of borrowing is that interest payments to lenders are tax-deductible. Thus, the government subsidizes part of the payments to the lenders. The negative side of borrowing comes from the costs associated with bankruptcy and financial distress.

The second theory is known as the *pecking order theory* and is based on the observed behavior of financial managers. Financial managers appear to prefer a hierarchy of financing sources and their order of preference runs as follows: first choice is internal funds (retained earnings), followed by external debt financing, and external equity being the last choice. This behavior can be explained by the *information asymmetry* between managers and investors.

KEY CONCEPTS IN THE CHAPTER

Corporate Taxes and Debt Policy: One of the most important deviations from the classic MM framework is the presence of corporate income taxes and the differential treatment meted out to interest payments on debt. Firms are allowed to deduct interest payments from their income subject to taxation. This creates a subsidy for borrowing and effectively expands the corporate pie available for distribution to investors (stockholders and bondholders). If a firm borrows D dollars at an interest rate of r_D the firm reduces its annual tax bill by $T_c(r_D D)$, where T_c is the corporate tax rate. If the debt is permanent, then the present value of this tax shield is:

$$T_c(r_D D)/r_D = T_c D$$

Thus, the firm's value can be increased by borrowing and the increase in value will equal T_cD. We can modify the MM proposition I to the following expression:

Value of firm = Value of all-equity-financed firm + T_cD

While the model is simple, it is less than satisfactory. The basic problem with this is that it leads to an optimal debt ratio of one hundred percent. This, of course, does not make any sense. In fact we find many successful companies with very little borrowing in their balance sheet.

Debt Policy and Corporate and Personal Taxes: The issue of taxes gets complicated when personal taxes are also considered. In a world where both corporations and individuals are taxed on their income, the firm does well by its investors when it minimizes not just the corporate taxes but the total taxes paid by the firm and its investors. Consider a firm with both debt and equity. Each dollar of operating income (income before taxes and interests) can be paid out either as equity income or as interest income. Let the tax rates on interest income and equity income be T_p and T_{pE} respectively. There are two ways you can pay the operating income to the investor – either as interest to the bondholder or as dividend to the stockholder. If it is paid out as dividends, the effective cash flow to the stockholder will be as follows:

Operating income	=	$1
less corporate taxes	=	$1 - T_c$
Personal tax on equity income	=	$T_{pE}(1 - T_c)$
Net of all taxes	=	$(1 - T_{pE})(1 - T_c)$

When a dollar of operating income is paid out to the bondholder, the firm saves corporate taxes and the bondholder gets $(1 - T_p)$. Under these conditions, the debt policy will be irrelevant, if:

$$1 - T_p = (1 - T_{pE})(1 - T_c)$$

This can happen only if the corporate tax rate, T_c, is less than T_p and T_{pE} is very small. This is what Merton Miller used to suggest that debt policy could very well be irrelevant. Miller suggested that the effective tax on equity income is very low as most of the income could be in the form of capital gains. Miller's arguments were formulated in the 1970s, when tax rates were very different from what they are now. The changes made in 1986 effectively reduced the personal tax rates on interest income and raised the tax on capital gains. This was followed by more changes in 1998, which reduced the advantage to debt as the effective tax on capital gains has been reduced to 20 percent. Since the investor can defer the tax on capital gain the effective tax rate on capital gain would be a lot less. However, considering the fact that part of the equity income comes as dividends, which are taxed at higher rates, debt will continue to have some advantage over equity in terms of taxes.

A practical rule on debt policy would be to structure debt and equity such that the total tax bill paid by the firm and the investors is minimized. In order to figure out the relative tax advantage of debt and equity funding, the text uses the following values for the different tax rates: $T_p = 33$

percent, T_{pE} = 16 percent, and T_c = 35 percent. The value for T_{pE} is computed using a tax rate of 10 percent on capital gains and 33 percent on dividend income. It is also assumed that 78 percent of the stock returns are received in the form of capital gains. With these assumptions, a dollar of pre-tax income paid out as interest would mean net receipts of 67 cents for the investor. A dollar of pre-tax income routed through equity will end up as 54 cents of after-tax income for the stockholder. Thus there is a moderate tax advantage of about 13 cents in favor of debt financing.

Note that these numbers are crude estimates and different assumptions can lead to different values for the comparative advantage to borrowing. In general, companies, which are unsure that the corporate tax shield will be used to its full advantage, have less incentive to borrow. Many firms have non-interest tax shields available, which will help them reduce their tax bills without resorting to debt financing.

Financial Distress and Debt Policy: The prospect of *financial distress* concerns investors and reduces the present value of the firm. Financial distress occurs when the firm cannot meet its obligations to the creditors. The ultimate in financial distress is *bankruptcy* and liquidation of the business. The risk and cost of financial distress increase as borrowing increases. Financial distress can be costly and leads to a loss in the value of the business. The fear of the prospect of financial distress affects the market value of the levered firm's stocks and bonds. The value of the firm can be written as:

$$\text{Value of firm} = \text{value if all-equity-financed} + \text{PV (tax shield)} - \text{PV(costs of financial distress)}$$

Financial distress costs include *bankruptcy costs*, costs of operating under the cloud of bankruptcy, and *agency costs*. Bankruptcy is the legal mechanism allowing creditors to take over the assets of the firm and control the business. Bankruptcy costs are the costs of using the system. These direct costs include the legal and accounting costs. These costs can be large and reduce the total payoff to shareholders and creditors. Evidence suggests that bankruptcy costs can be large absolutely and significant even relative to firm value. Smaller firms can have a much higher percentage of costs relative to their size.

Other financial distress costs vary with asset types and the nature of the firm. These costs arise from the difficulties of running a bankrupt firm. An airline facing potential bankruptcy will find it very difficult to hire able pilots. The market price adjustments when a firm enters bankruptcy are a significant cost to investors.

Agency costs are incurred when non-bankrupt, but financially troubled firms have to face create conflicts of interest between creditors and shareholders. Stockholders can "play" different games that can be costly to the lenders. These games include:

- Risk shifting or investing in risky but negative NPV projects,
- Refusing to contribute equity capital,
- Cash in and run or paying themselves cash dividends,

- Playing for time, and
- Bait and switch or issuing progressively more and riskier debt.

The lenders anticipate these sub-optimal behaviors on the part of the stockholders and attempt to rein-in the behavior by incorporating strict conditions in debt contracts. These, in turn, restrict stockholder flexibility and add to the costs of doing business.

The Trade-off Theory: The trade-off theory postulates that firms balance the benefits (tax-shield) and costs (financial distress costs) and arrive at an optimal debt ratio. Thus, the optimal debt ratio reflects a trade-off between tax shields and the costs of financial distress. The trade-off theory suggests that firms may have different target debt ratios. The optimal debt ratio will be a function of the type of assets and the ability of the firm to use the tax-shield provided by debt. Firms with assets, which are tangible and easily transferable to others, can be expected to borrow more. Examples of this type of firms include airlines, retailers, and banks. On the other hand, firms with high levels of intangible assets, which can lose value in financial distress, will not use much debt. Pharmaceutical companies, high tech firms, and software companies are typical examples of this kind.

Empirical studies find broad support for the trade-off theory. Companies with more tangible and easily transferable assets (e.g. airlines) tend to borrow more and firms with more intangible assets (e.g. high tech companies) borrow less. It is also seen that companies, which go private through leveraged buy-outs, are generally mature companies with cash-cow businesses. However, many profitable companies--those that would tend to benefit the most from tax shields--borrow very little and appear to ignore the potential benefits from debt financing. This phenomenon remains a puzzle and is not easily explained by the trade-off theory. The fact that corporate debt ratios are not much higher than now than what they were about a century ago does not fit well with the predictions of the trade-off theory. Debt ratios across countries also cannot be explained by tax differences.

The Pecking Order Theory of Financing Choices: The pecking order theory of capital structure is fashioned from the observed practice of companies. Firms appear to have a preferred order of financing choices—internal equity (retained earnings) being the most preferred and external equity being the least preferred. A formal framework for the theory uses *asymmetric information* between the manager and the investor as the basis for the theory. Given asymmetric information, it is rational for the manager to prefer the use of retained earnings first. The manager would also prefer to issue debt rather than common stock, as the common stock would be potentially under-priced.

The pecking order theory also suggests that managers would like to maintain a *financial slack*, which would provide flexibility of means for meeting future financing needs. Thus, they would hold reserves of marketable securities and have spare borrowing capacity. Firms also adapt their target dividend ratios to their investment opportunities while trying to avoid sudden changes in dividends.

WORKED EXAMPLES

1. Two firms are identical in all respects except that one firm is 100 percent financed by common stock and the other is 50 percent equity-financed and 50 percent debt-financed at 8 percent a year. The balance sheets of the two firms are as follows:

ALL EQUITY FIRM				EQUITY AND DEBT FIRM			
Assets	$10,000	Equity	$10,000	Assets	$10,000	Debt (8%)	$5,000
						Equity	5,000
Total	$10,000	Total	$10,000	Total	$10,000	Total	$10,000

Assume that the company has an operating income of $1,500. Show that the interest paid on debt is a tax shield.

SOLUTION

The income statements for the two firms can be shown as below:

	ALL EQUITY FIRM	EQUITY AND DEBT FIRM
Earnings before interest and taxes	1,500	$1,500
Interest expenses		400
Pretax income	1,500	1,100
Tax at 35 percent	525	385
Net income to stockholders	$ 975	$ 715
Total income to bond and stockholders	$975	$400 + $715 = $1,115
Interest tax shield (0.35 x interest)	$0	0.35 x $400 = $140

The interest tax shield is the difference between the streams of payments received by the investors of the two firms.

2. What is the present value of the tax shield as calculated in problem 1?

SOLUTION

Assume that the risk of the investment in the tax shield requires a rate of return equal to that paid on the debt, namely, 8 percent. If the financing is considered permanent, the problem is one of solving for the present value of a perpetuity.

Present value of tax shield = $140/0.08 = $1,750

Because the total amount of the debt is $5,000, the present value of the tax shield is the amount of the total debt that the government underwrites when it allows interest to be deducted as an expense. The difference between the total debt and the federal subsidy, $3,250 ($5,000- $1750), is the amount the company underwrites. Also, note that the present value of the tax shield is independent of the return on the debt. The cash difference between taxes paid, $140 ($525 - $385), makes going into debt a profitable investment, worth $1,750. Restated,

Present value of tax shield = $\dfrac{\text{corporate tax rate x expected interest payment}}{\text{expected return on debt}}$

$$= T_c(r_D D)/r_D = T_c D$$
$$= 0.35 \text{ X } (0.08 \text{ X } \$5,000)/0.08$$
$$= 0.35 \text{ X } \$5,000$$
$$= \$1,750$$

3. The balance sheet for Henry Coes Corp. is given below. The company has no long-term debt now and its balance sheet is shown below. Ignoring personal taxes, work out how much shareholders would benefit if the company borrowed $1,000 million of long-term debt and used it to repurchase stock.

Balance Sheet for Henry Coes Corp. ($ in millions)

Balance Sheet – Book Values			
Net working capital	500	Long-term debt	0
Long-term assets	2,100	Equity	2,600
Total assets	$2,600	Total liabilities and equity	2,600
Balance Sheet – Market Values			
Net working capital	500	Long-term debt	0
Long-term assets	6,500	Equity	7,000
Total assets	7,000	Total liabilities and equity	7,000

SOLUTION

Increase in value = $1,000 x 0.35 =$350 million.
This increase in value will accrue to the shareholders. Thus, while the book value of equity will decrease by the amount of repurchase ($1,000 million), the market value will decrease by only $650 million only. This is the net advantage to shareholders for going into debt. The book and market value balance sheets after the debt issue and stock repurchase are given below.

Balance Sheets for Henry Coes Corp. - After borrowing $1,000 m ($ in millions)

Balance Sheet – Book Values			
Net working capital	500	Long-term debt	1,000
Long-term assets	2,100	Equity	1,600
Total assets	$2,600	Total liabilities and equity	2,600
Balance Sheet – Market Values			
Net working capital	500	Long-term debt	1,000
Long-term assets	6,850	Equity	6,350
Total assets	7,350	Total liabilities and equity	7,350

SUMMARY

This chapter's main point is that *debt policy does matter,* once taxes, the probability of bankruptcy, financial distress, and potential conflicts of interest among the firm's security holders are factored in. The chapter considers, one by one, the main deviations from the MM perfect market framework and arrives at practical implications for corporate debt policy. We end up with two theories of capital structure – the trade-off theory and the pecking order theory. It should be kept in mind that the two theories are not mutually exclusive and corporate practice can reflect both theories.

Corporate taxes combined with the tax-deductibility of interest are compelling reasons why debt policy counts. Interest on debt is deductible before corporate taxes are paid and that creates a tax shield, which enhances the after-tax value of the firm. Tax shields are valuable assets; their value being the present value of reduced taxes. Personal taxes introduce additional complications. Miller's analysis reflects these and suggests that the advantage to debt may not be that significant.

While tax shield encourages borrowing, non-trivial costs of financial distress are the costs paid for the benefit of debt. Because promises made to creditors may be broken or honored only with substantial difficulty, a firm is not able to borrow as much as it may choose. Consequently, the prospective cost of financial distress reduces the value of the firm. These costs include the cost of bankruptcy, as well as, the indirect costs of time and effort to resolve a financially distressed condition. Further, whenever financial distress arises, there are a variety of tactics, which stockholders may resort to in order to minimize their risk exposure and gain at the cost of the lenders. These tactics or "games" represent the agency costs of borrowing and include risk shifting, refusing to contribute equity capital, taking cash out of the enterprise, and making decisions, which defer the day of reckoning. To forestall the possibility of such maneuvers, restrictive provisions are often incorporated into bond contracts, which in effect offset some of the benefits of debt financing.

The trade-off theory of capital structure suggests that a firm's debt-equity decision is really one of trading off interest tax shields against the cost of financial distress. This helps to explain, at least partially, why different companies have different debt-equity ratios. Empirical evidence supports the trade-off theory to an extent, though some observed practices in the real world contradict the predictions suggested by the theory. The pecking-order theory says that financial managers have a preferred, ordered set of financing options, and they go down that list in order of preference. The first choice is internal funds or retained earnings. This is followed by the safest external source of financing, usually debt. External equity is the least preferred source. In order to accommodate the choice of financing preferences, companies typically maintain somewhat sticky dividend policies and some financial slack. The hierarchy of preferences seems to reflect the information asymmetry between the mangers and the stockholders or investors.

Debt may or may not be a good alternative to equity financing. Factors to consider are the total tax liability to shareholders, a firm's business risk, the types of assets that produce operating income, and the need for financial slack.

LIST OF TERMS

Agency costs
Bankruptcy
Bankruptcy costs
Capital gains
Financial distress
Financial distress costs
Financial slack

Information asymmetry
Pecking order
Tax-deductible
Tax shield
Trade-off theory
Value of all-equity firm

EXERCISES

Fill-in Questions

1. The main benefit of corporate debt is that the interest is a(n) _____ expense.

2. An investor willing to lend at a before-tax return of 10 percent must be willing to lend at an after-tax return of _____ if her marginal income tax rate is 36 percent.

3. _____ between managers and investors forms the basis for the pecking order theory.

4. The direct costs of _____ consist of the present value of administrative, court, and legal fees, which reduce the total payoff to shareholders and bondholders.

5. The indirect costs of bankruptcy, which arise out of conflicts of interest, are called _____.

6. In a financially distressed firm, a project whose net present value is $200 will add (exactly, less than, more than) _____ $200 to the value of shareholders.

7. The bondholders of a financially distressed firm have (more, less) _____ to gain from investments, which increase firm value, the greater, the probability of default.

8. The effective rate of tax on _____ is often lower than the statutory rate since gains remain untaxed until they are realized.

9. Firms should strive to maximize the (after-tax, before-tax) _____ income of shareholders.

10. If $1 - T_p$ is greater than $(1 - T_{pE})(1 - T_c)$, corporate borrowing is (better, worse) _____ than personal borrowing.

11. It pays companies to issue more debt as long as the corporate tax shield (exceeds, is less than) _____ the personal tax cost to the marginal lender.

12. The _____ of capital structure says that firms attempt to find an optimal debt ratio by comparing the benefits and costs of leverage.

13. Firms whose assets are risky and mostly intangible tend to borrow (less, more) _____ than firms whose assets are tangible and relatively safe.

14. A preferred hierarchy of financing choices is called the _____ theory of capital structure.

15. _____ refers to the extent to which a firm has flexible opportunities for meeting its future financing needs.

Problems

1. Compute the present value of interest tax shields resulting from each of the following debt issues. Consider only corporate taxes, the marginal rate of which is 35 percent.
   a. A $1,000, 1-year loan at 9 percent.
   b. A 7-year loan of $1,000 at 9 percent. Assume principal is repaid at maturity.
   c. A $1,000 perpetuity at 8 percent.

2. The book and market value balance sheets of Bonnie Walker, Inc. are given below. Assume that: (1) the MM theory holds except for taxes, (2) no growth, (3) the debt is permanent, (4) 35 percent corporate tax rate, and (5) the interest rate on debt is 8 percent.

   a. How can the market value of the firm be greater than its book value?
   b. Demonstrate the extent to which the stockholders would be better off if the company were to sell additional debt at 8 percent, using the proceeds to purchase $40 of stock.
   c. Demonstrate the effects of replacing $40 of permanent, 8 percent debt with equity.

Balance Sheets for Bonnie Walker ($ in millions)

Balance Sheet – Book Values				Balance Sheet – Market Values			
Net working capital	$40	Long-term debt	$70	Net working capital	$40	Long-term debt	$70
Long-term assets	70	Equity	$40	Long-term assets	$110	Equity	$80
Total Assets	$110	Total liabilities and equity	$110	Total assets	$150	Total liabilities and equity	$150

3 Compute the total corporate and personal taxes paid on debt and equity income for each of the following cases. Assume a corporate income tax rate of 35 percent; realized capital gains are taxed at 20 percent and all cash dividends are taxed as ordinary income; the interest rate on debt is 10 percent; earnings before interest and taxes are $1,000; the levered firm borrows $1,000; and, where the condition calls for it, all earnings for shareholders are paid to them.

CASE	BONDHOLDERS' TAX BRACKET	STOCKHOLDERS' TAX BRACKET	FORM OF EQUITY INCOME
1	0	0	All dividends
2	0.15	0.15	All dividends
3	0.15	0.15	All unrealized capital gains
4	0.28	0.28	All dividends
5	0.28	0.28	All unrealized capital gains
6	0.36	0.36	All dividends
7	0.36	0.36	All unrealized capital gains

For each case, identify whether the levered or unlevered firm has the tax advantage? What implications do the differences you observe have for making financial decisions of the firm? For individual investors?

4. Moonshines, Inc., has serious problems and is facing bankruptcy. Its market value balance sheet is as follows:

Net working capital	$500	Bonds	$650
Long-term assets	200	Equity	50
	$700		$700

Evaluate the following actions the financial manager is contemplating. Present an objective evaluation of each action. Assume each action is independent of all other actions.

a. The company pays a cash dividend of $75.
b. The company sells its long-term assets for $100, collects $450 from its net working capital, closes its doors, and invests the cash of $550 in U.S. Treasury bills at the going rate of 8 percent.
c. The company is confronted with an investment opportunity, which has a net present value of $200 but decides not to undertake it.

d. The company is confronted with an investment project whose net present value is $200 and sells new equity to undertake it.

e. The company is confronted with an investment opportunity whose net present value is $200 and borrows $200 to undertake it.

f. The lenders agree to extend the due date of its debt from 1 year to 2 years. Or from 1 year to 5 years.

g. The lenders agree to extend the due date of its debt from 1 year to 2 years, provided the lenders control all working capital and investment decisions, as well as prohibiting the issuance of any further debt.

5. You are the financial manager of a Fortune 500 company. You are asked to demonstrate how interest tax shields may contribute to the value of the stockholders' equity. Assume that the company has a market value of about $30 billion, has about $2 billion of short-term debt, and very little long-term debt. Assume that debt can be issued at a rate equal to about 8 percent and that the corporation's income tax rate is 35 percent.

Essay Questions

1. Explain the trade-off theory of capital structure.

2. Explain MM's proposition I, as corrected for the presence of corporate income taxes.

3. Describe the pecking-order theory of capital structure. Compare the theory with the trade-off theory. Does it make sense for a company to follow the pecking order theory?

4. Select five Fortune 500 firms and describe their capital structure in terms of the two theories discussed in the chapter.

5. How can it be said that it may not be in the stockholders' self-interest to contribute fresh equity capital, even if that means foregoing positive net present value investment opportunities?

ANSWERS TO EXERCISES

Fill-in Questions

1. Tax-deductible
2. 6.4 percent
3. Information asymmetry
4. Financial distress
5. Agency costs
6. Less than
7. More
8. Capital gains
9. After-tax
10. Better
11. Exceeds
12. Trade-off theory
13. Less
14. Pecking order
15. Financial slack

Problems

1. a. Interest tax shield: 0.35($1,000 X 0.09) = $31.5; PV(tax shield) = $31.5/1.09 = $28.90.

    b. Present value of tax shield: N = 7, I = 9, PMT = $31.5, FV = 0; PV = solve = $158.54.

    c. PV(tax shield) = (0.35 x $1000 x .08)/0.08 = $350. Or, T_c x D = 0.35 x $1,000 = $350.

2. a. Book values are based largely on historical costs, whereas market values are based on expected profitability. Companies earning profits higher than their cost of capital will typically have market values higher than book value.

    b. PV of tax shield = T_cD = 0.35 X $40 = $14.00. The value of total assets will increase by this amount. $40 m of shares are repurchased. This amount less the tax shield will be the net change in the value of equity. The new market value balance sheet is shown below.

Net working capital	$ 40.00	Debt	$110.00
Long-term assets	124.00	Equity	54.00
	$164.00		$164.00

    c. This is the reverse of b above. Assets now decline by $14.00 and equity increases by only $26.00.

    Market value valance sheet after the equity issue:

Net working capital	$ 40.00	Debt	$ 30.00
Long-term assets	96.00	Equity	106.00
	$136.00		$136.00

3. a. Bond value falls, stockholders gain.
    b. Bondholders will get $550; stockholders will get nothing.
    c. Everyone loses.
    d. Bondholders gain because the debt ratio improves; stockholders also gain.
    e. Bondholders could gain or lose, depending on the risk of the project.
    f. Bondholders lose in both instances.
    g. Bondholders may gain in this case.

4. The details for case 5 are shown below. The results for all cases are summarized in the table below.

INCOME STATEMENTS

	TAX RATE	UNLEVERED FIRM	LEVERED FIRM
Earnings before interest and taxes		1,000	1,000
Interest		0	100
Pretax income		1,000	900
Corporate tax at	35%	350	315
Net income to stockholders		650	585
Total income to stockholders and bondholders (before tax)		650	685
Tax on firm		350	315
Tax on bondholders at	28%	0	28
Tax on stockholders	0%	0	0
Total income to stockholders and bondholders (after tax)		650	657
Total taxes paid:		350	343

Advantage to debt = $7 (on $1,000 debt at 10 percent interest)

The tax advantage to debt for the different cases is given in the table below.

Cases	Corporate Tax rate	Tax on bondholders	Tax on stockholders	Total Taxes Paid Unlevered Firm	Total Taxes Paid Levered Firm	Advantage to Debt
1	0.35	0	0	$350	$315	$35
2	0.35	0.15	0.15	$447.5	$417.75	$29.75
3	0.35	0.15	0	$350	$330	$20
4	0.35	0.28	0.28	$532	$506.8	$25.2
5	0.35	0.28	0	$350	$343	$7
6	0.35	0.36	0.36	$584	$561.6	$22.4
7	0.35	0.36	0	$350	$351	-$1.0

You can also calculate the effective advantage to debt as the difference between $1-T_p$ and $(1-T_{pE})$ x $(1-T_C)$, where T_p is the personal tax rate on interest income and T_{pE} is the personal tax rate on equity income and T_C is the corporate tax rate.

5. One billion dollars of debt, at an interest rate of 8 percent, enables the firm to reduce it annual tax bill by $28 million ($1,000 X 0.08 X 0.35). If the debt is permanent, the present value of this debt will be $350 million ($28/0.08). Assuming the effect of financial distress costs to be negligible, the firm value will increase by about $350 million. This increase in value will go the shareholders.

19
Financing and Valuation

INTRODUCTION

So far, we have treated investment and financing to be separate and have not considered any interaction between the two. This assumed the MM perfect market world where the investment decisions could be made without any reference to how the investments are financed. This chapter provides you with tools required to make investment decisions when they are affected by financing decisions. The chapter gives useful and practical pointers to deal with capital budgeting situations where investment and financing decisions interact. The chapter also explains how to handle the cash flows which are very safe or of low risk.

The chapter describes two equivalent approaches to incorporating the effects of financing interactions. The first approach uses the popular and widely used tool of the weighted-average cost of capital (WACC). WACC incorporates the effect of tax shields into the discount rate used to value the cash flows produced by a project. WACC is typically calculated using actual market data and balance sheets for companies or industries. Usually, WACC works quite well, if you know its limitations and potential pitfalls.

The second approach adds the present value of the financing effects to the base-case net present value and calculates the *adjusted present value or APV* of the project. The modified MM proposition I described in Chapter 18 is an example of the APV approach. The approach is very general and can be useful in cases where WACC does not work very well because the assumptions for the correct use of WACC are violated. The APV approach is also useful in cases where the project or the investment decision involves special or subsidized financing or costs of issuing securities needed to finance the project.

Before we begin the lessons of this chapter, it might be useful to have a quick review of the investment decision making process we have used so far. The following steps are involved in evaluating investment opportunities:

- Forecast the project's incremental after-tax cash flows.
- Assess the project's risk.
- Estimate the opportunity cost of capital.
- Calculate NPV, using the discounted-cash-flow formula.

Remember that the opportunity cost of capital reflects the projects business risk and does not include any effect of financial leverage. This chapter tells you how to incorporate the effect of borrowing.

KEY CONCEPTS IN THE CHAPTER

The Weighted-Average Cost of Capital: The weighted average cost of capital, (or more exactly, the after-tax weighted average cost of capital) incorporates the tax deductibility of borrowing into the discount rate used to evaluate project cash flows. Thus, WACC is the adjusted discount rate or cost of capital. The formula for WACC is:

$$WACC = r_D(1 - T_c)D/V + r_E(E/V)$$

where, r_D = Before-tax cost of debt,
       r_E = Cost of equity
       T_c = Marginal tax rate for the firm
       D/V = Debt to assets ratio
       E/V = Equity ratio

It is simply the cost of the source of funds weighted by the percentage of each source in the balance sheet. The formula is general and can easily be adapted to include preferred stock or even separate costs for short-term and long-term debts. For example, if a firm uses preferred stock in its financial mix, the WACC can be written as:

$$WACC = r_d(1 - T_c)D/V + r_P(P/V) + r_E(E/V),$$

where r_P is the cost of preferred stock and P/V is the ratio of preferred stock to assets.

In practice, WACC is typically calculated using actual balance sheet data for firms and all the variables used in the formula refer to the whole firm. Therefore, when it is directly used to evaluate projects, the following points should be kept in mind:

- WACC calculated from actual company data should be used for project evaluation only when the project is a carbon copy of the firm or represents the same average risk as the firm.
- The project supports the same debt ratio as the firm.
- WACC assumes that the debt ratio (D/V) is maintained by regular re-balancing.
- The debt ratio and equity ratio should be based on market values, rather than book values.
- When computing WACC from actual numbers, care has to be taken for properly adjusting or accounting for current liabilities, short-term debt, and deferred taxes. The usual approach is to net these out of the balance sheet. However, if the short-term debt is part of the permanent financing mix used by the firm, it should probably be included in the WACC.
- Industry costs might be better than individual firms' cost when used for project analysis, especially by firms outside the industry.
- Immediate source of funds for the project is of no relevance for computing the WACC.

WACC is very useful when it is properly used. It can be adjusted for changes in debt ratios or business risk changes by applying the equations from MM's propositions I and II. (See worked example 3.) The adjustments can be used for betas also using the following equations from chapter 9:

$$\beta_{asset} = \beta_{debt} (D/V) + \beta_{equity} (E/V)$$
$$\beta_{equity} = \beta_{asset} + (\beta_{asset} - \beta_{debt})D/E$$

These leverage adjustments should be kept within reasonable limits and should not be used for large changes in debt ratio.

Adjusted Present Value: Adjusted present value (APV) is an alternative to using the WACC. Technically, the APV is more general and can be used in cases where the WACC may not be able to capture all the side effects of financing decisions. The general expression for APV can be written as below:

APV = base-case NPV + sum of present values of all financing side-effects

The base-case NPV is the NPV of the project cash flows using the opportunity cost of capital. That is, you are assuming that the project is an all equity-financed mini-firm. Here are the steps involved in computing the APV.

- First, calculate the base-case NPV, i.e. without financing side effects.
- Identify the financing side effects. The effects can be from: issue costs, tax shields, special interest loans, etc.
- Compute the present values of all the side effects using the appropriate discount rates.
- Add the present values of the side effects to the base-case NPV to get the APV.

Generally, issue costs reduce the project's NPV, while tax shields or special financing deals add to the NPV. Care has to be taken when computing the present value of tax shields. The amount supported by the debt has to be estimated. The tax shield also depends on whether the debt is fixed in dollar terms or is assumed to be constantly re-balanced. The WACC approach follows the latter assumption. Following rule 1 generally gives a higher value for the present value of the tax shield and therefore a higher APV.

APV and Hurdle Rates: Using APV, we can work backwards to compute the hurdle rate that has to be cleared by the project cash flows in order to be acceptable. This will be the internal rate of return for which the project's APV = 0. This rate is called the *adjusted cost of capital* or discount rate (r^*) and can be used as the hurdle rate for projects with comparable risk and similar debt capacity. The project is acceptable if it gives positive NPV when the cash flows are discounted using the adjusted cost of capital.

Opportunity Cost of Capital, Adjusted Discount Rate, and WACC: The opportunity cost of capital is a return measure based on pure business risk and is not affected by the financial leverage carried by the project. It is the expected return offered by capital markets on comparable risk projects. This should be the discount rate used if the project is all-equity financed. An *adjusted discount rate* or *hurdle rate* can be computed using the APV. This rate will reflect the financing side effects measured by the APV. WACC is an *adjusted cost of capital* that captures the benefit of tax shields. Be careful when you use these terms, because strictly, they are not interchangeable.

Discounting Safe, Nominal Cash Flows: Safe, nominal cash flows are comparable to debt related cash flows. This is because the firm is committed to making the stipulated dollar cash flows. The correct discount rate to use, in such cases, is the after-tax unsubsidized borrowing rate.

This rule is useful in the evaluation of special or subsidized financing deals. Such deals could be viewed as equivalent loans. That is:

Equivalent loan = Present value of the cash flows needed to service the debt.

Again, this present value is calculated using the firm's after-tax borrowing rate. Thus, any subsidized loan at interest rates below the market rate will be like signing up for an equivalent loan less than the amount you are really able to borrow. The difference between the actual amount borrowed and the equivalent loan is the NPV of the special financing deal.

WORKED EXAMPLES

1. Goremann Corp. (GC) has a total market value of $524 million. The market value of equity is $300 million and the company carries debt valued at $224 million. The before-tax cost of debt is 9 percent and the cost of equity is estimated at 14 percent. The marginal tax rate is 35 percent. Estimate the weighted-average cost of capital for the company.

SOLUTION

The weighted average cost of capital = $r_D(1 - T_C)D/V + r_E E/V$
D = $224 million, E = $300 million, V = D + E = $524 million
D/E = 0.4275, V/E = 0.5725

Substituting these and other values into the equation for WACC,

WACC = 0.09(0.65)0.4275 + 0.14 (0.5725) = 10.52 percent

2. GC is considering a project, which is expected to produce $12.5 million in annual after-tax cash flows for the next 5 years. The project has the same risk as the company's existing operations and is expected to support the same debt capacity. What is the NPV of the project if the estimated investment required for the project is $45 million?

SOLUTION

NPV of the project = -45 + PV of cash inflows. Using a calculator, PV of $12.5 million for 5 years: N = 5, I = 10.52, PMT = $12.5, FV = 0, PV = solve = $46.762 million. NPV = -45 + 46.762 = $1.762 million.

3. GC is planning to spend large amounts of money on R & D over the next few years and feels that it may not be able to use all the tax shields generated by a 42.75 percent debt ratio. The company considers lowering the debt to 20 ratio percent. How will this change its WACC and cost of equity? Assume that the lower debt ratio will reduce the before-tax cost of debt to 8 percent.

SOLUTION

Note that the change in debt ratio will lower the cost of equity. The problem can be solved by using the "three step" process of unlevering and relevering the WACC.

Step 1: Unlever the WACC to calculate the opportunity cost of capital, r.

$r = r_D D/V + r_E E/V = 0.09(0.4275) + 0.14(0.5725) = 0.1186 = 11.86$ percent

Step 2: Calculate the cost of equity at 20 percent debt ratio.

$r_E = r + (r_A - r_D)D/E = 0.1186 + (0.11.86 - 0.08)0.2/0.8 = 0.1283 = 12.83$ percent

Step 3: Calculate the new WACC.

$WACC = 0.08(1 - 0.35)0.2 + 0.1283(0.8) = 11.30$ percent

4. Gary Teeker is the financial manager of Wosley Corp., a family owned firm. Mr. Teeker has been asked by the family members to value the firm. The business generates an after-tax cash flow of $1.5 million a year. This is expected to continue indefinitely at this level. The firm's marginal tax rate is 36 percent. The industry average data for comparable companies are as follows:

Cost of debt = 12 percent
Average beta for comparable companies = 1.5.
Risk free rate = 4.5 percent
Market risk premium = 9 percent.

The company's debt ratio at 40 percent is very close to the industry average. Help Mr. Teeker value the firm. Explain the steps used in valuation.

SOLUTION

We need to compute the cost of equity and then the weighted average cost of capital.
using the CAPM, $r_E = 4.5 + 1.5 (9) = 18$ percent.

227

$$\text{WACC} = r_D(1 - T_c)D/V + r_E(E/V)$$

where, r_D = the firm's current borrowing rate

T_c = the marginal corporate income tax

r_E = the expected rate of return on the firm's stock (a function of the firm's business risk and its debt ratio)

D, E = the market values of currently outstanding debt and equity

$V = D + E$ = the total market value of the firm

The weighted-average cost of capital for the firm is therefore:

$$\text{WACC} = 0.12(1 - 0.36)0.4 + 0.18(0.6) = 13.87 \text{ percent}$$

The value of the firm = $1.5 million/0.1387 = $10.8147 million

5. Rummy Corp. is considering an investment project, which will generate a level after-tax cash flow of $500,000 a year in the next 5 years. Returns on comparable risk investment opportunities are 14 percent. The investment requires a cash outlay of $1.5 million. Compute the net present value of this project.

SOLUTION

This straightforward capital budgeting problem requires you to find the present value of $500,000 a year for each of 5 years, using the discount rate of 14 percent. The cash outlay is then deducted from the present value of that stream of cash to obtain NPV. The calculations are:

$$NPV = -1,500,000 + \sum_{t=1}^{5} \frac{\$500,000}{(1.14)^t}$$

[Use the calculator for the PV computation: N = 5, I = 14, pmt = $500,000, FV = 0, PV = SOLVE, PV = $1,716,541]

$$NPV = -\$1,500,000 + \$1,716,541 = \$216,541$$

6. Rummy Corp. of problem 5 above does not have the cash available to undertake the project. Therefore, it is investigating the possibility of selling stock. The financial manager discovered that for issues of that size, the effective cost to the firm would be 16 percent of the gross proceeds to the company. How much must the company raise in order to net $1.5 million, and what impact does the cost of issuing common stock have on the project's NPV?

SOLUTION

This is a problem of determining the adjusted present value (APV) of the investment, taking into account the costs incurred when external financing is needed. First, find the amount of money that must be raised so that the company obtains the needed $1.5 million. The company will receive only 84 percent of the amount raised. Thus, the amount of money (gross proceeds) to be raised equals:

$$\text{Gross proceeds of the issue} = \$1,500,000/0.84 = \$1,785,714$$

$$\text{Issue costs} = \$1,785,714 - \$1,500,000 = \$285,714$$

Because this is an additional cash outlay prompted by this project, it must be included in the analysis. The APV will be:

$$\begin{aligned} \text{APV} &= \text{base-case NPV - issue cost} \\ &= \$216,541 - \$285,714 \\ &= -\$69,173 \end{aligned}$$

The issue cost makes the project unacceptable.

7. Rummy is comfortable with a 65 percent target debt ratio. It borrows at the rate of 12 percent, pays the principal in equal yearly installments, and pays interest based on the unpaid balance. Debt issue costs are 5 percent of the gross proceeds, and equity issue costs are those of problem 6. The tax on the corporation, bondholders, and shareholders is 30 percent. What does this do to APV?

SOLUTION

This extension of the basic problem requires you to incorporate the present value of the interest tax shield to make it complete. Let's go through it in steps.

Step 1. We already know the value of the base case is $216,541.

Step 2. Determine the issue cost. To calculate the issue cost of debt, determine how much will be needed. It is $975,000(0.65 X $1,500,000). Next, determine how much should be raised to obtain that amount: It is $1,026,316($975,000/0.95). The issue cost is determined by taking the difference between the amount that must he raised and the amount that is actually used: It is $51,316($1,026,316 - $975,000). The issue costs of equity are similarly determined. The amount needed is $525,000 ($1, 500,000 x 0.35). The amount to be raised is $625,000 ($525,000/0.84). The issue cost is $100,000($625,000 - $525,000).

Step 3. Determine the present value of the interest tax shield. Before you can do that, however, you must determine the annual installment payments, the annual interest payable in each year, the annual tax shelter, and the present value of the annual tax shelter. The annual installments are $205,263($1,026,316/5 years) plus interest on the remaining balance. The table is as follows. (Because the debt is not subsidized, it is evaluated at the 12 percent borrowing rate.)

YEAR	DEBT OUTSTANDING AT START OF YEAR	INTEREST	INTEREST TAX SHIELD	PRESENT VALUE TAX SHIELD
1	$1,026,316	$123,158	$36,947	$32,989
2	821,053	98,526	29,558	23,563
3	615,790	73,895	22,168	15,779
4	410,527	49,263	14,779	9,392
5	205,264	24,632	7,390	4,193
				$85,916

Combine all the PVs to obtain APV.

$$APV = \text{base-case PV} - \text{PV of issue cost} + \text{PV of tax shield}$$
$$= \$216,541 - (\$51,316 + \$100,000) + \$85,916$$
$$= \$151,141$$

Accept the project.

8. Lee Morgan Company is considering an investment project that costs $2 million and is expected to generate savings of $295,000 a year forever. The business risk of this project warrants a rate of return of 15 percent. Calculate the net present value of the project, assuming no tax shields. Then, calculate the project's NPV, assuming tax shields that arise because additional 12 percent debt may be issued in amounts equal to 30 percent of the cost of the project. The overall tax rate is 30 percent. Finally, determine the minimum acceptable base-case NPV, as well as, the minimum internal rate of return.

SOLUTION

The solution to this problem is straightforward. The base-case NPV is:

$$\text{Base-case NPV} = \text{cash outlay} + \text{present value of a perpetuity}$$
$$= -\$2,000,000 + (\$295,000/0.15)$$
$$= -\$2,000,000 + \$1,966,667$$
$$= -\$33,333$$

The project cannot be accepted as it is.

Present value of tax shield = ($600,000 X 0.12 X 0.30)/0.12 = $180,000

Now, the project is acceptable. It has a positive APV.
$$APV = \text{base-case NPV} + \text{PV tax shield} = -\$33,333 + \$180,000 = \$146,667$$

To find the minimum level of income *net* of the tax effects (of -$180,000):

$$-\$180,000 = -\$2,000,000 + (\text{annual income}/0.15)$$

Solving for annual income, we obtain:

$$\text{Annual income} = (\$2,000,000 - \$180,000) \times 0.15 = \$273,000$$

This is the minimum annual income this project must generate in order to make it acceptable. The minimum acceptable rate of return is:

$$\$273,000/\$2,000,000 = 0.1365 = 13.65 \text{ percent}$$

9. Euro-American Corp (EAC). is planning an investment in a European country. The local government has offered EAC a subsidized loan of $12 million for a term of 3 years. The loan will carry an interest rate of 3 percent annually. EAC's current borrowing rate is 8 percent. The company's marginal tax rate is 30 percent. EAC will pay interest only during the three years and the entire principal amount is repaid at the end of 3 years. The investment project has a base NPV of negative $600,000. Should EAC invest in the project?

SOLUTION

The after-tax unsubsidized borrowing rate is 5.6 percent. [0.08(1 - 0.30)]. This is the rate at which the loan cash flows are to be discounted. The table below gives the cash flows and their discounted values.

Period	0	1	2	3
Cash flow (in thousands)	12,000	-360	-360	-12,360
Tax shield		108	108	108
After-tax cash flow	12,000	-252	-252	-12,252
Marginal tax rate	30%			
Present value of outlays		-239	-226	-10,404
Sum of present values	-10,869			
NPV of loan financing	1,131			

APV of the project = -$600,000 + $1,131,000 = $531,000.

Accept the project.

SUMMARY

This chapter enables us to deal with the all too common cases of investment and financing interactions. We had investment decisions from chapters 2 through 12 and in all cases it was assumed that investment and financing could be clearly separated. However, when financing decisions give rise to side effects such as tax shields, they have to be accounted for. The chapter describes two basic approaches to deal with this problem. The first approach is to adjust the discount rate used to evaluate the cash flows. The second approach evaluates the financing effects and adds the present values of these effects to the all-equity financed project NPV.

The weighted-average cost of capital represents the first approach and is typically calculated using company balance sheets valued at market values of debt and equity. The weighted-average cost of capital approach to adjusting discount rates says the proper discount rate used to evaluate projects of risk identical to that of the firm is the market value weighted cost of capital. WACC is popular and is fairly easily computed.

As long its limitations are understood, WACC is very useful. Care has to be taken to use it right. Remember, that WACC computed from actual company balance sheets should be used only for projects that resemble the company as a whole pretty closely. WACC also assumes that the debt is maintained by regular re-balancing of the sources of funds.

WACC is flexible and versatile and can be adjusted for changes in leverage and business risk. WACC is an adjusted cost of capital, which captures the tax shield benefit of debt. The CAPM can be used to adjust or compute the cost of equity for changes in business risk or leverage.

The adjusted present value approach is an alternative to using the WACC. The APV is simply the base-case NPV of the project, which is assumed to be all-equity financed plus the present value of all financing side effects. APV can be adapted to deal with different types of side effects such as issue costs, tax shields, special financing deals, etc. While computing APV, care has to be taken to ensure the proper assumptions about financing. In general, the true value of the tax shield is invariably less than that implied by the corporate marginal tax rate.

As an alternative to APV, a single adjusted discount rate or cost of capital is often computed reflecting the present values of financing side effects. With this adjusted discount rate, one can calculate the APV directly discounting the project cash flows at the adjusted discount rate. WACC is but an example of an adjusted discount rate.

The chapter also presents rules for evaluating safe, nominal cash flows. The proper discount rate to use in such cases is the after-tax borrowing rate. The cash flows may be viewed as the amount of money needed to service an equivalent amount of debt. Two common examples of this type of cash flows are depreciation tax shields and payouts that are fixed by contract. The procedure of treating cash flows as debt-equivalent loans is consistent with adjusted-discount-rate approaches. The approach can be very useful in evaluating subsidies and special financing deals which go with some projects.

LIST OF TERMS

Adjusted cost of capital	Hurdle rate
Adjusted discount rate	Opportunity cost of capital
Adjusted net present value	Subsidized financing
Base-case NPV	Target debt ratios
Business risk	Value additivity
Corporate debt capacity	Weighted-average cost of capital

EXERCISES

Fill-in Questions

1. The adjusted net present value is equal to _____ plus the present value of the effects of financing decisions.

2. The _____ is the discount rate, which reflects only the business risk of the project and is used to calculate the base-case NPV.

3. The opportunity cost of capital depends on the _____ of the investment project to be undertaken.

4. The _____ is an opportunity cost or _____ adjusted for the financing effects.

5. The adjusted net present value analysis of a project has to take into account the change in _____ of the firm brought about by the project.

6. _____ is normally computed using the firm's market value balance sheets or the firm's _____.

7. The use of APV assumes that _____ holds.

8. The APV approach can be used to evaluate the value of _____.

Problems

1. The balance sheet of Barry Moore Corp. shows a debt ratio (debt to assets) of 35 percent. The company's cost of debt (before tax) is 8 percent and the beta of the company stock is 1.5. The risk free rate is 5 percent and the expected market risk premium is 8.5 percent. The marginal tax rate is 30 percent. Calculate the weighted-average cost of capital for the firm.

2. Ms. Moore, the CEO of the firm, suggests the company needs to increase debt to 45 percent of assets. The cost of debt will increase to 9 percent. What will be the effect this will have on the WACC?

3. Texas Incinerator Corp. (TIC) is evaluating a $1 million investment project, which is expected to generate level, after-tax cash flows of $300,000 a year in each of the next 6 years. Rates of return obtainable on investments of comparable risk are 12 percent. Compute the net present value of this project.

4. TIC will finance the project in problem 3 entirely by the sale of stock. The cost of floating the stock is 12 percent of the gross proceeds. How much must the company raise, and what impact does the flotation costs have on the net present value of the project?

5. The Perpetual Motion Company is evaluating a $6 million plant expansion, which it estimates will generate $750,000 in after-tax cash perpetually. The return obtainable on investments of comparable risk is 13 percent.

   a. Calculate the net present value of the project, assuming no tax shields.
   b. Calculate the project's net present value, assuming tax shields produced by the issuance of 9 percent debt in amounts equal to 40 percent of the project's cost. The company's marginal tax rate is 34 percent.
   c. Determine the minimum acceptable base-case NPV.
   d. Determine the minimum acceptable internal rate of return.

6. Using the data in problem 5, calculate the weighted-average cost of capital.

7. You are considering a project in an East European country. The project has an investment of $4 million. The government of the country offers a special incentive package for investments in the country, which includes tax rebates amounting to 10 percent of the initial investment for each of the first two years. The project is expected to generate enough taxable income during the first two years to fully use the tax rebate. Your company's borrowing rate is 10 percent and its tax rate is 30 percent. What is the value of the tax rebate?

Essay Questions

1. Describe the differences between opportunity cost of capital and weighted average cost of capital. What are the primary assumptions you make when you use the weighted-average cost of capital based on actual values from a corporate balance sheet?

2. Explain the APV approach to evaluating the financing effects. Are there cases where the financing side effects can be negative?

3. Your company has been offered a special loan by a state government to induce your company to invest in their state. Describe how you will calculate the value of this offer.

4. Discuss the following statement – "Any safe or low risk cash flow should be evaluated using the risk-free rate, as these cash flows are certain and have no risk."

5. Why is it often better to use industry weighted average cost of capital than individual firm's cost of capital?

ANSWERS TO EXERCISES

Fill-in Questions

1. Base-case net present
2. Opportunity cost of capital
3. Business Risk
4. Adjusted cost of capital (or adjusted discount rate), hurdle rate
5. debt capacity
6. Weighted average cost of capital, target debt ratio
7. Value additivity
8. Subsidized financing

Problems

1. Cost of equity = $r_E = r_f + \beta(r_m - r_f) = 5 + 1.5(8.5) = 17.75$ percent
   Cost debt = $r_D = 8$ percent
   WACC = $0.08(1 - 0.30)0.35 + 0.1775(0.65)$
   $\qquad = 0.0196 + 0.1154$
   $\qquad = 13.50$ percent

2. Use the three-step process to unlever and relever the WACC.

   Step 1: Unlever the WACC to calculate the opportunity cost of capital, r.
   $\qquad r = r_D D/V + r_E E/V = 0.08(0.35) + 0.1775(0.65) = 0.1434 = 14.34$ percent

   Step 2: Calculate the cost of equity at the 45 percent debt ratio.
   $\qquad r_E = r + (r_A - r_D)D/E = 0.1434 + (0.1434 - 0.09)0.45/0.55 = 0.1871 = 18.71$ percent

   Step 3: Calculate the new WACC.
   $\qquad$ WACC = $0.09(1 - 0.3)0.45 + 0.1871(0.55) = 0.1313 = 13.13$ percent

3. Use the Cash flow and NPV worksheet: $CF_0 = -\$1,000,000$, $CO_1 = \$300,000$, $FO_1 = 6$;
   NPV: I = 12, NPV = \$233,422

4. Proceeds needed: $\$1,000,000/(1 - 0.12) = \$1,136,364$
   Issue cost: $\$1,136,364 - \$1,000,000 = \$136,364$
   APV = base-case NPV - issue cost
   $\qquad = \$233,422 - \$136,364 = \$97,058$

5. a. Base-case NPV $= -\$6,000,000 + \$750,000/0.13$
   $\qquad\qquad\qquad = -\$6,000,000 + \$5,769,231$
   $\qquad\qquad\qquad = -\$230,769$

b. Amount borrowed: $6,000,000 X 0.4 = $2,400,000
   Tax shield = $2,400,000 X 0.09 X 0.34 = $73,440
   APV = base-case NPV + PV of tax shield
   $$= -\$230,769 + (\$73,440/0.09)$$
   $$= -\$230,769 + \$816,000$$
   $$= \$585,231$$

c. Acceptable minimum base-case NPV = -$816,000
   Minimum annual income = (cash outlay + minimum base case NPV) x required return
   $$= (\$6,000,000 - \$816,000) \text{ X } 0.13 = \$673,920$$

d. Minimum return = $673,920/$6,000,000 = 11.23%

6. Before we can calculate the weighted-average costs of capital, we need to first calculate the r_E using the equation:

$$r_E = r + (r - r_D)D/E = 0.13 + (0.13 - 0.09)0.4/0.6 = 0.13 + 2.67 = 0.1367 = 15.67 \text{ percent}$$

$$\text{WACC} = r_D(1 - T_c)D/V + r_E(E/V)$$
$$= 0.09(1 - 0.34)0.4 + 0.1567 (0.6)$$
$$= 11.78 \text{ percent.}$$

7. The value of the incentive package can be calculated by discounting the resulting cash flows by your after-tax borrowing cost. Your after-tax borrowing rate r^* is:

$$r^* = r_D(1 - T_C) = 0.10(1 - 0.3) = 0.07 = 7 \text{ percent.}$$

The cash flows from the package will be $1 million for each of the first two years.
Present value: N = 2, I = 7, PV = solve, PMT = $0.4 million, FV = 0, PV = $0.7232 million

20

Understanding Options

INTRODUCTION

This is the first of four chapters dealing with options. Options are important innovations of modern finance and an understanding of the theory and practice of option valuation and applications will help the financial manager do his or her job better. This chapter gives you a detailed introduction to the two basic options, *calls* and *puts*. The chapter helps you understand the working of options through *position diagrams* which shows the pay-off of different positions in calls, puts, or shares held by an investor. Although the chapter focuses primarily on exchange-traded options on stocks the concepts and valuation principles are general and can be extended to options on different assets and liabilities. While formal valuation of options is left to the next chapter, this chapter gives you an intuitive description of what determines an option's value. Chapter 22 deals with the applications of option theory to real options and chapter 23 describes warrants and convertible bonds, which are examples of options commonly used in corporate financing.

Most stock options are traded in exchanges and are not controlled by the corporations on whose stocks these options are based. These options do not directly affect the companies or their balance sheets. However, a financial manager needs to understand options and their valuation, as these are very useful in managing and understanding risk associated with many management decisions. Nearly all corporate securities are options themselves or have some kind of options embedded in them. Financial managers will also have to deal with options related to commodities, exchange rates, and interest rates. Corporate bonds often have call features and other options attached to them. Options are also part of many capital budgeting decisions, which involve *embedded* options to expand, abandon, or, in other ways, modify the project cash flows. A clear understanding of the principles of option valuation will help the manager understand the trade-off involved and arrive at the optimal decision.

KEY CONCEPTS IN THE CHAPTER

Calls and Puts: There are two basic options: *calls* and *puts*. A call option gives its owner the right to buy an asset at a specified *exercise price*, or *strike price*, during a specified period. A put option gives its owner the right to sell an asset at a specified exercise price during a specified period. A *European* option is exercisable only at maturity while an *American* option is exercisable any time up to its expiration date. Here are some terms associated with options.

- *Underlying asset* – e.g. an option on one share of IBM.
- *Type of option* – call or put.

- *Exercise price* or *strike price* – the price at which the buyer of the option gets the right to buy (call) or sell (put) the asset to the seller of the option. The seller of the option is often called the *writer* of the option.
- *Maturity* or *expiration date* – the date till (American) or on (European) which the option can be exercised.
- *Option premium* – This is the price paid to buy the option.
- *Asset price* – The price of the underlying asset.
- *In-the-money* or *out-of-the-money* – An option is said to be in-the-money if the exercise of the option makes money for you at that moment. A call option will be in-the-money if the share price is above the exercise price and a put option will be in-the-money if the share price is below the exercise price.

Calls, Puts, Shares, and Combinations: Position diagrams show the pay-off from an option, or for that matter, holding any asset. These are very useful in understanding the value of owning derivative securities based on an asset and the exposure the owner has relative to the changes in value of the asset. Learn to draw the position diagrams for the simple options and assets first and then graduate to the different combinations of options and assets. Given below are pay-off diagrams form holding a share, a put and a call. Your pay-off is on the vertical axis and the stock price is on the horizontal axis.

| Buy a share | Buy a Put | Buy a call |

Note that the position diagrams are not profit diagrams, as they do not include the original cost or price paid for the options or the asset. Studying different combinations of options and positions in shares enables us to understand options and their pay-offs better. Figure 20.5 in the text gives some interesting combinations. Consider the following four positions: buying a call, buying a put, buying a share and depositing an amount equal to the present value of the exercise price. Note that the combination of buying a call and investing the present value of the exercise price in a safe asset gives you a pay-off identical to buying a put and buying the share. Thus, of the four positions, only three can have independent values. In other words, you can always create the fourth asset or security by a combination of the other three. This helps in the valuation of options. The relationship among these four assets is called the *put-call parity*. This can be expressed as:

Value of a call + present value of exercise price = value of put + share price

238

We can rearrange this in several different ways to express the value of a call or a put in terms of the other three.

Value of call = value of put + share price - present value of exercise price

Value of put = value of call - value of share + present value of exercise price

The relationship can be stated in words in different ways:

- Buying a call and selling a put is identical in pay-off to buying a share and borrowing the present value of the exercise price.
- Buying a put is identical in pay-off to buying a call, selling a share, and investing the present value of the exercise price.

Bonds and Stocks as Options: Stocks and bonds issued by limited liability corporations can be seen as special cases of options. When a firm borrows, the lender, in effect, acquires the company, and shareholders obtain a call option to buy it back by paying off the debt. The shareholders will walk away if the assets of the firm are worth less than the promised payment to the bondholders. Again, there are different ways of looking at the stockholder-bondholder relationship in the options framework.

- Bond value = asset value - value of call
- Bond value = present value of promised payments to bondholders - value of put
- Stock value = value of call with the exercise price equal to promised payment to bondholders
- Firm value = asset value

In general, we can say that the bondholders have bought a safe or risk-free bond and then sold a put option to the stockholders. The stockholders will exercise this right if the value of the assets goes down below the face value of the bonds.

Identifying Options: Options are not always easy to identify. Warrants and conversion features are obvious options. As long as there is a pay-off, which is contingent on the value of another asset, an option is present. You come across a number of options in everyday life some of which may not be obvious. Some examples include:

- The right to drop a course within the first two or three weeks for a full refund of fees paid.
- A money-back guarantee on articles purchased.
- The right to get a ticket for your university's homecoming football game.
- A fully refundable air ticket.

Try identifying the options in the above (see worked example 4 for answers).

239

Determinants of Option Value: Formal valuation of options is discussed in chapter 21. This chapter gives you a clear understanding of the basic determinants of the value of an option. The value of a call at expiration is simply the difference between the stock price and the exercise price, with a minimum value of zero. For example, an IBM option with an exercise price of $105 will be worth $5 if the stock price is $110. If the stock price is less than $105 the option is worth nothing. At anytime before expiration, the option will be worth more than the difference between the exercise price and the asset price. Review figure 20-10, which shows the value of a call option at different values of the stock price. Note that the figure applies to an option that has some time to expiration, so that the option has a "time premium." As long as there is time left to maturity and potential volatility in the option, an option will have value above the value at expiration. An option will never be worth more than the price of the stock, which is an upper bound for the value of a call option. The lower bound for an option's value is zero or the difference between the stock price and the exercise price, whichever is higher. An option value equals zero when the value of the underlying asset is equal to or less than the exercise price. Option values tend to increase as the value of the underlying asset exceeds the exercise price. Here are some additional facts on a call option value:

- For a given exercise price, the value of an option increases as the stock price increases.
- When the stock price becomes high relative to the exercise price, the option value approaches the stock price less the present value of the exercise price. As the stock price increases the probability of exercise also increases and when the stock price is sufficiently higher than the exercise price, exercise is almost certain.
- The value of an option increases with the rate of interest (r_f). This is because holding an option is equivalent to getting an interest free loan equal to the exercise price. Higher the interest rate, higher is the value of this loan.
- The value of an option increases with the time to expiration (t).
- The value of an option increases with the variability of the share prices. Higher the probability of large stock price changes, higher the value of the option. In other words, an option on a stock with high standard deviation of returns (σ) will be worth more than an option on a stock with lower variability of returns.

The table below summarizes the effect of changes in the key variables on the value of a call option.

Variables	Change in the value of a call option when the variable increases
Stock price (P)	Positive
Exercise Price (EX)	Negative
Interest rate (r_f)	Positive
Time to expiration (t)	Positive
Volatility (σ)	Positive

WORKED EXAMPLES

1. Find the value of a call option, given that the present value of the exercise price is $35, the value of the put is $10, and the share price is $33.

SOLUTION

Use the put-call parity:

Value of call + present value of exercise price = value of put + share price,

Value of call = value of put + share price - present value of exercise price
$$= \$10 + \$33 - \$35$$
$$= \$8$$

2. Find the implied present value of the exercise price of a 13-week call, given that the value of the call option is $8, the value of the put option is $5, and the market price is $20.

SOLUTION

Present value of exercise price = value of put + share price - value of call
$$= \$5 + \$20 - \$8$$
$$= \$17$$

3. Given below are recent quotations for options on IBM shares. IBM stock was selling at 106.50 and the call money rate (charged to brokers on stock exchange collateral) was 3.25 percent.

Strike Price	Call Price	Put Price
$105	$5.30	$3.60
110	3.00	6.40

a. Which options are in-the-money and which is out-of-the-money?
b. Assume that there is exactly 40 days to expiry. What values would put-call parity imply for European puts? What reasons might account for the traded ones being worth slightly more?

SOLUTION

a. The $105 call and the $110 put are in-the-money. The other options are out-of-the-money.
b. The 40 day discount factor for the 3.25 percent call money rate = $1/(1.0325^{40/365}) = 0.9965$. The values of European puts are given by:

241

Value of put = PV (exercise price) + V (call) – share price
V ($105 put) = $105 X 0.9965 + 5.30 - $106.5 = $3.43
V ($110 put) = $110 X 0.9965 + 3.00 - $106.5 = $6.12

The traded options are American options. The early exercise feature of these puts is valuable, and more so if the option is in-the-money.

4. Can you identify the options included in the following situations:

    a. The right to drop a course within the first two or three weeks for a full refund of fees paid.
    b. A money-back guarantee on articles purchased.
    c. The right to get a ticket for your university's homecoming football game.
    d. A fully refundable air ticket.

SOLUTION

    a. The right to drop a course is a put option. You are "selling" the course back to the university.
    b. A money-back guarantee is also a put option as you are selling the article back to the shop.
    c. This would be a call option.
    d. Another put option.

5. Here are prices quoted for a series of call options on Money Machine.com (all with the same expiration date):

Exercise Price	Option price
$50	$4
$60	$8
$70	$13

Can you suggest a trading strategy, which will make money for you?

SOLUTION

The prices do not seem to be real. If they are, you can easily make money by buying the $50 option and selling the other two contracts. In the real world, higher exercise price call options would sell at lower prices.

6. Mary Stiller, the new CEO of World Grossing Corp, a global trading firm, was offered the following bonus package based on World Grossing stock price at the end of the year. Ms. Stiller will get $10,000 for every dollar of price increase above a base stock price of $50 with

a maximum bonus of $100,000. Can you identify the combination of options, which will give the same pay-off as the bonus package?

SOLUTION

The bonus package is equivalent to a combination of the following: Buying 10,000 call options with exercise price of $50 and selling 10,000 call options with exercise price of $60. Check this out for different stock prices:

Stock price	$50	$55	$60	$65	$70
A. Value of $50 options	$0	$50,000	$100,000	$150,000	$200,000
B. Value of $60 options	$0	0	0	$50,000	$100,000
Net value = A - B	$0	$	$100,000	$100,000	$100,000

SUMMARY

The chapter is the beginning of the coverage of options in the book and describes the two basic types of options – calls and puts. The use of position diagrams helps us understand the pay-off for calls, puts and various combinations of owning stocks, and the options. These help you identify options embedded in many real life situations and construct packages for different pay-off situations. The chapter explains the various characteristics of options and the effects of the changes in the different variables affecting the value of an option. The value of a call option is a function of the exercise price, the stock price, the risk-free rate of interest, time to expiration, and the volatility of returns measured by the standard deviation of returns. While a higher exercise price would mean a lower call option value, all the other variables have a positive relationship with the value of a call. Note that the value of the option is not affected by the expected return on the stock.

Options are an important and ever-present part of modern corporate finance. Most corporate securities have features of options or have options embedded in them. The financial manager will have a number of uses for options. Some of these include capital budgeting decisions, financing decisions, and risk management. A good understanding of the way options work and the knowledge of how to value them will be very useful for a corporate financial manager.

LIST OF TERMS

American option
Call option
European option
Exercise price
In-the-money
Out of the money

Position diagram
Put option
Put-call parity
Strike price
Volatility

EXERCISES

Fill-in Questions

1. A(n) _____ gives its owner the right (without the obligation) to buy an asset at a specified exercise price, or _____ price.

2. A(n) _____ gives its owner the right to sell stock at a specified price.

3. _____ call options may be exercised only on the expiration day, whereas _____ call options may be exercised on or before the expiration day.

4. For European options, the value of a call option plus the present value of the _____ equals the value of the _____ plus the share price.

5. The best way to show the effect of using combinations of options is to draw a _____.

6. When a firm borrows, (shareholders, creditors) _____ acquire the company and (shareholders, creditors) _____ obtain an option to buy it back.

7. The value of limited liability lies in the option to default and is the value of a (put, call) _____ option on the firm's assets with an exercise price equal to the promised payment to (creditors, owners) _____.

8. If the following variables decrease, the changes in the call option prices are (positive, negative):

Stock price	_____
Exercise price	_____
Interest rate	_____
Time to expiration	_____
Stock price volatility	_____

9. When an asset's value exceeds the strike price, then the call option on it is said to be (in, out of) _____ the money and the put option is said to be (in, out of) _____ the money.

10. This relationship -- value of call + present value of exercise price = value of put + share price -- is called _____.

11. In the language of option pricing, the annualized standard deviation of the return on the underlying asset is called its _____.

Problems

1. Find the value of a call option, given that the present value of the exercise price is $26, the value of the put is $2, and the share price is $30.

2. Find the implied present value of the exercise price of a 26-week call, given the value of the call option is $1, the value of the put option is $7, and the market price is $35.

3. Identify the options involved in the following:

   a. The CEO of Crazy Fox gets 10,000 shares when he is hired. He can sell the shares back to the company at a price of $40 if he is fired within the next two years.

   b. A cereal manufacturer has a long-term contract with an agricultural trading company for the supply of corn and wheat. The transactions would normally be at market prices. However, the contract stipulates a minimum price the cereal company will pay if the market price falls below that price. The contract also stipulates a ceiling price, if the market price goes above that price.

4. The following are recent quotes for call options on General Electric shares expiring in 35 days.

Exercise Price	Call price
$37.50	$3.40
$40.00	$1.75
$45.00	$0.15

   Assume an interest rate of 3.25 percent. The stock price was $40.41. Use the put-call parity to estimate the prices for the put options. Do you expect these prices to be different from the prices quoted in the market?

5. Mary Stiller, the new CEO of World Grossing Corp. is offered the following bonus package (instead of the one in worked example 6): She will get $75,000 if the share price closes at $50 or higher in six months time. Can you identify the combination of options or other securities that will give this pay-off?

6. Given below are the pay-off diagrams for certain combinations of options or securities. Can you identify the combinations?

| Figure A | Figure B | Figure C |

Essay Questions

1. Explain the following statement – "Shares of a limited liability corporation can be viewed as call options or put options depending on how you look at them."

2. Explain why financial managers should be interested in options.

3. List and explain the key elements, which determine the value of options.

4. Describe the typical corporation's debt and stockholders' equity as options.

ANSWERS TO EXERCISES

Fill-in Questions

1. Call options; strike
2. Put option
3. European, American
4. Exercise price; put option
5. Position diagram
6. Creditors; shareholders

7. Put; creditors
8. Negative, positive, negative, negative, negative
9. In; out of
10. Put-call parity
11. Volatility

Problems

1. Value of call = value of put + share price - PV of exercise price
   = $2 + $30 - $26 = $6

2. PV of exercise price = value of put + share price - value of call
   = $7 + $35 - $1 = $41

3. a. A put options with exercise price of $40.

   b. The two parties have sold each other a call option and a put option. The cereal manufacturer has bought a call option (sold by the trading firm) with the exercise price equal to the ceiling price. The agricultural trading firm has bought a put option (sold by the cereal manufacturer) with the exercise price equal to the minimum price.

4. The 35 day discount factor for the 3.25 percent call money rate = $1/(1.0325^{35/365}) = 0.9969$. The values of European puts are given by:

Value of put = PV (exercise price) + V(call) – share price

$V(\$37.5 \text{ put}) = \$37.5 \times 0.9969 + 3.40 - \$40.41 = \$0.38$

$V(\$40 \text{ put}) = \$40 \times 0.9969 + 1.75 - \$40.41 = \$1.22$

$V(\$45 \text{ put}) = \$45 \times 0.9969 + 0.15 - \$40.41 = \$4.60$

These are the values for European options. Quoted prices available in the market are for American puts and these are likely to be somewhat higher.

5. If you buy 75,000 calls with exercise price of $49 and sell 75,000 calls with exercise price of $50, you will almost always get the payoff stipulated in the bonus package. The payoff will be different if the stock price ends up between $49 and $50. You could narrow the difference between the option combinations and the bonus by fine tuning the option exercise prices in the combination as follows: 150,000 contracts each with exercise prices of $49.50 and $50; 300,000 contracts each with exercise prices of $49.75 and $50; or 750,000 contracts each with exercise prices of $49.90 and $50.

6. Figure A pay-off is for the following combination: Buy one call with exercise price of $30, sell two calls with exercise price of $35 and buy one call with exercise price of $40. Figure B involves a combination of buying a call with exercise price of $30 and selling a call with exercise price of $50. Figure C is the payoff you get when you buy both a call and put with the same exercise price of $45.

21
Valuing Options

INTRODUCTION

This chapter picks up from where we left off in chapter 20 and explains the valuation of options from the first principles. We start with the simplified version of the binomial method for valuing options. This approach uses option-equivalent portfolios using ownership in stock and borrowing. Alternately, one could the risk-neutral method, which involves computing the probability of stock price changes under the assumption of risk-neutral investors. The two methods are equivalent and give the same valuation. The general binomial method and its applications are presented later. This is followed by the Black and Scholes formula, which is easier and more accurate than the binomial method. The formula is illustrated with a clear worked out example. The chapter also reviews the application of the binomial option-pricing model to American options. Remember that the Black-Scholes model was derived for the European call option. Valuation of American options as well as European options on stocks paying dividends need to be adapted or modified to the specific situation. In some cases, the step-by-step binomial method may the only right approach.

KEY CONCEPTS IN THE CHAPTER

A Simple Option Valuation Model: We learned in chapter 20 the basic properties of options and the key determinants of the value of an option. We now approach the important problem of computing the value of an option. So far, the discounted cash flow approach has been the basic procedure we used for valuation. However, discounted cash flows will not work for options, because:

- Difficulty in forecasting cash flows from an option, though it is possible to do.
- Impossible to find the correct opportunity cost of capital because an option's risk changes every time its price changes. An in-the-money option is safer than one out-of-the-money and a stock price increase raises option prices and reduces risk, and vice versa, each time stock prices change.
- Options are always riskier than the underlying stock because they have higher betas and higher standard deviations of return.

The problem of option valuation is solved by creating an option equivalent portfolio by combining the stock and borrowing. Initially, we simplify the problem by assuming that the stock can take only two possible values when the option expires. A portfolio of the stock and a loan is constructed such that it gives the same pay-off as the option at the time of expiration. Thus, the value of the option can be written as:

Value of call = value of the number of shares in the equivalent portfolio – borrowed amount.

The number of shares needed to replicate one call is the *hedge ratio* or *option delta*. This ratio is computed as follows:

$$\text{Option delta} = \frac{\text{spread of possible option prices}}{\text{spread of possible share prices}}$$

An equivalent, but alternative, approach is to assume that the investors are *risk-neutral*. With this assumption, we can get the investors to be satisfied with the risk-free rate of return on their stock investment. We can now estimate the *probability of stock price* going up or down and thereby calculate the value of the option.

$$\text{Probability of rise in stock value} = \frac{\text{interest rate - downside change}}{\text{upside change - downside change}}$$

This value is the probability of the price change in the risk-neutral world. Note that this is not the real probability, but a synthetic construct, which enables us to value the option.

The Binomial Method: The above approaches to valuation are somewhat simplistic and assume that the stock will have just two possible values (one up and one down) in the next period. The approach is general and is a simplified version of the *binomial* method. Essentially, we assume the possible changes over the next period to be just two - an "up" value and a "down" value. We can extend the binomial method by assuming shorter time intervals and then replicate the process. That is, we can break down a one-month option into a series of 30 one-day options and ultimately into shorter and shorter intervals so that you end up with continuous changes. While doing this type of option valuation manually will be cumbersome, one can find computer programs that will make the computations less time consuming.

The General Binomial Method: The basic approach in the binomial method involves specifying two (and only two) possible asset value changes per unit of time under consideration. We then assume that the investors will be risk-neutral and will be satisfied with a rate of return equal to the risk-free interest rate. Given these conditions, it is easy to calculate the implied probability (p) that the asset will rise (the probability of a fall in value will be, of course, 1-p). We can find the pay-off for the option for the two asset values and calculate the expected value of the option. There are generalized formulas to determine asset value changes based on the standard deviation of asset returns.

$$1 + \text{upside change} = u = e^{\sigma\sqrt{h}}$$

$$\text{upside change} = e^{\sigma\sqrt{h}} - 1$$

$$1 = \text{downside change} = d = 1/u$$

Downside change $= (1/u) - 1$

Where,

e = base for natural logs = 2.718
σ = standard deviation of (continuously compounded) annual returns on asset
h = interval as a fraction of a year

As the number of intervals is increased, the values you obtain from the binomial method should get closer and closer to the Black-Scholes value.

The Binomial Method and Decision Trees: The application of the binomial method looks and feels a lot like the decision trees we have seen in the capital budgeting chapters. However, the binomial method is not another application of decision trees. Option pricing theory is needed to solve the problems described in this chapter. Discounted cash flows will not work because there is no single discount rate, which will capture the changing risk involved. The option theory is more powerful and will provide simpler solutions where decision trees cannot or become too complex.

The Black-Scholes Formula: Extension of the binomial approach to larger and larger number of sub-periods comprising smaller and smaller intervals will ultimately result in a smooth continuous distribution of stock price changes. Black and Scholes achieved this theoretically and derived a formula for the value of an option. The formula can be written as :

$$\text{Value of option} = [\text{delta x share price}] - [\text{bank loan}]$$
$$= [N(d_1) \times P] - [N(d_2) \times PV(EX)]$$

where:

$$d_1 = \frac{\log[P / PV(EX)]}{\sigma\sqrt{t}} + \frac{\sigma\sqrt{t}}{2}$$

$$d_2 = d_1 - \sigma\sqrt{t}$$

$N(d)$ = cumulative normal probability density function
EX = exercise price of option
PV(EX) is calculated by discounting at risk-free interest rate for t-periods in the usual way.
t = number of periods to exercise date
P = price of stock now
σ = standard deviation per period of (continuously compounded) rate of return on stock
Notice that the Black-Scholes formula has all the properties we expected. It increases with P, σ, and t, and decreases with PV(EX). It also increases smoothly as a function of P from C = 0 for small P up to P – PV(EX) for large P.

Using Black-Scholes Model: Using Black-Scholes model is not particularly difficult, once the values of the variables are known. See the worked examples and the problems at the end. $N(d_1)$ and $N(d_2)$ can be calculated from the tables for the probability tables for normal distribution (Appendix A - Table 6 in the Brealey and Myers book). Alternately, you can use the NORMDIST function in the Excel spreadsheet program. For example, if you want to find the value for $N(d_1)$ where $d_1 = 0.501$, type in "= NORMDIST(0.501, 0,1, TRUE)" in the EXCEL spreadsheet, you will get the value $N(d_1) = 0.308$. Once you get the values of $N(d_1)$ and $N(d_2)$, you can substitute these in the Black-Scholes formula and get the option value. See worked examples 4 and 5. The values for $N(d_1)$ and $N(d_2)$ for all the solutions were calculated using the EXCEL spreadsheet program.

The Black-Scholes formula is more accurate, easier to use and realistic than the binomial method. Note that from given market prices for options and other parameters, one can estimate the variability of stock returns using the Black-Scholes formula.

Option Values at a Glance: The Black-Scholes formula applies to the European call on stocks, which do not pay any dividends. In order to apply this for the valuation of American calls as well as dividend paying stocks, you will have to modify the model or apply the general binomial method. Here is a summary of these situations.

American call--no dividends: In the absence of dividends, the value of a call option increases with the time to maturity. An American call should not be exercised before maturity. Therefore, the value of the American call will be same as that given by the Black-Scholes model for the European call.

European Puts - no dividends: Using the put-call parity, you can derive the value of a European put.

$$\text{Value of put} = \text{Value of call} - \text{Value of stock} + \text{PV(Exercise price)}$$

American put--no dividends: It sometimes pays to exercise an American put before maturity in order to reinvest the exercise price. An American put is always more valuable than a European put. The Black-Scholes formula does not allow for early exercise and thus, cannot be used to value an American put exactly. We can use the step-by-step binomial method by checking at each point whether the option is worth exercising the option ahead of its maturity.

European Calls on Dividend-paying stocks: For European calls on dividend-paying stocks, the value obtained by the Black-Scholes model will overstate the value of the option as part of the share value is composed of the present value of dividends, which the option holder does not receive. Therefore, the share price will need to be reduced to reflect the present value of the lost dividends.

American calls on dividend-paying stocks: The fact that a stock pays dividends does not necessarily imply that the option should be exercised early. The dividend gain is to be compared with the interest lost by the early exercise. Again, the best approach to valuing the option is to use the step-by-step binomial method and check at each stage whether the option is more valuable if exercised just before the ex-dividend date or held for at least one more period.

WORKED EXAMPLES

1. MBM Corp shares are currently trading at $105. You are required to value a six-month call option on MBM shares. The exercise price is given as $105. You are also told to assume that the stock can take only one of two possible values: $84 or $131.25. Assume an interest rate of 3.5 percent. Value the option using the option equivalent portfolio and the risk-neutral method.

SOLUTION

We can represent the situation six months from now as follows:

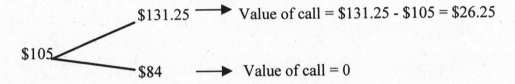

This pay-off for the options can be replicated by a portfolio of stock and loan.

Number of shares in the portfolio = Option delta or hedge ratio = $\dfrac{\$26.25 - 0}{\$131.25 - \$84}$ = 0.5556

A portfolio of 0.5556 shares and a loan $45.87 will give the same payoff as the option as shown below. Note that the interest rate for six months = 3.5%/2 = 1.75%

	Low stock price = $84	High stock price = $131.25
Value of 1 call option	0	$26.25
0.5556 shares	0.5556x$84 = $46.67	0.5556x$131.25 = $72.92
Loan + Interest on a loan of $45.87	$45.87x1.0175 =$46.67	$45.87x1.0175= $46.67
Total pay-off	0	$26.25

Note: The loan amount is set such that the portfolio will have the same payoff as the option.

Value of call = 0.5556 shares - $45.87 = $58.34 - $45.87 = $12.47

Risk-neutral method: The upside change in the stock price is 0.25 and the downside change is -0.20. Therefore, if the investors were risk-neutral, they would expect to get a return of 1.75 percent for the six-month period. We can compute the probability from the following equation:

$$p(0.25) + (1-p)(-0.2) = 0.0175$$

$$p = \frac{0.0175 + 0.20}{0.25 + 0.2} = 0.4833$$

The value of the option in six months is $26.25.
Current value = $26.25 x 0.4833/1.0175 = $12.47

2. Data for an option valuation problem are given below. Explain the Black-Scholes option valuation formula and compute the value of a European call option with exercise price of $120. Also, value a European put with the same exercise price. Show all steps.

Time	3 years
Standard deviation of continuously compounded return on asset	0.635
Current asset price	$100
Option exercise price	$120
Interest rate	8 %

SOLUTION

Basic Black-Scholes formula can be written as below:

$$\text{Value of option} = [\text{delta x share price}] - [\text{bank loan}]$$
$$= [N(d_1) \times P] - [N(d_2) \times PV(EX)]$$

where:

$$d_1 = \frac{\log[P / PV(EX)]}{\sigma\sqrt{t}} + \frac{\sigma\sqrt{t}}{2}$$
$$d_2 = d_1 - \sigma\sqrt{t}$$

$N(d)$ = cumulative normal probability density function
EX = Exercise price of option = $120, PV(EX) = $120/(1.08^3) = $95.26
t = number of periods to exercise date = 3 years
P = price of stock now = $100
σ = standard deviation per period = 0.635

$d_1 = 0.5941$, $N(d_1) = 0.7238$
$d_2 = -0.5058$, $N(d_2) = 0.3065$

$$\text{Value of call} = 0.7238 \times \$100 - 0.3065 \times \$95.26 = \$72.38 - \$29.20 = \$43.18$$

$$\text{Value of put} = \text{Value of call} + \text{PV(EX)} - \text{stock price}$$
$$= \$43.18 + \$95.26 - \$100 = \$38.44$$

3. Karl Cahn Partners (KCP), a private take-over specialist firm, has embarked on an acquisition strategy to buy several other privately held companies. It presently has an opportunity to buy RRK Inc., but needs another six months to complete its analysis. It has instructed the CFO to negotiate an option to buy RRK. What price should the CFO be willing to pay for the option? The estimated standard deviation of RRK is 0.60, the value of its shares is $50 apiece, and the estimated equivalent to an exercise price is $70. Assume the interest rate is 7 percent.

SOLUTION

Summary of data:

Price of stock = $50
Exercise price = $70
PV (EX) = $70/(1.07^{0.5}) = $67.67
Standard deviation = 60 percent
Years to maturity = 0.5 years
Interest rate = 7 percent

$d_1 = -0.5012$, $N(d_1) = 0.3081$
$d_2 = -0.9255$, $N(d_2) = 0.1774$
$V \text{ (call)} = N(d_1) P - N(d_2) \times \text{PV(EX)}$
$\qquad = 0.3081 \times \$50 - 0.1774 \times \$67.67$
$\qquad = \$15.40 - \$12.00 = \$3.40$

4. Refer to problem 3 above. If RRK has been issued a put option by KCP with the same exercise price, how much is it worth?

SOLUTION

Use the put-call parity, beginning with:

$$\text{Present value of exercise price} = \text{value of put} + \text{share price} - \text{value of call}$$
$$\text{Value of put} = \text{present value of exercise price} - \text{share price} + \text{value of call}$$
$$= \$67.67 - 50.00 + 3.40 = \$21.07$$

5. Suppose you are offered a 1-year option to buy the Euro at the exchange rate of $0.90 = 1 Euro. You have the following additional information:

Maturity of option	$t = 1$
Exercise price	$E = \$0.90$
Current exchange rate (price) of Euro	$P = \$0.90$
Standard deviation of exchange-rate changes	$\sigma = .15$
Dollar interest rate	$r_\$ = .05$
Euro	$r_E = 0.06$

SOLUTION

To value the call option, you must first reduce the current price of the Euro by the amount of the lost interest.

Adjusted price of Euro, $P^* = $ current price$/(1 + r_E) = 0.90/1.06 = \$0.85$

Price/PV(exercise price) $= P^*/[E/(1 + r_\$)] = 0.85/(0.90/1.05) = 0.9906$

$d_1 = \log[P/PV(EX)]/\sigma\sqrt{t} + \sigma\sqrt{t}/2;$ $d_2 = d_1 - \sigma\sqrt{t}$

$\sigma = 0.15,$ $t = 1$ year, $\sigma\sqrt{t} = 0.15$
$d_1 = -0.0118$ $d_2 = -0.1382$
$N(d_1) = 0.5047$ $N(d_2) = 0.4450$
Value of the call option $= N(d_1)P - N(d_2) \times PV(EX)$
$\qquad\qquad\qquad\qquad = 0.5047 \times \$0.85 - 0.4450 \times 0.86$
$\qquad\qquad\qquad\qquad = \$0.0471 = 4.71$ cents/Euro

SUMMARY

This chapter is an extension of chapter 20 and applies the lessons learned in the last chapter to valuation of options. First, a simplified version of the binomial method is presented. The chapter also reviews the general binomial method, which is a very versatile tool in option valuation. By applying it over shorter and shorter periods, the binomial method approaches the Black-Scholes method in terms of accuracy. The chapter also presents the more rigorous Black-Scholes model. The model is not too difficult to apply, once you learn how to calculate the normal probability distribution values required in the formula.

The Black-Scholes formula is easier to use and more accurate than the binomial method. However, the model strictly applies only to European call options on to non-dividend paying stocks. European puts on non-dividend paying stocks can be valued using the Black-Scholes formula for the call option and then the put-call parity learned in the last chapter. American calls on non-dividend paying stocks can be valued using the Black-Scholes formula, as the value of both types of options would be same in this case. For options on dividend paying stocks, the Black-Scholes formula need to be applied with some modification or the step-by-step binomial method should be used.

LIST OF TERMS

American Option
Binomial method
Black-Scholes
Currency Option

European Option
Hedge ratio
Option delta

EXERCISES

Fill-in Questions

1. The number of shares needed to create the option equivalents from buying and selling common stocks and borrowing is called the _____ or _____.

2. The _____ method shows how to replicate the outcomes from an option for the evolution of the stock price.

3. The _____ formula assumes lognormal distribution of stock price changes. The formula is derived for the European call options.

4. An option to buy British pounds at a stipulated exchange rate is a(n) _____ option.

5. As the number of intervals for analyzing options is increased from 1 to 52, the _____ method produces results that are very close to the _____ model.

6. An American call option on a stock, which pays no dividends should not be exercised before maturity; therefore, its value is the same as a _____ call.

7. A(n) _____ put is always more valuable than a(n) _____ put.

Problems

1. XYZ, Inc., has a 3-month option to acquire a publicly traded company, ABC Corp. Here are the assumptions the CFO made to analyze how to construct option equivalents.

   Exercise price $70
   Current price of ABC stock $70
   Price may move only up or down:
       Estimated low price $59.50
       Estimated high price $82.40
   1-year interest rate   6%

   Demonstrate how to replicate the pay-off from a call option.

257

2. Use the Black-Scholes model to evaluate the $105 IBM call option expiring in 40 days. IBM stock is selling at 106.50 and the call money rate (charged to brokers on stock exchange collateral) was 3.25 percent. Assume a standard deviation of 26 percent.

3. Use the Black-Scholes model to evaluate the following IMK Corp option: Exercise price = $135, Stock price $130, Volatility = 26 percent, time to expiration = 3 months, and the risk-free interest rate = 6.25 percent.

4. Private, Inc.(PI), has an opportunity to buy Family Corp. (FC) another privately held company. PI needs more time to evaluate the deal and has negotiated a 60-day option to buy the company. The exercise price is set at $75. How much is the option worth to PI given that the estimated standard deviation of FC is 40 percent and the estimated value of each share of FC is $60. Assume the risk-free rate is 4.5 percent.

5. Refer to problem 4 above. FC persuades PI to write a put option with the same exercise price. How much is this option worth to FC?

6. You are offered a 1-year option to buy Mambian Crusados at $0.50/Crusado. The current exchange rate is $0.55/Crusado. You have the following information:

Maturity of option	$t = 1$
Standard deviation of exchange-rate changes	$\sigma = 0.16$
Dollar interest rate	$r_\$ = 0.05$
Crusado interest rate	$r_M = 0.08$

What is the value of this currency option?

Essay Questions

1. Explain the technique of creating option-equivalent combinations using stocks and bank loans.

2. Describe the general binomial method. How does this method compare with the Black-Scholes model?

3. Explain the approach you would take to value an American call on a dividend paying stock.

4. "An American call option should never be exercised before its maturity." Discuss this statement.

5. "The Black-Scholes formula applies only to European calls on on-dividend paying stocks." Discuss this statement.

ANSWERS TO EXERCISES

Fill-in Questions

1. Hedge ratio; option delta
2. Binomial
3. Black-Scholes
4. Currency

5. Binomial; Black-Scholes
6. European
7. American, European

Problems

1. The pay-off for the call option for the high and low values of the stock and for a portfolio of equivalent stock + loan combination are given in the table below. The number of stocks required to duplicate the option pay-off is calculated using the hedge ratio or option delta formula.

$$\text{Hedge ratio} = \text{option delta} = \frac{\text{spread of possible option values}}{\text{spread of possible share values}}$$
$$= \$12.50/\$22.90 = 0.5415$$

Thus, if you buy 0.5415 shares and borrow $31.74, the pay-off for the option is duplicated. See the table below.

	Low stock price = $59.5	High stock price = $82.40
Value of 1 call option	0	$12.40
0.5415 shares	$32.22	$44.62
Loan + Interest on a loan of $31.74	$32.22	$32.22
Total pay-off	0	$12.40

Value of one call option = 0.5415 x $70 – $31.74 = $37.91 - $31.74 = $6.17

2. Summary of data needed:

Price of stock = $106.4
Exercise price = $105
Standard deviation = 26 percent
Years to maturity = 40/365 = 0.1096 years
Interest rate = 3.25 percent
PV (EX) = $105/(1.035$^{0.1096}$) = $104.60

Black-Scholes formula: V (call) = N(d$_1$) x P – N(d$_2$) x PV (EX)

$$d_1 = \frac{\log[P / PV(EX)]}{\sigma\sqrt{t}} + \frac{\sigma\sqrt{t}}{2}$$

$$d_2 = d_1 - \sigma\sqrt{t}$$

$$d_1 = \frac{\log[\$106.5 / \$104.63)}{0.26\sqrt{0.1096}} + \frac{0.26\sqrt{0.1096}}{2}$$

$d_1 = 0.2516$, $d_2 = 0.1656$, $N(d_1) = 0.5993$, $N(d_2) = 0.5658$
Value of call = 0.5993 x \$106.5 – 0.5658 x \$104.60 = \$4.65

3. $d_1 = \log[P/PV(EX)]/\sigma\sqrt{t} + (\sigma\sqrt{t})/2$
     = -0.1087

   $d_2 = d_1 - \sigma\sqrt{t} = -0.2387$

   $N(d_1) = 0.4567$, $N(d_2) = 0.4057$
   Value of call $= N(d_1) \times P - N(d_2) \times PV(EX)$
                 $= 0.4567 \times \$130 – 0.4057 \times 132.97$
                 $= \$5.43$

4. $d_1 = -1.2502$, $d_2 = -1.4124$
   $N(d_1) = 0.1056$, $N(d_2) = 0.0789$
   Value of call $= 0.1056 \times \$60 – 0.0789 \times \$74.46 = \$0.46$

5. Using the put-call parity:
   V(put) = V(call) + PV(EX) – share price
          = \$0.46 + \$74.46 - \$60 = \$14.92

6. To value the call option, you must first reduce the current price of the Crusado by the amount of the lost interest.

   Adjusted price of Crusado, $P^* $ = current price/$(1 + r_M)$ = 0.55/1.08 = \$0.5093
   Price/PV(exercise price) = $P^*/[E/(1 + r_\$)]$ = 0.5093/(0.50/1.05) = 1.0695

   $d_1 = \log[P/PV(EX)]/\sigma\sqrt{t} + \sigma\sqrt{t}/2$; $d_2 = d_1 - \sigma\sqrt{t}$

   $\sigma = 0.15$,   t = 1 year, $\sigma\sqrt{t} = 0.15$
   $d_1 = 0.4999$ $d_2 = 0.3399$
   $N(d_1) = 0.6914$ $N(d_2) = 0.6330$

   Value of the call option $= N(d_1)P – N(d_2) \times PV(EX)$
                             $= 0.6914 \times \$0.5093 – 0.6333 \times 0.4762$
                             $= \$0.051$ or 5.1 cents/Mark

22
Real Options

INTRODUCTION

This chapter uses and extends the lessons learned in chapters 20 and 21 to evaluate the real options of different types, which are often encountered by the corporate financial manager. Real options can be very valuable and can add value to the firm, if they are understood correctly and acted upon. Chapter 10 provided a brief introduction to the four common real options typically found in many capital investment projects. These are:

- The option to expand and make follow-on investments.
- The option to abandon or shrink a project.
- The option to wait and learn before investing.
- The option to change the input, the output or the production methods.

These options need to be considered as part of the capital investment project and included in the value of the project. The chapter provides a number of examples of valuing these options using the Black-Scholes or the binomial method. The options approach to valuation of these special situations associated with capital budgeting decisions is necessitated by the fact that simple discounted cash flow (DCF) analysis does not work very well in these cases. The DCF analysis is designed for analyzing investments, which do not change their nature during the life of the project. It is ideally suited for evaluating passive investments like bonds and stocks. Most corporate assets or investment projects are, on the other hand, actively managed by the manager. Projects can very often change their nature in terms of risk, cost structure, and expansion or abandonment possibilities. A smart manager will respond appropriately to these changes. These situations are best valued as options, which permit multiple decision points. The additional rounds of decisions give the manager more choices and enable the firm to capitalize on good fortune or to mitigate losses. The choices create uncertainty, which often makes the option more valuable.

KEY CONCEPTS IN THE CHAPTER

The Value of Follow-on Investment Opportunities: Many capital budgeting projects have expansion or follow-on investment opportunities attached to them. These expansion or follow-on projects are real options and should be considered while evaluating the original project. A pure DCF analysis of the follow-on project will not do justice to it. Even when the follow-on project is a negative NPV project, it can add value to the original project. It can be seen as an out-of-the-money call option. Note that such an option will have higher value if the uncertainty is higher and time to expiration is longer. These are properties that are somewhat counter-intuitive and the opposite of what one would find in the DCF analysis. Typical investments with follow-on projects include R & D projects and investments in new markets, foreign countries, and new technology. Remember that the uncertainties associated with the follow-on project actually make the value of options even more attractive.

As mentioned before, DCF analysis cannot do justice to the follow-on projects. This is because managers are actively involved in the management of both the initial project and the follow-on projects. The company will take up the follow-on projects only if they are found attractive or become in-the-money at the time the investment is called for.

The follow-on projects can be evaluated as call options. The investment required in the project is the exercise price and the present value of cash flows from the project is the asset price. The volatility of the project cash flows is to be measured as the standard deviation of the return on a stock with characteristics similar to that of the project. It may not be easy to find a stock with these characteristics, but the company's experience from the past might be of some help.

The Timing Option: Most investment projects have built-in timing option in that the firm can make the investment now or some time in the future. A project with a positive net present value with a timing option is in effect a mutually exclusive project with itself with a later starting date. The cost of delaying the investment is the lost cash flow during the delay; but the important benefit is that you can learn a lot more about the prospects of the project and uncertainties surrounding the project might be cleared up. Delaying the investment might be the right choice if the value of the option is significant.

Valuing the timing option is simple when there is no uncertainty. One can calculate the project's NPV at various dates of project commencement and pick the one date with the highest NPV. When there is uncertainty involved, as is in most cases, the option is best valued as a call option. The option associated with the timing of the project can be valued using the binomial method and the risk-neutral technique. The present value of the cash flows from the project will be the asset value and the investment required for the project is the exercise price. Cash flows from the project are similar to dividends on a stock. By delaying the exercise of the option, you are loosing the current cash flows, but gaining the time premium of the option. This premium will be a function of the volatility and time. These options can be valued using the step-by-step binomial method

The Option to Abandon: This is the opposite of the option to expand. The option to reduce the size of the project or scrap it altogether, when things do not turn out as expected, is very valuable and enhances the project's value. The abandonment option can be seen as a put option and can be analyzed in terms of the possible project outcomes. The valuation of the abandonment option can be done using the binomial method. You start by estimating the present value of the project without the option to abandon. This is done by using the standard DCF approach. The steps to create a binomial tree giving the values for various possible project outcomes follow this. The "up" and the "down" values are computed for the different nodes on the tree. You then compute the risk-neutral probability for the upside change and the downside change. Using these probabilities and working back-wards from the end point of the project one can complete the tree by estimating the value of project for different nodes of the tree. Given the salvage value for the assets of the project at the various points in the project life, you can compute the value of the abandonment option for the different nodes. For each node you have two values for the project - one is the present value of the future cash flows and the other the salvage or abandonment value. The higher of the two is the effective value of the project at each node. We can work backwards to compute the effective value of the project incorporating the abandonment value. The difference between this value and the simple DCF present value of the project is the value of the abandonment put option.

Abandonment value and project life: For most projects, the effective project life is not known at the time the project is being evaluated. One makes specific assumptions about project life based on past experience with similar projects. This assumption is needed when one uses the standard DCF procedure for evaluation of capital budgeting projects. A real options approach will enable the project analyst to go beyond the one project life assumption. Essentially, one has to build a binomial tree extending to a point well beyond the usually assumed project life and then follow the procedure described above to find the optimal life for the project.

Temporary Abandonment: Often businesses face situations when it makes sense to abandon assets temporarily for possible use in future. Plants are shutdown when demand falls to a point where it does not make sense to operate them. The plants are mothballed with the expectation of being restarted when the demand picks up again and operations are profitable. In general mothballing of assets and reactivating them costs money. It will pay to mothball an asset if the value of the mothballed asset is more than the value of the asset in operation plus the cost of mothballing it. Similarly, a mothballed asset will be put back in service when the value of the asset in operation exceeds the value of the mothballed asset plus the cost of reactivating it.

Flexible Production Facilities: Flexibility in manufacturing, procurement or other operating activities can have significant option value. Flexibility in production or manufacturing can be designed and built into a plant or manufacturing system. While such a plant or system can cost more than a plant or system without the flexibility, the former is more valuable because of the flexibility option. The flexibility may be with respect to any of the following: switching machine set ups to produce different products, switching from one source (or type) of raw material, or even switching the location of manufacturing from one country to another. These options are somewhat more complicated than the abandonment or follow-on options, but the principles learned in the chapter can be used to evaluate them. The options are more valuable if the uncertainty relating to the inputs of the system is high. For example an option to switch feedstock from natural gas to a liquid fuel is very valuable if the ratio of the prices of the two is very volatile. Another option that can be very valuable is the option relating to the procurement of key inputs to the business. An interesting example is the one discussed in the text, which describes an option on the purchase of airplanes by airlines. Most long-term procurement decisions involve three possible choices - a firm commitment now, a contract with a variable procurement option, or a commitment later. Again the value of the option will be a positive function of the uncertainty surrounding the component to be procured and the variability in the benefits and costs relating to it.

A Conceptual Issue: Option pricing models assume creation of option-equivalent portfolios constructed from the asset and a loan. This is valid for stocks and other financial assets, which are widely traded in the market. The real options discussed in this chapter involve real assets, which are seldom widely traded in the market. This raises the question of the validity of using the option pricing models for the valuation of the real options. However, this should not be a serious problem as long as there are traded assets or portfolios of risk characteristics identical to that of the assets included in the real option. The assumption is similar to what is made in the standard capital budgeting evaluation procedures used.

WORKED EXAMPLES

1. Conner Canary Corp. (CCC) is considering a new technology for an ultra-electronic combination internal combustion electric engine. The technology is expected to revolutionize automobile industry and could lead to the ultimate zero emission cars. The net present value of the initial project is negative and is estimated at -$15 million. However, the company's chief technologist is keen on the project because the project will open up opportunities for the next generation of combination engines, which are expected to produce zero emission vehicles (ZEV). The estimated NPV of the ZEV project is -$25 million. Investment decision in the ZEV project must be made in 2005 (3 years from now). The other details of the ZEV project are given below:

Investment required in 2005	= $360 million
PV of cash flows expected (in 2005)	= $335 million
Standard deviation for comparable projects	= 35 percent
Required rate of return for the typical combination engine projects	= 16 percent
Interest rate	= 6 percent

CCC's CEO, Jose Mendez needs to make a decision on the initial project. Evaluate the project.

SOLUTION

The problem is an example of a project with a follow-on investment. The fact that the follow-on project has a negative NPV does not necessarily mean that it should be rejected. The follow-on project is a call option and has to be evaluated as such. We can use the Black-Scholes model to evaluate the value of the option.

Value of the call option = $N(d_1)P - N(d_2) \times PV(EX)$;

where $d_1 = \log[P/PV(EX)]/\sigma\sqrt{t} + /\sigma\sqrt{t}/2$, $d2 = d_1 - \sigma\sqrt{t}$

$P = \$335/(1.16)^3 = \$214.623$ million
This is the value of the cash flow from the project. This should be discounted using the required rate of return for the project.

PV (EX) = $360/(1.05)$^3^ = $302.26 million

PV (EX) = $360/(1.05)^3 = $302.26 million

This is part of the option pricing process and the rate used to find the PV should be the interest rate.

σ = 0.35, t = 3 years, $\sigma\sqrt{t}$ = 0.6062, d_1 = -0.2617; d2 = -0.8680

$N(d_1)$ = 0.3968, $N(d_2)$ = 0.1927

Value of the call option = $N(d_1)P - N(d_2)$ X PV(EX) = 0.3968 x $214.623 - 0.1927 x $302.26

= $26.92 million

The value of the option when added to the NPV of the project, gives a positive value for the project: -$20 million + $26.92 million = $6.92 million.

2. Figure 22-1 summarizes the possible payoffs from the new project being considered by ABC Inc. The project is worth $30 million based on the cash flows projected. If things go well, the project will be worth $45 million by the end of the first year. If things do not go well, the business will be worth only $20 million. The company can get $25 million for the plant and machinery in the worse case scenario. Calculate the value of the abandonment option. Assume an interest rate of 10 percent.

Value = $30 million

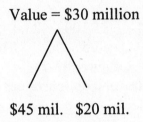

$45 mil. $20 mil.

Figure 22-1

SOLUTION

Using the risk-neutral approach, we can calculate the probability of a rise in the asset value. (Note: This is the notional probability in a risk-neutral world for option valuation; not the real probability. This value should not be used to calculate present value of the cash flows.)

The probability of a rise is:

p = (r – down side change)/(upside change – down side change);
where r = the interest rate = 0.10
upside change = (45/30) - 1 = 0.50
downside change = (20/30) - 1 = -0.33
p = 0.43/0.83 = 0.52

The value of the put option is zero for the upside change and $5 million for the downside change ($25 - $20). The expected future value of the put = 0.52 X 0 + 0.48 X $5 = $2.40 million

Current value = $2.40/1.10 = $2.182 million

3. Rainbow Rivet Company has a project, which requires a cash outlay of $75 million. The company has the option to delay the project for up to 2 years. The project's current cash flow is $15 million, and the cost of capital is 15 percent. The company estimates that the project's cash flows may decrease by 20 percent or increase by 25 percent. Assume that the investment cannot be postponed beyond the end of the second year. The risk-neutral rate is 5 percent. Value the option.

SOLUTION

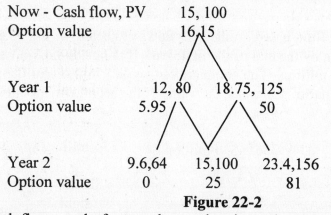

Now - Cash flow, PV	15, 100
Option value	16,15

Year 1	12, 80	18.75, 125
Option value	5.95	50

Year 2	9.6,64	15,100	23.4,156
Option value	0	25	81

Figure 22-2

Cash flows, end-of-year values and option values are all in million dollars.

Figure 22-2 shows the project's possible cash flows, end-of-year values and the option values at the different points in time. With a cash flow of $15 million, the value of the project is $100 million, when discounted at the market-required rate of 15 percent. If demand turns out to be low in year 1, the cash flow is only $12 million, and the remaining value of the project falls to 12/0.15 = $80 million. If demand is high in year 1, the cash flow is $18.75 and the value rises to 18.75/0.15 = $125 million. A second year of low demand would cause the cash flows to fall to $9.6 and the project value to fall to $64, and so on.

Notice that if you undertake the investment right away, you capture the first year's cash flow ($12 or $18.75). If you delay, you miss out on this cash flow, but you now have more information on how the project is likely to work out. In addition, that information has value.

If demand is high in the first year, the company has a cash flow of $18.75 million and a value of $125 million at the end of the first year. The total return is (18.75 + 125)/100 - 1 = 0.4375, or 44 percent. If demand is low, the cash flow is $12 and the year-end value is $80. Total return is (12 + 80)/100 - 1 = -0.08, or - 8 percent.

266

The probability of a rise is:
$$p = [0.05 - (- 0.08)]/[0.44 - (-0.08)]$$
$$= 0.25$$

The probability of a decline = $1 - p = 1 - 0.25 = 0.75$

To find the call option value on the project with an exercise price of $75, begin at the end and work backwards. If the project value is $64, the option to invest is worthless. (Asset price is less than the exercise price.) At the other two points, the option is worth $25 million ($100 - $75), and $81 million ($156 - $75).

At the end of year 1, we need to calculate the option value as the higher of the following: i) value if the investment option is exercised ($5 million on the left branch ($80 - $75), and $50 on the right branch ($125 - $75) and ii) the expected value of the options from the end of year 2. The values are given in Figure 22-2. The value for the left branch for the options = $5.95 = ($25 x 0.25)/1.05. For the right branch, the value of the options from the next year will work out to $37.14 million [($25 x 0.75 + $81 x 0.25)/1.05]. This is lower than the value of the option if exercised at that point ($50 million = $125 - $75).

The value of option now = ($5.95 x 0.75 + $50 x 0.25)/1.05 = $16.15 million

This, however, is less than the value if the option is exercised now: $25 million = $100 - $75 million. Thus, the company should go ahead and invest in the project right now.

SUMMARY

This chapter is an extension of chapter 21 and applies the lessons learned in the last two chapters to the analysis and valuation of real options faced by corporate financial managers. These real options are: the option for follow-on investment, the abandonment option, the timing option, and the option to vary production or other resources to achieve flexibility in production or procurement or other operating activities. These options can be valued using the Black-Scholes or binomial method with the risk-neutral approach as appropriate. These options are extremely valuable and a manager's ability to understand and correctly value these options will enable him (her) to manage the corporate resources better. Note that the real options compliment the DCF analysis of many capital budgeting situations rather than replace it. Also, real options are more valuable when the uncertainty involved is higher and the time to expiration of the option is longer. Care and judgment will have to be used in obtaining the parameters required for valuation of these options.

LIST OF TERMS

Abandonment option   Put option
Call option   Real options
Flexible production facilities   Timing option

EXERCISES

Fill-in Questions

1. Capital budgeting decisions often involve _____ options.

2. A(n) _____ option is an insurance policy that pays off when the value of the asset is less than the option's exercise price.

3. An abandonment option is a(n) _____ option with an exercise price equal to the sales value of the assets.

4. Decisions concerning the timing of investments and the value of follow-on investments are examples of _____ options.

5. The _____ option is essentially one of choosing the optimal point for investment.

6. Real options may be provided by _____ where inputs or outputs may easily be varied.

Problems

1. Burgers & Burgers Corp. (BBC) is considering a new technology for a new hybrid burger with high protein and very low fat content. The net present value of the project is negative and is estimated at -$10 million. However, the company's chief food-technologist is keen on the project because the project will open up opportunities for the next generation of burgers, which are expected to be of zero fat content. The estimated NPV of the ZB (for Zero fat content burger) project is -$65 million. Investment decision must be made in 2004 (two years from now). The other details of the ZB project are given below:

Investment required in 2004	= $250 million
PV of cash flows expected (in 2004)	= $185 million
Standard deviation for comparable projects	= 45 percent
Required rate of return for the typical high-tech burger projects	= 18 percent
Interest rate	= 8 percent

BBC's CEO, Ms. Marie Hunt has asked you, the CFO, to help her decide on the investment. What would you do?

2. TVS Corp. has a project with the following estimated values: $10 million by the end of the first year, if the things work out well; and $2.7 million if things do not turn out well. In the latter case, the company can sell the assets for $3 million. There is a 50 percent chance that the business will succeed. Assets of comparable risk carry a required return of 23 percent.

    a. Based only on the above information, calculate the present value of the project. Round up as you go through the steps.

    b. Does this analysis incorporate the option embedded in the project? Should it? Why? If so, what is the option worth? That is, what is the present value of the firm with the embedded option?

3. Refer to problem 2. Suppose now that in each 6-month period the firm may either rise in value by 40 percent or fall by 30 percent. Assume further that the company has the option to sell the project at the end of the year for $3 million. What option values emerge?

4. The percentage change for upside and downside changes in problem 2 work out to 92 and -48 percent. What is the implied volatility? How will the upside and downside value change if the period of analysis is six months and the implied volatility is the same.

Essay Questions

1. What are real options? Describe two types of real options and tell how you would value them.

2. Describe the step-by-step approach of evaluating abandonment option associated with a project.

3. Rocky D. Feller, the CEO of a large American automobile company and is convinced that the long-term prospects of automobile industry in China and India are very good. However, the projects proposed for these two countries turn out to be negative NPV projects. He feels that the project analysis does not do justice to future expansion possibilities in the two countries. Identify the real options involved in the projects and suggest an evaluation approach, which will take into account future prospects available in foreign markets.

4. Discuss the following statement. "All capital budgeting projects include options of various kind. Therefore, it is better to evaluate them using option valuation techniques rather the DCF approach."

ANSWERS TO EXERCISES

Fill-in Questions

1 Real	4. Call
2 Abandonment	5. Timing
3 Put	6. Flexible production facilities

Problems

1. The problem is an example of a project with a follow-on investment similar to the worked example 1. The follow-on project is a call option and has to be evaluated as such. We can use the Black-Scholes model to evaluate the value of the option.

Value of the call option $= N(d_1)P - N(d_2) X \; PV(EX)$

$d_1 = \log[P/PV(EX)]/\sigma\sqrt{t} + /\sigma\sqrt{t}/2, \; d_2 = d_1 - \sigma\sqrt{t}$
$P = \$185/(1.18)^2 = 132.86; \; PV(EX) = \$250/(1.08)^2 = \$214.33$

$\sigma = 0.45, \; t = 2$ years, $\sigma\sqrt{t} = 0.6364, \; d_1 = -0.4332; \; d_2 = -1.0696$
$N(d_1) = 0.3325; \; N(d_2) = 0.1424$

Value of the call option $= N(d_1)P - N(d_2) X \; PV(EX)$
$= 0.3325 \; X \; \$132.86 - 0.1424 \; X \; 214.33$
$= \$13.66$ million

The value of the option when added to the NPV of the project, gives a positive value for the project: -\$10 million + \$13.66 million = \$3.66 million.

2. a. With a 50 percent chance that the business will succeed, the expected value in year 1 is $(0.50 \; X \; 10) + (0.5 \; X \; 2.7) = \$6.4$ million. At a discount rate of 23 percent, the present value is $6.4/1.23 = \$5.2$ million. The rest of the problem deals with valuing a put option. Begin with a diagram such as Figure 22-3 and the following information.

Figure 22-3
Expected cash flow = [(probability of high demand X 10) + (probability of low demand X 2.7)]

$$= (0.5 \times 10) + (0.5 \times 2.7) = 6.4 \text{ million}$$

Present value
$$= 6.4/1.23 = 5.2 \text{ million}$$

b. Present value of business without option to abandon $5.2 million
    Exercise price $3.0 million
    Maturity   1 year
    Interest rate   5 percent
    Better-case scenario: Future value with high demand $10.0 million
    Worse-case scenario: Future value with low demand $2.7 million

Percentage change in the value of the business:

$$\text{Upside} = (10.0/5.2) - 1 = 0.92 = 92\%$$
$$\text{Downside} = (2.7/5.2) - 1 = 0.46 = -48\%$$

Next, calculate the probability that value will rise:

$$p = (r - \text{downside change})/(\text{upside change} - \text{downside change})$$
$$= [0.05 - (-0.48)]/[0.92 - (-0.48)]$$
$$= 0.53/1.48 = 0.38$$
$$1 - p = 0.62$$

If the project is successful, the option to abandon = 0. If it is unsuccessful, the company can sell the assets and net 3.0 - 2.7 = 0.3 million.

The expected value of the option one period from now is:

$$(\text{probability of rise} \times 0) + [(1 - \text{probability of rise}) \times 0.3]$$
$$= (0.38 \times 0) + (0.62 \times 0.3)$$
$$= \$186,000$$

The current value of the option to abandon is:

$$(\text{expected future value})/(1 + \text{interest rate}) = 186,000/1.05 = \$177,143$$

Value of business with abandonment option= value of business without abandonment option
$$+ \text{value of option}$$
$$= 5.2 + 0.177$$
$$= 5.38 \text{ million}$$

3. Figure 22-4 shows the possible firm values by the year-end. When the firm is worth 2.548 million, the option is worth:

Exercise price - firm value = 3 - 2.548 = 452,000

$$p = (r - \text{downside change})/(\text{upside change} - \text{downside change})$$
$$= [0.05 - (- 0.30)]/[0.40 - (-0.30]$$
$$= .35/.70 = 0.5$$
$$1 - p = 0.5$$

Now	Firm Value		5.2	
	Option value		(0.107)	
Month 6	Firm value	3.64		7.28
	Option value	(0.22)		(0)
Month 12	Firm Value	2.548	5.096	10.190
	Option value	(0.452)	(0)	(0)

Figure 22-4

Figures in parentheses show the values of an option to sell the firm's assets for $3 million.

In month 6, firm value is 3.64 million, and there is a 50-50 chance that, at the end of the year, the option will be worthless or worth $0.452 million.

Expected value of option at end of year = (0.5 x 0) + (0.5 x 0.452) = $0.226 million

Value at month 6 = 0.226/1.025 = $0.220 million

Option Value Now: Figure 22-4 contains values in parentheses for each step.
The expected value of the option
   in month 6 = [(Probability of rise) x 0] + [(1 - probability of rise) x 0.220]
         = (0.5 x 0) + (0.5 x 0.220) = $0.110 million

Value today = (expected value of option at month 6)/(1 + interest rate)
         = 0.110/1.025 = $0.107 million

4. Upside change = u = 0.92; 1 + u = 1.92 = $e^{\sigma\sqrt{h}}$

h = 1; Taking Log of both sides; $\log(1.92) = \sigma\sqrt{h} = 0.652$; $\sigma = 0.652 = 65.2$ percent.

The implied volatility or standard deviation of the annual returns is 65.2 percent.

The upside and downside changes for 6-month intervals are:
   Upside change (6-month interval) = $e^{0.652\sqrt{0.5}} - 1 = 1.586 - 1 = 0.59$
   Downside change = (1/u) - 1 = 1/1.586 - 1 = 0.631 - 1 = -0.37

23

Warrants and Convertibles

INTRODUCTION

Corporations have always been on the lookout for new types of securities. Warrants and convertible securities are among the earliest of corporate financial innovations. The most common warrant is a long-term call option that is attached to a bond or a stock issue. It usually gives its holder an option to *buy for cash* another security of the company, usually its common stock. The typical convertible security is a long-term option that is attached to a bond or a preferred stock and it gives its holder the option to exchange the bond or preferred stock for another security of the company, usually common stock.

Warrants are typically of shorter duration than convertible bonds. They are also detachable from the securities from which they are issued and require cash payment of the exercise price when exercised. The Black-Scholes option valuation formula may be used to place a value on warrants, but care must be taken to allow for the effects of dividends and changes in the number of shares outstanding. Warrants are frequently issued with private placement bonds and occasionally with public bond issues. They are also occasionally used as compensation for investment bankers and as part of restructuring packages for firms reorganizing after bankruptcy.

The value of a convertible bond is equal to the value of the bond component plus the value of the option component. While the holders of convertible bonds and the warrants are not entitled to receive any cash dividends paid before exercise of the option, the exercise prices are automatically adjusted for any stock split or stock dividends. Corporations usually have call options on the convertible bonds they issue. This allows them to call the bonds in order to force conversion of the bonds. The optimal rule for calling convertible securities would be to call them when, and only when, the value of the convertible security reaches the call price.

KEY CONCEPTS IN THE CHAPTER

Warrants: Warrants are usually detachable, meaning that they may be sold and exercised apart from the security with which they were offered. Warrant holders are not entitled to vote, nor do they receive cash dividends. Their interest in the company is usually protected against stock splits and stock dividends. Often, the exercise price is stepped up over the life of the warrant. Usually, the life of a warrant is shorter than the conversion feature of a convertible bond. The Black-Scholes options valuation formula may be used to value on a warrant provided it contains no unusual features and does not pay cash dividends. Cash dividends and dilution arising from the additional shares from the exercise of the warrants, however, present difficulties in using the Black-Scholes model. Consequently, adjustments for dilution are required. The binomial method is needed to value stocks with cash dividends.

<u>Valuation of Warrants:</u> Warrants are American call options and can be valued using the Black-Scholes model. Like any other American option, the value depends on the share price, exercise price, the volatility, the interest rate, and the time to maturity. Warrant valuation needs to be adjusted for the fact that the exercise of the warrant results in an increase in the number of shares outstanding. This causes dilution and needs to be adjusted for.

The value of a warrant at maturity can be written as:

$$\text{Value at maturity} = \frac{1}{(1+q)} \max imum(\frac{V}{N} - EX, 0),$$

Where q = number of warrants issued per share outstanding
    N = number of shares outstanding
    EX = exercise price of the warrant
    V = value of the equity of the firm *after the issue* of the warrant

In effect, the warrant is worth 1/(1+q) times the value of a call option written on the stock of an alternate firm with the same equity V and outstanding shares N, but with no warrants. This would require calculating the value of the share price of this notional firm and also adjust the volatility (standard deviation) of its equity to reflect the balance sheet of the notional firm. Problem 1 of the worked examples shows the calculations involved.

Convertible Bonds: Convertible bonds resemble warrants because they are options to acquire common stock. The warrant and conversion options differ in that warrants are exercised by the payment of cash to the issuing firm, whereas holders of convertible securities exchange them for common stock on predetermined terms. The value of convertible bonds consists of the value of the bond as a bond and the value of the conversion feature, itself being evaluated as an option. Thus, the price of convertible securities has two lower bounds: the value as a security standing apart from the conversion feature and the value of the conversion feature itself. The conversion option is evaluated just as warrants are, making certain to adjust for cash dividends and potential dilution. The bonds are evaluated like any bond. Here are the terms commonly used with convertible bonds:

- *Conversion price*: the price at which the bond is convertible
- *Conversion ratio*: the number of shares received in exchange for each bond
- *Conversion value:* the value of the bond if converted = conversion ratio X share price.

Remember that the value of a convertible bond depends on the value of the bond portion and the value of the convertible (option) portion. The bond-value is simply the present value of the coupon payments and the face value. This establishes a floor. The other floor is the conversion value. Low firm value and low bond values go together.

Convertible securities come in different forms. These include complicated securities like a Liquid Yield Option Note (LYON), which is a zero coupon convertible bond, which is also callable and putable (meaning the bondholder can sell it back to the issuer at a specified price). In recent years, some issuers have issued convertible preferred or bonds, which are automatically converted (mandatory convertible).

Forced Conversion: Convertible bonds always carry the *call feature* that permits the issuer to call the bond at a specified price, and typically, a few years after bond issue. This feature enables the firms to force conversion by calling the bonds for redemption. Ideally, the firms should do this once the bond's conversion value exceeds the call price. Empirical evidence indicates that financial managers do not consistently follow the optimal rule. They appear to wait a while and it is not uncommon to find convertible bonds with conversion values far exceeding their call price.

The Difference Between Warrants and Convertibles: While warrants and convertibles share many similarities, they are also different in many ways. Here is a list.

- Warrants are usually issued privately; convertibles are usually issued publicly.
- Warrants are usually detachable and exercisable alone; when a convertible bond is exercised, both the bond and the option are given up.
- Warrants may be issued alone; convertible securities always consist of the security and the conversion option.
- Warrants are exercised for cash; convertible securities are not.
- The cash receipts from exercised warrants may be taxable; there are no unusual tax features with convertible securities.

Rationale for Issuing Warrants and Convertibles: Why do companies issue warrants and convertibles? You will hear reasons like: they lower interest costs or they allow a firm to issue stocks at a higher price. These do not make sense and assume inefficient markets and incorrect pricing of the securities. The real reasons could be more complex. Typically, convertibles and warrants are issued by smaller and more risky firms, who have trouble getting unsecured and subordinated debt at reasonable costs. The market, on account of asymmetric information, tends to overestimate the risk of these firms. By offering convertibles or warrants, the firm is giving a piece of the action to the investors and is thus able to lower its agency costs. These securities do a better job of assuring the investors that the management will not act against bondholders' interest. Since the lenders participate in any gains accruing to the shareholders from excess risk-taking or other actions not in the interests of the bondholders, lenders are less concerned about management "misbehavior."

WORKED EXAMPLES

1. The table below contains information about Mory Corp.'s recently issued subordinated bonds with detachable warrants.

a. Calculate the cost of the warrants.
b. Calculate the call option value without the dilution effects.
c. Calculate the call option value with the dilution effects. (Assume the alternative firm's standard deviation of stock price changes is 39 percent.)

Details of Warrants Issued by Mory Corp.

Item	Value
Amount of loan	$120,000,000
Debt value without warrants	$105,000,000
Number of shares outstanding (N)	12,000,000
Current stock price	$40.00
Value of firm before debt issue	$540,000,000
Existing loans	$60,000,000
Number of warrants issued/share outstanding (q)	0.10
Total number of warrants issued	1,200,000
Exercise price of warrants (EX)	$52.00
Years to expiration of warrants (t)	5
Annual standard deviation of stock price changes	0.36
Rate of interest	6.00%

SOLUTION

1. a. Cost of warrants = total amount of loan - value of loan without warrants
   = $120 million - $105 million = $15 million
   Cost per warrant = 15/1.2 = $12.50 per warrant

   b. Since we are not concerned about the dilution effect, we calculate the value of the option as if it were a regular call option on the stock.

   $$\sigma\sqrt{t} = 0.36\sqrt{5} = 0.8050, \quad PV(EX) = \frac{\$52}{(1.06)^5} = \$38.86$$

   Share price/PV(EX) = $40/$38.36 = 1.0294

   $d_1 = \log[P/PV(EX)]/\sigma\sqrt{t} + \sigma\sqrt{t}/2$
   $= \log 1.0294/0.8050 + 0.8050/2 = 0.4385$
   $d_2 = d_1 - \sigma\sqrt{t} = -0.3665$
   $N(d_1) = 0.6695; \quad N(d_2) = 0.3570$ (Values obtained using Excel spread-sheet.)

   Value of call option value = $N(d_1) \times P - N(d_2) \times PV(EX)$
   $= 0.6695 \times \$40 - 0.3570 \times \$38.86 = \$12.91$

276

c. To calculate the value of the warrant with the dilution effect, we use the value of the stock of the alternate firm where the stock price = V/N. The value of the warrant is 1/1+q times this option value.

Equity (V) of the alternate firm = original firm's total assets - value of loans
$$= \$660 \text{ million} - \$165 \text{ million} = \$495 \text{ million}$$

Current share of alternative firm = V/N
$$= \$495 \text{ million}/12 \text{ million shares}$$
$$= \$41.25 \text{ per share}$$

$\sigma\sqrt{t} = 0.39\sqrt{5} = 0.8721$

Share price/PV(EX) = $41.25/$38.86 = 1.0616

$d_1 = \log 1.0616/0.8721 + 0.8721/2 = 0.50465$
$d_2 = d_1 - \sigma\sqrt{t} = -0.3675$
$N(d_1) = 0.6931; N(d_2) = 0.3566$

Value of call option value = $N(d_1)$ X P – $N(d_2)$ X PV(EX)
$$= 0.6931 \text{ x } \$40 - 0.3566 \text{ x } \$38.86$$
$$= \$14.73$$

Dilution factor = 1/1+q = 1/1.1
Warrant value of original firm with dilution = [1/(1 + q)] x value of call on alternative firm
$$= (1/1.1) \text{ x } \$14.73$$
$$= \$13.39$$

2. Rhea Mare Corp. (RMC) issued a 5.5 percent convertible bond, which matures 25 years from now. The conversion price is $36, and the bonds are callable at 106.25. The market price of the common stock is $42 per share.

   a. What is the conversion ratio of the bonds?
   b. If the conversion ratio were 33.33, what would be the conversion price?
   c. At the current market price for common shares, what is the conversion value of the convertible? Explain your answer.
   d. If bonds of comparable risk to those of RMC were selling at a return of 10 percent, at what price would you expect the bond to be selling if it did not have the conversion feature? Assume interest is payable annually.
   e. Based on your answer in d, what part of the bond's total value is ascribable to the value of the bond alone and what part is ascribable to the conversion feature? Explain fully.
   f. Should the financial manager call the bonds? Why or why not?

SOLUTION

2. a. Conversion ratio = $\dfrac{\text{face value of convertible security}}{\text{conversion price}}$

    = $1,000/$36

    = 27.78 shares

b. Using the formula for the conversion ratio in (a) immediately above, the setup is:

    33.33 = $1,000/conversion price

    Conversion price = $1,000/33.33

    = $30

c. Conversion value of the convertible:

    Security = conversion ratio X market price of common shares

    = 27.78 shares X $42 per share

    = $1,166.76

    In other words, one convertible bond may be exchanged for $1,166.76 worth of common stock and must be worth at least this value.

d. Solve for the bond value using calculator:
    N = 25, I = 10, PV =solve, PMT = $55, FV = $1,000; PV = $591.53

e. Conversion value of bond $1,166.76
    Value of bond alone   591.53
    Value of conversion feature $ 575.23

f. Yes, because the conversion value exceeds the call price.

SUMMARY

Warrants and convertibles are a class of hybrid securities issued by firms. Warrants are often sold with a package of other securities, typically bonds. Both are call options and can be valued using the Black-Scholes model after making adjustments for the fact that, on exercise, they cause dilution by increasing the number of shares of the firm. The types of the hybrid securities have proliferated into a menagerie of convertibles or option-type securities with names like LYON. The motives for issuing convertibles and warrants can be traced to information asymmetry between the firm's management and the lenders. Many of the firms, which issue these types of securities are either small, young companies or companies with relatively higher risk compared to firms able to issue unsecured straight bonds. Convertibles and warrants allow the lenders to participate in the firm's future prospects without having to be equity holders. This type of arrangement protects the bondholders' interests better. Thus, they reduce the bondholder-shareholder conflict in an efficient way.

LIST OF TERMS

Bond value

Conversion price

Conversion ratio

Conversion value

Convertible bond

Detachable warrant

Fully Diluted

Liquid yield option note (LYON)

Mandatory Convertible

Non-detachable warrants

Warrant

EXERCISES

Fill-in Questions

1. A(n) _____ gives its owner the right to (buy, exchange) _____ stock for cash, whereas a convertible security gives its owner the right to (buy, exchange) _____ the bond for stock.

2. A(n) _____ is a zero coupon, convertible bond that is callable and putable.

3. A warrant, which is sold, originally with bonds but which may be resold apart from the bonds is called a(n) _____ warrant.

4. Benoit Corporation has a number of $1,000 convertible bonds outstanding, each of which is convertible to 40 shares of common stock. The (conversion ratio, conversion price) _____ is _____ dollars and the (conversion ratio, conversion price)_____ is _____ shares.

5. The value of a convertible bond depends on both its _____ and its _____.

6. A _____ is automatically converted into the firm's shares at the end of a certain date.

7. According to accounting guidelines, firms with a significant number of warrants outstanding have to report their earnings on a _____ basis.

Problems

1. The table below contains information about Brady Corp.'s recently issued bonds with detachable warrants.

   a. Calculate the cost of the warrants.
   b. Calculate the call option value without the dilution effects.

c. Calculate the call option value with the dilution effects. (Assume the alternative firm's standard deviation of stock price changes is 34 percent.)

Brady Corp. – Details of Warrants

Item	Value
Amount of loan	$30,000,000
Debt value without warrants	$25,000,000
Number of shares outstanding	3,000,000
Current stock price	$36.00
Value of firm before debt issue	$128,000,000
Existing loans	$20,000,000
Number of warrants issued per share outstanding	0.12
Total number of warrants issued	360,000
Exercise price of warrants	$42
Years to expiration of warrants	6
Annual standard deviation of stock price changes	0.32
Rate of interest	6 %

2. Right-O Corp. issued an 8 percent convertible bond, par value of $1,000 at par. The bonds mature in 21 years. The conversion price at the time of issue was $35 and is stepped up as follows: $40 - five years after issuance, $45 - ten years after issuance, and $50 - thereafter. The bonds are presently callable at 105, and the common stock's current price is $55 a share.

a. What is the bond's present conversion ratio?

b. What is the conversion ratio in each of the other periods?

c. At the current market price for common shares, what is the conversion value of the convertibles? Explain fully.

d. If the market price of the common shares declined to $25 a share and comparable bonds were selling to return 8 percent, what is the lowest price at which you would expect the bonds to sell?

e. If the market price of the common shares were $50 and comparable bonds were selling to return 11 percent, at what price would you expect the bonds to be selling if they did not contain the conversion feature? Assume interest is payable annually.

f. Based on your answer in part e, what part of the bond's minimum value is ascribable to the value of the bond alone and what part is ascribable to the conversion feature? Explain fully.

g. Is it financially smart to call in the bonds, given the conditions in part e above?

Essay Questions

1. Explain how you would use the Black-Scholes model to value a warrant.

2. Compare the major characteristics of a convertible bond with a bond possessing a detachable warrant.

3. It has been well stated that convertible bonds have a floor or lower limit to their price. What is this floor and how is it determined? Is there more than one floor? Is there also an upper bound? If so, what is it and how is it determined?

4. "The way I see it, financial managers should call in outstanding convertible bonds when their value reaches the call price. Yet, empirical evidence suggests that many financial managers don't do this. The managers are not acting smart!" Discuss.

5. Discuss the following statement: "Convertible bonds have lower interest costs and therefore they are better than straight bonds. Even when the bond is converted, the conversion comes at a premium compared to the current stock price. Under the circumstances, I do not see why more companies are not issuing convertibles."

ANSWERS TO EXERCISES

Fill-in Questions

1. Warrant; buy; exchange
2. Liquid yield option note
3. Detachable
4. Conversion price; 25; Conversion ratio; 40

5. Bond value; conversion value
6. Mandatory convertible
7. Fully diluted

Problems

1. a. Cost of warrants = $30 million - $25 million = $5 million
   Cost per warrant =%5 million/0.36 = $13.89 per warrant

   b. $\sigma\sqrt{t} = 0.32\sqrt{6} = 0.7838$
   $PV(EX) = \$42/(1.06)^6 = \$29.61$

   Share price/PV(EX) = $36/$29.61 = 1.2159

   $d_1 = \log 1.2159/0.7838 + 0.7838/2 = 0.6413$
   $d_2 = d_1 - \sigma\sqrt{t} = -0.1426$
   $N(d_1) = 0.7393$; $N(d_2) = 0.4433$

   Value of call option = $N(d_1) \times P - N(d_2) \times PV(EX)$
   $= 0.7393 \times \$36 - 0.4433 \times \$29.61 = \$13.49$

   c. Dilution factor = 1/(1 +q) = 1/1.12
   Current equity value V = $158 million - $45 million = $113 million
   Current share price of alternative firm = $113 million/3 million = $37.67 per share

$\sigma\sqrt{t} = 0.34\sqrt{6} = 0.8328$

Share price/PV(EX) = \$37.67/\$29.61 = 1.2723

$d_1 = \log 1.2723/0.8328 + 0.8328/2 = 0.7056$
$d_2 = d_1 - \sigma\sqrt{t} = -0.1273;$ $N(d_1) = 0.7598;$ $N(d_2) = 0.4494$

Value of call option = $N(d_1)$ x P – $N(d_2)$ x PV(EX)
                                    = 0.7598 x \$37.67 – 0.4494 x \$29.61
                                    = \$15.31

Warrant value of original firm with dilution = (1/1.12) X \$15.31 = \$13.67

2. a.   Conversion ratio = face value/conversion price
                                        = 1,000/40
                                        = 25

   b.   1,000/35 = 28.57
        1,000/40 = 25.00
        1,000/45 = 22.22
        1,000/50 = 20.00

   c.   Conversion value is \$55 X 25 = \$1,375

   d.   Conversion value is \$625, but the bond value of \$1,000. Therefore the bond will be selling at \$1,000.

   e.   Calculator valuation: N = 21, I = 11, PV = solve, PMT = \$80, FV = \$1,000. The bond value = PV = \$757.75.

   f.   \$1,375 - \$757.75 = \$617.25 is ascribable to the conversion feature.

   g.   Yes

24

Valuing Debt

INTRODUCTION

This chapter provides fundamental insights into the valuation of debt and explains why we see many different interest rates in the market. The five sections in the chapter describe the following:

  i) the relationship between nominal rates and real interest rates,
  ii) the term structure (or variation of interest for different maturities) of interest rates,
  iii) the concept of duration and how it affects the bond values when interest rates change,
  iv) the theories of term structure, and
  v) the risk structure and debt value.

The chapter is important and gives you answers to some vexing questions you would have on interest rates, debt values and their changes from time to time. Financial managers have to deal with the valuation of debt at some point or other and it is necessary that they understand the basic theoretical principles, which explain the relationship among the term structure, risk structure, and debt values.

The chapter begins with Irving Fisher's classical theory of interest. Fisher postulated that real rates of return are determined by the equilibration of the supply of and demand for real capital and are reasonably constant over time, and therefore, changes in nominal rates essentially reflect changes in inflation expectations. This insight has been fundamental to our understanding of changes in interest rates over time. While economists debate the validity of the strict version of Fisher's theory, it appears that the broad relationship among inflation, nominal interest rates, and real interest rates support Fisher's ideas.

KEY CONCEPTS IN THE CHAPTER

Real and Nominal Interest Rates: Most debt securities promise a fixed *nominal* interest rate. Fisher postulated that real rates are not affected by changes in inflation. According to Fisher, the relationship between real interest rates and nominal or money rates of interest rate is given by:

$$1 + r_{money} = (1 + r_{real})(1 + i)$$

From this we can derive the approximate relationship:
real rate = money (nominal) rate - inflation rate.

It follows that a change in the expected inflation rate will cause the same change in the money rate or *nominal interest rate*. Critics of Fisher's theory argue that real rates are affected by inflation rates. Historically, real rates have changed over time. Unfortunately, real rates are not observable. What is observed is the difference between nominal rates and inflation. Again, part of the problem is Fisher's theory is in terms of expected inflation, which cannot be observed. Empirical studies indicate that inflation expectations have been the principal causes of nominal interest rate changes. Fisher's theory appears to hold in broad approximation. Remember that the real rate is an expected rate. The actual realized real rates may be different from what you expected to get when you bought a T-bill or some other investment. Also, the real rates have varied over time.

Spot Rates, Term Structure, and Yield to Maturity: The spot rate is the rate of interest obtainable on a bond at the present, or spot, time period. The series of spot rates of different maturities results in a term structure of interest rates; typically, the term structure is upward sloping, with long-term rates higher than short-term rates. The term structure is a series of spot rates $r_1, r_2, \ldots r_i, \ldots$ for different maturities. If $C_1, C_2, \ldots C_i$ are the cash flows received from a bond investment, the value of the bond is:

$$PV = \frac{C_1}{(1+r_1)} + \frac{C_2}{(1+r_2)^2} + \ldots \frac{C_i}{(1+r_i)^i} + \ldots ,$$

where r_i is the spot rate for the "ith" year.

This is how each bond is valued in the market. However, we use the yield to maturity as a summary measure. The PV of a bond can be expressed by the following equation:

$$PV = \frac{C_1}{(1+y)} + \frac{C_2}{(1+y)^2} + \ldots \frac{C_i}{(1+y)^i} + \ldots$$

where y = yield to maturity. The yield to maturity is an internal rate of return and unambiguous and easy to calculate. The problems with yield to maturity include:

- Assumes that yield to maturity does not change.
- Assumes a constant reinvestment rate of return.
- Yield to maturity does not determine price; it is vice versa.

The term structure of government bonds can be estimated using a series of zero coupon "strips". This is the yield curve you see in the Wall Street Journal every day. This provides the spot rates for different maturities.

Interest Rates, Bond Prices, Duration and Volatility: When interest rates change the prices of long-term bonds vary more than short-term bonds. In other words, long-term bonds are more sensitive to interest rate changes than the short-term bonds. *Duration* and *volatility* are two useful measures, which enable us to formalize this relationship. Duration is the average time for the total cash flow to be realized from an asset, such as a bond. It is actually a weighted average,

284

where the date to each cash flow is weighted by the ratio of its present value to the total value of the bond. The other statistic, called volatility, is easily obtained from duration. In fact, it is just duration discounted by one time period. Volatility measures the sensitivity of the asset price (in percent) to a (unit) change in its yield. Both of these measures are extremely important for understanding the riskiness of bonds and portfolios containing bonds.

$$\text{Duration} = \frac{1 \times PV(C_1)}{V} + \frac{2 \times PV(C_2)}{V} + \ldots + \frac{i \times PV(C_i)}{V} + \ldots$$

where V is the total value of the bond.

$$\text{Volatility (percent)} = \frac{\text{Duration}}{1 + \text{yield}}$$

<u>Managing Interest Rate Risk:</u> Volatility and duration are useful practical measures, which help in managing interest rate risk. The risk management techniques use the properties of duration and try to match the duration of their asset and liability portfolios. Note that the changes in bond prices are given by the following relationship:

Change in bond price = Volatility x change in interest rates

The last relationship is often called the *one-factor model* of bond returns and is very useful in understanding changes in bond values. It should be mentioned that the relationship holds across different maturities only when the yield curve makes parallel shift. That is, interest rate changes are same at all maturities. In practice, changes in short-term interest rates and long-term rates are not always same and therefore the one-factor model may explain only part of the changes in bond values.

Explaining the Term Structure: The term structure is not constant. While most of the times, the yield curve is up-ward sloping, occasionally; you find short-term rates to be higher than long-term rates. The term structure shows not only the spot rates for different maturities (r_1, r_2, r_3,...), it also implies one-period rates of returns or *forward* interest rates for different points in time. For example, if r_1 and r_2 are the spot rates for 1-year and 2-year maturity, then the implied forward rate for year 2, $f_2 = (1 + r_2)^2/(1 + r_1) - 1$. Theories of term structure attempt to explain the term structure by defining the relationship between the forward rate and the expected future spot rate. The three primary theories are the *expectations* theory, the *liquidity preference* theory, and the *inflation premium* theory.

The expectations theory says that the forward rate must equal expected future spot rate. In other words, an investor interested in a two-year investment can get the same return investing either in a two-year bond or a one-year debt now and followed by another one-year debt next year. Expectations theory suggests that an upward sloping yield curve is the result of expected higher interest rates in the future. Empirical support for the expectations theory is limited and the historic returns on long-term Treasury bonds have been consistently higher than the returns on short-term T-bills. Expectations theory implies risk neutral investors, who would treat short-term and long-term investments same. It appears, though, that investors want higher returns for holding long-term bonds.

The liquidity preference theory suggests that investors would want a liquidity premium for holding long-term debt, as they consider long-term bonds more risky. This premium is the difference between forward rates and expected future spot rates. The liquidity premium theory would suggest a generally upward sloping yield curve, though one can explain a downward sloping term structure as being caused by an expected fall in future spot rates.

The presence of inflation adds extra uncertainty about the real returns from long-term bonds and thus makes long-term bonds more risky compared to short-term investments. Thus, if investors generally expect inflation, it is likely that they would demand an inflation premium for investing in long-term bonds.

Note that none of these explanations is totally satisfactory. Term structure analysis is static; it catches a slice of time and fixes interest rates of like kind and quality bonds. Bond traders are interested in changes in bond prices. Recent theories and analyses incorporate interest rate changes and bond returns. One system shows financial managers how to replicate one bond by using two others, given that interest rates may change.

Default Risk: Interest rates differ not only across maturities, but also across borrowers. Bonds have market-related risks and firm-specific default risks. When the value of bonds and the term structure of interest rates are determined, default risk must also be considered. The threat of default adds uncertainty to the payments expected from the bond investment. The *expected cash flow* from a risky bond is less than the *promised cash flow* and the *expected yield* will be less than the *promised yield*. In practical terms, investors would demand higher returns on a bond that has the risk of default. Bond ratings attempt to measure the risk of default.

Bond Ratings and Junk Bonds: Bond ratings are assigned by the rating agencies based on their analysis and judgment of the firm's financial and business prospects and probable default. Moody's and Standard and Poor are the well-known rating agencies for long-term bonds. The ratings range from the highest rated AAA (Aaa by Moody's) to the lowly C for bonds with high probability of default. Bond ratings generally reflect the probability of default quite well and can be seen as a proxy for the default risk.

Junk bonds are bonds with ratings less than investment grade (BBB by Standard and Poor or Baa by Moody's). Before the eighties, most of the junk bonds were the fallen angels or investment grade bonds, which slipped in rating because of the issuers' financial distress. Since the 1980s there is a wider acceptance of bond issues with ratings lower than investment grade and this has helped many young, growing and risky companies raise debt capital to finance their growth or acquisitions. The default rate on junk bonds have varied from a low of 2 percent in boom times to a high of 10 percent during the early nineties' recession. It appears that junk bonds are here to

286

stay and serve many companies, which otherwise would not have been able to raise debt at reasonable rates in the capital market.

Debt as Options: When option pricing is extended to debt analysis, corporate bonds become the equivalent to risk-free lending combined with giving stockholders a put option on the firm's assets. Thus, the value of a bond consists of the value of a risk-free debt less the value of the put option. The maturity for the option equals the maturity of the bond and the exercise price equals the promised payment to the lenders. The value of the put equals the value of the limited liability of stockholder's right to walk away from the firm's debt in exchange for handing over the firm's assets to creditors. We have discussed this in chapter 20. The relationship can be written as:

Bond value = bond value with no chance of default - value of put

Generally, the value of the put option increases (and the bond value decreases) with increased leverage and maturity. However, for firms already in financial distress the value of the option may decrease (and the bond value increase) as the maturity of debt increases. This can happen if the longer term improves the probability of the firm's recovery from financial distress.

Government Guaranteed Debt: Government loan guarantee eliminates the risk of default and essentially make the debt risk-free. As these guarantees often do not involve any cash subsidies, it is naively assumed that this is cost free for the taxpayers. However, the loan guarantee is the same put option on the firm's assets discussed above. In effect the government is giving the put option back to the lenders, thus making the debt default risk-free.

WORKED EXAMPLES

1. Find the real rate of interest, given that the nominal rate is 7 percent and the inflation rate is 3 percent.

SOLUTION

The solution is obtained by using the formula:

$$1 + r_{money} = (1 + r_{real})(1 + i)$$

where

r_{money} = nominal or money rate of interest
r_{real} = real rate of interest
i = inflation rate

Substituting in the equation, we obtain: $1 + 0.07 = (1 + r_{real})(1 + 0.03)$

We then solve for r_{real}:

$$1 + r_{real} = (1 + r_{money})/(1 + i) = 1.07/1.03 = 1.0388$$
$$r_{real} = 0.0388 = 3.88 \text{ percent}$$

One can also use the approximate relationship: Nominal rate = real rate + inflation rate. This would give a value for real rate of: 7% - 3% = 4%.

2. Calculate the yield to maturity on a 10-year bond carrying a coupon rate of 7 percent. Assume par value of $1,000, that the interest is payable annually and the bond is selling at 97.

SOLUTION
Here is the BA-II Plus calculator solution:

N = Number of coupons = 10, I = yield to maturity = solve, PV = price of the bond = -$970, PMT = coupon payments = $70, FV = principal paid at maturity = $1,000, I = yield to maturity = 7.44%

3. It is 2002 and you notice that the yields to maturity of your company's two bonds, 5s of 2006 and 9s of 2006, are selling at 87.44 and 100.71 respectively, which results in yields to maturity of 8.87 and 8.78 percent. Your financial manager is puzzled as to why two bonds of the same quality and same maturity do not have the same yield to maturity. What reasonable answer will you give?

SOLUTION

The answer lies in estimating the spot rates for each of the remaining years and taking the present value of the payments to be received. This is done in the table below using a set of assumed spot rates. Each year's coupon payments and the principal payments are discounted using the respective spot rates, not the yield to maturity. It clearly shows that the two bonds are valued correctly by the market. The yield to maturity is different because the two bonds have different cash flow patterns. The lower coupon bond has more of its cash flows coming later. Remember that the market uses spot rates for different periods (not the yield to maturity) to discount the cash flows for different years. Yield to maturity is a measure of convenience used by us – not the one that actually gets into the discounted cash flow for the bonds.

Present-Value Calculations

			5s of 2006		9s of 2006
Period t	Interest rate r_t	C_t	PV at r_t	C_t	PV at r_t
1	0.06	$ 50	$ 47.17	$ 90	$ 84.91
2	0.07	50	43.67	90	78.61
3	0.08	50	39.69	90	71.44
4	0.09	1050	743.85	1090	772.18
			$874.38		$1,007.14

4. Calculate the duration of 8 and 14 percent, 5-year Treasury bonds whose yields are 7.85 percent.

SOLUTION

Duration = $[1 \times PV(C_1)/V] + [2 \times PV(C_2)/V] + [3 \times PV(C_3)/V] + \ldots\ldots$

Yield = 7.85%, Coupon = 8.00%

Year	C_t	$PV(C_1)$ at 7.85%	Proportion of Total Value $[PV(C_t/V]$	Proportion of Value x Time
1	80	74.18	0.0737	0.0737
2	80	68.78	0.0684	0.1368
3	80	63.77	0.0634	0.1902
4	80	59.13	0.0588	0.2352
5	1,080	740.16	0.7357	3.6785
Totals	1,400	1,006.02	1.00	4.3144

Yield 7.85%, Coupon 14.00%

Year	C_t	$PV(C_t)$ at 7.85%	Proportion of Total Value $[PV(C_t)/V]$	Proportion of Value X Time
1	140	129.81	0.1041	0.1041
2	140	120.36	0.0966	0.1932
3	140	111.60	0.0895	0.2685
4	140	103.48	0.0830	0.3320
5	1,140	781.27	0.6268	3.1340
Totals	1,700	1,246.52	1.00	4.0318

5. What is the impact of a 0.5 percentage point increase and decrease in interest rates on the present value of each of the two bonds in problem 4? Compute their volatilities and compare with what you would have estimated from their duration.

SOLUTION

The yields are now 7.35 percent or 8.35 percent. The results of the computations are as follows:

	8% Bonds		14% Bonds	
	New Price	% Change	New Price	% Change
Yield falls to 7.35	1,026.40	2.026	1,270.13	1.894
Yield rises to 8.35	986.15	-1.975	1,223.51	-1.846
Difference	40.25	4.001	46.62	3.740

The percentage change is, for example, the present value of the 8 percent bond yielding 7.35 percent divided by the present value of the 8 percent bond yielding 7.85 percent; that is, percentage change $[(\$1026.40/\$1006.02) - 1] \times 100 = 2.03$ percent.

The volatility results for the two bonds are as follows:

289

Bond	Duration	Volatility (from duration)	Volatility (direct)
8 percent	4.3144	4.001	3.999
14 percent	4.0317	3.740	3.739

6. Determine the better financial strategy when confronted with a 2-year spot rate of 9 percent, a 1-year spot rate of 8 percent, and an expected spot rate on 1-year bonds 1 year from now of 10 percent. Assume you do not need your money for 2 years and are not bothered by risk.

SOLUTION

To find the answer, you want to know the expected return of each strategy. The setup is:

$$\$1,000(1 + r_1)[1 + E(_1r_2)] \text{ compared with } \$1,000(1 + r_2)^2$$

where:

r_1 = 1-year spot rate
$E(_1r_2)$ = expected spot rate on 1-year bonds 1 year from now
r_2 = 2-year spot rate

Substituting the values above, we obtain:

$$\$1,000(1 + 0.08)(1 + 0.10) \quad \text{compared with} \quad \$1,000(1 + 0.09)^2$$
$$\$1,000(1.08)(1.10) \quad \text{compared with} \quad \$1,000(1.09)^2$$
$$\$1,000(1.188) \text{compared with} \quad \$1,000(1.1881)$$
$$\$1,188 \text{compared with} \$1,188.10$$

For all practical purposes, there is no difference between the two outcomes; therefore, you would be indifferent about this investment.

If you wish to lock in the final outcome of $1,188, say, because of your queasiness about the expected 1-year spot rate, choose the 9 percent, 2-year spot rate. You should also note that the implied forward rate is:
$$(1 + r_2)^2 = (1+r_1)(1 + f_2)$$

where f_2 is the implied forward rate. Substituting the above values, we obtain:

$$(1 +0.09)_2 = (1 + 0.08)(1 + f_2)$$
$$(1.09)_2 = (1.08)(1 + f_2)$$
$$1.1881 = 1.08(1 + f_2)$$
$$1 + f_2 = 1.1881/1.08 = 1.1000$$
$$f_2 = 0.1000 = 10.00 \text{ percent}$$

As expected, the implicit forward rate is almost exactly equal to the expected future spot rate, again indicating a condition of relative indifference.

SUMMARY

This chapter explores the full complexities of valuing debt. The chapter attempts to answer fundamental questions on interest rates, term structure, and risk structure. It starts with the basic relationship between inflation and nominal interest rates. Irving Fisher's theory still forms the basis for the widely accepted rule of thumb:

$$\text{Real interest rate} = \text{Nominal interest rate} - \text{inflation.}$$

Keep in mind that only the nominal rate is observed and the other two are expectations. Fisher's theory should be seen as a broad approximation.

The three term structure theories are explored. The expectations theory ignores the possibility of risk and lacks convincing empirical support. There appears to be a risk premium in the term structure and the forward interest rates are, on average, higher than future spot rates. This risk premium can be on account of inflation or general risk based on future uncertainty. New theories are taking a different approach and would probably gain currency as more work is done.

Bond values reflect present values of cash flows produced discounted by the series of spot rates over the bond's maturity. For convenience, the yield to maturity is used as a summary measure. It is important to understand that the yield to maturity is derived from the price of the bond and the other way around. Duration and volatility are useful measures of the sensitivity of a bond's value to changes in interest rates.

Lastly, the risk structure of bonds is explored. Bond ratings capture the default risk of corporate bonds fairly well. A risky bond can be seen as the combination of a risk-free bond less the value of a put given to the shareholders. Thus, the value of a government guarantee to a private corporation is the value of this put.

LIST OF TERMS

Bond ratings	Money rate of interest
Duration	Nominal interest rate
Expectations theory	Promised yield
Forward rate	Real interest rate
Inflation premium	Spot rate
Junk bonds	Strips
Liquidity preference theory	Term structure of interest rates
Liquidity premium	Yield to maturity

EXERCISES

Fill-in Questions

1. _____ include a premium for anticipated inflation.

2. The nominal rate of interest must equal the _____ plus the _____.

3. If the money (nominal) rate of interest is 10 percent and the anticipated inflation rate is 10 percent, the real rate of interest is _____.

4. Under Fisher's scheme of interest rates, if the forecasted inflation rate is 5 percent and the real interest rate is 3 percent, the nominal interest rate is _____.

5. The real rate of interest is equal to the _____ minus the _____.

6. Any interest rate, which is fixed today, is called the _____.

7. The term structure of interest rates consists of a series of _____ on bonds of comparable risk.

8. A bond's internal rate of return is called _____.

9. When government bonds are repackaged into mini-bonds, each of which makes only one payment; they are known as _____.

10. _____ measures the average time that the total cash flow from an asset is realized over the life of that asset.

11. _____ measures the percentage change in the price of a bond or other asset corresponding to a unit change in its yield.

12. The _____ rate between two dates is the interest rate we can lock into between buying them today and by selling discount bonds for those two dates.

13. The _____ of the term structure of interest rates says the only reason for an upward-sloping term structure is that investors expect future spot rates to be higher than current spot rates.

14. The difference between forward rates and expected future spot rates is called _____.

15. The _____ theory of term structure of interest rates takes into account risk, whereas the explanation does not.

16. The _____ theory of the term structure of interest rates assumes that the risk from holding bonds comes only from uncertainty about expected inflation rates.

17. When one assumes that bonds create options, the bond value is equal to the value of the bond, assuming no chance of default, minus _____ .

18. A loan guarantee may be valued as a(n) _____ on the firm's assets.

19. High-yield bonds are also called _____ bonds and are usually rated at _____ or lower.

20. The _____ on junk bonds is typically much higher than the _____ .

Problems

1. Find the real interest rate, given that the nominal rate is 9 percent and the inflation rate is 5 percent.

2. If the money rate of interest is 9.3 percent and the real rate is expected to be 5 percent, what is the implied inflation rate? How realistic is it to assume that the real rate will be 5 percent?

3. How different is your inflation estimate in Problem 2 if you use the approximate formula, subtracting one rate from the other?

4. Calculate the yield to maturity on a 15-year bond carrying a coupon rate of 9 percent. Assume that the interest is payable annually and the bond is selling at 92.

5. As the financial manager of Fab Corp. you estimate the following spot interest rates on Treasury securities: $r_1 = 4.00$, $r_2 = 5.00$, $r_3 = 5.60$, $r_4 = 7.20$, $r_5 = 6.50$. Your company's bonds have an 11 percent coupon rate, interest is payable annually, and they mature in exactly 5 years.

    a. Assuming the bond to be risk-free, estimate the present value of the bond?
    b. Calculate the present values of the following Treasury issues: (1) 5 percent, 3-year bond; (2) 8 percent, 3-year bond; and (3) 6 percent, 5-year bond.
    c. Determine the yield to maturity of each of the bonds.
    d. Explain the differences between the yields to maturity you observe.

6. Calculate the duration and volatilities of 9 and 13 percent; 5-year Treasury bonds whose yields are 8.00 percent.

7. Find the impact of a 0.5 percentage point increase and decrease in interest rates on the present value of each of the two bonds in problem 6. Use this to compute their volatilities and compare with your answer from problem 6.

8. Please refer to problem 5. You know that Fab Corp debt is risky and the following default premiums are considered reasonable: 0.2 percent for year 1 and year 2, and 0.4 percent for years 3, 4 and 5. Estimate the present value of the bond and the yield to maturity.

Essay Questions

1. Explain the term structure of interest rates and the theories that attempt to explain the term structure.

2. How are nominal rates of interest adjusted for the effects of inflation? Explain fully, using whatever equations you feel are necessary.

3. Explain the relationship between the price of a bond and the yield to maturity. Does the yield determine the price or is it the other way around? What really determines the price of a bond in the market?

4. Why are there bond ratings, and what influence do you think they have on the value of bonds?

5. Government guarantees do not cost the taxpayer anything as they are rarely invoked. Discuss.

ANSWERS TO EXERCISES

Fill-in Questions

1. Nominal interest rates
2. Real rate; inflation premium
3. Zero
4. 8 % (approximate), 8.15 % (exact)
5. Nominal rate on Treasury bills; expected inflation rate
6. Spot rate
7. Spot rates
8. Yield to maturity
9. Strip
10. Duration

11. Volatility
12. Forward
13. Expectations theory
14. Liquidity premium
15. Liquidity preference
16. Inflation premium
17. Value of a put
18. Put option
19. Junk; BB
20. Promised yield; expected yield

Problems

1. $1 + r_{real} = (1 + r_n)/(1 + i) = 1.09/1.05$, $r_{real} = 3.81$ percent

2. $1 + I = (1 + r_n/(1 + r_{real}) = 1.093/1.05$; $I = 4.10$

Assumption of a real rate of 5 percent is not very realistic, because it is well above the historical (1926-1994) arithmetic average of 0.6 percent.

3. $i = r_n - r_{real} = 9.3$ percent - 5.0 percent = 4.30 percent; 20 basis points different from 2 above.

4. 10.00 percent

5. a.

PERIOD	INTEREST RATE	CASH FLOW	PRESENT VALUE
1	4.00	110	105.77
2	5.00	110	99.77
3	5.60	110	93.41
4	7.20	110	83.29
5	6.50	1,110	810.17
			1,192.41

b.

	PERIOD	INTEREST RATE	CASH FLOW	PRESENT VALUE
(1)	1	4.00	50	48.08
	2	5.00	50	45.35
	3	5.60	1,050	891.66
				985.09
(2)	1	4.00	80	76.92
	2	5.00	80	72.56
	3	5.60	1,080	917.13
				1,066.61
(3)	1	4.00	60	57.69
	2	5.00	60	54.42
	3	5.60	60	50.95
	4	7.20	60	45.43
	5	6.50	1,060	773.67
				982.16

c. Using the values the different bonds above the yield to maturity can be calculated as below:

Fab Corp Bond	6.38 %
T-Bond 1	5.55 %
T-Bond 2	5.53 %
T-Bond 3	6.43 %

d. The yields to maturity are different because of the differences in coupon rates and the timing of cash flows for the different bonds.

6.

Yield = 8.00%, Coupon = 9.00%

Year	C_t	PV(C_t) at 8.00%	Proportion of Total Value [PV(C_t)/V]	Proportion of Value x Time
1	90	83.33	0.0801	0.0801
2	90	77.16	0.0742	0.1484
3	90	71.44	0.0687	0.2061
4	90	66.15	0.0636	0.2544
5	1,090	741.84	0.7134	3.5670
Totals	1,450	1,039.92	1.00	4.2560

Yield = 8.00%, Coupon = 13.00%

Year	Ct	PV(C_t) at 8.00%	Proportion of Total Value [PV(C_t)/V]	Proportion of Value x Time
1	130	120.37	0.1003	0.1003
2	130	111.45	0.0929	0.1858
3	130	103.20	0.0860	0.2581
4	130	95.55	0.0797	0.3186
5	1,130	760.06	0.6411	3.2054
Totals	1,650	1,190.63	1.00	4.0682

Discounting by their yields, we find that the volatilities of the two bonds are:

9.00% bond: 3.941, 13% bond: 3.767.

7. The yields are now 7.50 or 8.50 percent. We obtain:

	9% Bonds		13% Bonds	
	New Price	% Change	New Price	% Change
Yield falls to 7.50	1,060.69	1.997	1,222.51	2.678
Yield rises to 8.50	1,019.70	-1.944	1,177.33	-1.117
Difference	40.99	3.941	45.18	3.767

The percentage change is, for example, the present value of the 9 percent bond yielding 7.50 percent divided by the present value of the 9 percent bond yielding 8.00 percent; that is, percentage change = (($1060.69/$1039.92) - 1] X 100 = 2.00 percent.

The volatility results for the two bonds are as follows:

Bond	Volatility (direct)	Volatility (from problem 5)
9 percent	3.941	3.941
13 percent	3.767	3.767

8. The computations are given below

PERIOD	INTEREST RATE	CASH FLOW	PRESENT VALUE
1	4.20	110	105.66
2	5.20	110	99.39
3	6.00	110	92.36
4	7.60	110	82.06
5	6.90	1,110	795.12
			1,174.50

Yield to maturity: Solve for I, given -
N = 5, PV = -$1,174.50, PMT = $110, FV = $1,000; I = SOLVE = Yield = 6.77 %

25

The Many Different Kinds of Debt

INTRODUCTION

This chapter describes the many different types of debt securities available for corporations and other borrowers. The number and variety of debt instruments, which are used in global finance today, are amazing. One might wonder, why so many different forms? The answer lies in the fact that selling securities to raise money is essentially a marketing problem and investment bankers and corporations try to appeal to potential lenders in many different ways; just like an auto-manufacturer offers so many different models with different market segments in mind.

Debt is broadly differentiated as public issue bonds, private debt, asset-backed securities, and project financing. All are promissory notes, although each has characteristics peculiar to it. The bond contract contains the specific terms, called covenants; to which borrowers and lenders agree. Bonds contain such features as being fully registered, unsecured, subordinated, mortgage, collateral trust, a variety of repayment provisions, and restrictive provisions. Debt is either sold publicly or placed privately. Privately sold debt is less costly to issue, contains nonstandard features, and imposes more restrictive terms on the borrower. Debt securities can be issued within one's own country or overseas and in many different currencies. Financial innovation is alive and well in debt markets with corporations coming up with new types of debt all the time.

The chapter also describes the typical provisions and covenants seen in debt contracts and the rationale for these. Financial managers should have the general awareness and knowledge of the common provisions contained in debt contracts and understand the need for the same. The manager's familiarity will help her understand why a certain kind of debt might be of better value for the company in a certain situation. Here are a few points to keep in mind:

- Each financial manager should know the type of debt and its covenants that are best for him or her or the company. There is no "one size fits all" approach in financing.

- Be aware of the major distinctions between debt sold to the public and privately placed debt. The former contract is more complex and the characteristics and formats are more standardized. However, the restrictive covenants of publicly sold debt are less severe than privately placed debt. Issue costs for the former is higher, but the interest rate may be somewhat less.

The Appendix to the chapter provides a description of the bankruptcy procedures and the different options available to firms in financial distress. The specific option chosen by the distressed firm will depend on the extent of distress and the future prospects.

KEY CONCEPTS IN THE CHAPTER

The chapter is descriptive and explains the many terms and phrases commonly used in global bond markets. We summarize the main points of the different sections.

Domestic Bonds, Foreign Bonds, and Eurobonds: U.S. firms may borrow either domestically or in foreign bond markets. The international market for long-term debt, typically debt sold in many different countries, is called the Eurobond market. Among some of the nuances that concern financial managers is the currency in which the principal or interest will be paid and local security markets regulation (or lack thereof).

The Eurobond market started as an innovation to get around government regulations and is technically defined as bonds in a currency sold outside its "home" jurisdiction (e. g. Japanese Yen outside Japan). Today, this market has broadened and expanded with major currencies for borrowing being the U.S. dollar, the British pound, the Euro, and the Japanese yen and the bonds are sold in different countries at the same time. Be careful not to confuse a Euro bond (one denominated in Euro) with a Eurobond (can be in any currency).

The Bond Contract: All bonds are promissory notes or "IOUs." All publicly issued bonds are covered by bond indentures, which are included in the registration statement and whose main provisions are contained in the prospectuses. Foreign issuers of bonds (or stocks) are not required to disclose nearly as much information as U.S. publicly offered ones.

Bond prices are quoted as a percentage of their face value. Sometimes they are sold at a discount from their face value. Most often interest payments, called coupons, are fixed for the life of the bond, although recently, more and more floating-rate notes have been issued. Bonds may or may not be registered.

The details of the contract terms are found in the *indenture* or *trust deed*, a copy of which is in the registration statement and a condensed version of which is in the prospectus. Here is a brief summary of some of the more common terms.

Accrued interest is the interest accrued between the last coupon date and the date of sale of a bond. The buyer of the bond will pay this to the seller. The price, excluding the accrued interest, is the *clean price*.

Underwriting fee is the difference between the offering price to the public and the price to underwriters. Most bonds are underwritten. Underwriters provide the service of distributing the bonds and advice the firm on other matters related to the bond issue.

Coupon payments are the interest payments made usually semiannually in the U.S. Eurobonds and bonds issued in continental Europe pay interest annually.

Bearer securities are bonds (or other securities), which are not registered, and possession of the certificate is the evidence of ownership. Almost all bonds in the U.S. are registered, but many Eurobonds and bonds in some foreign countries are issued in the bearer form.

Security and Seniority: The significance of the legal security and seniority of bonds depends largely on the extent to which assets and earnings are available to meet the legal obligations of semiannual interest payments as well as the repayment of principal when due. *Debenture* bonds are unsecured general credit of the company and have no legal security other than the general bill-paying ability of the company. *Secured debt*, by contrast, has a specific claim on specific assets and is often called m*ortgage* bonds. *Collateral trust* bonds have a claim on other securities. *Equipment trust certificates* are used to finance railroad rolling stock, trucks, ships, and aircraft. The ownership of the equipment remains with a *trustee*; the company makes an initial down payment and the balance is paid through a series of trust certificates. Ownership is transferred to the company only after the last certificate has been paid off. The repayment of the principal claims of some debt holders may be *subordinated* to those of other debt holders.

Asset-backed Securities: These are securities backed by cash flows from a group of assets. Typical examples of assets packaged include: home mortgages, car payments, credit card payments, etc. Companies combine a group of assets and sell the cash flows from these assets to a separate company and this company sells *mortgage pass through certificates*. The mortgage payments are passed on to the security holders. Often, companies issue a series of this type of securities called *collateralized mortgage obligations* (CMOs).

Repayment Provisions: Some of the key repayment provisions included in typical bond contracts are briefly summarized below:

Sinking fund requires issuers to repay on a regular basis some of the principal of the debt before maturity. Payment may be in cash, which would be used to retire bonds called by lottery. Alternately, the firm may buy back the required number of bonds in the market and retire them. The latter option, if provided for in the bond indenture, is a valuable option for the firm. Sinking fund requirements may be mandatory, optional, or both. Sinking fund provisions may mean a test of firm solvency, unless the firm is allowed to purchase them in the open market. This would be like lowering the bar progressively, as the bonds of a company in financial distress will be selling at a discount.

Call provision allows the borrower to call in or retire its bonds, invariably at a premium, before they mature. The option generally starts a few years after the issue of the bond. This is a valuable option because when it is invoked under the proper conditions--when the market price equals the call--it tends to minimize the value of the bonds, which is equivalent to saying that it tends to maximize the value of the firm's stock.

Restrictive Covenants: Because the company has the valuable option to default on its bonds, restrictive bond provisions are the order of the day. Maintaining an adequate ratio of assets to debt, minimum working capital requirements, ensuring that all subsequent debt will be

301

subordinated to existing debt, incorporating a negative pledge clause, restricting the amount of cash dividends paid, and requiring a minimum level of net worth are typical restrictive provisions, all of which are intended to enhance the security of bondholders. The leveraged buy-outs (LBOs) of the 1980s ushered in an era in which many restrictive covenants--especially the prohibition on the use of debt of equal or senior claim to that already outstanding and the easing of dividend restrictions--were forgone in exchange for higher than normal yields. Some common covenants seen in most bonds include the following:

- *Negative pledge clause* undertakes not to give greater security to other parties. For example, the company is not permitted to have any lien without equally securing the debt securities.
- *Restrictions* on debt issues and dividend payments unless certain conditions are satisfied.
- *Cross-default clause* will make default on one issue an act of default on all issues.
- *Affirmative covenants* require the company to do certain things to protect lenders. These range from the innocuous providing of copies of accounts to agreeing to maintain particular levels of working capital or net worth.

Project Finance: Project finance involves loans that finance particular projects through a parent company or one of its major subsidiaries. Project loans rely on the project itself for the repayment of principal and the payment of interest. Because that may not be sufficient security for lenders, tangible property, production payments, completion guarantees, and recourse to stockholders are commonly incorporated into the lending agreement. This type of financing is typically used for joint ventures, such as electric power companies, in which the project's outputs are split among the participants. Project finance deals typically involve large projects, which are physically isolated from the parent and provide tangible security for the lender. The main benefits of project finance are the sharing of risk with parties who are in the best position to share specific kinds of risk.

Innovations in the Bond Market: Bond market innovations keep flowing at an amazing pace. Some of them succeed and others fail. Many of the innovations appeal to specific clientele with specific needs. Think of these as creation of new products designed to satisfy the special needs and demand by lenders and borrowers. Investment banks turn a profit by matching the special needs of the borrowers and lenders. For example, the regulation of the Japanese insurance industry created special types of yen bonds. On the other side of these bonds were probably European investors investing in Japan, but wanting to limit their risk. When the innovation survives, it is usually because of economies of scale, widened investor choices, and changes that accommodate changing perceptions of investor risk.

Bankruptcy Procedures (Appendix): The U. S. bankruptcy laws provide two options to firms in financial distress and seeking to file for bankruptcy. Chapter 7 is generally used by small firms, which do not expect to reemerge from the bankruptcy proceedings as a going concern. A trustee appointed by the bankruptcy judge oversees the orderly liquidation of the business and the proceeds are distributed to the creditors according to the hierarchy of their claims. Secured creditors' claims take precedence over that of unsecured creditors and among unsecured creditors, claims by the U. S Treasury, followed by court decrees, precede other claims.

Chapter 11 filing is used typically by larger firms, which expect to emerge from the bankruptcy as viable business after reorganizing and restructuring its assets and liabilities. The laws provide for rules and procedures for the reorganization and restructuring. The company is expected to file a reorganization plan within a specified time limit and this plan to has to be approved by at least one half of the creditors, with the added provision that the creditors approving the plan must control at least two-third of the value of total claims against the firm.

The process of bankruptcy reorganization is not necessarily the most economically efficient as the different claimants have conflicting interests. While liquidation may be in the best interest of secured creditors, reorganization and restructuring would benefit unsecured lenders and equity holders. Considerable amount of money is spent in legal, accounting and other costs of settling the disputes among various claimants.

WORKED EXAMPLES

Assume semi-annual coupons for all problems.
1. Duke Box Corp.'s 8 percent debenture matures in 10 years and the yield on comparable risk bonds is 6 percent. At what price would you expect the bonds to be selling?

SOLUTION

Using the BA II-Plus, compute the value of the bond as follows:

Solve for PV given, N = 20, I = 6, (SET P/Y =2), PMT = $40, FV = $1,000,
      PV = $1,148.77

2. If the bonds in problem 1 are callable at 106, what should the financial manager do?

SOLUTION

The financial manager should call the bond because the present value of the bond ($1,148.77) is greater than the present value of the call price ($1,060.00).

3. Given the call provision of 2 above, what is the maximum price you would expect the bond to achieve when bonds of comparable risk are selling to yield 6 percent?

SOLUTION

The bond will sell for no more than the call price, which is $1,060. The difference between the present value of the bond without the call provision and $1,060 is the value of the call provision (option), or $88.77.

4. Rumsmeer Corp.'s bonds have a provision, which stipulates that the ratio of senior debt to total assets will never fall below 45 percent. If the company is at the limit of that ratio and it wishes to issue another $25 million in senior debt, how much additional equity capital must it raise to comply with this restrictive provision?

SOLUTION

The required ratio of 45 percent senior debt implies that equity (or junior debt) must be 55 percent. So the ratio of senior debt to equity is 45 percent to 55 percent. If they desire to issue $25 million of new debt, the amount of new equity required, x, will be determined thus:

$$0.45/0.55 = \$25 \text{ million}/x$$
$$x = 25 \times 0.55/0.45 = \$30.556 \text{ million}$$

5. A security dealer in New York offers to sell you a bond currently yielding 8.5 percent. A dealer from London offers a Eurobond of equivalent risk and similar features at a yield of 8.6 percent. Which one would you buy?

SOLUTION

The New York bond will have interest semiannually and thus have an effective yield of 8.68 percent ($1.0425^2 - 1$). The Eurobonds interest is annually and the effective yield is the same as the quoted yield. The New York bond is better.

SUMMARY

The chapter gives you an overview of the global debt market with all the varieties and kinds of debt securities. There is also coverage of the contractual provisions of typical bond indentures. As a financial manager, you should be familiar with the bond market scene, the terms, and terminology so that you are able to evaluate any prospective debt offering you would like to make for your company. The chapter also covers the continuing innovation going on in the bond markets. The innovators attempt to create value by offering specialized products, which would appeal to different market segments. Innovation is also the result of trying to get around government regulations. Keep in mind that all innovations do not necessarily succeed. The trick is to understand which would create value and which is merely packaging old stuff in new colors.

The Appendix to the chapter provided a description of the two alternate filings financially distressed firms could use. Chapter 7 filing is used by firms, which do not expect to survive as a going concern. Generally larger firms, hoping to reemerge from the bankruptcy proceedings use chapter 11 filing. The firms hope to reorganize and restructure the firm's assets and liabilities to the satisfaction of the creditors. The procedures are far from economically efficient, as they have to content with the conflicting claims of different claimants on the firm's assets.

LIST OF TERMS

Affirmative covenant	Floating-rate notes (FRN)
Call provision	Indenture
Chapter 7 filing	Mortgage bonds
Chapter 11 filing	Mortgage pass-through certificates
Clean price	Negative pledge clause
Collateral trust bonds	Original issue discount bonds
Collateralized mortgage obligations	Pay-in-kind bonds (PIKs)
Cross-default clause	Project finance
Debenture bonds	Registered bonds
Equipment trust certificates	Sinking fund
Eurobond	Zero coupon bonds

EXERCISES

Fill-in Questions

1. The international market for foreign bonds is called the _____ market.

2. The document in a public issue of bonds, which incorporates all the contract provisions between the borrower and lender, through an agreement with a trust company, is called a(n) _____.

3. Fully _____ bonds pay interest and principal to bondholders whose names appear on the records of the company as being owners of the bonds, whereas the _____ bonds pay interest and principal to those have coupons in their possession.

4. A bond, which is unsecured and relies on the general credit of the corporation, is called a(n) _____.

5. If an issue of bonds has a(n) _____, then if interest rates fall, the company may be able to retire them for less than their present value.

6. A _____ provides for a periodic allocation of cash or bonds to retire debt before its maturity.

7. The covenant in which a company undertakes not to give greater security to other parties is known as a _____.

8. If a company defaults to one set of creditors, then other bondholders are likely to be protected by a _____ clause.

9. Agreeing to provide copies of accounts to bondholders or to maintain a particular level of net worth are examples of _____.

10. Bonds, whose rate of interest is contingent on the rate of interest paid on Treasury bills, or other benchmarks, are called _____.

11. It is often attractive to use _____ to fund large projects, which are physically isolated from the parent and can offer tangible security to the lender.

12. Bonds, which have the option to pay interest in the form of either cash or more bonds, are called _____ bonds, the acronym for which is _____.

13. The _____ bonds do not pay any interests and are issued as _____.

14. The _____ are _____ created by companies packaging assets like home mortgages and car loans and the interest and principal payments pass through to the investors.

15. Small firms under financial distress with no hope of remerging from bankruptcy use _____, while distressed larger firms hoping to survive as going concern generally use _____ filing.

Problems

1. If Mare Corp.'s 6 percent debenture bonds mature in 8 years and the yield on comparable-risk bonds is 10 percent, at what price would you expect the bonds to be selling, all else the same?

2. If Brown Collie, Inc. has 10 percent mortgage bonds maturing in 9 years and comparable risk bonds are selling to yield 8 percent, at what price would you expect the bonds to be selling if they were non-callable? If they were callable at 105?

3. What is the value of the right to call a 10-year, 10 percent coupon bond at a price of 106 when bonds of comparable risk yield 6 percent?

4. Rudy Hill, Inc.'s bond indenture contains a provision stipulating that the ratio of senior debt to total assets must be kept at 35 percent at all times. If the company is at the limit of that ratio, determine how much more additional equity capital it must raise in order to float an additional $70 million of bonds.

Essay Questions

1. Differentiate between a debenture bond, a subordinated bond, and a mortgage bond.

2. In what sense, if any, may subordinated debt be viewed as equity capital?

3. Why does a call provision have value to the financial manager?

4. Explain what a sinking fund is and how it is most likely to work.

5. Why is the option to default on a corporate bond valuable? Explain fully.

6. When would innovations in the financial markets create value?

ANSWERS TO EXERCISES

Fill-in Questions

1. Eurobond
2. Indenture
3. Registered; bearer
4. Debenture
5. Call provision
6. Sinking fund
7. Negative pledge clause
8. Cross-default
9. Affirmative covenant
10. Floating-rate notes
11. Project finance
12. Pay-in-kind, PIK
13. Zero coupon; original issue discount
14. Mortgage pass-through certificates; collateralized mortgage obligations
15. Chapter 7, Chapter 11

Problems

1. Solve for PV, given: N = 16, I = 10 (P/Y = 2), PMT = $30, FV = $1,000; PV = $783.24

2. Solve for PV, given: N = 18, I = 8 (P/Y = 2), PMT = $50, FV = $1,000; PV = $1,126.59
   Value without the call = $1,126.59; If callable = $1,050.00

3. First find the value of the bond.
   Solve for PV, given: N = 20, I = 6 (P/Y = 2), PMT = $50, FV = $1,000; PV = $1,297.55
   Bond value = $1,297.55
   Call price = $1,060.00
   Bond value less call price = value of call provision
   Value of call provision = $1,297.55 - $1,060 = $237.55

4. 0.35/0.65 = $70 million/x; Equity needed = $70 X 0.65/0.35 = $130 million

26
Leasing

INTRODUCTION

The chapter provides an introduction to leasing and describes the various types of leases and terms associated with leasing. Operating leases are short-term leases, often cancelable and entered into for reasons of convenience and non-financial reasons. Financial leases are leases that cover most of an asset's estimated economic life. These leases are non-cancelable by the lessee or cancelable only if the lessor is reimbursed for expected losses arising from forgone income. Financial leases are essentially considered as substitutes for buying the asset and financing the same by borrowing the money required. Leasing and borrowing can be seen as financing alternatives.

The focus of this chapter is the valuation of a financial lease and to determine whether, and to what extent, it tends to enhance the value of the firm. The decision rule that emerges is: a financial lease is superior to buying and borrowing if the financing provided by the lease exceeds the present value of the liability it creates. An equivalent approach is to discount all lease cash flows using the after-tax borrowing rate and consider the NPV of the leasing. Use leasing if the NPV is positive.

KEY CONCEPTS IN THE CHAPTER

Terms to Know: Before you embark on an analysis of leases, you must know a variety of terms. The more important ones are summarized below:

Lessee is the renter or the user of the asset. Lessee contracts to make a series of payments to the lessor, and in return, gets to use the asset for the lease term.

Lessor is the legal owner and normally is entitled to the tax privileges of ownership like depreciation deductions or investment tax credits, if they are available. At the end of the lease period, the equipment reverts to the lessor.

Operating lease is a short-term lease, cancelable at the option of the lessee. These are usually engaged into for convenience and flexibility. Generally, this is not considered a substitute for ownership and long-term use of the asset.

Financial or full-payout leases are non-cancelable, long-term leases for most of the asset's useful life. Failure to make the lease payments can get the lessee into serious trouble, and in that sense, lease obligations are like debt obligations. This form of leasing is considered a source of financing and a substitute for debt.

Full-service or rental lease is one where the lessor maintains, insures, and pays taxes on the equipment. On the other hand, in a n*et lease* the lessee maintains, insures, and pays taxes on the property. *Sale and leaseback* is an arrangement where a firm sells an asset to the lessor and then leases it back from the buyer. *Leveraged leases* are financial leases where the lessor borrows part of the purchase price using the leased equipment as collateral.

Significance of Financial Leases: Financial leases are studied in depth because they are a source of financing and are similar to debt. With financial leases, the lessee (the user) assumes the risks and rewards of ownership. Leasing displaces debt. The ownership of the asset makes a difference as to who gets the salvage value at the end of the lease period and who gets the tax privileges. When bankruptcy and reorganization occur, the lessee loses the asset's use, whereas the lessor does not. Financial leases will, normally, have to be reported in the balance sheet as equivalent ownership of the asset with the lease obligations capitalized and shown on the liability side.

Why Lease: Some motivations for leasing can make a lot of sense, while others appear dubious and imply market myopia and inefficiency. Those, which are rational and make sense include:

- Convenience,
- Cancellation options are valuable,
- Maintenance is provided,
- Tax shields may be advantageous, and
- Could help avoid alternative minimum tax.

Some dubious reasons for leasing include:

- Avoid capital expenditure controls,
- Preserves capital,
- Off-balance sheet financing; this may no longer be possible as leases must be capitalized and their estimated present values called as an asset and a liability, if they fall under certain guidelines, and
- Affects book income positively

The dubious reasons imply that markets and the investor could be fooled by appearances.

Operating Leases: Operating leases may make sense when an asset is required over an extended period and the lessor can buy and manage the asset cheaper than the lessee; for example, a truck-leasing company. The option to cancel the lease is sufficiently important to the lessee.

Valuing Financial Leases: Valuing financial leases are similar to valuing any set of cash flows. Essentially, you identify all the cash flows involved and then calculate the present values at the appropriate discount rates. Add up the present values to find the NPV; accept if the NPV is positive. For convenience, we will adopt the usual practice of analyzing a lease from the lessee's perspective. If you are interested in the lessor's perspective, all you need to do it is just reverse the signs – a positive cash flow to the lessee is negative for the lessor. The main cash flows resulting from a lease transaction are:

- At the start (time 0), the lessee saves the cost of purchasing the asset. This is the main positive cash flow for the lessee.
- During the lease term, the lessee promises to pay regular lease payments. These could be annual, or more frequent, and in some cases start at time 0. The lease payments are tax-deductible.
- The lessee loses the tax privileges associated with ownership. This means that the tax deductions from depreciation are not available.
- At the end of the lease period, the lessee does not own the asset and thus, loses the remaining value of the asset.
- There may be other cash flows such as maintenance costs. These will have to be accounted for.

The basic approach to valuing the lease is to find the present value of all the above cash flows and sum them up. The only issue, which remains, is the discount rate to be used. The accepted practice is to use the after-tax borrowing rate to discount all the cash flows, except the salvage value. The salvage value may be discounted at the company cost of capital.

An alternate approach involves calculating the equivalent loan. The equivalent loan is the loan that exactly matches the lease liability at each point in time, i.e., commits the firm to exactly the same cash outflows as the lease would. Compare the financing by the lease with the financing provided by the equivalent loan and accept the lease if the value of the lease is positive.

Value of lease = cash flows from leasing - cash flows from equivalent loan

For the lessee, the main positive cash flow from leasing is simply the purchase price of the asset. The two approaches would give exactly the same answer. In general, a financial lease is superior to buying and borrowing if the financing provided by the lease exceeds the present value.

Financial leasing decisions are an example of the interaction between financing and investing decisions. Therefore, for any investment project with the possibility of leasing the project assets, the adjusted net present value should be determined before the investment decision is made.

APV = NPV of the project + NPV of lease

What this suggests is that if the equipment for a project is available under lease financing, the project NPV should be adjusted to reflect any positive NPV from the lease transaction. This could, in some cases, result in turning a negative NPV project into an acceptable project because of the benefits of the lease.

The evaluation methods discussed above will show that if all the factors are identical for the lessee and the lessor, then the values of the lease to the lessor and lessee would be equal but of opposite signs. This would mean that it is not possible to have a mutually beneficial lease transaction if the lessee and the lessor have the same tax rates, the same cost of the asset, and the same discount rate. Thus, a lease would make sense only if the lessee and the lessor have different tax rates. Of course, it might also make sense if the cost of the asset or the discount rate is different; but then this is not a reason for leasing. Any such difference would qualify the lessor to be a seller (lower cost of asset) of the asset or a lender (lower discount rate). In short, it is generally agreed that tax differentials drive financial leases in many cases.

WORKED EXAMPLES

1. Main Street Corp. (MSC) is evaluating the lease of a minicomputer, which, if purchased, would cost $150,000. Its estimated useful life is 5 years, at the end of which time it will be obsolete. The annual lease payments are $35,000, payable in six installments, the first being payable when the contract is signed. The company is in the 35 percent marginal income tax bracket. Set up a statement of cash-flow consequences of the lease contract. If MSC's before-tax borrowing rate on long-term debt is 12 percent, estimate the net present value (NPV) of the lease.

SOLUTION

The table below gives the cash flows and present values. Note that the depreciation schedule is contained in that portion of the table (from Chapter 6 of the text). Leasing displaces debt and the risk of the cash flows from leasing approximates the risk of the cash flows that would have been incurred had the firm borrowed. The current after-tax borrowing rate is the appropriate rate at which to evaluate the lease. That is $12(1 - 0.35) = 7.80$ percent. This is the rate used to calculate the present values. Discounting at this rate, we obtain a NPV of -$10,210.

Cash Flows for Lessee from the Lease Contract (in $1,000)

	Year 0	Year 1	Year 2	Year 3	Year 4	Year 5
Cost of computer	150.00					
Lost depreciation tax shield	-10.50	-16.80	-10.08	-6.05	-6.05	-3.02
Lease payment	-35.00	-35.00	-35.00	-35.00	-35.00	-35.00
Tax shield of payment	12.25	12.25	12.25	12.25	12.25	12.25
Cash flow	116.75	-39.55	-32.83	-28.80	-28.80	-25.77
NPV at 7.80%	-10.21					
Tax depreciation rate	0.20	0.32	0.192	0.1152	0.1152	0.0576
Borrowing cost	12%					
Tax rate	0.35					
After-tax rate	7.80%					

Note that:
Lost depreciation tax shield = cost x depreciation rate x marginal tax rate

312

For year 1- Lost depreciation tax shield = 150 x 0.32 X 0.35 = 16.80

2. Calculate the equivalent loan of the lease given in problem 1.

SOLUTION

The equivalent loan is simply the present value of the lease cash outflows discounted at the after-tax borrowing rate. From the table above, present value of the cash out flows (exclude the positive cash flow at the start) = $126, 960. What this means is that for the same cash flows you are committing to the lease, you can actually get a loan of $126,960. As this is more than the cash flow provided by the leasing at the start ($116,750), you are better off rejecting the lease.

NPV of lease = $116,750 - $126,960 = -$10,210

3. What is the value of the above lease to the lessor?

SOLUTION

The cash flows to the lessor are the same as those to the lessee except the signs are reversed. Thus, the NPV to the lessor is a positive $10,210.

4. Assume the lessee's tax rate is zero. What is the value of the lease now?

SOLUTION

The table below shows the results. It is still a negative NPV deal, actually a little worse.

				Year		
	0	1	2	3	4	5
Cost of computer	150.00					
Lost depreciation tax shield	0.00	0.00	0.00	0.00	0.00	0.00
Lease payment	-35.00	-35.00	-35.00	-35.00	-35.00	-35.00
Tax shield of lease payment	0.00	0.00	0.00	0.00	0.00	0.00
Cash flow of lease	115.00	-35.00	-35.00	-35.00	-35.00	-35.00
NPV	-11.17					
Tax depreciation rate on cost	0.2000	0.3200	0.1920	0.1152	0.1152	0.0576
Required return	12.00%					
Marginal tax rate	0.00%					
After-tax discount rate	12.00%					

5. Indian County Memorial Hospital (ICMH) is considering installing an integrated patient information system costing $435,000 to replace the hospital's existing information system.

313

The initial evaluation of the project showed that the NPV of the project is negative. The present value of benefits from the project was estimated at $401,000. So the CEO of ICMH rejected the project. It appears that the supplier of the system is offering a five-year lease as an alternative to purchasing the system. The lease terms involved 6 annual payments of $80,000 with first payment due on signing the lease. The supplier also offered to sell the system to ICMH at the end of the lease for the expected salvage value of $20,000. Evaluate the project. ICMH does not pay taxes and its borrowing cost is 9 percent.

SOLUTION

NPV of the project without leasing = -$435,000 +$401,000 = -$34,000

So the rejection of the project by the CEO is understandable. However, since leasing has been offered, we need to evaluate the APV of the project as follows:

APV of the project = NPV of the cash flows + NPV of the lease.

NPV of lease: Since ICMH does not pay taxes, the only cash flows involved are the cost of the system, the annual lease payments and the final payment of $20,000 to buy the asset at the end of the lease period. These are shown below:

Year	Cash flows
0	+$355,000 = $435,000-$80,000
1	-$80,000
2	-$80,000
3	-$80,000
4	-$80,000
5	-$100,000 = -$80,000-$20,000

Compute present value using the cash flow worksheet:
CF_0 = +$355,000, CO_1 = -$80,000, FO_1 = 4, CO_2 = -$100,000, FO_1 = 1
Go to NPV: worksheet: I = 9, NPV = $30,829.

APV = -$34,000 + $30,829 = - $3,171

APV is negative. The project should be rejected.

SUMMARY

This chapter provides an overview of the different types of leases. It then focuses on the evaluation of financial leases, which are considered a source of financing. Financial leasing can be considered as an alternative to buying the asset and borrowing the cost of the asset. The evaluation of financial leases assumes the same format as the evaluation of any other cash flows. The direct cash flows are discounted at a tax-adjusted rate appropriate to the level of risk, which is typically and conveniently assumed to be the firm's present borrowing rate. The present borrowing rate is used because the lease displaces debt in the company's financial structure but has no effect on the required amount of equity financing.

Two equivalent approaches to evaluating financial leases are presented. The first approach to evaluating leases is to discount all the cash flows at the after-tax interest rate of the firm. The sum of these present values gives you the NPV of the lease transaction. The alternate approach computes the equivalent loan that would be supported by the cash outflows produced by the lease payments. If the equivalent loan is less than the financing provided by the lease, the lease would be a good deal.

Leasing an example of the interaction between investing and financing decisions. For any investment project with potential leasing of assets, the adjusted present value should be considered before finalizing the investment decision.

LIST OF TERMS

Capital leases
Direct lease
Equivalent loan
Financial lease
Full-service lease
Lease
Lessee

Lessor (owner)
Leveraged leases
Net lease
Off-balance-sheet financing
Operating lease
Sale and leaseback

EXERCISES

Fill-in Questions

1. The user of a leased asset is called the _____, whereas the owner of a leased asset is called the _____.

2. Leases, which are short-term and cancelable during the contract period at the option of the _, are called _____ leases.

3. Leases which are long-term or extend over the economic life of the asset and which cannot be canceled or can be canceled only if the _____ is reimbursed for losses are called _____ leases.

4. When the lessor promises to maintain and insure the leased assets and pay property taxes on it, they have provided a(n) _____ lease.

5. When the _____ agrees to maintain the leased asset, insure it, and pay properly taxes due on it, the lease is known as a net lease.

6. When the lessee identifies the equipment to be used and arranges for the leasing company to buy it from the manufacturer, the signed contract is called a(n) _____ lease.

7. When a firm sells an asset it owns and leases it back to the buyer, the arrangement is known as _____.

8. When lessors borrow part of the purchase price of a leased asset and use the lease contract as security for the loan, the entire financing scheme is known as a(n) _____ lease.

9. Generally accepted accounting standards no longer allow _____ financing; rather, lease payments of _____ leases must be _____, which is to say that the present value of the lease payments must be estimated and shown as debt on the right-hand side of the balance sheet.

10. A(n) _____ is one that exactly matches the lease liability, or to put it another way, one that commits the firm to exactly the same cash outlays as a lease would.

Problems

1. Beans Mayo Corp (BMC) decided to lease additional computer equipment for the next 5 years. The deal requires annual lease payments of $66,000 commencing on the day the contract is signed. Had the equipment been purchased, it would have cost $320,000. The company's marginal tax bracket is 35 percent, and its long-term borrowing rate is 10 percent. Calculate the net present value of the lease and its equivalent loan.

2. Provide an equivalent loan analysis for the situation of problem 1.

3. BMC's treasurer suddenly realizes that BMC is unlikely to pay taxes in the next five years. How does this affect the NPV of the lease?

4. Utopia University of Nevada (UUN) is considering installing a new computer network connecting its three campuses. The total cost of the network is estimated ad $785,000 and the present value of benefits from the project was estimated at $765,000. So the university President rejected the project. The supplier of the system is offering a 4-year lease as an alternative to purchasing the system. The lease terms involved 5 annual payments of $180,000 with the first payment due on signing the lease. The supplier also offered to sell the network to UUN at the end of the lease for the expected salvage value of $50,000. Evaluate the project. UUN does not pay taxes and its borrowing cost is 12 percent.

Essay Questions

1. How can it be said that financial leases are a source of financing? Explain fully.

2. In what sense may lease payments be viewed as the equivalent of interest payments?

4. Some people say that long-term lease obligations should be regarded as debt, even though they may not appear on the balance sheet. What rationale can you give for this point of view?

6. List and explain some of the reasons that make leasing dubious and offer an explanation for each item.

6. Usually the direct cash flows from the lease are assumed to be safe and are discounted at roughly the same rate of interest as obtainable on a secured bond issued by the lessee. Why?

ANSWERS TO EXERCISES

Fill-in Questions

1. Lessee; lessor
2. Lessee; operating
3. Lessor; financial
4. Full-service
5. Lessee

6. Direct
7. Sale and leaseback
8. Leveraged
9. Off-balance-sheet; financial; capitalized
10. Equivalent loan

Problems

1. The analysis is provided in the table below. The NPV is negative (-$1,610). Reject the lease.

Cash Flow Analysis of the Lease (in $1,000s)

	Year 0	Year 1	Year 2	Year 3	Year 4	Year 5
Cost of computer	320.00					
Lost deprn tax shield	-22.40	-35.84	-21.50	-12.90	-12.90	-6.45
Lease payment	-66.00	-66.00	-66.00	-66.00	-66.00	-66.00
Tax shield of pmt	23.10	23.10	23.10	23.10	23.10	23.10
Cash flow	254.70	-78.74	-64.40	-55.80	-55.80	-49.35
NPV at 6.5%	-1.60					
Tax deprn rate	0.2	0.32	0.192	0.1152	0.1152	0.0576
Borrowing cost	10 %					

After-tax borrowing rate 10(1-0.35) = 6.50 %

2. The equivalent loan is equal to the present value of the cash outflows produced by the lease.

Equivalent Loan Analysis (in $1,000s)

	Year 0	Year 1	Year 2	Year 3	Year 4	Year 5
Cash flow	254.70	-78.74	-64.40	-55.80	-55.80	-49.35

Equivalent Loan = Present value at 6.5% of cash flows from year 1 to year 5 = $256.30

Net benefit from the lease = Financing provided by the lease - Equivalent Loan
$$= \$254{,}700 - \$256{,}300 = -\$1{,}600$$
Reject the lease.

3. The analysis is given in the table below. The NPV of the lease is positive at $3,810. The company's zero tax rate now makes the lease beneficial.

(In $ 1,000s)

	Year 0	Year 1	Year 2	Year 3	Year 4	Year 5
Cost of computer	320.00					
Lost deprn tax shield	0.00	0.00	0.00	0.00	0.00	0.00
Lease payment	-66.00	-66.00	-66.00	-66.00	-66.00	46.00
Tax shield of pmt.	0.00	0.00	0.00	0.00	0.00	0.00
Cash flow	254.00	-66.00	-66.00	-66.00	-66.00	-66.00
NPV at 10%	3.81					
After-tax borrowing rate	10.00					

4. NPV of the project without leasing = -$785,000 +$765,000 = -$20,000

APV of the project = NPV of the cash flows + NPV of the lease.

Since UUN does not pay taxes, the only cash flows involved are the cost of the system, the annual lease payments and the final payment of $50,000 to buy the asset.

Year	Cash flows
0	+$605,000 = $785,000-$180,000
1	-$180,000
2	-$180,000
3	-$180,000
4	-$230,000 = -$180,000-$50,000

Compute present value using the cash flow worksheet:
$CF_0 = +\$605{,}000$, $CO_1 = -\$180{,}000$, $FO_1 = 3$, $CO_2 = -\$230{,}000$, $FO_1 = 1$
Go to NPV: worksheet: I = 12, NPV = $26,501,
APV = -$20,000 + $26,501 = + $6,501

The APV is positive, so the project may be accepted.

27
Managing Risk

INTRODUCTION

This is the first of two chapters in the book dealing directly with risk management. Businesses face risk every day and it is not possible to earn significant returns for stockholders without taking risk. However, managers would like to reduce or eliminate the kinds of risk that does not give additional returns for taking the risk. These types of risk may relate to key inputs like raw materials, the main products of the business, or financial variables like interest rates or foreign exchange rates. Risk reduction of controllable risk allows financial managers to worry about the things that are worth worrying about and they are in the best position to handle. This chapter focuses on business related risk from commodity prices and interest rate changes. Thanks to financial innovation and development of financial derivatives, corporate financial managers have considerable flexibility in deciding the kind of risk they want to be exposed to and the kind of risk they want to hedge.

Hedging offsets risk and is accomplished with futures, forward contracts, options or and often with custom designed derivatives. Risk management through hedging with appropriate financial tools is the focus of this chapter. The primary purpose of hedging is to control individual risks thereby controlling a firm's total risk. Such hedging techniques are part and parcel of today's financial manager's tool book. The point of hedging is to minimize the risks the manager is not equipped to handle. Typically hedging involves finding the number of units of an asset (or liability) that is needed to offset changes in the value of an obligation (or asset) and then taking the appropriate derivative position to reduce or eliminate the risk.

KEY CONCEPTS IN THE CHAPTER

Insurance: One simple way of hedging some kinds of risk is to go out and buy insurance. Insurance as a way of reducing or hedging risk has been around for a long time. However, the kind of risk, which can be insured, is rather limited. This depends on the type of risk and the extent to which insurance companies have a relative advantage in dealing with it. Before they underwrite insurance for any risk, insurance companies would like to have a reasonable estimate of the probability of the risk-causing event. They would also like to have a large enough pool of customers seeking the insurance for the risk. If these two conditions are not satisfied, the insurance will be too costly to write. It is unlikely that you will want to insure risks for which the premium is too expensive. Insurance will also be inefficient if the presence of insurance gives you less incentive to reduce the risk yourself.

In general, the insurance companies have the following relative advantages:

- They are skilled at estimating risks.
- They are skilled at advising on reducing risk.
- They can pool (or diversify) risks.

Insurance companies also face some disadvantages. These include:

- They have to overcome their administrative costs, including legal costs of disputes.
- They encounter the *adverse selection* problem, where those at greater risk are more likely to buy insurance.
- *Moral hazard* is another problem, which means that those who insure have less incentive to reduce their exposure to risk.

Homemade insurance like options or future contracts might work better in some cases.

Hedging with Futures: Futures, forwards, swaps, and options are ideal hedging tools. These are known as *derivatives*, because their value is derived from the value of an underlying asset. A futures contract is an exchange-traded agreement to buy or sell something at a future date for a price agreed upon today. When a financial manager hedges with futures, he or she agrees to deliver or accept a specified "commodity" at a specified price, location, and time. Futures contracts are available for a wide range of commodities, financial instruments, and foreign currencies. The commodities traded in the futures markets include grains and oilseed, livestock and meat, food and fiber, and metals and petroleum. Financial instruments traded include various stock market indexes and a number of interest related instruments. Most major foreign currencies have exchange traded futures contracts.

Futures contracts allow one to hedge the risk of a present or expected position by buying (the long hedge) or selling (the short hedge) the contract for future delivery. A farmer expecting to have wheat or corn in a few months can lock in a price by going short or selling futures contract for delivery close to the date of his expected crop. Similarly, a miller could lock in a price for his expected future purchase by buying futures contracts. Excess demand for or supply of futures contracts is absorbed by speculators. Futures contracts are important for the management of risk relating to prices of physical commodities, stock prices, and interest rates. By hedging with futures, financial managers can lock in fix prices on commodities or financial instruments that will not be available until some time in the future.

The Mechanics of Futures Trading: When financial futures are bought (or sold), one does not pay (or receive) the price of the contract till the date of delivery. The transactions require the buyer or seller to make a margin deposit in cash or securities. This serves as collateral for performance of the contract. Each day futures contracts are marked to market to determine profits or losses. Any gain that accrues on the re-pricing of the futures contracts is not available to the parties to the contract, till the contract is settled.

Setting up a futures hedge is similar to any other hedge. First, you identify your risk exposure. For example, let us say that you are expected to need cotton fiber in November. You can find the futures contracts with the closest relationship to cotton and establish a long position in the futures market. In this case, you can actually use cotton fiber futures and buy them for delivery in November.

Here are some important points about futures and futures hedging:

- Futures contracts are standardized as to the date, quantity, and specifications of the underlying asset.
- They are traded through organized exchanges and you are required to keep margin deposits as security for your position.
- Speculators are essential to futures contract markets because they take up the imbalances between futures contract supply and future contract demand.
- Spot prices are prices for immediate delivery of the contracts.
- As the delivery date for futures contracts approaches, the contracts become more and more like spot contracts and the prices approach the spot price.

Spot and Futures Prices: The price of a futures contract will have a definite relationship with the spot price of the same financial instrument or the commodity. Financial futures, for example, differ from buying exactly the same item in the spot market in that the buyer does not pay for the security at the time the order is placed and can earn interest during the interim. The buyer also does not receive dividends or interest normally paid to the holder of the actual instrument. Thus we get:

$$\frac{\text{Futures price}}{(1 + r_f)^t} = \text{spot price} - \text{PV(dividends or interest payments forgone)}$$

Foreign exchange futures are important to firms dealing in international markets. The price of a currency future will be related to the spot exchange rate as follows:

$$\frac{\text{Futures price of foreign currency}}{1 + r_\$} = \text{spot price} - \text{PV(foregone interest on foreign currency}$$

Note that PV(forgone interest) = $(r_{fc} \times \text{spot price})/(1 + r_{fc})$.

Commodity fixtures are more complicated than financial futures. When one is dealing in commodity futures, payment is not made immediately for the entire contract, and interest may be earned. In addition, the purchaser of the contract does not incur any storage fees. The *convenience yield* is forgone, however, when one buys commodity futures because the commodity is not available for immediate use. In other words, the futures contract does not help you use the commodity for any current needs. Thus the relationship between spot and future prices for commodities can be written as:

$$\frac{\text{Futures price}}{(1 + r_f)^t} = \text{spot price} + \text{PV(storage costs)} - \text{PV(convenience yield)}$$

= spot price - PV(net convenience yield)

Net convenience yield reflects the net amount of convenience yield and storage costs. A commodity in temporary short supply will see its spot price run high indicating high convenience yield. The storage cost is a function of the nature of the commodity and its value to weight ratio. If storage costs are high relative to convenience yield, the net convenience yield will be negative. Note that the above relationship will not apply for "commodities" which cannot be stored. For these, there may not be a clear relationship between spot and future prices. Futures contracts on electricity are good examples.

Forward Contracts: A high degree of liquidity exists in futures markets because futures contracts are standardized and mature on a limited number of specified dates each year. But what about financial managers who wish to customize futures contracts to suit their special needs or make deals that mature on dates other than those found on organized futures markets? The answer is to construct a forward contract, which is the equivalent of a homemade futures contract. In other words, forward contracts are customized futures contracts. The forward rate agreement (FRA) is one way to customize futures contracts. Most forward contracts arise from dealings in foreign exchange currency markets. A financial manager may manufacture a forward loan by borrowing short-term and lending long-term. Such homemade forward contracts may occur either in foreign exchange or in loans. For example, we can get a 1-year forward interest rate by borrowing for 2 years and lending (depositing the money) for one year. The relationship can be expressed as:

$$1 \text{ year forward interest rate} = \frac{(1 + 2 \text{ year borrowing rate})^2}{1 + 1 \text{ year lending rate}} - 1$$

Swaps: A swap is created when two companies enter into an agreement to exchange cash flows set by fixed or variable interest rates. In effect the two parties are lending each equivalent loans, but on different basis for interest rates. The different bases for interest rate may be fixed rate and floating rate or just interest rates in different currencies. The rationale for swap follows from the fact each of the two parties to a swap may have "competitive advantage" in one of the markets, but would want to borrow in the market other than the one they have advantage in. For example, an American company may be interested in borrowing Japanese yen, while a Japanese firm may be interested in US dollar loans. Each firm is likely to be better known in its home market. An optimal arrangement can be worked out whereby each firm issues debt in its home country, receive that currency, and then swap it for the other country's currency. This is a currency swap. Swaps also exist on loans in which a fixed interest-rate loan is exchanged for a floating-rate loan, or involve two floating-rate loans tied to different base rates. In practice swaps are arranged through a third-party dealer and would involve some transaction costs. Note that a mutually beneficial swap can be arranged whenever there is a relative advantage to one party in one market and for the other party in the second market.

Credit Derivatives: Credit derivatives allow lenders to transfer default risk to other parties. These enable banks and other financial institutions to reduce their risk in specific loan markets.

Many credit derivatives are *default swaps*, where one party pays the other if there is default on a loan or a group of loans. This is similar to buying default insurance.

How to Hedge: There are a number of general principles involved in hedging. The most important one is how to think about the relationship between the risks you want to reduce and the kinds of contracts available to hedge it with. It is likely that no contract will give a perfect hedge: There will generally be residual (or basis) risk between the risk and the hedge. Hedging commodity prices, exchange rates, interest rates, and stock market levels are all very similar. Many risks change continuously through time, so their hedges have to be adjusted as a dynamic hedge quite frequently through time.

Here are the steps involved in setting up a hedge:

- Find the relationship between the commodity or asset position (say, A) you want hedged and the futures contract (B). You can study the historic relationship between the two and it may be expressed as follows:

$$\text{Expected change in value of A} = a + \delta \, (\text{change in value of B})$$

- Delta (δ) measures the sensitivity of A to changes in the value of B.

- It is called the *hedge ratio*. It is the number of units of B, which should be purchased to hedge a position in each unit of A.

- Duration hedging is very similar. Duration measures sensitivity to a parallel shift in interest rates (chapter 24).

Options, deltas and betas: We learned about options and option deltas in chapter 20. Options can be used to hedge positions in stocks or commodities. The option delta is similar to the delta in the hedging relationship described above. Note that δ is the number of shares equivalent to position in each option. For each option you hold, you will get a perfect hedge if you sell δ shares. If you want to hedge a position in one share you will have to sell $1/\delta$ options. Option deltas change as the stock prices change, so that in order to remain hedged one will have to change the position continuously. Betas of stock portfolios also express similar relationship. If you have a portfolio with a beta of 1, you can hedge by selling index futures contracts of equal amount.

The Role and Use of Derivatives: Derivatives provide an extremely flexible set of instruments, which enable many kinds of risks to be hedged. They can also be used for speculative purposes, and this has brought some companies into serious trouble and caused questions to be asked about the derivatives markets themselves. The chapter provides some commonsense guidelines for making sure you only use derivatives in a way, which helps your company. Senior management of companies should be aware of the risks they are taking and ensure that control systems exist to prevent anyone from taking excessive risk. Companies should only venture into areas where they have comparative advantage. In other words, know what you are getting into and do not go beyond your depth of understanding.

WORKED EXAMPLES

1. Jean Grahn has $200,000 of Tixar Corp. stock and that she wants your help in determining how much of the Standard & Poor's 500 Index (S&P 500) she should sell in order to hedge the market-related risk to which she is exposed. The historical relation between the stock's change in price and the change in price of the market index is

Monthly change in value of Tixar shares $= a + \delta$ (monthly changes in market index)
$= 0.05 + 1.5$(monthly changes in market index)

SOLUTION

To hedge her position, Jean must sell futures contracts worth $300,0000 (1.5 x $200,000). This hedges position.

2. The S&P 500 stock index 2-month futures are trading at 1,125.40 and the spot S&P 500 index is at 1,122.73. The 2-month interest rate is 4.3 percent, and the average annual dividend yield on the index is 2.80 percent. Are these rates consistent?

SOLUTION

$$\frac{\text{Future price}}{(1 + r_f)^t} = \text{spot price} - \text{PV(dividends)}$$

Dividend yield for 2 months = 2.80/6 = 0.4667%; Dividends = $1,122.73 x 0.004667 = $5.24

$$\text{PV(Futures price)} = \frac{1,125.40}{(1 + 0.043)^{(2/12)}} = \$1117.53$$

Spot price - PV(dividends) $= \$1,122.73 - \$5.24/(1.043^{(2/12)})$
$= \$1122.73 - \$5.20 = \$1,117.53$

The two values are same. There is no arbitrage opportunity.

3. Mercury Motor Company is able to borrow at an annual rate 8 percent for 2 years, using its automobile loans as collateral. The loans are made from Mercury Acceptance Corporation, a wholly owned subsidiary. It estimates that its overall annual return from car loans is 10 percent. If the average automobile loan is 3 years in length, what forward interest rate is implied by this homemade forward contract?

$$\text{Forward interest rate} = \frac{(1+3 \text{ year rate})^3}{(1+2 \text{ year rate})^2} - 1 = \frac{1.10^3}{1.08^2} - 1$$

$$= 14.11 \text{ percent}$$

4. Grey Mare Company (GMC) plans to set up a machine tools plant in Italy and needs 20 million Euros. It finds it can get better financing terms if it borrows in the United States than in any other country. It issues $18 million 5-year, 10 percent notes in the U.S. capital markets. Simultaneously, it enters into a swap agreement with its Italian bank, for an equivalent Euro loan carrying 12 percent interest rate. The details of the agreement are: (1) GMC is to swap its dollar liabilities into Euro (2) the bank pays GMC sufficient dollars to service the debt; and (3) GMC agrees to make annual payments in Euro to cover the Euro loan. What is the result of this currency swap? Assume an exchange rate of $0.90/Euro.

SOLUTION

20 million Euros = 20 x 0.9 million dollars = $18 million

(cash flows in millions)

	Year 0		Years 1 - 4		Year 5	
	$	Euro	$	Euro	$	Euro
Issue dollar notes	+18	0	-1.8	0	-19.8	0
Swap $s for Euros	-18	20.0	+1.8	-2.4	+19.8	-22.4
Net cash flow	0	20.0	0	-2.4	0	-22.4

GMC has effectively converted its 10 percent dollar loan into a 12 percent Euro loan.

5. Sheen Parts Corp. (SPC), a Dallas based auto parts manufacturer is planning an expansion into Germany and wants to borrow in Euro. Zeit Zimmer Gmbh (ZZG), a German car manufacturer plans to move into the US market and wants to borrow in US dollars. SPC can get US dollar loans at 9% and Euro loans at 11 percent. ZZG can obtain US dollar loans at 9 percent and Euro loans at 8 percent. Design a swap such that SPC gets 30 percent of the total cost savings and ZZG gets 70 percent of the total cost savings.

SOLUTION:

First let us find the total cost saving likely to result from a swap between the two. Note that SPC has comparative advantage in the US market and, ZZG has advantage in the German market. Without the swap, SPC will borrow in Germany at a cost of 11 percent and ZZG will borrow in the US at 9 percent. The total cost will be 11 + 9 = 20 percent. If each party borrows in the market of their relative advantage, the total cost in annual interest rates will be: SPC's dollar loans at 9 percent + ZZG's Euro loans at 8 percent = 17 percent. Thus there is a cost saving of 3 percent. If ZZG is to get 70 percent of this, the swap should lower its borrowing cost to: 9 - 2.1 = 6.9 percent. Similarly SPC should lower its cost by 0.9 percent to: 11 - 0.9 = 10.1 percent. The details of the swap can be designed in many different ways, but all of which require that SPC borrows in the US and ZZG borrows in Germany and each swap the flows to the other. You can be set up the details as to the exact interest flows in many ways. Here is one, which will satisfy the condition of the 70/30 split of the savings:

SPC borrows US dollars at 9 percent and charges ZZG 9 percent.
ZZG borrows Euros at 8 percent and charges SPC 10.1 percent.

Net cost to SPC = 9% - 9% + 10.1% = 10.1%
Net cost to ZZG = 8% - 10.1% + 9% = 6.9%

Note that transaction costs and the risk of counter party default are ignored.

6. Two-month gold futures contract is quoted at $301.1/ounce. The spot price is $300. What is the net convenience yield? Assume an interest rate of 4.3 percent.

SOLUTION

We can use the relationship: PV(Futures price) = Spot price - PV(Net convenience yield)

$$PV(\text{Futures price}) = \frac{301.10}{(1 + 0.043)^{(2/12)}} = \$299.00$$

PV(Net convenience yield) = Spot price - PV(Futures price) = $300 - $299 = $1

7. Jamie Milan owns $100,000 in a mutual fund, which has a very high correlation to the S & P 500 index and a beta close to 1. Jamie wants to sell his fund now, but was advised by his tax consultant to wait for another six to take advantage lower rates next year. Suggest a hedging strategy for Jamie.

SOLUTION

Since the correlation with S & P 500 is very high and the fund's beta is close to 1, Jamie can effectively hedge his position by selling S &P 500 Index futures contracts worth $100,000.

SUMMARY

Managers and businesses are in the business of taking risks. However, they are better off taking the risks they are best equipped to handle and where they have expertise and skill. Hedging enables businesses to reduce the risks, which are not related to their areas of expertise or are unrewarding. Managers can choose the risk they want to reduce or hedge. They can use either insurance or hedging tools available in the market.

The hedge is established by buying futures, forwards, swaps, or even options contracts. The use of all these is explained in the chapter. Because hedging mitigates the risk of individual assets, the firm's total risk is also reduced. Hedging tactics are important because they allow financial managers to concentrate their energies on decisions whose risks are not easily hedged or diversified away.

LIST OF TERMS

Adverse selection
Arbitrageurs
Basis risk
Convenience yield
Counterparty
Delta
Derivative instruments
Forward contract
Forward rate agreement (FRA)
Futures contract
Hedge

Hedge ratio
Immunized
Jump risk
Long hedge
Marked to market
Moral hazard
Net convenience yield
Short hedge
Spot price
Storage costs
Swap

EXERCISES

Fill-in Questions

1. A(n) _____ offsets risks by trading assets or liabilities for other assets.

2. _____ measures the sensitivity of one asset's value to changes in the value of another.

3. Futures, forwards, swaps, and options are called _____ instruments, because their value depends on the value of other assets.

4. The problem that insurance tends to be bought by those most at risk is called the problem of _____.

5. The problem that once you have insurance you have less incentive to reduce the risks you take is called _____.

6. _____ contracts are contracts traded on organized exchanges to buy or sell commodities or securities in the future on terms fixed today.

7. Futures contracts are _____ daily to determine profits and losses.

8. The delta of the relationship between the risk and the hedging instrument establishes the _____ for the hedge.

9. When a hedge has been established, the position is said to have been _____ against that particular source of risk.

10. When the prices of two commodities are not likely to move exactly together, a perfect hedge is not possible. The remaining risk is called _____ and the hedge ratio is greater than, less than) _____ one.

11. Selling futures contracts is a(n) _____.

12. Buying futures contracts is a(n) _____.

13. Today's price of a commodity is called the _____.

14. The discounted futures price of a commodity equals the spot price plus the present value of_____ and minus the present value of the _____.

15. The difference between the convenience yield and the storage cost is called the _____.

16. Financial managers who wish to trade in futures contracts, which are non-standardized or which mature at dates other than those traded in the futures markets must use _____.

17. A(n) _____ is an agreement with a bank in which an interest rate today is locked in for a loan to be delivered from the bank at some future date.

18. If significant price differentials exist between forward and futures markets, _____ will buy and sell contracts so that such discrepancies will be eliminated.

19. Firms that issue debt in the country in which they are well known, receive that currency, and then exchange it for another country's currency are said to have engaged in a currency _____.

20. The persons or companies taking the two sides of a swap transaction are referred to as _____.

21. Many insurance risks are _____ and are probably the type of risk that would like to have covered by insurance rather than by hedging.

Problems

1. Chester Malloy is your friend and he tells you how he shorted $3 million of Myra Images Corp. stocks. He wants your help in determining how much of the Standard & Poor's 500 Index (S&P 500) he should buy in order to hedge the market-related risk to which he is

exposed. The historical relation between the stock's change in price and the change in price of the market index is

Monthly change in value of Myra Images = a + δ(monthly changes in market index)
= 0.35 + 2.2(monthly changes in market index)

2. ABC Corp. is able to borrow at 10 percent for 1 year, using its credit card receivables as collateral. It estimates that its overall return from the credit card loans is 12 percent. If the average credit card loan is of 2 years maturity, what forward interest rate is implied by this homemade forward contract?

3. Mayo Corp. plans to modernize its German manufacturing facility. The estimated financing needs are 30 million Euros. It finds it can get better financing terms if it issues $27 million of 6-year, 8 percent notes in the U.S. capital markets. Simultaneously, it enters into an agreement with its German bank for an equivalent Euro loan swap. The Euro loan carries 10 percent interest rate. Assume an exchange rate of $0.90/Euro. Demonstrate the "numbers" of this currency swap.

4. Borza Corp. and Mettle, Inc. can borrow fixed or floating rate loans as below:

	Borza Corp.	Mettle, Inc.
Fixed rate loans	8%	10.0 %
Floating rate loans	T-bill + 1%	T-bill +2%

Borza wants to borrow at floating rate and Mettle wants to get a fixed rate loan. Can you design a swap, which will lower borrowing costs for both companies? Assume that the cost savings from the swap are shared equally.

5. Recent quotations from the Coffee, Sugar and Cocoa Exchange show the following:

	Spot Price	5-month futures price
Coffee	$0.52/lb	$0.59/lb
Sugar	$0.071/lb	$0.053
Cocoa	$1,790/ton	$1,492/ton

The short-term interest rate is 4.5 percent. Estimate the net convenience yield for each commodity. Comment on the net convenience yield numbers you get. Does it look like there is a shortage in any of the commodities?

Essay Questions

1. Discuss the statement. " Managers are paid to take risk.".

2. Describe the difference between adverse selection and moral hazard, and explain why they cause problems for insurance companies.

3. Describe the process of hedging through financial futures, giving examples.

4. Demonstrate how forward contracts may be constructed to suit a particular need you can think of.

5. Discuss the statement. "Derivatives have improved the hedging opportunities for managers."

6. Your company is a one of the largest packaged food producer in the world and consumes large quantities of corn, wheat, pork bellies, etc. Devise a hedging strategy for the firm, explaining why you might want to hedge the risk in your primary supplies.

ANSWERS TO EXERCISES

Fill-in Questions

1. Hedge	12. Long hedge
2. Delta	13. Spot price
3. Derivative	14. Storage costs; convenience yield
4. Adverse selection	15. Net convenience yield
5. Moral hazard	16. Forward contract
6. Futures	17. Forward rate agreement (FRA)
7. Marked to market	18. Arbitrageurs
8. Hedge ratio	19. Swap
9. Immunized	20. Counterparties
10. Basis risk; less than	21. Jump risk.
11. Short hedge	

Problems

1. To hedge the short sale, Chester must set aside $6,6,00,000 (2.2 x$3,000,000).

2. Forward interest rate = $[(1.12)^2/1.10] - 1 = 14.04$ percent

3.

Cash flows in millions

	Year 0		Years 1 - 5		Year 6	
	$	Euro	$	Euro	$	Euro
Issue dollar notes	+27.0	0	-2.16	0	-29.16	0
Swap for Euros	-27.0	30.0	+2.16	-3.00	+29.16	-33.00
Net cash flow	0	30.0	0	-3.00	0	-33.00

The swap has resulted in a Euro loan carrying 10 percent interest.

4. Borza's comparative advantage is in the fixed rate market as it can borrow at 2 percent lower than Mettle. Mettle has comparative advantage in the floating rate market as it has to pay

330

only 1 percent higher than the rate paid by Borza. Note that Borza has a lower rate or absolute advantage compared to Mettle in both markets. Each party can benefit by borrowing in the market of their comparative advantage and swapping the loans to get their preferred type of loan. The total cost of each company borrowing directly in their preferred market: T-bill+1% + 10% = T-bill + 11 %. If each borrows in the market of comparative advantage, the total cost will be: 8% + T-bill + 2% = T-bill + 10 %. Thus, the swap should give a total saving of 1 percent. If the saving is shared equally, Borza should end up with a floating rate loan of T-bill + 0.5% and Mettle should have a fixed rate loan of 9.5%. This can be accomplished as follows:

Borza borrows fixed rate at 8% and passes it on to Mettle at 9.5%.
Mettle borrows floating rate at T-bill+2 % and passes it on to Borza at the same rate.
Borza's effective cost = 8% - 9.5% + T-bill+2% = T-bill+0.5%.
Mettle's effective cost = T-bill+2 - (T-bill+2) + 9.5% = 9.5%.

5. The table below shows the spot price, futures price, (PV(futures price) and the net convenience yield.

$$\text{PV (futures price)} = \frac{\text{Futures price}}{(1+045)^{5/12}}$$

Net convenience yield = Spot price - PV(futures price).

Commodity	Spot price	Futures price	PV(futures price)	Net convenience yield
Coffee	$0.52/lb	$0.59/lb	$0.5793/lb	-7.93 cents/lb
Sugar	7.1 cents/lb	5.3 cents/lb	5.20 cents/lb	1.9 cents/lb
Cocoa	$1,790/ton	$1,492/ton	$1,464.9/ton	$325.1/ton

For coffee, it appears that storage costs dominate the net convenience yield. For both sugar and cocoa, the net convenience yield is fairly high compared to the spot price, perhaps indicating a temporary shortage.

28
Managing International Risks

INTRODUCTION

This chapter covers management of risks brought on by international exposure of one kind or another. Exposure to international risks has become very common on account of the expanding global trade and investment. A company with investments and real operations overseas obviously faces significant international risks. Even those companies, which operate within their home countries, are not immune from international risk, as they would have customers, suppliers, and/or competitors from abroad. In other words, there are very few purely "domestic" operations, which will not be affected by international risks such as changes in exchange rates, global market conditions for major commodities, and significant geopolitical events.

International risk arises from one of three broad sources: exchange rate changes, interest rate differences and political risk. An understanding of the exchange markets is the first step in understanding exchange risk. The chapter begins with a description of the foreign exchange markets. It then goes on to explain a set of basic relationships covering exchange rates, interest rates and inflation across countries. This is followed by sections on hedging currency risk, international investments and political risk.

KEY CONEPTS IN THE CHAPTER

Foreign Exchange Markets: The foreign exchange market is global and has no one central trading place. Trading takes place all over the world, though most of the trading is done in centers like New York, London, and Frankfurt. The daily volume of currency transactions in these markets exceeds over 1 trillion dollars. International banks and some large multinational corporations are the major players in currency markets. The transactions can be spot or forward. Spot transactions are for immediate delivery and forward transactions are completed at future points in time at prices agreed upon now.

An e*xchange rate* is the price of one currency in terms of another. A *direct quote* (for Americans) is the dollar price of 1 unit of the foreign currency. For example $0.90/Euros and $1.44/British pound are direct quotes. An *indirect quote* is given as units of foreign currency needed to buy one dollar (e.g. Yen 131/$). Indirect quotes are commonly used for most currencies. The British pound sterling and the Euro are the exceptions and are quoted in direct terms. There is also an organized futures market for currencies. Futures are (as we saw in chapter 27) standardized forward contracts and are available for most major currencies. You can also buy options on the futures contracts. Banks sell custom designed option contracts on currencies. There are also more complicated contracts combining features of a forward contract and options.

The forward rate for currency reflects the market's expectation about the change in the currency's expected future spot rate. A currency is said to have a *forward premium* (*discount*) if the forward rate in direct terms is higher (lower) compared to the spot rate. Normally, the premium is computed as an annualized percentage.

Some Basic Relationships: If individuals are not worried about risk and there are no barriers to international trade, exchange rates would be governed by four fundamental relationships. These relationships cover the current spot and forward exchange rates, the interest rates in the two countries, the inflation rates in the two countries, and the expected future spot rate. The four relationships are interdependent. The difference in interest rates between two currencies is equal to the difference in the expected inflation rates, which in turn is equal to the expected change in spot rate. This change in spot rate is equal to the difference between the forward and spot rates, which in turn is equal to the difference in interest rates between two different currencies. These relationships are based on the economic argument that the real rate of return on invested capital among all countries tends to equilibrate even though nominal interest rates may differ on account of inflation.

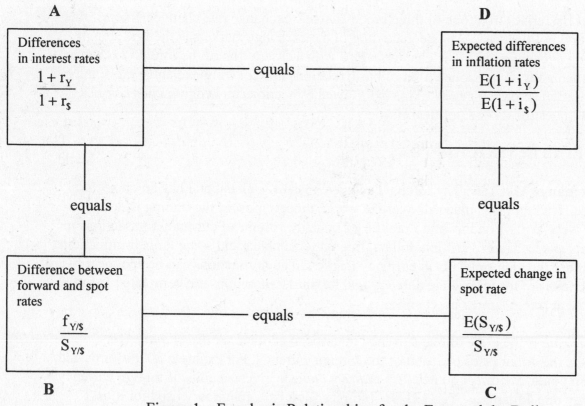

Figure 1 – Four basic Relationships for the Euro and the Dollar

Note that the exchange rates are expressed in indirect terms of Yens/$. Each of the above relationships is reviewed below.

Interest rates and exchange rates (boxes A and B): This is known as the *interest-rate parity*. The difference between interest rates must equal the differential between the forward and spot exchange rates. This relationship seems to hold pretty well when taxes and government regulations are absent. This is the case in international markets (Eurocurrency markets). If the relationship does not hold, one can make money by borrowing in one currency, lending in the other, and covering the exchange rate risk with forward contracts.

The forward premium and changes in spot rates (boxes B and C): This relationship (the *expectations theory*) implies that the expected change in spot rate should equal the current forward premium (or discount). This theory ignores risk. On average the forward rate can be expected to equal the future spot rate. The relationship may not hold exactly and the forward price may be an over or underestimate.

Changes in the exchange rate and inflation rates (boxes C and D): If goods flow freely across borders, then the prices should roughly be equal across countries. This is often called the *purchasing power parity* (PPP) implying that similar goods should be priced roughly the same in each country. This also means that the differences in inflation rates get reflected in exchange rates. That is if the inflation rate is 3 percent in the US and 2 percent in Japan, the yen will appreciate by about 1 percent or the number of yens required to buy a dollar will fall by about 1 percent. The PPP holds broadly in the long run, but short run deviations are not uncommon. The estimated difference in relative inflation rates between two countries can be seen as a rough estimate of the expected change in the spot exchange rate.

Interest rates and inflation rates (boxes D and A): Capital tends to flow to its highest and best use and in equilibrium expected real return on capital should be the same in different countries. Thus the money rate of interest will reflect expected inflation and differences in money rates should equal the expected differences in inflation rates. This is known as the international Fisher effect.

The four relationships in practice:

Interest-rate parity: Works well in international markets, but not so well in domestic markets because of government regulations and taxes.

The expectation theory of forward rates: On average the forward rate equals the future spot rate; however it often overshoots one way or the other. Forward rate is seen as a better predictor than exchange forecasting services.

Purchasing power parity: Generally holds well over the long term. It is also seen that where there are large differences in inflation between countries (example - Bolivia and the US in the eighties), the adjustment is more rapid.

Real interest rates across countries: High inflation countries have higher interest rates and real rates seem to converge, though in the short-term a disparity in real rates might exist especially where government regulations and taxes are significant factors. Part of the problem in testing this theory is that we cannot observe expected inflation rates and expected real rates.

Currency Risk: Most companies engage in some form of exchange risk hedging. Exchange risk is often classified as either *transaction exposure* or *economic exposure*. Transaction exposure is the risk of unfavorable exchange rate movements affecting known commitments in foreign currency. For example, a company, which is expecting a payment in a foreign currency from an export transaction, is facing a transaction exposure. Transaction exposure can be easily hedged through different means as discussed below. Economic exposure is refers to the overall impact on the business from changes in exchange rates. This is harder to quantify and managing this risk should be part of the firm's overall global business strategy.

Transaction exposure can be hedged using futures or forward contracts. Hedging can also be done using options, which protect against adverse currency movements without affecting any possible gains form favorable movement of exchange rate. In theory one can also hedge by lending or borrowing in the foreign currency depending on the direction of the exposure (borrow if you are expecting a foreign currency cash flow in future; lend if you have to pay in foreign currency at a future date.) If the interest rate parity holds, hedging by forward/futures contracts or through lending/borrowing should give essentially the same results.

The main advantage of hedging transaction exposure is that the firm is free to concentrate on the main business. Hedging can also be done at a relatively low cost. Foreign exchange markets are reasonably efficient in the major currencies. This means that the cost of hedging is likely to be low. Remember that cost of hedging is not the difference between today's spot rate and forward rate, but the expected spot rate and the forward rate.

International Investment Decisions: Overseas investments are evaluated by discounting estimated cash flows at the opportunity cost of capital with adjustments for subsidized financing or other effects. There are two ways to calculate net present value. One converts the foreign currency cash flows into home currency cash flows. These cash flows are discounted using the home country opportunity cost of capital to get the project NPV in the home currency. This method requires a forecast of foreign exchange rates. The other method discounts the foreign currency cash flows at the foreign currency cost of capital to obtain the project NPV in the foreign currency. This is then converted into the home currency using the spot exchange rate. The latter method implicitly assumes that the currency flows are hedged. The two approaches to evaluating foreign projects are summarized below.

	Approach 1	Approach 2
Step 1	Estimate cash flows in foreign currency.	Estimate cash flows in foreign currency.
Step 2	Convert to home currency using forecasted exchange rates.	Calculate the net present value using the foreign currency discount rate.

| Step 3 | Calculate net present value using the home country discount rate | Convert the NPV to home currency using the current spot rate |

Approach 1 requires exchange rates forecast, while approach 2 does not. However, approach 2 requires computation of opportunity cost for the project in the foreign currency. This approach ignores exchange rate risk. The two approaches should result in the same NPV value. If they do not, it would mean you have used an exchange rate forecast different from that given by the market. The project should be justified based on its cash flows and not on any exploitation of presumed market inefficiency.

The Cost of Capital for Foreign Investment: The cost of capital for foreign projects was discussed in chapter 9. The basic approach involves estimation of beta for the foreign project relative to the company's *home market index* and then the calculation of the home currency required rate of return. This rate of return can then be converted into the foreign required rate of return using the following relationship:

$$\frac{1 + \text{home currency return}}{1 + \text{home currency interest rate}} = \frac{1 + \text{foreign currency return}}{1 + \text{foreign currency interest rate}}$$

Remember that diversification is valuable and international diversification may be even more valuable. In general, it is wiser to adjust estimated cash flows for foreign risks than to adjust the discount rate.

Political Risk: In a general sense, political risk is not confined to foreign investments. Businesses always face the risk of unanticipated government action, which affect their business adversely. The important difference about foreign political risk is that the risk arises from the fact that your company is a foreign company in that country and may be treated differently because it is a foreign company. The extreme case of political risk is the risk of expropriation. If foreign governments change the rules after you have made your investments, your business profitability gets affected. The key to "managing" political risk is understanding the nature of the risk and then structuring the business, its operations and financing in a way that the probability of adverse foreign government action is reduced. If any adverse action does take place, the effect on the business value should be minimized.

WORKED EXAMPLES

1. The Wall Street Journal reported the following spot and forward rates on April 11, 2002:

	Spot Rates	6- month forward rate
Japanese Yen	Y131.47/$	130.84
British Pound	$1.4383/pound	1.4306
Swiss Francs	$0.6026/Fr.	0.6031

Calculate the forward premium (discount) for each of the currencies.

SOLUTION

The forward premium (discount) for each currency can be calculated as follows:

$$\text{Forward premium (discount)} = \frac{\text{spot rate } - \text{ forward rate}}{\text{forward rate}} \times \frac{12}{\text{months to expiration}}$$

Please note that this is the formula used for indirect quotes. For direct quotes, the formula is modified as below:

$$\text{Forward premium (discount)} = \frac{\text{forward rate } - \text{ spot rates}}{\text{spot rate}} \times \frac{12}{\text{months to expiration}}$$

The premium is always reported as an annualized number.

$$\text{Premium for Japanese yen} = \frac{131.47 - 130.84}{130.84} \times 4 = 1.93 \text{ percent}$$

$$\text{Discount for British pound} = \frac{\text{forward rate } - \text{ spot rate}}{\text{spot rate}} \times 4 = \frac{1.4306 - 1.4383}{1.4383} \times 4 = -2.14 \text{ percent}$$

$$\text{Premium for Swiss Franc} = \frac{0.6031 - 0.6026}{0.6026} \times 4 = 0.33 \text{ percent}$$

Note that the quotes for the British pound and Swiss Franc are in direct terms and the formula was reversed to reflect that.

2. Use the spot exchange rates given in problem 1 and check if the interest rate parity holds or not given the following 3 month interest rates:

US dollar interest rate	2.24 percent
Japan	0.40 percent
Britain	4.20 percent
Switzerland	2.00 percent

SOLUTION

According to interest rate parity, the relationship among the spot, forward and interest rates can be written as:

$$\frac{\text{forward rate}}{\text{spot rate}} = \frac{1 + \text{foreign interest rate}}{1 + \text{dollar interest rate}}$$

We can write the foreign interest rate = $\dfrac{\text{forward rate} \times (1 + \text{dollar interest rate})}{\text{spot rate}} - 1$

This is the formula for indirect quotes. For direct quotes, the formula would be:

$\dfrac{\text{spot rate} \times (1 + \text{dollar interest rate})}{\text{forward rate}} - 1$

Also, note that the interest rate should be for the period of the forward contract. So the dollar rate should be: 2.24/4 = 0.56 percent

Japanese interest rate = [(130.84 x 1.0056)/131.47] – 1 = 0.08 percent/3 months
$\qquad\qquad\qquad$ = 0.32 percent (annual)

The British interest rate = [(1.4383x1.0056)/1.4306] – 1 = 1.1 percent/3 months
$\qquad\qquad\qquad$ = 4.4 percent (annual)

The Swiss interest rate = [(0.6026x1.0056)/0.6031] – 1 = 0.48 percent/3 months
$\qquad\qquad\qquad$ = 1.92 percent (annual)

None of the interest rates reported exactly matches the ones calculated by the interest rate parity.

3. The one-year dollar interest rate is 2.9 percent. The one-year spot and forward rate for the Euro is $0.8831 and $0.8771. Estimate the one-year Euro interest rate.

SOLUTION

Using the interest rate parity relationship, we can write the Euro interest rate as:

$\qquad$ = [(0.8831x1.029)/0.8771] – 1 = 3.6 percent

4. The expected annual inflation in Mexico is 5 percent. The expected inflation for the US is 1.5 percent. If the spot rate for the peso is 9.91 pesos/$, estimate the expected 1-year future spot rate.

SOLUTION

$\qquad$ Expected spot rate = $\dfrac{(1 + \text{inflation rate for Mexico}) \times (1 + \text{spot rate})}{(1 + \text{inflation rate for US})} = \dfrac{1.05 x 9.91}{1.015}$

$\qquad\qquad$ = 10.252 pesos

5. Dos Amigos Brewery (DAB) exports Mexican beer to the United States. They expect to receive a payment of $875,000 in about 3 months time from their wholesaler in Texas. The spot and forward rates for the peso are 9.91 pesos/$ and 10.00 pesos/$. DAB has banking relationship with a Houston bank and the bank is willing to lend money to DAB at the US

prime rate of 5 percent. DAB's cost of funds in Mexico is 8 percent. Suggest two ways of hedging DAB's dollar exposure. Compare the cash flows resulting from each hedging approach.

SOUTION

DAB can hedge by either: i) sell dollar forward or ii) borrow dollars from its Houston bank and convert the dollars at the spot rate and pay back the bank using its dollar cash receipts 3 months from now. The cash flows of the two approaches are shown below:

Hedging with forward contract:

DAB sells $875,000 forward at 10 pesos/$. Cash flow in 3 months = 875,000 x 10
$$= 8,750,000 \text{ pesos}$$

Present value of the cash flow (annual cost of 8%, quarterly cost = 2%) = 8,750,000/1.02
$$= 8,578,431 \text{ pesos}$$

Hedging through bank loan

DAB borrows the present value of $875,000 to be received in 3 months. The loan amount is converted into pesos now using the spot rate. The loan is paid off by the dollars received in 3 months. First, calculate the loan amount. Annual interest rate of 5 percent converts to 1.25 percent per 3 months.

Loan amount   = $875,000/1.0125 = $864,198
Peso cash flow   = 864,198 x 9.91 = 8,564,202 pesos

DAB is better off with the forward contract hedging. Its loan rate in the US is too high relative to its cost of funds in Mexico. There appears to be a deviation from the interest rate parity.

6. Barton Restaurants, a large US hamburger chain, is planning to open a number of restaurants in Gardinia. The initial investment is estimated at 25 million Gardinian kronas. Stacy Appleton, the CFO of Barton is evaluating the project on an expected project life of 5 years. The expected annual cash flows for five years are 7.5 million kronas. Stacy collected following additional information:

Current exchange rate = $1/krona
Current US interest rate = 4.5 percent.
Gardinian interest rate = 6.5 percent
US Opportunity cost of the project = 12 percent

Evaluate the project.

SOLUTION

We can use two approaches to evaluate the project. The first approach involves conversion of all cash flows into US dollar and discounting the cash flows with the US opportunity cost of 12 percent. The second approach discounts the foreign cash flows using the foreign opportunity cost and converting the resultant NPV into dollar NPV using the current spot rate. Approach 1 requires forecast of exchange rates for each of the next five years. Approach 2 requires estimation of the foreign opportunity cost.

Approach 1: We can use the interest rates to forecast the future exchange rates. The exchange rate forecasts and the dollar cash flows from the project are given below:

Year	Forecasted Exchange rate	Cash flow in $million
Current	spot rate = $1/kr	25.000
Year 1	$1 \times 1.045/1.065 = \$0.9812/kr$	7.359
Year 2	$1 \times (1.045/1.065)^2 = \$0.9628$	7.221
Year 3	$1 \times (1.045/1.065)^3 = \$0.9447$	7.085
Year 4	$1 \times (1.045/1.065)^4 = \$0.9270$	6.953
Year 5	$1 \times (1.045/1.065)^5 = \$0.9096$	6.822

Use the cash flow worksheet:
$CF_0 = -25$, $CO_1 = 7.359$, $FO_1 = 1$, $CO_2 = 7.221$, $FO_2 = 1$,
$CO_3 = 7.085$, $FO_3 = 1$, $CO_4 = 6.953$, $FO_4 = 1$, $CO_5 = 6.822$, $FO_5 = 1$
Use NPV worksheet: $I = 12\%$, NPV = $0.6598 million

Approach 2:

We need to estimate the krona opportunity cost of capital for the project. This can be estimated from the following relationship:

$$\frac{1 + \text{home currency return}}{1 + \text{home currency interest rate}} = \frac{1 + \text{foreign currency return}}{1 + \text{foreign currency interest rate}}$$

$$\text{Krona opportunity cost} = \frac{1.12 \times 1.065}{1.045} - 1 = 14.14\%$$

First compute the krona NPV: $CF_0 = -25$, $CO_1 = 7.5$, $FO_1 = 5$; Compute NPV, given $I = 14.14\%$
NPV = kr0.6617 million = $0.6617 million.

(The difference in the NPV values for the two approaches is due to rounding of the opportunity cost and the conversion cash flows.)

SUMMARY

This chapter covered the basics of managing the risks associated with international operations. International operations add three additional elements of risk to a company's business: risk caused by changes in exchange rates, risk caused by different interest rates in different countries and political risk. Financial managers should understand the nature of each of these risks. The nature and complexity of each element of risk will be a function of the type of the business, the size of the firm and the nature of international operations.

Understanding the workings of foreign exchange market is a necessary first step to understanding exchange rate risk. There are four basic economic relationships, which govern the changes in exchange rates. These relationships link the spot and forward exchange rates, the interest rates and the inflation rates across countries. The relationships ignore investor' risk aversion, transaction costs, taxes and other form of government intervention and other market imperfections. Therefore, the empirical validity of the relationships is less than perfect. However, they are reasonable accounts of the relationships involved and are useful for anyone interested in the direction and magnitude of changes in exchange rates. Financial managers would do well to learn the four basic relationships or parity theories as they are often called.

Exchange rate changes affect cash flows of businesses involved in international operations. Businesses are exposed to two types of exchange risk: transaction exposure and economic exposure. Transaction exposure is the exposure given by known or committed transactions is quantifiable and can be, in most cases, fully hedged. The cost of hedging should be seen in terms of expected future spot rates rather than current spot rates. Economic exposure, on the other hand, is the long and medium term impact on the firm's business caused by the changes of exchange rates. This is difficult to quantify and hedge. The best approach to managing economic exposure is to treat it as part of the firm's overall risk and develop strategies to control and minimize the impact of the exposure.

International capital investment decisions are no different from any other investment decision. You accept positive NPV projects. The only complexity is that you have cash flows in a foreign currency and these need to be evaluated using the "foreign discount' rate. Alternately, you can convert the foreign currency cash flows into your home currency cash flows and use the home currency discount rate.

The last part of the chapter discusses political risk. Foreign operations are subject to an extra dimension of political risk because it is possible that a foreign company might be treated differently than a domestic firm in the same business. The key to managing political risk is to understand it fully and then design the business operations and financing structure to reflect and minimize the effect of any adverse political action. The nature and level of political risk is a function of not only the country involved but also the industry and the current economic and political situation in the country.

LIST OF TERMS

Direct quote

Economic exposure

Eurocurrency market

Expectations theory of exchange rates

Forward market

Indirect quote

Interest rate parity theory

Purchasing power parity

Spot exchange rate

Transaction exposure

EXERCISES

Fill-in Questions

1. An exchange rate quotation for the price of a currency for immediate delivery is known as
    _____.

2. Financial managers who buy and sell currency for future delivery do it in the
    _____ market for foreign currencies.

3. The relationship between the interest-rate differential and the annual forward premium or
    discount is known as the _____

4. The _____ theory of exchange rates says that the percentage difference between
    the forward exchange rates and the spot exchange rates is equal to the expected change in the
    spot rate.

5. The _____ suggests that expected changes in the spot exchange rate is
    approximated by estimated differences in relative _____ rates.

6. The international market for short-term loans that is virtually free of government regulation is
    called the _____ market.

7. Most currency quotations are given as _____ quote, and give the number of units of
    foreign currency needed to buy one United States dollar.

8. The Euro and the British pound are normally quoted using the _____ quote, which gives
    the number of US dollars needed to buy one unit of foreign currency.

9. The risk from an exchange rate movement on currency receipts/payments already contracted
    is known as _____.

10. The risk from an exchange rate movement on the value of the entire business is known as
    _____.

Problems

1. Given below are quotes for the Canadian dollar and the Euro. Calculate the forward premium or discount.

	Spot rate	6-month Forward rate
Canadian dollar	$0.6297/C$	$0.6280/C$
Euro	$0.90/Euro	$0.8867/Euro

    Also, compute the C$/E cross rates (spot and forward).

2. The current dollar one-year interest rate is 3.6 percent. The one-year interest rate in India is 7.5 percent. The spot exchange rate for the Indian rupee is Rs. 49/$. Estimate the likely one-year forward exchange rate for the rupee, assuming interest rate parity.

3. Meyer GmbH is a Munich based sports good manufacturer. They export archery equipment to the US. The company is expecting a payment of $5 million in 3 months. The spot and forward rate for the Euro are $0.8800 and $0.8776 respectively. Meyer has an opportunity cost of funds of 6.5 percent in Germany. It can also borrow dollars from its New York bank at the rate of 4.5 percent. Suggest the best hedging approach for Meyer.

4. Sun Motors Corp. (SMC), a Korean auto parts company is planning an investment in India. The initial investment is estimated to cost 560 million Indian rupees. Soyul Kim, the CFO of SMC Barton is evaluating the project on an expected project life of 6 years. The expected annual cash flows for six years are 135 million rupees. Soyul collected the following additional information:

    Current exchange rate = Rs.26/Korean Won
    Current Koran interest rate = 9.5 percent.
    Indian interest rate = 7.5 percent
    Korean Opportunity cost of the project = 15 percent

    Evaluate the project.

ANSWERS TO EXERCISES

Fill-in Questions

1. Spot rate
2. Forward
3. Interest-rate parity
4. Expectations theory
5. Purchasing power parity, inflation
6. Eurocurrency
7. Indirect
8. Direct
9. Transaction exposure
10. Economic exposure

Problems

1. Both quotes are given in the direct quotes format. The forward premium can be calculated using the following formula

$$\text{Forward premium (discount)} = \frac{\text{forward rate - spot rate}}{\text{spot rate}} \times \frac{12}{\text{months to expiration}}$$

$$\text{Forward premium or discount for C\$} = \frac{0.6280 - 0.6297}{0.6297} \times 2 = -0.54 \text{ percent}$$

That is the Canadian dollar is at a discount of 0.54 percent.

$$\text{Forward premium or discount for the Euro} = \frac{0.8867 - 0.9000}{0.9000} \times 2 = -2.96 \text{ percent}$$

The Euro is at a discount of 2.96 percent.

$$\text{Cross rate C\$/Euro} = \frac{\text{Dollar price of Euro}}{\text{Dollar price of C\$}}$$

Spot C\$/Euro = 0.9000/0.6297 = C\$1.4293/Euro
Forward rate = 0.8867/0.6280 = C\$1.4119/Euro

$$\text{Forward premium or discount} = \frac{1.4119 - 1.4293}{1.4119} \times 2 = -2.45 \text{ percent}$$

The Euro is at a discount of 2.45 percent relative to C\$.

2. The one-year forward rate for Rupee $= \dfrac{49 \times 1.075}{1.036} = \text{Rs.50.84/\$}$

3. Meyer can hedge in two ways. See the worked example problem 5. The quarterly German interest rate would be 6.5/4 = 1.625 %, and the corresponding US rate 1.125%.

Hedging through forward contracts: Meyer sells \$5,000,000 forward at the rate of \$0.8776/Euro. Present value of this can be computed as below:

$$\text{Cash flow from forward hedging} = \frac{5,000,000}{0.8776} \times \frac{1}{1.01625} = 5,606,255 \text{ Euros}$$

Hedging through dollar loan: Meyer can borrow the present value of \$5,000,000 now and convert the loan amount at the spot rate of \$0.88/Euro. The loan will be repaid by the receivable cash flow.
Loan amount = \$5,000,000/1.01125 = \$4,944,376
Euro cash flow by conversion using spot rate = \$4,944,376/0.88 = 5,618,609 Euros

The latter is a slightly better alternative.

4. See worked example 6. We can use the same two approaches to evaluate the project. The first approach involves conversion of all cash flows into Korean wons and discounting the cash flows with the Korean opportunity cost of 15 percent. The second approach discounts the rupee cash flows using the Indian opportunity cost and converting the resultant NPV into Korean won NPV using the current spot rate. Approach 1 requires forecast of rupee exchange rates for each of the next five years. Approach 2 requires estimation of the Indian opportunity cost.

Approach 1: We can use the interest rates to forecast the future exchange rates. The exchange rate forecasts and the Korean won cash flows from the project are given below. Note that the exchange rate is an indirect quote (rupee/won); so the formula used in the worked examples is reversed:

Year	Forecasted Exchange rate	Cash flow in million Wons
Current	spot rate = Rs26/won	-21.5385
Year 1	26 x 1.075/1.095 = Rs.25.525	5.6807
Year 2	26 x $(1.075/1.095)^2$ = Rs.25.059	5.7864
Year 3	26 x $(1.075/1.095)^3$ = Rs.24.601	5.8940
Year 4	26 x $(1.075/1.095)^4$ = Rs.24.152	6.0037
Year 5	26 x $(1.075/1.095)^5$ = Rs.23.278	6.1154
Year 6	26 x $(1.075/1.095)^6$ = Rs.22.853	6.2291

Use the cash flow worksheet:
CF_0 = -21.5385, CO_1 = 5.6807, FO_1 = 1, CO_2 = 5.7837, FO_2 = 1, CO_3 = 5.8940, FO_3 = 1, CO_4 = 6.0037, FO_4 = 1, CO_5 = 6.1154, FO_5 = 1, CO_6 = 6.2291, FO_6 = 1

Use NPV worksheet: I = 15 %, NPV = 0.8181 million wons

Approach 2:

We need to estimate the rupee opportunity cost of capital for the project. This can be estimated from the following relationship:

$$\frac{1 + \text{home currency return}}{1 + \text{home currency interest rate}} = \frac{1 + \text{foreign currency return}}{1 + \text{foreign currency interest rate}}$$

Rupee opportunity cost = $\dfrac{1.15 \times 1.075}{1.095} - 1 = 12.9\%$

First compute the rupee NPV: CF_0 = -560, CO_1 = 145, FO_1 = 6; Compute NPV, given I = 12.9%
NPV = Rs.21.2625 million = 0.8178 million wons.

This is practically the same as Approach 1.

346

29

Financial Analysis and Planning

INTRODUCTION

This chapter shows us how to use a firm's financial statements to analyze past performance and assess its current financial condition. Financial analysis includes the use of accounting statements to measure and interpret past performance. While past performance is no guarantee of future performance, it can help us understand the future. The chapter demonstrates the use of financial ratios and discusses the limitations of financial analysis. Ratios are convenient summary measures and always have to be viewed with a dose of healthy skepticism. The ratios commonly used for financial analysis, however, help you to ask the right questions about a firm's financial performance.

The chapter also provides an introduction to financial planning. Growth and financial planning go hand in hand. Financial planning helps identify the financing requirements needed to fund growth and the need for external financing. While financial planning models use little finance theory, they help focus on the funding needs of the firm for given growth plans.

KEY CONCEPTS IN THE CHAPTER

Financial Statements: Financial or accounting statements are prepared with the objective of providing detailed information to the various stakeholders of a corporation. These stakeholders include shareholders, lenders, suppliers, customers, employees, and others. The standards and norms used for the preparation of accounting statements differ across countries and are largely a function of the relative importance given to the different stakeholders. The US and the British standards emphasize the stockholders' perspective, while in Germany and some countries in continental Europe the emphasis is on lenders. While uniform international standards are emerging, each country's standards are driven by its history and the stage of evolution of its capital markets and financial institutions.

Balance Sheet: A company's balance sheet gives a snap shot of what the company owns (assets), and what it owes (liabilities and shareholders' equity) as of a specific date. The date would be the last date of the reporting period. Reporting convention requires that the assets and liabilities be shown in declining order of their liquidity or currency. Short-term assets and liabilities are shown first in their respective columns ahead of the long-term assets or liabilities are shown. The values of assets and liabilities are almost always reported in book value or cost terms.

Income Statement: The income statement is an account of the operating revenues, the costs and the profit or loss earned during the reporting period. While the balance sheet is as of one date, the income statement captures what transpired during the whole quarter or year. Typically, subtotals are shown at various points in the statement to identify different definitions of profit such as earnings before interest and taxes (EBIT), earnings before taxes, etc. Note that the US accounting and tax rules permit the company to report income differently than the one reported in tax filing. The differences in tax income and the income reported to shareholders are mainly due to different depreciation charges used and some other charges.

Sources and Uses of Funds: The sources and uses of funds statement can be prepared from the balance sheet and income statement data. The statement shows the details of financing raised by the company during the year and how the funds raised were used. Sources of funds include net operating income, depreciation, and external capital like issue of debt or equity. Uses of funds are mainly investments in current or long-term assets and payment of dividends. Note that financial planning involves projecting sources and uses of funds for the plan period.

Financial Analysis: Financial analysts use a number of ratios derived from the financial statements and market information. These ratios are grouped according to the kind of questions they help answer. Five classes of financial ratios are typically used. These are leverage ratios, liquidity ratios, efficiency ratios, profitability ratios, and market value ratios. Note that most of the ratios use book or accounting values of the various assets and liabilities. It is also common practice to use averages of the beginning and ending values of the assets and liabilities to compute the profit and efficiency ratios to get a more accurate view of profit or efficiency performance for the period. The different classes of ratios are described briefly below.

Leverage Ratios: These ratios tell us about a firm's financial leverage or use of debt financing and its ability to service its debt obligations. Some commonly used leverage ratios are given below:

Debt ratio = (long-term debt + value of leases)/(long-term debt + value of leases + equity)

Debt-equity ratio = (long-term debt + value of leases)/equity

Times interest earned = (EBIT + depreciation)/interest

The last ratio provides a measure of a firm's ability to service its interest payments.

Liquidity Ratios: These ratios attempt to measure the short-run ability of the firm to meet its current liabilities. Reserve borrowing power may mean more than any of these ratios. Common liquidity ratios are the following:

Net working capital to total assets = net working capital/total assets

Current ratio = current assets/current liabilities

Quick ratio = (cash + marketable securities + receivables)/current liabilities

Cash ratio = (cash + marketable securities)/current liabilities

<u>Efficiency Ratios:</u> These ratios measure how efficiently the firm uses its assets.

Sales to Assets (Asset Turnover) = sales/average total assets

Days in Inventory = (Average inventory/cost of goods sold) x 365

Average collection period = average receivables/average daily sales

<u>Profitability:</u> Various measures of profitability are used. One ratio alone is likely to be misleading. The entire set of ratios, trends, and comparison with the benchmarks are likely to provide better insights.

Net profit margin = (EBIT - tax)/sales

Return on total assets = (EBIT - taxes)/average total assets

Return on equity = earnings available for common/average equity

Payout ratio = dividends per share/earnings per share

<u>Market Value Ratios:</u> These are often used to measure a firm's market performance. Some analysts prefer them to other performance measures precisely because they use market data and because capital markets send information to a firm's management. The commonly used market-based ratios are given below:

Price-earnings ratio = stock price/earnings per share

Dividend yield = dividend per share/stock price

Market-to-book ratio = stock price/book value per share

Tobin's q = market value of assets/estimated replacement cost

<u>Benchmarks:</u> A ratios by itself does not tell you much. One has to use benchmarks to compare performance of the firm and evaluate the same. Typical benchmarks used include the following: the same firm's past, industry averages, a select group of firms, a peer firm or the best firm in the industry. You have to be cautious and careful about the ratios you select and the benchmarks you use. Keep in mind the pitfalls of comparisons across firms with different accounting norms or standards.

<u>The Du Pont System:</u> The Du Pont system, pioneered by the eponymous firm, shows the linkages among key profitability and efficiency ratios. The Du Pont equations are expressed in terms of the return on assets (ROA) or the return on equity (ROE).

$$ROA = \frac{EBIT - tax}{assets} = \frac{sales}{assets} \, x \, \frac{EBIT - tax}{sales}$$

$$ROE = \frac{EBIT - tax - \mathrm{int}\, erest}{equity}$$

$$= \frac{assets}{equity} \, x \, \frac{sales}{assets} \, x \, \frac{EBIT - tax}{sales} \, x \, \frac{EBIT - tax - \mathrm{int}\, erest}{EBIT - tax}$$

Firms would like to earn high ROA. ROA is the product of the sales to assets ratio and profit margin. Generally, the ratios are determined by the type of industry the firm is in, the level of competition, and the firm's own competitive strength. ROE includes the effect of leverage also. Again, this is a function of the industry and firm's own choice of leverage. The Du Pont equation breaks down the profitability performance measure (ROA or ROE) into its basic components and provides a very useful tool for comparative performance evaluation of two companies or a company with some benchmark.

Financial statements provide most of the data required for financial analysis. Care and caution need to be exercised before the data from the financial statements are used and when the ratios are interpreted. The following cautionary comments are in order. Note that even within a country, accountants enjoy considerable discretion and flexibility as to the treatment of intangible assets as well as many other elements, which go into an accounting statement. When you calculate financial ratios and make comparisons, you need to look below the surface to see how particular items have been treated. Some of the items, which could make significant differences on ratios, depending on how they are treated include: depreciation, deferred tax, intangible assets, goodwill, off-balance-sheet debt, pensions, derivatives and foreign accounting practices.

Financial Planning: The primary objective of financial planning is to ensure that the firm will have the needed funds to meet the expansion plans. Financial planning is part of overall corporate planning process. Financial plans project the funds requirement for the firm's projected growth plan. Planning helps focus on the need for financing and prepare the firm for the future. Identification and tying up the right sources for the funds needed are essential parts of the plan. Normally, firms prepare alternate plans reflecting different scenarios and this would help avoid unpleasant surprises.

Financial Planning Models: Financial planning models use the simple sources and uses relationship to project the external funding requirement:

Total external funds needed = Total uses of funds - operating cash flow
Total uses of funds = Investment in fixed assets + investment in net working capital + dividends

?mple 4-step approach can be used. First, project operating cash flow based on the projected ?nd cost assumptions. Then, project funds needed by estimating the investments in fixed and current assets needed to meet the sales projections. The third step involves estimating the additional financing needed. This is the difference between the investments in assets and the operating cash flow less the dividends to be paid. The last step is preparing the pro-form balance sheet based on the projected increase in assets, the needed financing and a plan for raising the needed funds. It is possible that the plan may need to be revised if the projected balance sheet does not fit debt ratio or other targets.

These projections can be carried out easily using spreadsheet programs. Sophisticated models are often used, which help in making varied projections based on different assumptions. In most cases, the simple "percentage of sales" approach can work very well. This assumes a constant relationship of key parameters to the projected sales level.

<u>Finance and Financial Planning</u>: Planning models do not emphasize the accepted tools of financial analysis such as net present value or market risk. Financial planning typically uses goals and objectives based on accounting or other sets of numbers. Examples include sales or profit margin levels, absolute profit targets, market share goal, etc. These rarely relate to any finance theory or the normative corporate objective of shareholder wealth maximization. It is possible that firms choose the above goals as proxy for the shareholder wealth, though such plans may run the risk of chasing after the proxies rather than the real objective of shareholder wealth maximization.

Growth and External Financing: Two measures of growth are often used to indicate the level of growth that can be financed without having to resort to external financing. The first, *internal growth rate*, gives the growth rate that can be sustained without any external financing. This can be calculated as follows:

$$\text{Internal growth rate} = \frac{\text{retained earnings}}{\text{total assets}}$$

This can be expressed in an alternate form, which gives better insight into the measure:

$$\text{Internal growth rate} = \frac{\text{retained earnings}}{\text{net income}} \text{ x } \frac{\text{net income}}{\text{equity}} \text{ x } \frac{\text{equity}}{\text{total assets}}$$
$$= \text{plowback ratio x return on equity x (equity/total assets)}$$

The internal growth rate implies that the firm will not use *any external funding*. A more practical measure is the *sustainable growth rate,* which measures the growth that can be sustained without any *external equity* financing.

$$\text{Sustainable growth rate} = \text{plowback ratio x return on equity}$$

WORKED EXAMPLES

1. Conduct a financial ratio analysis of Burl and Hurl Corp. Use the data given below:

Burl and Hurl Corp: **Balance Sheet**   **($s in million)**

	2001	2000
Cash & short-term securities	175	100
Receivables	500	350
Inventories	750	755
Other current assets	100	75
Total current assets	1,525	1,280
Plant and equipment	1,105	1,170
Other long-term assets	150	50
Total assets	**2,780**	**2,500**
Debt due	25	35
Payables	510	405
Other current liabilities	15	10
Total current liabilities	550	450
Long-term debt and capital leases	375	425
Other long-term liabilities	225	175
Preferred stock	250	250
Shareholders' equity	1,380	1,200
Total liabilities & equity	**2,780**	**2,500**

Income Statement

	2001	2000
Net sales	3,465	3,210
Cost of goods sold	2,252	2,119
Other expenses	346	314
Depreciation	77	62
Earnings before interest and tax (EBIT)	790	715
Net interest	40	46
Tax	285	254
Net income	465	415
Preferred stock dividend	25	25
Earnings applicable to common stock	440	390
Common dividends	260	260
Earnings retained	180	130

Other Financial Information

Market value of equity	6,675
Average number of shares (million)	100
Earnings per share	4.40
Dividends per share	2.60
Share price	66.75

SOLUTION

Leverage ratios:
   a. Debt ratio = ($375 + $225)/($375 + $225 + $1,380) = 30.3%
   b. Debt-equity ratio = ($375 + $225)/$1,380 = 43.5%
   c. Times interest earned = ($790 + $77)/$40 = 21.7 times

Liquidity ratios:
   a. Net working capital to total assets = ($1,525 - $550)/$2,780 = 35.1%
   b. Current ratio = $1,525/$550 = 2.77
   c. Quick ratio = ($175 + $500)/$550 = 1.23
   d. Cash ratio = $175/$550 = 0.32
   e. Interval measure = ($175 + $500)/[($2,252 + $346)/365] = 94.8 days

Efficiency ratios:
   a. Sales to total assets = $3,465/[($2,780 + $2,500)/2] = 1.3
   b. Sales to net working capital = $3,465/{[($1,525 - $550) + ($1,280 - $450)]/2} = 3.84
   c. Average collection period = [($500 + $350)/2]/($3,465/365) = 44.8 days
   d. Inventory turnover = $2,252/[($750 + $755)/2] = 3.0

Profitability ratios
   a. Net profit margin = ($790 - $285)/$3,465 = 14.6%
   b. Return on total assets = ($790 - $285)/[($2,780 + $2,500)/2] = 19.1%
   g. Return on equity = $440/[($1,380 + $1,200)/2] = 34.11%
   h. Payout = $2.60/$4.40 = 59.1%
   i. Plowback = 100% - 59.1% = 40.9%
   j. Sustainable growth rate = 0.409 x 0.341 = 14.0%

Market value ratios:
   a. Price-earnings ratio = $66.75/$4.40 = 15.2 times
   b. Dividend yield = $2.60/$66.75 = 3.90%
   c. Market-to-book = $66.75/($1,380/100) = 4.8 times

2. Doughty Barker Corp. had sales of $1,450 million last year and total assets of $900 million. The company earned a net income of $136 million and paid dividends of $48 million. The net equity for the firm was $576 million. Calculate the internal growth rate and the sustainable growth rate for the firm.

Retained earnings = Net income - dividends = $136 million - $48 million = $88 million
Internal growth rate = retained earnings/total assets = $88 million/$900 million = 9.78 percent
Plowback ratio = $88 million/$136 million = 64.7 percent
ROE = $136 million/$576 million = 23.6 percent
Sustainable growth rate = plowback ratio X ROE = 0.647 X 23.6 = 15.3 per cent.

353

3. Margi Genetics, a fast growing biotech firm has been growing at an annual rate of 45 percent for the last several years. The total assets of the company stood at $475 million at the end of fiscal year 2001. The firm is all-equity financed. The company earned a net income of $88 million on sales of $350 million. Ten percent of the earnings are paid out as dividends. For the next three years the company has projected an annual growth rate of 40 percent and is confident that it can earn the same profit margin.

    a. What is the internal growth rate for the firm?
    b. What is the sustainable growth rate?
    c. Prepare a financial plan for meeting the expansion needs of the firm for the three year period, assuming that all the financial ratios will remain same.
    d. Project a balance sheet as of the year-end 2004.

SOLUTION

    a. Internal growth rate = retained earnings/ total assets = ($88 x 0.9)/$475 = 16.67 %
    b. Since the firm is all-equity financed, the internal growth rate and sustainable growth rate will be same. You can check this by computing the sustainable growth rate using the formula, plowback x ROE. Plowback = 0.9, ROE = $88/$475 = 18.53%, Sustainable growth rate = 0.9 x 18.53 % = 16.67%
    c. We can prepare simplified proforma (projected) income statements for the three-year period as shown below.

$ in million

	Fiscal 2002	Fiscal 2003	Fiscal 2004
Sales	490.00	686.00	960.40
Net income	123.20	172.48	241.47
Dividends	12.32	17.25	24.15
Retained earnings	110.88	155.23	217.32

If the sales-to-assets ratio remains same, the firm would need by the end of 2004:

Total assets = (960.4/350) x 475 = $1,303.40 million
Additional financing during the three year period = 1303.40 - 475 = $828.40 million
Retained earnings available = 110.88 + 155.23 + 217.32 = $483.43 million
External financing needed = 828.40 - 483.43 = $344.97 million

    d. The balance sheet would show total assets = $1,303.40, Equity = $1,303.40

4. A firm has $24,000 in inventory. If this represents, 15 days sales, what is the annual cost of goods sold? What is the inventory turnover ratio?

Annual cost of goods sold = $24,000 x 365/15 = $584,000
Inventory turnover ratio = 365/15 = 24.33

5. Claire Menem Corp. has the following balance sheet for the year ending December 31, 2001:

Assets	$ million	Liabilities & net worth	$ million
Cash	41	Accounts Payable	24
Receivables	89	Notes payable	125
Inventories	70	Accruals	12
Total current assets	200	Total current liabilities	161
Net Fixed Assets	915	Long term loan	264
		Common Stock	117
		Retained Earnings	573
Total assets	1,115	Total liabilities & net worth	1,115

Company's sales for 2001 were $2,350 million. Net income was $125 million. The company paid dividends amounting to $65 million in 2001. Sales are projected to increase to $2,750 million in 2002. The company informs you that, except for cash balance all assets would have to be increased in proportion to sales to meet the expansion needs for 2002. You are also told that the firm plans to finance the funds needed through a mix of additional equity (50 percent of the external funds needed) and long-term debt (50 percent of the external funds needed). Calculate the additional funds needed in 2002. Assume accounts payable and accruals will increase in proportion to sales. Project a balance sheet as of the year-end 2002 incorporating the financing of the additional funds.

SOLUTION
The sales are expected to grow by $(2,750/2,350) - 1 = 17.02\%$
Uses of funds:
Total assets for 2002 = 41 + (1,115 - 41) x 1.1702 = 41 + $1,256.80 = $1,297.80 million
Increase in assets = $1,297.81 m - $1,115 m = $182.80 million

Sources of funds:
Net income for 2002 = 2,750 x (125/2,350) = 146.28 million
Dividends = 146.28 x (65/125) = $76.06 m
Net operating cash flow in 2002 = 146.28 - 76.06 = $70.22 million
Accounts payable in 2002 = 24 x 1.1702 = $28.08 million
Accruals in 2002 = 12 x 1.1702 = $14.04 million
Funds from accounts payable and accruals = 28.08 - 24 + 14.04 - 12 = 6. 12
Net funds needed from new equity and debt = 182.80 - 6.12 - 70.22 = 106.46 = $106.46 million
New debt   = $53.23 million.
New equity = $53.23 million

(Note that depreciation is not considered as a source of funds as the increase in fixed assets is projected from the net fixed assets level.)

The projected balance sheet is given below:

Claire Menem - Pro forma Balance Sheet for 2002

Assets	$ million	Liabilities & net worth	$ million
Cash	41.00	Accounts Payable	28.08
Receivables	104.15	Notes payable	125.00
Inventories	81.91	Accruals	14.04
Total current assets	227.06	Total current liabilities	167.12
Net Fixed Assets	1,070.74	Long term loan	317.23
		Common Stock	170.23
		Retained Earnings	643.22
Total assets	1,297.80	Total liabilities & net worth	1,297.80

SUMMARY

The chapter introduces financial analysis and planning. The five classes of financial ratios commonly used in financial analysis, are described. Of course, financial analysis is a lot more than the simple computation of ratios and tabulating the same. The ratios should be used to analyze past performance, for assessing current financial standing, and to understand the future prospects. Remember that the ratios do not provide answers, but only provide the basis for asking the right questions. One has to be careful and selective in the use of financial ratios. Also, limitations of accounting data should be kept in mind when interpreting financial ratios.

The chapter also provides a brief look into financial planning. Financial planning helps a firm prepare for meeting the financial needs for future growth. The simple percentage of sales model can work well. More sophisticated models are available, which might be useful to analyze the impact of and the financing needs for different alternative growth projections. The planning process should also include tying up the sources of funding and evaluating the proposed financing plans. Two useful growth measures, the internal growth rate and the sustainable growth, can tell you the extent of the growth that can be pursued with no external funding or no external equity financing, respectively.

Note that most financial planning models use very little finance theory. Goals and objectives used in the plans typically include accounting or sales goals such as earnings per share, profit margin growth, market share or sales targets. These goals are meant to be proxies for the ultimate corporate objective of maximizing stockholder value. The financial manager should ensure that the goals do not become substitutes for the real objective of stock value maximization.

LIST OF TERMS

Average collection period
Current assets
Current liabilities
Current ratio
Debt ratio
Debt-equity ratio
Dividend yield
Inflation premium
Internal growth rate
Leverage ratio

Net profit margin
Net working capital
Payout ratio
Price-earnings ratio
Quick ratio
Return on equity (ROE)
Return on total assets (ROA)
Sales-to-assets ratio
Sustainable growth rate
Tobin's q

EXERCISES

Fill-in Questions

1. The difference between current assets and current liabilities is called _____.

2. _____ measure the firm's financial leverage.

3. Long-term debt and the value of leases are included in the (numerator, denominator) _____ of both the _____ ratio and the _____ ratio.

4. Times interest earned is a (liquidity, profitability, leverage) _____ ratio.

5. Assets that are in cash or will be turned into cash in the near future are called _____.

6. Liabilities that are to be paid in the near future are called _____.

7. The _____ ratio is the same as the _____ ratio except inventories and "other current assets" are dropped from the numerator.

8. Merry-Go-Round's cash dividend per share was $2 and its earnings per share were $6, so its _____ ratio was 33.3 percent. The market price per share is $72, so its _____ ratio is 12 times and its _____ is 2.78 percent.

9. The extent to which a firm's assets are being turned over is captured by the _____ ratio.

10. _____ measures the percentage of sales, which finds its way into profits.

11. The speed with which customers pay their bills is measured by the _____.

357

12. One overall measure of financial performance is captured by the _____ ratio.

13. The _____ ratio is computed by relating earnings available to common to (average, ending, beginning) _____ equity.

14. The growth that can be financed without resorting to any external equity financing is called the _____.

15. The growth rate that can be achieved without resorting to any external financing is the _____.

16. If BRC Corp.'s equities and liabilities have a market value of $240 million and a replacement cost of $160 million, its _____ is 1.5.

Problems

1. Balance sheet, income statement and other relevant information for Picardi Brews, Inc. are given below. Compute a complete set of financial ratios for 2001.

($ in million)

Picardi Brews, Inc. - **Balance Sheet**	2001	2000
Assets		
Cash & short-term securities	150	135
Receivables	480	435
Inventories	860	775
Other current assets	110	152
Total current assets	1,600	1,497
Plant and equipment	1,611	1,420
Other long-term assets	150	100
Total assets	**3,361**	**3,017**
Liabilities & Net Worth		
Debt due	55	45
Payables	615	565
Other current liabilities	45	30
Total current liabilities	715	640
Long-term debt and capital leases	375	425
Other long-term liabilities	225	175
Preferred stock	100	100
Shareholders' equity	1,946	1,677
Total liabilities & equity	**3,361**	**3,017**

Income Statement

Net Sales	5,750	5,180
Cost of goods sold	4,125	3,710
Other expenses	750	515
Depreciation	64	57
Earnings before interest and tax (EBIT)	811	898
Net interest	43	47
Tax	292	323
Net income	476	528
Preferred stock dividend	9	9
Earnings applicable to common stock	467	519
Common dividends	198	198
Earnings retained	269	321

Other Financial Information

Market value of equity	6,188
Average number of shares	110
Earnings per share	4.25
Dividends per share	1.80
Share price	56.25

2. Cherry Blossom Corp. had sales of $220 million last year. The company' sales to assets ratio was 1.25. The net income for the year was $11 million. The company paid a dividend of $3 million. The ROE was 12.5 percent. Calculate the internal growth rate and the sustainable growth rate.

3. Keynes Corp. has $145,000 in receivables. If this represents, 22 days sales, what are the annual sales? What is the receivable turnover ratio?

4. Lacks Corp. had a net profit margin of 12 percent in 2001. Its sales were $36 million and assets amounted to $54 million. The debt to equity ratio for the firm was 1. Compute the return on assets and return on equity. The interest paid amounted to $1.32 million.

5. Neptune Company has the following balance sheet for the year ending June 30, 2001:

Assets	$ million	Liabilities & net worth	$ million
Cash	35	Accounts Payable	45
Receivables	75	Notes payable	55
Inventories	95	Accruals	15
Total current assets	205	Total current liabilities	115
Net Fixed Assets	185	Long term loan	65
		Common Stock	20
		Retained Earnings	190
Total assets	390	Total liabilities & net worth	390

Company's sales for 2001 were $850 million. Net income was $68 million. Company paid dividends amounting to $34 million in 2001. Sales are projected to increase to $1 billion in 2002. Calculate the additional funds needed to finance the expansion. Project a balance sheet as of the year-end 2002 incorporating the financing of the additional funds. Assume that the firm is operating at full capacity and all assets would need to be increased in proportion to sales. Also, assume that accounts payable and accruals would increase in proportion to sales.

Essay Questions

1. Explain the use of the Du Pont system.

2. Describe how a bank lending officer might use ratio analysis. Select five ratios that would be most useful for the purpose.

3. Discuss the statement – "Financial planning models have no finance in them."

4. What is the practical significance of internal growth rate and sustainable growth rate? Which, if any, should be the goal for growth for a company?

5. You are a newly hired financial analyst at an investment firm specializing in web commerce. Your first task is to review all the studies the firm produced and to recommend a system by which to compare individual companies. You are somewhat perplexed because the "industry" is not well defined and most of the companies are new and small and do not have any earnings. What do you do? Do the ratios contained in the text help? Explain fully.

ANSWERS TO EXERCISES

Fill-in Questions

1. Net working capital
2. Leverage ratios
3. Numerator; debt; debt-equity
4. Leverage
5. Current assets
6. Current liabilities
7. Quick; current
8. Payout; price-earnings; dividend yield

9. Sales to assets
10. Net profit margin
11. Average collection period
12. Return on total assets
13. Return on equity; average
14. Sustainable growth rate
15. Internal growth rate
16. Tobin's Q

Problems

1. Picardi Brews - Ratios for 2001
   Leverage ratios:

a. Debt ratio = ($375 + $225)/($375 + $225 + $1,946) = 23.6%
b. Debt-equity ratio = ($375 + $225)/$1,946 = 30.8%
c. Times interest earned ($811 + $64)/$43 = 20.4 times

Liquidity ratios:
a. Net working capital to total assets = ($1,600- $715)/$3,361 = 26.3%
b. Current ratio = $1,600/$715 = 2.24
c. Quick ratio = ($150 + $480)/$715 = 0.88
d. Cash ratio = $150/$715 = 0.21
e. Interval measure = ($150 + $480)/[($4,125 + $750)/365] = 47.2 days

Efficiency ratios:
a. Sales to total assets = $5,750/[($3,361 + $3,017)/2] = 1.8
b. Sales to net working capital = $5,750/{[($1,600 - $715) + ($1,497 - $640)]/2} = 6.60
c. Inventory turnover = $4,125/[($860 + $775)/2] = 5.1
d. Average collection period = [($480 + $435)/ 2]/($5,750/365) = 29.0 days

Profitability ratios
a. Net profit margin = ($811 - $292)/$5,750 = 9.0%
b. Return on total assets = ($811 - $292)/[($3,361 + $3,017)/2] = 16.3%
c. Return on equity = $467/[($1,946 + $1,677)/2] = 25.8%
d. Payout = $1.80/$4.25 = 42.4%
e. Plowback = 100% - 42.4% = 57.6%
f. Sustainable growth rate = 0.576 x 0.258 = 14.9%

Market value ratios:
a. Price-earnings = $56.25/$4.25 = 13.2 times
b. Dividend yield = $1.80/$56.25 = 3.20%
c. Market-to-book = $56.25/($1,946/110) = 3.2 times

2. Net income = $11 million
Retained earnings = $11 million- $3 million = $8 million
Assets = sales/(sales/asset ratio) = $220 million/1.25 = $176 million
Internal growth rate = retained earnings/assets = $8 million/$176 million = 4.55 percent
Plowback ratio = $8 million/$11 million = 0.73
Sustainable growth rate = plowback X ROE = 0.73 X 12.5 = 9.1 percent

3. Annual sales = $145,000 x 365/22 = $2,405,682
Receivable turnover ratio = 365/22 = 16.6

4. Return on assets = net profit margin x sales/assets = 0.12 x (36/54) = 8 percent.
Return on assets = (EBIT - tax - interest)/equity
EBIT - tax - interest = 0.12 s $36 million - $1.32 = $3 million
Equity = $54 million x 0.5 = $27 million

361

Return on equity = $3 million/$27 million = 11.1 %

5. The sales are expected to grow by (1,000/850) -1 = 17.65%

Uses of funds:
Total assets for 2002 = $390 million x 1.1765 = 458.82
Increase in assets = $458.82 - $390 = $68.82 million

Sources of funds:
Net income for 2002 = 1,000 x (68/850) = $80 million
Dividends = (80 x 34/68) = $40 million
Net operating cash flow in 2002 = 80 -40 = $40 million
Accounts payable in 2002 = 45 x 1.1765 = $52.94 million
Accruals in 2002 = 15 x 1.1765 = $17.65 million
Funds from accounts payable and accruals = 52.94 + 17.65 - 45 + 15 = $10.59 million
Net funds needed from new equity and debt = 68.82 - 10.59 - 40 = $18.23 million

We assume that this will be financed as follows:
New debt   = $9.12 million.
New equity = $9.11 million.

(Note that depreciation is not considered as a source of funds as the increase in fixed assets is projected from the net fixed assets level.)

The projected balance sheet is given below:

Projected Balance Sheet of Neptune Company

Assets	$ million	Liabilities & net worth	$ million
Cash	41.18	Accounts Payable	52.94
Receivables	88.23	Notes payable	55.00
Inventories	111.76	Accruals	17.65
Total current assets	241.17	Total current liabilities	125.59
Net Fixed Assets	215.65	Long term loan	74.12
		Common Stock	29.11
		Retained Earnings	230.00
Total assets	458.82	Total liabilities & net worth	458.82

30
Short-Term Financial Planning

INTRODUCTION

This chapter focuses on short-term financial planning. Short-term financial decisions differ from long-term financial decisions in two important ways. First, they are easily reversed in most cases. Second, there is far less uncertainty about the decision variables as you are concerned with the next few months rather than years. This does not mean that short-term financial decisions are any less important. Short-term financial decisions ensure the firm's liquidity and are critical to the short-term survival of the business.

Firms finance their operations from short-term and long-term sources. Although short-term financial decisions almost always involve short-lived assets, there is a linkage between short-term and long-term financing decisions arising from a firm's cumulative capital requirements. If you have a surplus of long-term financing, you would need less short-term funds. Ordinarily, financial managers try to match the maturity of capital sources with the life of the assets funded by them. For example, some minimum level of working capital is needed permanently in the business and is financed from permanent sources, whereas the seasonal increase in working capital typically is financed from short-term sources.

The chapter also provides a brief review of important sources of short-term financing. The primary short-term funding sources are loans from commercial banks and direct market borrowing through commercial paper issues. Commercial banks provide different types of loans and lines of credit and remain a major source of funding for corporations, though their market share has decreased significantly in the last two decades.

KEY CONCEPTS IN THE CHAPTER

Components of Working Capital: *Current assets* and *current liabilities* together are known as working capital. The term *net working capital* is used to denote the difference between current assets and current liabilities. Current assets include cash and marketable securities, *accounts receivable* and *inventory*. Current liabilities include *accounts payable*, which reflects the credit obtained from suppliers, and any other short-term obligation including short-term loans.

Working capital management (sometimes also referred to short-term financial management) involves decisions on the levels and mix of current liabilities. Persons other than the financial manager will be actively involved in management decisions with respect to specific components of working capital. For example, the production manager has comparative advantage over the financial manager in determining how much to invest in inventories in order to minimize stock outs, storage costs, risks of spoilage and obsolescence, and the opportunity costs of tying up money in inventories. Details of management of current assets and liabilities are discussed in the next two chapters.

Links between Long- and Short-Term Financing Decisions: Businesses require funds for investments in fixed assets and current assets. Over time, the capital requirements tend to increase steadily but mostly irregularly. These cumulative capital requirements are financed by a combination of long-term and short-term capital sources. The decision to use one type of funding necessarily affects the other. Long-term loans are less risky, but more expensive. Short-term loans work the other way - more risky but less expensive. Usually many companies try to match the maturities of assets and financing. Financing of the seasonal requirements of current assets and the comfort level for surplus cash are discretionary decisions. Too much comfort level cash is not good as the return on cash holdings is zero.

Changes in Cash and Working Capital: The changes in cash and working capital can be traced through the sources and use statement discussed in chapter 29. The statement tells us the overall changes in cash and other assets and how they were financed. Note that profits and cash flows are not the same. The term cash flow from operations is often used to describe the sum of net income and depreciation. This can be very misleading, as the amount does not represent the actual cash flow produced by the operations during the period. To the extent that part of the sales has not been collected or there are other changes in current assets or current liabilities, the simple cash flow measure would underestimate or overestimate the actual cash flow produced by the operations of the business. Understanding the changes in the firm's net working capital is the best way to understand the changes in the liquidity of the firm. A firm's operating cycle essentially is the movement from one current asset to another - from cash to raw-material inventory to finished goods inventory to receivables and back to cash. Thus changes in working capital represent the net liquidity position, which is not affected by the seasonal or other changes across the different current assets and liabilities.

Cash Budgeting: A cash budget is a weekly, monthly, or quarterly forecast of cash inflows and outflows. The budget indicates deficient or excessive cash balances, and financing plans are formulated based on it. Remember that this is a budget of cash flows and not expenses booked in the ledger. The steps involved in preparing cash budgets are:

Step 1: Estimate cash inflows, which typically include:

- Present cash sales.
- Estimated collections of prior receivables.
- Sale of assets.
- Tax refunds.

Step 2: Estimate cash outflows, which include:

- Payments on accounts payable,
- Labor, administrative, and other expenses,

- Capital expenditures, and
- Taxes, interest, and dividends.

Sum the cash flows and find the net inflow. Estimate the amount that must be financed, including a minimum cash balance.

The Short-Term Financial Plan: The estimated financing needs from the cash-budget forms the basis for the short-term financing plan. Some large cash flows may be the result of seasonal or other factors, such as tax payments, capital expenditures, etc. Note that the cash budget is a forecast based on the best judgment of the manager and the uncertainty involved in the estimation process has to be kept in mind while using the budget for decision making. Each proposed plan is evaluated for its compatibility and costs and the need to maintain required ratios. Note that simulation and optimization models help, but they rely heavily on the reality of their underlying assumptions.

Financial managers have two major options for financing short-term cash deficiencies:

- Borrow from banks, perhaps through an unsecured line of credit with a compensating balance.
- Stretch out payments on accounts payable. This may be expensive, as using trade credit beyond the minimum period allowed may mean forgoing valuable trade discounts.

Here are some typical questions, which need to be asked before finalizing the plan:

- Is the cash reserve too large?
- Are the current and quick ratios satisfactory?
- What are the intangible costs of stretching payables, such as lost discounts?
- Does the plan produce a financially sound result?
- Is there a real need for long-term financing rather than short-term funding?
- What about adjusting operating and investment plans?
- What about selling receivables to a commercial finance company?

<u>Short-term Financial Planning Models:</u> Short-term financial planning models often need to be worked out for different scenarios and assumptions. These involve tedious and complex computations, which are best done by computer spreadsheets and simulation models. The usefulness of the forecasts is, of course, determined by the reasonableness and accuracy of the assumptions rather than the complexity of the model itself.

Sources of Short-term Borrowing: The primary sources of short-term funding include commercial banks, finance companies and direct borrowing in capital market. Finance companies provide short-term loans for financing receivables and inventories. Direct market borrowing includes short-term commercial paper as well as medium term notes.

Bank loans: Bank loans can come in many forms. Often banks can guarantee availability of credit through formal *commitment* and charge a commitment fee for a line of credit. These are in the form of revolving lines of credit. The line of credit may be *evergreen (*without maturity*)* or for a specified term. Banks may offer a short-term *bridging* loan for the purchase of equipment or other needs as an interim financing until longer term financing is tied up. While most bank loans are for short maturity, banks often provide *term loans* with maturity extending up to 5 years. Interest on bank loans may be fixed or tied to benchmarks like the prime rate or LIBOR (London Inter-Bank Offer Rate). It is also possible to get an international loan in a foreign currency.

Bank loans for very large amounts are often *syndicated* or shared by a number of banks. Large money-center banks sell some of their loans to other institutions through loan *participations* or *assignments*. Participation can be for one loan or a number of similar loan transactions can be combined and packaged into marketable securities. This process of transforming loans and other receivables into tradable securities is known as *securitization*.

Secured bank loans usually require collateral, usually receivables or inventory. Although almost all trade accounts receivables are acceptable collateral for loans, not all kinds of inventory are. Some unsecured loans are *self-liquidating*, as the sale of goods and services for which the loan was made provides the cash to repay the loan.

Commercial Paper: Commercial paper is unsecured short-term debt issued directly to investors by well-known, large, and safe companies. The maximum maturity for commercial paper can be 270 days though most are issued for 60 days or even shorter maturity. Registration with the SEC is not required. The interest on commercial paper is well below prime rate and is usually only 1 percent or so higher than comparable maturity government debt. Thus considerable cost savings are achieved by issuing commercial paper as a source of financing. The firm has to be of very high financial standing and very low risk to be able to issue commercial paper. Firms, which issue commercial paper, generally have a back-up line of credit from banks to ensure high rating for the paper.

Medium-Term Notes: Medium-term notes (MTN) are typically of longer maturity than commercial paper, but well below that of long-term bonds. These are unsecured notes and are popular with finance companies and large blue-chip issuers. Like the commercial paper, the MTNs are issued through dealers, and not underwritten. They permit considerable flexibility for the issuer.

WORKED EXAMPLES

1. The table below contains the balance sheets and income statement for Meadowbrook Corp. Complete a statement of sources and uses of funds for 2001.

Meadowbrook Corp. - Balance Sheet

	2000	2001
Current assets		
Cash	15	31
Marketable securities	5	0
Inventory	25	17
Accounts receivable	20	35
Total current assets	65	83
Fixed assets		
Gross investment	75	85
Less depreciation	-15	-17
Net fixed assets	60	68
Total assets	125	151
Current liabilities		
Bank loans	10	15
Accounts payable	35	30
Total current liabilities	45	45
Long-term debt	15	20
New worth (equity and retained earnings)	65	86
Total liabilities and net worth	125	151

Income Statement	2001
Sales	300
Operating expenses	245
	55
Depreciation	-2
	53
Interest	-3
Pretax income	50
Tax at 34 percent	-17
Net income	33
Note:	
Dividend	12
Retained earnings	21

SOLUTION

Analysis of the balance sheet and cash generated from operations provides valuable information for financial planning. Here is the step by step procedure for the preparation of the sources and uses statements:

Step 1: Compare the differences in each balance sheet account.

Step 2: Determine whether those differences increase or decrease the cash or funds of the firm.

Step 3: Under the caption "Sources," list all the items, which increased the amount of cash or funds. Under the caption "Uses," list all the items, which decreased cash or funds.

Step 4: Sum both sources and uses.

Step 5: Take the difference between sources and uses to determine the net change in the cash position of the firm.

The table below indicates the impact each change has on the sources and uses of cash. A plus indicates source and minus indicates use of funds.

	2000	2001	Sources (+) and Uses (-)
Current assets			
Cash	15	31	-16
Marketable securities	5	0	5
Inventory	25	17	8
Accounts receivable	20	35	-15
Total current assets	65	83	-18
Fixed assets			
Gross investment	75	85	-10
Less depreciation	-15	-17	2
Net fixed assets	60	68	-8
Total assets	125	151	-26
Current liabilities			
Bank loans	10	15	5
Accounts payable	35	30	-5
Total current liabilities	45	45	0
Long-term debt	15	20	5
New worth (equity and retained earnings)	65	86	21
Total liabilities and net worth	125	151	26

Income Statement

	2001	Sources/Uses
Sales	300	
Operating expenses	245	
	55	
Depreciation	-2	2
	53	
Interest	-3	
Pretax income	50	
Tax at 34 percent	-17	
Net income	33	33
Note:		
Dividend	12	-12
Retained earnings	21	21

Note that anything that is a source of funds is a plus; anything that uses funds is a minus. The summary statement for sources and uses of cash is given below:

Sources and uses of cash for Meadowbrook Corp.

Sources
Sold marketable securities	5
Reduced inventories	8
Increased bank loan	5
Issued long-term debt	5

Cash from operations:
Net income	33
Depreciation	2
Total sources	58

Uses
Increased accounts receivable	15
Invested in fixed assets	10
Reduced accounts payable	5
Dividends	12
Total uses	42
Change in cash balance	16

2. Refer to problem 1. What are the changes in the net working capital?

SOLUTION

Sources of funds:
    Issued long-term debt   5
    Cash from operations:
        Net income   33
        Depreciation   2
    Total   40

Uses of funds:
    Invested in fixed assets   10
    Dividends   12
    Total   22

Changes in net
    working capital   18

The changes in current assets and current liabilities (or net working capital) are the result of long-term financing and investment decisions, as well as current operations.

3. The table below gives the forecasted budget data for Yang Corp.

(Figures in $ 1,000)

	March	April	May	June
Sales	580	640	720	610
Purchases - Cash	128	144	122	116
Purchases - Credit	320	360	305	390
Salaries and wages	44	44	44	50
Rent, Utilities, and other expenses	50	50	50	50
Interest and Dividends	32	24	24	32
Taxes	36	0	0	36
Capital expenditure	0	0	120	120

Seventy percent of the sales are cash sales and the remaining thirty percent is collected in the following month. Cash purchases are paid in the month of purchase and the credit purchases are paid in the following month. Prepare a cash budget for the months of April, May and June. Daisy Yang, the CFO of the firm uses a target cash balance of $30,000 for budgeting. Ms. Yang is negotiating a new line of credit with her bank. Estimate the amount she would need in her line of credit.

SOLUTION

The preparation of cash budget is a fairly simple exercise of listing all inflows and outflows. First, we need to compute the collections for each month. The worksheet below shows the details:

(Figures in $ 1,000)

	March	April	May	June
Receivable at start of period	X	174	192	216
Sales	580	640	720	610
Cash sales	406	448	504	427
Collection of receivables	X	174	192	216
Total collections	X+406	622	696	643
Receivables at end of period	174	192	216	183

The cash budget is given in the table below. Note that the firm has a cash surplus above the target operating cash balance amount of $30,000 for April and May. The firm would need to borrow an amount of $50,000 in June. So the line of credit should be at least for $50,000. Ms. Yang may like to set a higher limit, say, $60,000 for covering forecasting errors.

Cash Budget for Yang Corp. (Figures in $ 1,000)

	April	May	June
Sources of Cash			
Cash sales	448	504	427
Collections on accounts receivable	174	192	216
Total Sources	622	696	643
Uses of cash			
Payments for cash purchases	144	122	116
Payments for accounts payable	320	360	305
Salaries and wages	44	44	50
Rent and utilities	50	50	50
Interest and dividends	24	24	32
Taxes	0	0	36
Capital expenditure	0	120	120
Total uses of cash	582	720	709
Sources - uses = change in cash balance	40	-24	-66
1. Cash at start of period	30	70	46
2. Change in cash balance	40	-24	-66
3. Cash at end of period = 1 + 2	70	46	-20
4. Minimum operating cash balance	30	30	30
5. Cumulative short-term financing = 4- 3	-40	-16	50

Note: A negative number for cumulative borrowing indicates cash surplus.

4. Little Valley Corporation (LVC) needs $10 million, and the company's bank has offered to make a loan at 8.5 percent annually, provided the company maintains a 10 percent compensating balance. The manager of a competing bank indicated that she would lend the company the needed funds for 9.25 percent with no compensating balance. Which bank is making the better offer? Explain fully. Would your answer be different if LVC normally maintained a $200,000 cash balance?

SOLUTION

The compensating balance is $1,000,000 ($10,000,000 x 0.10) and the amount of funds actually available for use is $9,000,000. The amount of interest charged is $850,000 ($10,000,000 x 0.085). Thus, the cost of the loan is the interest cost of $850,000 divided by the effective amount of money available for use is:

$$\text{Effective cost} = \frac{\$850,000}{\$9,000,000} = 0.0944 = 9.44 \text{ percent}$$

This is more expensive than the offer from the second bank.

If the financial manager normally kept an average of $200,000 on deposit, the amount normally available for use increases to $9,200,000 and the cost per annum is only 9.24 percent and is slightly cheaper than the offer from the second bank.

5. Jones and Company needs to borrow about $50 million of short-term financing for the next year. The firm is considering the following two options:

- Commercial paper issued at a discount rate 4 percent, 360-day basis. The issues will be for 90 days, but refinanced every 90 days with a new issue. Issues expenses are 0.25 percent for each issue. The firm will also need a back-up line of credit to ensure good credit rating for the commercial paper. The back-up line of credit costs 0.2 percent on an annual basis.

- A bank loan at prime rate less 0.25 percent. The prime rate is currently 5.75 percent.

Compute the effective costs for the two alternatives and advice the firm.

SOLUTION

We will assume that the interest rates on the commercial paper and the prime rate remain constant for the one-year period.

Cost of commercial paper:
The paper is issued at a discount of 4 percent.
The proceeds from the issue = 50 - 50 x 0.04 x 90/360 = $49.5 million
Less issue expenses   = 0.0025 x 50 = $0.125 million
Net proceeds   = $49.375 million

In effect, the company receives $49.375 million and repays $50 million in 90 days.

$$\text{Nominal cost excluding cost of back-up credit} = \frac{0.625}{49.375} \times \frac{365}{90} = 5.13 \text{ percent}$$

Effective annual cost, assuming rollover every 90 days $= \left(\dfrac{50}{49.375}\right)^{(365/90)} - 1$

$$= 5.23 \text{ percent}$$

Cost including cost of back-up credit = 5.23 + 0.2 = 5.43 percent.

Cost of the bank loan = 5.75 - 0.25 = 5.5 percent.

The commercial paper costs slightly less than the bank loan. Note that both rates can change during the year and it is possible that the actual cost advantage might change depending on the commercial paper rate at the time of each issue and how the bank loan rate is reset.

SUMMARY

This chapter provided an overview of short-term financial planning and leads to the next two chapters, which deal with the details of short-term assets and liability management. Short-term financial decisions are easier than the long-term financial decisions for the simple reason that they are often easily reversed. They are however, no less important. Short-term planning ensures liquidity and the very survival of the firm. The uses and sources statement analyzes changes in working capital and is very useful tool to evaluate the liquidity and financial position of the firm.

The chapter provides a step-by-step description of the cash budgeting process. The cash budget is a useful planning tool that helps in short-term financing decisions. A cash budget shows the amount of financing needed at various times during the plan period. It also highlights the major inflows and outflows, which could create huge surpluses or deficits.

The chapter provides a brief review of key sources of short-term funding. Commercial banks are the main source of much of the unsecured borrowing by corporations. Bank loans come in many forms with different maturities, different ways of charging interest, and other fees. When computing costs of any financing, all costs, including the opportunity cost of compensating balances, should be considered. Corporations with excellent credit rating are able to borrow directly from the market by issuing commercial paper or medium-term notes.

LIST OF TERMS

Bridging loan	Matching maturities
Cash budget	Medium-term notes (MTNs)
Commercial paper	Revolving credit
Compensating balance	Self-liquidating loans
Evergreen credit	Stretching payables
Line of credit	Term loan
Loan assignment	Working capital
Loan participation	

EXERCISES

Fill-in Questions

1. The concept of _____ is at work when short-lived assets are financed from short-term sources and long-lived assets are financed from long-term sources.
2. A forecast of short-term cash inflows and cash outflows is called a(n) _____.

3. Changes in _____ are captured by the sources and uses of cash statement, whereas the sources and uses of funds statement captures changes in _____.

4. The percentage of a loan that must be retained on deposit is called a(n) _____.

5. A prearranged maximum borrowing capability at specified interest rates is known as a(n) _____.

6. Extending the payment dates for bills from suppliers is called _____.

7. Commercial paper rates usually are (below, equal to, greater than) _____ the prime rate charged by banks.

8. The principal form of medium-term debt financing from banks is called _____.

9. Unsecured notes issued by companies and maturing within nine months are called _____.

10. An unsecured loan is called a _____ when the sale of goods will provide the cash to repay the loan.

11. A legally assured line of credit with a bank, which provides a put option to borrow on fixed terms for up to three years, is known as _____.

12. Large money center banks often sell their loans to other banks through _____ or _____.

13. A _____ is an interim loan given for a specific purpose till other financing is arranged.

Problems

1. Using the balance sheets and income statement given below for Feld and Cramer, Inc., work out a complete sources and uses of cash and a sources and uses of funds statement for 2001.

Year-End Balance Sheets, In Millions	2000	2001
Current assets:		
Cash	$ 13	$ 2
Marketable securities	0	5
Inventory	17	22
Accounts receivable	35	48
Total current assets	$ 65	$ 77
Fixed assets:		
Gross investment	$ 85	$ 85
Less depreciation	-17	-19
Net fixed assets	68	66
Total assets	$133	$143
Current liabilities:		
Bank loans	$ 15	$13
Accounts payable	30	37
Total current liabilities	$ 45	$ 50
Long-term debt	$ 20	$18
Net worth (equity and retained earnings)	68	75
Total liabilities and net worth	$133	$143

Income Statement, In Millions

Sales	$320
Operating expenses	-289
	$ 31
Depreciation	-2
	$ 29
Interest	-3
Pretax income	$ 26
Tax at 50 percent	13
Net income	$ 13
Cash dividends	$6
Retained earnings	$7

2. Mark Zoubi is preparing a cash budget for his family-owned skiing and sports goods business. Here are the data.

	September	October	November	December
Sales	1,250	1,400	1700	1850
Purchases - Cash	140	170	180	150
Purchases - Credit	630	765	833	675
Salaries and wages	105	105	105	115
Rent, Utilities, and other expenses	120	140	155	165
Interest	40	50	70	90
Taxes	250	120	120	250
Capital expenditure	400	300	0	0

Eighty percent of the sales are cash and credit card sales, which are effectively collected in the month of sales. The remaining twenty percent is collected in the following month. Cash purchases are paid in the month of purchase and the credit purchases are paid for in the following month. Prepare a cash budget for the months of October, November and December. Mark uses a target cash balance of $120,000 for budgeting purpose. Would the firm need any credit facility? If so, by what amount?

3. Wackers's Corp.'s primary bank has offered to lend the firm $8 million at an annual rate of 10 percent, provided the company maintains a compensating balance of 15 percent. The financial manager also approached a competitor bank and it offered him an $8 million loan at 11.5 percent annually with no compensating balance requirement. Which is the better deal?

4. Refer to problem 3 above. What would be the better deal if Wacker's usually kept on deposit an average of $200,000?

5. Smith and Daughters Corp. needs to borrow $20 million in short-term funding for next year. The firm has the following two choices:

- Commercial paper issued at a discount rate 3.5 percent, 360-day basis. The issues will be for 180 days, but refinanced every 180 days with new issue. Issues expenses are 0.2 percent for each issue. The firm will also need a back-up line of credit to ensure good credit rating for the commercial paper. The back-up line of credit costs 0.3 percent on an annual basis.

- A bank loan at LIBOR less 0.25 percent. The current LIBOR is currently 4.5 percent.

Compute the effective costs for the two alternatives and advice the firm.

Essay Questions

1. What is meant by matching maturities?

2. Discuss the following statement. "Short-term financial decisions are easily reversed and they are not very important."

3. Explain the importance of the cash budget. What is the ideal budgeting period for a small retail business?

4. Discuss the following statement: "Because the middle man is eliminated, or at least most of his functions are eliminated, when commercial paper is issued, there is a significant reduction in the cost of funds when commercial paper is used."

5. What is meant by a self-liquidating loan? Interim financing? Line of credit?

6. What provisions are typically found in a line of credit? Explain why you think they are there.

7. What characteristics should be possessed by assets that are used as collateral for inventory loans?

ANSWERS TO EXERCISES

Fill-in Questions

1. Matching maturities
2. Cash budget
3. Cash; net working capital
4. Compensating balance
5. Line of credit
6. Stretching payables
7. Below

8. Term loans
9. Commercial paper
10. Self-liquidating loan
11. Revolving credit
12. Loan assignments; loan participation
13. Bridging loan

Problems

1. From the balance sheet:

Cash	+11
Marketable securities	-5
Inventory	-5
Accounts receivable	-13
Total current assets	-12
Gross investment	0
Depreciation	+2
Net fixed assets	+2
Total assets	-10
Bank loans	-2
Accounts payable	+7
Total current liabilities	+5
Long-term debt	-2
Net worth	+7
Total liabilities and net worth	+ 10

From the income statement:

Depreciation	+2
Net income	+13
Cash dividends	-6
Retained earnings	+7

Sources and uses of funds and cash:

Sources:

Depreciation	$2
Net income	13
Increased accounts payable	7
Total sources	$22

Uses:

Bought marketable securities	$5
Increased inventories	5
Increased receivables	13
Decreased bank loans	2
Reduced long-term debt	2
Dividends	6
Total uses	$33

Reduction in cash	$11

2. The worksheet below shows the details of collections for each month:

(Figures in $ 1,000)

	September	October	November	December
Receivable at start of period	X	250	280	340
Sales	1250	1400	1700	1850
Cash sales	1000	1120	1360	1480
Collection of receivables	X	250	280	340
Total collections	X+1000	1370	1640	1820
Receivables at end of period	250	280	340	370

The cash budget is given in the table below. The firm would need to borrow an amount of $245,000 in October, $305,000 in November and $98,000 in December. A line of credit of $320,000 or so is in order.

Cash Budget for Zoubi family business (Figures in $ 1,000)

Sources of Cash	October	November	December
Cash sales	1120	1360	1480
Collections on accounts receivable	250	280	340
Total Sources	1370	1640	1820

Uses of cash			
Payments for cash purchases	170	185	160
Payments for accounts payable	630	765	833
Salaries and wages	105	105	115
Rent and utilities	140	155	165
Interest and dividends	50	70	90
Taxes	120	120	250
Capital expenditure	400	300	0
Total uses of cash	1615	1700	1613
Sources - uses = change in cash balance	-245	-60	207
1. Cash at start of period	120	-125	-185
2. Change in cash balance	-245	-60	207
3. Cash at end of period = 1 + 2	-125	-185	22
4. Minimum operating cash balance	120	120	120
5. Cumulative short-term financing = 4- 3	245	305	98

3. Bank 1: $8,000,000 x 0.15 = $1,200,000   (compensating balance)
        $8,000,000 x 0.10 = $800,000   (dollar cost)
            Cost = $800,000/$6,800,000 = 11.76 percent

The cost of the loan from the second bank is 11.5 percent and is cheaper.

4. Bank 1: $800,000/$7,000,000 = 11.43 percent.

This is slightly cheaper than the offer from the second bank.

5. We will assume that the interest rates on the commercial paper and the prime rate to remain constant for the one-year period.

Cost of commercial paper: The paper is issued at a discount of 3.5 percent.

The proceeds from the issue   = 20 - 20 x 0.035 x 180/360 = $19.65 million
Less issue expenses   = 0.002 x 20 = $0.04 million
Net proceeds   = $19.61 million

In effect, the company receives $19.61 million and repays $20 million in 180 days.

Nominal cost excluding cost of back-up credit $= \dfrac{0.39}{19.61} \times \dfrac{365}{180} = 4.03$ percent

Effective annual cost, assuming rollover every 180 days $= \left(\dfrac{20}{19.61}\right)^{(365/180)} - 1$

$\qquad\qquad\qquad\qquad\qquad = 4.07$ percent

Cost including cost of back-up credit = 4.07 + 0.3 = 4.37 percent.

Cost of the bank loan = 4.5 - 0.25 = 4.25 percent.

The bank loan is cheaper. This assumes that the rates do not change during the year.

31
Cash Management

INTRODUCTION

This chapter deals with cash management, which comprises three parts. First, the cash flowing in and out through a firm's collection and disbursement systems create unusable transit balances and these need to optimized through efficient management of the inward and outward systems. Second, a firm needs to maintain an appropriate level of cash balance to ensure its liquidity, but cash is a zero-return asset and one should hold only just the needed level. Third, the financial manager needs to find the right assets to invest part of the firm's idle cash balances of the firm. The object of efficient cash management is to ensure the solvency of the enterprise and to add to the value of the firm. Financial managers trade-off the interest on invested money in exchange for liquidity and attempt to ensure the proper balance between too little and too much cash or liquidity.

The chapter also surveys the short-term investments available, which can be used to park surplus cash balances and earn some return. The marketplace in which these instruments are traded is known as the *money market*. The method of calculating yields on most money-market investments is different from that on other types of investment, because they are sold on a discount from their face value. The difference between the purchase price and the discount is the interest earned.

KEY CONCEPTS IN THE CHAPTER

Cash Collection and Disbursement: Managing collection and disbursement is a very important part of the cash management function. This revolves around check collections and disbursement as check written on bank accounts form the dominant means of payments for most small and medium value transactions.

Float and Float Management: Checks create *floats* or lags as they pass between the payer and the payee and through the banking system. Different terms are used to describe the different sources of the lag. *Mail float* arises on account of the transit time. There is *processing* float at the receiving end. Once the check is processed and deposited in a bank, the bank puts a hold on the availability of funds to allow time for the clearing of the check. This gives rise to *availability float*. The other side of the availability float is the *presentation float* impacting the payer. Collectively, the payer (or the writer of the check) enjoys *payment float*, which is the total lag between the time the check is written and the time the amount is debited to the payer's account. The mirror image of this is the *collection float* for the payee. Note that while float is time lag, it is also quantified in terms of dollars held in transit or processing.

Essentially, managing collection and disbursement means managing the float. Financial managers estimate the net float between payment float and the availability float and adjust cash balances accordingly. Managing float means speeding up collections and optimizing (not to say slowing down) disbursement. Corporations use different systems for speeding up collections. These include:

- *Concentration banking* with centralized accounts and bank accounts close to customers so that checks are likely to clear faster.
- *Lock-box systems*, which have optimized collection locations and speedy processing of incoming checks. The system is often used in conjunction with concentration banking so that collected checks are deposited into one account for optimal disbursement and control.
- Controlled and optimal disbursement.
- Use of information technology, which reduces transaction costs, speeds up transfers, and automates record keeping.

Electronic Funds Transfer: Fedwire and CHIPS are efficient means of transferring very large sums of money at a nominal cost. Fedwire operated by the Federal Reserve uses the gross system (i.e. each transaction is paid off separately) and CHIPS operates as a net system (cross payments are netted out). The Automated Clearinghouse (ACH) system can be used for routine transfers of bulk transactions like wages, dividends, regular payments to suppliers, etc. ACH can transfer funds in two to three days.

International Cash Management: Efficient cash management across the borders is complicated by the differences in currency, banking systems, and legal structures. Regional systems are typical with local concentration accounts with a bank in each country, surplus cash is then swept into multi-currency accounts in a single center, from which marketable securities can be bought and sold. A company may have several accounts with the same bank in different countries, in different currencies, or both. The bank may agree to take all the accounts together when it calculates the interest it pays or charges. Electronic transfers and computer-based cash management systems are especially valuable in international business.

Banks and Banking Services: Banks play a major role in cash management. Most of the transactions and cash flows go through the banking system. They also provide a whole host of other services such as lock-box systems, lines of credit and foreign exchange related services. Thus, relationships with banks are important. Compensating balances are essentially unusable amounts left in demand deposit accounts as a way of compensating the bank for its services. Explicit fees or direct charges for services rendered are also becoming common and seem to be more popular. Good banking relations are essential to efficient cash management.

Optimal Cash Balance: Firms hold cash because cash provides liquidity. Liquid balances are needed to meet the daily transaction needs. This liquidity comes at the cost of lost interest. What is the optimal balance that a firm should hold? Economists and management scientists have tried to model the trade-off of holding cash against the lost interest. Several inventory models have been developed to solve the problem of how much cash or cash substitutes to keep on hand. In the Baumol model, the three variables of concern are the interest forgone from holding cash, the fixed administrative expenses of buying and selling highly marketable securities, and the rate of cash disbursement or cash consumption. At the margin, *order costs* are reduced when larger and larger orders are placed, but *carrying costs* rise. Thus there is trade-off between the order costs and the carrying costs. The optimal balance or the inventory of cash is when the marginal reduction in order cost equals the marginal carrying cost. The order cost in this case is the transaction costs associated with the selling of securities and the carrying cost is the lost interest on the cash held.

For most large firms the practical relevance of the Baumol model is somewhat limited. The assumption of steady depletion is unrealistic. Firms typically face lump sum demands very often. Also the transaction cost of converting securities into cash is relatively small, when large amounts of securities are sold. Firms also hold cash at least partly to compensate banks for the services rendered by them. Decentralized management of operations also results in the need for a higher level of cash than if the system were to be totally centralized. Efficient cash management does imply centralization and most corporations have centralized systems for collections and disbursement.

Investing Idle Cash: Corporations typically carry a lot more cash than what is suggested by the transactions based model discussed above. These surplus cash are usually invested in marketable securities, which can be converted back to cash when needed.

The Money Market: The market for short-term, liquid, safe investments is known as the money market, which comprises banks, other financial institutions and dealers connected electronically and through telephones. A wide variety of investments are available and large corporations typically manage their own investments. Smaller firms can professional money managers or even use money market mutual funds.

Valuing Money-market Investments: The money market instruments are characterized by their low risk, high liquidity and very short maturity. There are however, significant differences in perceived default risk as well as the liquidity for the different investments. The US government securities are considered to be free of default risk and have the highest liquidity. These are followed by the federal agency securities and high-grade corporate securities. The returns on the different investments will reflect the perceived default risk and liquidity.

Most money-market investments are issued as pure discount securities. In other words, you get your return from the price appreciation of the investment and not from coupons. Returns are quoted as discount yields, which are computed on the face value of the investment (and not on the actual price) and use 360-day year to annualize the returns. The worked examples 4 and 5 show how the effective annual returns can be computed.

The International Money-Market: Money-market transactions and investments are not confined to national boundaries. Traditionally, dollar transactions outside the US were referred to as

Eurodollar transactions. This was also true for any currency transaction outside its home jurisdiction - e.g. Euroyen deposits. Since, the new common European currency is named *Euro*, it might be necessary to drop the old term Eurodollar and change it to simply "international dollar." International transactions carry some advantages in the form of less regulations and possible tax savings. A common international benchmark interest rate is the LIBOR (London Inter Bank Offer Rate), which is the rate at which banks lend or borrow from each other in the international markets. This is used to price international (and sometimes domestic) floating rate loans.

As a general response to the rising international transactions outside the US, the US regulatory banking laws have permitted American banks to create *international banking facilities (IBF)*. IBFs are located inside the US but are relieved of some regulatory burdens and are not required to keep reserves with the Federal Reserve.

Money-Market Investments: The chapter surveys the major money investments, which are ideally suited for short-term investments. As mentioned before the yield on these investments depend on the perceived risk, maturity, and the relative liquidity. Here is a brief summary of the major investments.

Treasury Bills: The dominant money-market instrument is the U.S. Treasury bill, which have maturities of 4 weeks, 3 months, and six months. The T-bills are sold at auction either competitively or at the average price of successful competitive bids. The T-bills are the safest and the most liquid investment and naturally offer the lowest yield. The T-bill rate serves as the primary benchmark for many floating rate loans.

Federal Agency Securities: Next in importance are United States government agency securities. These include issues by the various government-sponsored organizations such as the Federal Home Loan Bank, the Federal National Mortgage Association (Fannie Mae), the Student Loan Mortgage Association (Sallie Mae), etc. Although they are not backed by the full faith and credit of the United States government, their quality is considered very high.

Short-term Tax-exempt Investments: Securities issued by state and local agencies enjoy tax-exempt status so that investors do not pay income tax on the interest income received from these issues. Because interest income is exempt from federal income taxation, municipals are very desirable for investors in a high marginal income tax bracket. This class includes both short-term securities as well as the long-term issues with variable interest rates, known as the variable-rate demand bonds (VRDB).

Deposits: Although they are insured up to $100,000 by the Federal Deposit Insurance Corporation and similar agencies for non-bank financial institutions, regular commercial time deposits are not typically thought of as money-market investments. They do not have an active secondary market. They are not sold at a discount from face value and are not negotiable. Negotiable deposits at commercial banks are called certificates of deposit and have denominations of $100,000 or more, minimum maturity of 30 days, and a maximum maturity of 270 days.

Commercial Paper: Commercial paper is unsecured short-term debt issued directly by only the best-known, largest, and safest companies. These were discussed in chapter 30. The secondary market is limited, but generally the dealer will repurchase the paper.

Bankers' Acceptances: Bankers' acceptances are demands written on a bank which, when accepted, become negotiable money-market instruments. When the bank accepts them, they become high quality and the returns on them are slightly more than those available on Treasury bills.

Repurchase Agreements: Repurchase agreements are frequently used for investing very short-term cash (overnight money). They are loans secured by a government security dealer and are highly liquid.

Floating-Rate Preferred Stock: A recent innovation, these securities take advantage of the preferentially low tax to corporations of dividend income (70 percent). The rates are typically tied to the prime lending rate. Since most of the investors are corporations eligible for tax-exempt dividends, the rate on these is typically lower than that available on other short-term investments.

WORKED EXAMPLES

1. Mehta Trading Company's ledger balance is $29,500. The bank ledger balance showed an amount of $34,200 and the available balance is given as $28,300. Calculate the payment float, availability float and the net float.

SOLUTION

Payment float = bank ledger balance - company ledger balance = $34,200 - $29,500 = $4,700
Availability float = bank ledger balance - available balance = $34,200 - $28,300 = $5,900
Net float = payment float - availability float = $4,700 - $5,900 = -$1,200.

2. Homer Corp. has a disbursement float of 2 days and on average sends out $50,000 worth of checks a day. The average return obtainable in the year is 8 percent. What is the annual dollar return obtainable from investing the "payment float" portion of your checking account?

SOLUTION

The average amount available = payment float x daily flow
= 2 X $50,000 = $100,000

Interest earned = $100,000 X 0.08/365 = $21.92

3. Your company is offered a lock box system with the following details

> Average number of daily payments   300
> Average size of payments $1,200
> Daily interest rate   0.02%
> Saving in mailing time   1.3
> Saving in processing time   0.7
> Bank's charge per check processed $0.30

Assume 250 processing days per year. Evaluate the attractiveness of the lock-box system.

SOLUTION

The lock-box system reduces float and saves interest. The cost is the cost of processing charged by the bank.

Reduction in float = 1.3 + 0.7 = 2 days

Reduction in cash in transit   = 2 days x number of checks per day x average check
                                          = 2 x 300 x $1,200 = $720,000

Daily interest savings   = $720,000 x 0.02/100 = $144

Daily cost   = number of checks processed x processing charge/check
                                          = 300 x $0.28 = $84

Net daily savings   = $144 - $84 = $60

Annual benefit   = $60 x 250 = $15,000

The system saves money for the firm.

4. Fisher Corp sells fishing and other recreational gear through mail order. Currently the firm uses centralized billing and collection from its Montana headquarters. The company is considering setting up a concentration banking and lock-box system to improve its cash management. The City Bank has offered a complete collection and concentration banking system, which is expected to reduce the float in collections by 3 days and also save the company $24,000 in administrative costs. Other details of the system are given below:

> Annual fixed fee   = $72,000
> Number of lock-box locations   = 20
> Check processing charge   = 20 cents per check processed
> Wire transfer fee   = $9/location/transfer

The borrowing cost for the company is 8%. The company collects about $600,000 per day. Average amount per check is $600. Assume that there are 250 collection days in a year. Wire transfers will be made at the end of the day from each lock-box location. Evaluate the proposal.

SOLUTION

You can compare the benefits and costs of the system and decide. The benefits include the administrative cost savings and the reduced investment in cash and the resultant interest saved or gained.

Interest savings	= reduction in float x daily cash flow x cost of funds
	= 3 x $600,000 x 0.08 = $144,000
Total annual benefits	= $24,000 + $144,000 = $168,000

The costs of the system include the fixed fee plus the check-processing fee plus the cost of the wire transfers. Details are given below:

Fixed fee	= $72,000
Check processing fee	= Number of checks/day x processing days x processing charge/check
	= ($600,000/600) x 250 x 0.20 = $50,000
Wire transfer fees	= $9 x 20 x 250 = $45,000
Total costs	= $167,000

The benefits exceed the cost by $1,000. This may be a close call and the details need to be checked out.

4. If a 91-day Treasury bill is quoted at a discount of 2 percent, at what price must it be selling?

SOLUTION

The general formula is:

$$\text{Discount yield} = \frac{100 - \text{price}}{100} \times \frac{360}{91} = 0.02$$

Price = 100 - 100 x 0.02 x (91/360) = 99.4944

Or a $10,000 Treasury bill will sell for $9,949.44. The dollar amount of the discount, $50.56 is the interest earned. It is taxed as ordinary income, not as a capital gain.

5. What is the annual simple interest return on the Treasury bills discussed in problem 4? What is the effective compound rate of return?

SOLUTION
91-day return = $50.56/$9,949.44 = 0.5082 percent

Simple annual return = 0.5082 x (365/91) = 2.038 percent

The effective annual return $= \left(\dfrac{10,000}{9,949.44} \right)^{(365/91)} - 1 = 2.054$ percent.

6. Marge Pupper is a multi-millionaire, who made her money as a very successful screenplay writer for Hollywood movies. She expects her marginal tax rate to be 36 percent. Help her choose the best short-term investment from the following:

   a. High-grade commercial paper yielding effective pre-tax return of 3.6 percent.
   b. A municipal note yielding pre-tax return of 2.4 percent.
   c. A variable rate-preferred stock of Master Motors Corp. yielding 3.9 percent.

SOLUTION

Choose by after-tax return. So we will calculate the after-tax return on each investment:

After-tax return on the commercial paper = 3.6 x (1-0.36) = 2.30 percent.
After-tax return on the municipal note = same as pre-tax return = 2.4 percent.
After-tax return of the preferred stock = 3.9 x (1-0.36) = 2.5 percent.

The preferred stock has slightly higher returns. Assuming the three investments to be of equal risk, Marge can maximize her return by investing in the variable rate preferred stock.

SUMMARY

Cash management is an important part of the financial management function and includes three broad components. The three are: management of the flow of cash, determining the optimal levels of cash and marketable securities to hold, and finding the right mix of safe, short-term marketable securities. The first deals with the optimizing of the collection and disbursement systems. Collection and disbursement systems are designed for managing both the collection float and disbursement float. Centralized collection systems using concentration banking, lock boxes, and electronic transfers of excess cash are commonly used.

Cash provides liquidity, but does not pay any interest. The balance held by the firm should be optimized. Inventory based models can be used, though this may not work very well for large corporations, which face insignificant transaction costs relative to the level of cash holdings. Further, companies often hold more cash than needed for purely transaction needs and suggested by models like the Baumol model.

The third component of cash management deals with choosing the right investments to park the idle balances companies like to hold. The chapter lists a variety of money market instruments, which will serve as good investment assets with varying degrees of risk and return. The U.S. Treasury bills have the lowest risk, highest liquidity, and the lowest return. You can do better in terms of return with the agency securities, commercial paper, negotiable CDs, and so on. Of course, the risk increases and liquidity decreases.

LIST OF TERMS

Agency securities
Automated Clearinghouse system (ACH)
Bankers' acceptances
Carrying costs
Certificate of Deposit (CD)
CHIPS
Commercial paper
Concentration banking
Electronic funds transfer

Float
Floating rate preferred stock
International banking facility (IBF)
Lock-box system
Money market
Municipal securities
Repurchase agreement
Variable rate demand bonds (VRDB)

EXERCISES

Fill-in Questions

1. The two costs of holding inventory are _____ cost and _____ cost.

2. The _____ is used for transfer of routine and regular payments such as wages and dividends.

3. The _____ and the _____ are two means of electronic funds transfer.

4. The main cost of holding cash is _____.

5. The (higher, lower) _____ the interest rate, the higher the optimum amount of Treasury bills sold.

6. The time lag in the checks that have been written but have not yet cleared is called _____.

7. _____ banking requires customers to make payments to a local bank rather than directly to the company.

8. Renting a post office box to which customers make payments and from which the bank collects the payments is known as the _____ system of cash management.

9. In general, the default risk for money-market securities is (greater, less) _____ than it is for long-term debt.

10. Most money-market investments are _____ securities.

11. Noncompetitive bids for Treasury bills are filled at the (lowest, average) _____ price of the successful competitive bids.

12. The income from securities of states and other municipalities is (exempt, nonexempt) _____ from federal income taxes.

13. Time deposits are invariably insured by the Federal Deposit Insurance Corporation up to _____.

14. Negotiable certificates of deposit come in denominations of _____ or more.

15. A certificate providing evidence of a bank time deposit is called a _____.

16. A written demand that has been accepted by a bank to pay a given sum at a future date is called a _____.

17. A purchase of Treasury securities from a securities dealer with an agreement that the dealer will repurchase them at a later date at a specified price is a _____.

Problems

1. Betty Muhler, the CFO of Coleman-Muhler, Inc. is worried about the excessive float her firm has. The firm's current ledger balance is $485,000. The bank's ledger showed a balance of $520,000 in the company's account, but the available balance is $455,000. Calculate the payment float, availability float and the net float.

2. Detmer Corp uses a centralized billing and collection from its Florida headquarters. It has customers in all the fifty states, Washington D. C., Puerto Rico and Canada. The company is considering setting up a concentration banking and lock-box system to improve its cash management. Atlantic Bancorp has offered a complete collection and concentration banking system, which is expected to reduce the float in collections by 2 days and also save the company $45,000 in administrative costs. Other details of the system are given below:

Fixed fee	= $8,000/month
Number of lock-box locations	= 48
Check processing charge	= 24 cents per check processed
Wire transfer fee	= $8/location/transfer

The borrowing cost for the company is 12%. The company collects about $960,000 per day. Average amount per check is $800. Assume that there are 250 collection days in a year. Wire transfers will be made at the end of the day from each lock-box location. Evaluate the proposal.

3. A 30-day commercial paper issued by GMAC is selling at a discount yield of 2.4 percent. What is the price of the paper? What is the annual simple return of the bills? What is the annual compound rate of return?

4. Jules Coulomb Corp. (JCC) has marginal tax rate of 35 percent. It is considering the following short-term investment alternatives for its securities portfolio:

    a. Floating rate preferred stock with effective pre-tax return of 3.2 percent
    b. California State VRDB yielding pre-tax return of 2.6 percent.
    c. Corporate commercial paper yielding 4.4 percent.

    What is the best investment choice for JCC?

5. If JCC is located in California and is required to pay state income taxes at the marginal rate of 10 percent, in addition to the federal tax rate of 35 percent, on the income from both the preferred and the commercial paper, how would your advice change?

Essay Questions

1. What rationale can you give for holding cash, especially when it is considered that no interest is earned? Explain fully.

2. Describe the importance of float management clearly explaining how float may work either for or against a business.

3. Describe how companies manage collection and disbursement systems

4. Briefly describe the money market and the investments that are traded there.

5. What does it mean when we say, "Money-market investments are pure discount securities"?

ANSWERS TO EXERCISES

Fill-in Questions

1. Carrying; ordering
2. Automated Clearinghouse (ACH)
3. CHIPS; Fedwire
4. The interest foregone
5. Lower
6. Float
7. Concentration
8. Lock-box
9. Less
10. Discount
11. Average
12. Exempt
13. $100,000
14. $1,000,000
15. Certificate of deposit (CD)
16. Banker's acceptance
17. Repurchase agreement (or repo)

Problems

1. The different floats can be calculated as below:

Payment float	= bank ledger balance - company ledger balance
	= $520,000 - $485,000 = $35,000
Availability float	= bank ledger balance - available balance
	= $520,000 - $455,000 = $65,000
Net float	= payment float - availability float
	= $35,000 - $65,000 = -$30,000.

2. The benefits include the administrative cost savings and the reduced investment in cash and the resultant interest saved or gained.

Interest savings	= reduction in float x daily cash flow x cost of funds
	= 2 x $960,000 x 0.12 = $230,400
Total annual benefits	= $45,000 + $230,400 = $275,400

The costs of the system include the fixed fee plus the check-processing fee and the cost of the wire transfers. Details are given below:

Fixed fee	= 12 x $8,000 = $96,000
Check processing fee	= No. of checks/day x processing days x processing charge
	= ($960,000/800) x 250 x 0.24 = $72,000
Wire transfer fees	= $8 x 48 x 250 = $96,000
Total costs	= $264,000

The benefits exceed the cost by $11,400.

3. The general formula is:

$$\text{Discount yield} = \frac{100 - \text{price}}{100} \times \frac{360}{30} = 0.024$$

Price = 100 - 100 x 0.024 x (30/360) = 99.80

Or a $100,000 paper will sell for $99,800. The dollar amount of the discount, $200 is the interest earned. It is taxed as ordinary income, not as a capital gain.

30-day return = $200/$99,800 = 0.2004 percent

Simple annual return   = 0.2004 x (365/30) = 2.44 percent

The effective annual return = $\left(\dfrac{100,000}{99,800} \right)^{(365/30)} - 1 = 2.47$ percent.

4. Choose by after-tax return. Note that the only 30 percent of the preferred dividends are taxable, while the California bonds are tax-exempt.

After-tax return on floating-rate preferred = 3.2 - 3.2 x 0.3 x 0.35 = 2.864 percent.
After-tax return on the California VRDB = same as pre-tax return = 2.6 percent.
After-tax return of commercial paper = 4.4 x (1-0.35) = 2.86 percent.

The preferred stock has higher returns. Assuming the three investments to be of equal risk, the preferred stock would be the best choice.

5. If JCC is subject to California state income tax on the preferred dividends and the commercial paper return, their returns will be lower than what were computed in 4 above. The after-tax return on the preferred will be (assuming the state laws does not give the partial tax exemption permitted under the federal rules) = 2.864 - 3.2 x 0.10 = 2.544 percent. The return on the commercial paper will also be lower and will = 2.86 - 0.44 = 2.42 percent. Now, the state VRDB becomes the best choice.

32

Credit Management

INTRODUCTION

Credit policy is very important because companies use credit as a significant tool for expanding sales and profitability. The chapter describes the five key elements of credit policy in some detail and reviews the trade-off faced by the business in deciding on each element of credit policy. Credit starts with the terms of sale, which set forth the details of how the customers are required to pay for their purchases. The credit terms also specify the credit period and discount offered, if any. The second element of credit policy deals with the evidence of indebtedness or how the firm formalizes the debt owed to it by the customers. Companies do informal or formal credit analysis (the third element) to qualify customers for offer of credit and then decide the amount of credit (the fourth element) to be offered. The last component deals with the procedures for collection of delayed and delinquent payments.

Credit policy should be seen in the broad context of the operational and strategic management of the firm. The primary objective of the credit policy should be in line with the corporate management objective of shareholder wealth maximization. To this end, the policy details should aim at maximizing the overall profits rather than narrower goals such as sales maximization or bad debt minimization.

KEY CONCEPTS IN THE CHAPTER

Terms of Sale: The terms of sale indicate the method by which customers pay for goods and services. Most goods and services are sold on credit, usually with a cash discount being offered if payment is received within a short time, but with the entire amount nonetheless due at the end of a specified period. Cash on delivery (COD) and even cash before delivery (CBD) may be appropriate policy in certain cases, but in most industries credit is common for business customers. Industry practice plays an important part in determining the credit terms. A term of 2/10, net 30 means the customer will get a 2 percent discount if the bill is paid within 10 days from the invoice date. If the customer chooses not to take the discount, payment is required within 30 days from the invoice date. The discount terms may start from the end of the month in cases where the purchases are recurring. Credit terms can be part of an overall sales strategy and the sales manager should be part of the decision process.

Commercial Credit Instruments: Businesses use a variety of ways to formalize the debt owed by the customers. The most common approach is the open account, which is simply a record on the books of the firm showing the customer's liability to the firm. In some cases the open account may be supported by formal receipts of delivery of the goods supplied. Depending on the nature of the business and one's customers, other commercial credit instruments may be used, such as promissory notes, commercial drafts, bank acceptances, and letters of credit. A *commercial draft* is a Bill of Exchange and the customer *accepts* as record of debt before delivery of the goods. The actual payment may be immediate for a *sight draft* or after a period of credit for a *time draft*. The customer's acceptance creates a *trade acceptance,* which is either held to maturity or can be discounted for immediate payment when used as collateral for a loan.

Credit Analysis: Ordinarily, credit analysis precedes credit extension. Credit analysis often starts with simple analysis of the prospective customer's financial statements. For more rigorous analysis, the financial manager may hire the services of a credit agency, such as Dun and Bradstreet. These firms provide credit reports and credit scores giving details of the prospective customer's past credit history and experience with other businesses. Commercial banks and financial institutions use the system developed by the consulting firm, Fair Isaacs, to evaluate individual customers for credit card and other personal credit. The system uses a summery credit score capturing a wealth of details in one single measure. This may be appropriate for a firm dealing with a large number of small businesses or individual customers. For customers who have publicly traded bonds and stocks, market prices of the securities can provide information about the firm's financial strength or weakness.

Financial ratio analysis discussed in chapter 29 can be used to check the customers' creditworthiness. More sophisticated measures of creditworthiness of customers and risk indexes have been derived from the information included in financial statements. Altman's Z score is based on the statistical technique known as *multiple discriminant analysis*. Altman used multiple discriminant analysis to study the financial ratios of firms, which went bankrupt and compared them with the ratios of non-bankrupt firms. He developed an index of credit worthiness, called the Z score, given as:

$$Z = 0.72 \frac{\text{net working capital}}{\text{total assets}} + 0.85 \frac{\text{retained earnings}}{\text{total assets}} + 3.1 \frac{\text{EBIT}}{\text{total assets}}$$
$$+ 0.42 \frac{\text{shareholders equity}}{\text{total liability}} + 1 \frac{\text{sales}}{\text{total assets}}$$

Firms with Z-score of less than 1.2 were predicted to go bankrupt. Scores above 2.9 indicated financial strength and scores between 1.2 and 2.9 were considered in the gray area. Updated and modified versions of Z scores have been developed, but are proprietary information and may be available for use. The model was originally developed for predicting bankruptcy and not default on trade credit and thus one has to be careful in using to decide the trade credit worthiness of a customer.

The Credit Decision: After the foregoing steps have been taken, the credit decision is made. Every credit decision involves the trade-off between the expected profit when the customer pays and the loss on default by the customer. The profit can be expressed as REV - cost, where REV is the additional revenue from the sale. This trade-off can be expressed as:

Expected profit = p x PV(REV - cost) - (1 - p)PV(cost), where p is the probability of payment and PV is present value.

If the credit manager can identify the value of p for every customer, the credit decision becomes very easy. However, credit analysis is expensive and no credit manager can afford to do detailed credit research on every prospective customer. Usually the probability of default, as well as the size of the order, when compared with the gain from not extending credit, forms the basis for the analysis. If there is a possibility of repeat orders, this has to be accounted for by including the present value of the expected profit from the second order in the analysis.

A reasonable credit policy is based on three principles. First, the goal should be to maximize expected profits as a proxy for maximizing shareholder value. Narrower goals such as minimizing bad debt or maximizing sales should not be pursued. Second, concentrate efforts on those accounts most likely to pose a threat to the financial welfare of the firm, either because of their size or because of their doubtful paying ability. Third, possibility of repeat orders should be factored into the overall decision because they have a bearing on long-run sales and profits.

Collection Policy: A firm's collection policy lays out the details on when to treat an account as delinquent and the course of action to be taken for such accounts. When an account becomes delinquent, the firm's collection policy is enforced. By reviewing the aging data on accounts receivable, the manager can identify delinquent accounts. Collection policy should set the guidelines for the action, which needs to be taken. The action will depend on the status of the account and would follow a set sequence depending on the progress made by the account. In the worst case, when the account becomes un-collectable, the firm might decide turn the case over to its lawyers or an outside collection firm, specializing in collecting bad debts. These are costly alternative to collecting directly and usually resorted to as the ultimate step.

Most large firms manage their accounts receivable in-house. Smaller firms, which do not have the resources for extensive credit analysis, can use the services of *factors*. Factors are usually finance companies or subsidiaries of large banks, specializing in credit management and collection. They buy receivables from firms and absorb the credit risk. Factors do their own credit analysis and generally approve the customer for credit before the sale is authorized. Factoring services can include financing *(old-line factoring)* or the factor will pay the firm on due date *(maturity factoring)*. For some export transactions, it might be possible to buy credit insurance, usually sponsored by government agencies.

WORKED EXAMPLES

1. Find the effective annual cost of forgoing taking cash discounts for each of the following terms of sale: 2/10, n/30, and 5/20, n/60.

SOLUTION

The object is first to determine the effective cost of the loan arising from not taking the cash discount. For convenience, let's deal in increments of $100 of sales, and let's take the case of 2/10, n/30. Recognize that during the first 10 days you obtain a "free ride" on the seller's credit (although it is not cost-free, the cost of the free ride most probably being built into the sale price). Also note that if you do not take the cash discount, in effect you are borrowing the difference between the total amount billed, $100, and the amount of the cash discount, $2, which, of course, is $98; it costs you $2 each time you borrow the $98. You are borrowing the $98 for 20 days. If you repeat this process throughout the year, you will borrow 18.25 times because there are 18.25 20-day periods in a 365-day year (365/20).

The cost of the 20-day, $98 loan is:

Per period cost of loan   = dollar cash discount/dollar amount of loan
           = \$2/\$98 = 0.0204 = 2.04 percent

Simple annual rate = (\$2/\$98) x (365/20) = 37.24 percent.

If the firm is using this as a source of financing on a recurring basis, it is paying 2.04 percent for each of the 18.25 periods. The effective annual cost is the compound return on the 2.04 percent, namely,

Effective annual cost of foregoing cash discounts = $(1 + \text{per period rate})^{\text{number of periods per year}} - 1$

$$= (1 + 0.0204)^{18.25} - 1 = 0.4456 = 44.56 \text{ percent.}$$

This is very expensive by anyone's standards. Note that it is incorrect to estimate the cost of not taking the discount by merely estimating the cost as 2 percent (\$2/\$100) and multiplying that by the number of periods to obtain an answer of 36.5 percent (2 percent x 18.25) because that procedure ignores the effective amount that is borrowed and the compounding effect of the forgone interest.

The calculations for the other terms of sale are as follows:
5/20, n/60:
      Per period cost of loan = \$5/\$95 = 5.26 percent
      Simple annual rate = (\$5/\$95) x (365/40) = 48.03 percent.

      Effective annual cost = $(1 + 0.0526)^{365/40} - 1 = 0.5964 = 59.64$ percent

2. Corn Syrup Corp. has currently bad debts at 8 percent of sales. The CFO of the firm is considering tightening up credit policy. The new policy is expected to lower sales by 10 percent, but drop the bad debt ratio to 3 percent. The cost of goods sold is 78 percent of sales. Evaluate the proposed change in credit policy.

SOLUTION

Assume sales are S. The current net revenue after costs will be the net sales after bad debts less the cost of goods sold = S (1- 0.08) - 0.78S = 0.92S - 0.78S = 0.14S

The net revenue less costs for the new policy $\quad$ = 0.9S(1-0.03) - 0.78x0.9S
$$= 0.873S - 0.702S = 0.171S$$

The new policy is better.

3. Runnymede Corp.'s credit manager studied the bill-paying habits of its customers and discovered that 95 percent were prompt payers and 5 percent were slow payers. The records also showed that 15 percent of the slow payers and 2 percent of the prompt payers subsequently defaulted. The company now has 3,500 accounts on its books, none of which has yet defaulted. What is the total number of expected defaults, assuming no repeat business is on the horizon?

SOLUTION

To solve this problem, first categorize the number of prompt and slow payers. They are

Prompt payers	= 3,500 x 0.95 = 3,325
Slow payers	= 3,500 x 0.05 = 175

Next, multiply the probability of default for each class to obtain the expected number for each class.

Default from prompt payers	= 3,325 x 0.02	= 66.5
Default from slow payers	= 175 x 0.15	= 26.25
Total expected default		= 92.75

A total of 92.75 (say, 93) accounts (2.65 percent of the total) is expected to default.

4. Given the data in problem 3, revenues from sales of $1,800, and cost of the sales of $1,560, what is the expected profit (loss) from extending credit to slow payers?

SOLUTION

Expected profit = p x PV(revenues - cost) - (1 - p)(cost) = 0.85($1,800 - $1,560) - 0.15($1,560)
$$= \$204 - \$234 = -\$30$$

Clearly, it is not profitable to extend credit to slow payers.

5. Estimate how much Runnymede would have to increase prices to make it just worthwhile to extend credit to slow payers in problem 4.

SOLUTION

Estimate the revenues (left-hand side) needed to cover the costs (right-hand) side:

$$0.85(\text{revenues} - \$1,560) = 0.15 \times \$1,560$$
$$0.85 \times \text{revenues} - \$1,326 = \$234$$
$$\text{Revenues} = (\$234 + \$1,326)/0.85 = \$1,835$$

At average revenues of about $1,835, a price increase of about 2 percent, the firm is likely to just break even from extending credit to all customers.

6. Is it worthwhile for the credit manager of Runnymede Corp., to engage in a credit search to determine whether customers are slow or prompt payers if the cost of the search is $8, the probability of identifying a slow payer is 0.10, and the expected loss from a slow payer is $30?

SOLUTION

If the slow payer is identified and credit is denied, the firm will save $30. Therefore,

Expected payoff from credit check = (probability of identifying a slow payer x gain from not extending credit) - cost of credit check
= (0.10 x $30) - $8 = $3 - $8 = -$5

It is not worthwhile to engage in the credit check.

7. At what level of sales per customer would the credit manager in problem 6 be indifferent?

SOLUTION

If the expected loss from a slow payer were $80, the credit check would be worthwhile.

Set expected payoff from credit check (0.10 x X) - $8 equal to zero and solve for X, that is, $0.10X = 8$; $X = \$80$.

8. We expect that one of our slow-paying customers in problems 3-7 will subsequently place a repeat order. If the customer pays on the first order, we estimate a probability of 0.90 of no default on the second order. Assuming investments of comparable risk return 15 percent, how would you evaluate the extension of credit?

SOLUTION

Let's take this in steps. First, calculate the expected profit on the initial order.

$$\text{Expected profit on initial order} = p_1 \times PV(\text{revenues} - \text{cost}) - (1 - p_1)PV \times (\text{cost})$$
$$= (0.85 \times \$240) - (0.15 \times \$1,560)$$
$$= \$204 - \$234$$
$$= -\$30$$

Second,

$$\text{Next year's expected profit on repeat order} = p_2 \times PV(\text{revenues} - \text{cost}) - (1 - p_2)PV \times (\text{cost})$$
$$= (0.90 \times \$240) - (0.10 \times \$1,560)$$
$$= \$216 - \$156 = \$60$$

Third, calculate the present value of the total expected profit.

$$\text{Total expected profit} = \text{expected profit on initial order} + (\text{probability of payment and repeat}$$
$$\text{order} \times PV \text{ of next year's expected profit on repeat order})$$
$$= -\$30 + 0.85PV(\$60) = -\$30 + [(0.85)(\$60)]/1.15$$
$$= -\$30 + \$44.35 = \$14.35$$

It is worthwhile to extend credit if there is a chance of repeat order.

SUMMARY

The chapter deals with credit management. Credit management involves five steps:

- Deciding the terms of sale.
- Using the appropriate credit instruments as evidence of indebtedness.
- Designing the right credit analysis tools and techniques.
- Making the right credit decisions.
- Managing the collection.

Credit policy is also part of the overall marketing and sales strategy and the sales/marketing managers should be part of the decision process. The credit manager should clearly understand the trade-off involved. The ultimate objective should be profit maximization as proxy for shareholder wealth maximization. The manager should be willing to tradeoff higher sales or lower bad debts for higher profits. Credit analysis is not an exact science and companies will have to use their experience and industry wisdom to design the best policy. Sophisticated credit scoring techniques may not be relevant or the right ones to use in every case.

LIST OF TERMS

Aging of receivables   Open account credit
Cash discount   Promissory note
Commercial draft   Sight draft
Factor   Time draft
Multiple-discriminant analysis   Trade acceptance

EXERCISES

Fill-in Questions

1. _____ are often used to induce customers to pay their bills before the end of the free payment period.

2. When the buyer accepts the Bill of Exchange, you have a _____.

3. A _____ is a credit instrument used to get the buyer to acknowledge the credit before delivery.

4. A commercial draft may be a(n) _____ or a(n) _____, depending on when the payment is made.

5. A simple _____ may be used to record the customer's indebtedness.

6. Ordinarily, a credit manager (does, does not) _____ subject each customer to the same credit analysis. Rather, efforts should be concentrated on the (large, small) _____ and doubtful orders.

7. A firm, usually part of a commercial bank, which purchases accounts receivable is called a(n) _____.

8. The statistical procedure known as _____ was used to estimate the likelihood of financial failure.

9. Most trade credit is given on _____ rather than on promissory note or other commercial instruments.

10. Financial managers are said to be _____ when they classify their credit sales according to the percentage of the total that pay their bills in 1, 2, 3, or more than 3 months.

Problems

1. Find the effective annual cost of not taking the cash discounts on the following terms of trade: 3/10, n/30, and 1.5/15, n/40.

2. Jar of Pickles, Inc. has currently bad debts at 12 percent of sales. The CFO of the firm is considering tightening up credit policy. The new policy is expected to lower sales by 9 percent, but drop the bad debt ratio to 5 percent. The cost of goods sold is 82 percent of sales. Evaluate the proposed change in credit policy.

3. Crummer Crumpets Corp. (CCC)'s credit manager studied the bill-paying habits of its customers and found that 90 percent of them were prompt. She also discovered that 22 percent of the slow payers and 5 percent of the prompt ones subsequently defaulted. The company has 2,000 accounts on its books, none of which has yet defaulted. Calculate the total number of expected defaults, assuming no repeat business is on the horizon.

4. Given the data in problem 3, revenues from sales of $1,300, and the cost of sales of $1,100, what is the expected profit or loss from extending credit to slow payers?

5. Estimate the average level of revenues that makes it just worthwhile to extend credit to slow payers in problem 4.

6. Is it worthwhile for the credit manager of CCC to engage in a credit search to determine whether customers are slow or prompt payers if the cost of each search is $11, the probability of identifying slow payers is 0.06, and the expected cost of a slow payer is $86? Show all calculations.

7. At what sales level would the credit manager in problem 6 be indifferent? Show all calculations.

8. Say there is a 0.92 probability that a repeat customer of CCC will not default. How should the credit manager evaluate the original extension of credit to a customer who has been identified as a slow payer but also as certain to place a repeat order? The required return on an investment of this risk is 12 percent.

Essay Questions

1. Discuss the statement: "A firm may extend trade credit to a customer who may not be credit worthy by the standards of a typical bank loan officer."

2. What role does financial ratio analysis play in credit evaluation? Explain both the advantages and disadvantages of financial ratio analysis.

3. What should be the primary goal of credit policy?

4. "I don't know about other financial managers, but as the credit manager of Runnymede Corp., I consider maximization of profits, concentration on dangerous accounts, and repeat orders to be the most influential of my credit decisions." Evaluate this statement.

ANSWERS TO EXERCISES

Fill-in Questions

1. Cash discounts
2. Trade acceptance
3. Commercial draft
4. Sight draft, time draft
5. Promissory note

6. Does not; large
7. Factor
8. Multiple-discriminant analysis
9. Open account
10. Aging receivables

Problems

1. 3/l0, n/30: Per-period cost = dollar cash discount/dollar amount of loan

$$= \$3/\$97 = 3.093 \text{ percent}$$

Simple annual cost $= 3.093 \times 365/20 = 56.44$ percent

Number of periods $= 365/20 = 18.25$

Effective annual cost $= (1 + 0.0309)^{18.25} - 1 = 0.7426 = 74.26$ percent.

1.5/15, n/40: Per-period cost = dollar cash discount/dollar amount of loan

$$= \$1.5/\$98.5 = 1.52 \text{ percent}$$

Simple annual cost $= 1.52 \times 365/25 = 22.23$ percent.

Effective annual cost $= (1 + 0.0309)^{(365/25)} - 1 = 0.2464 = 24.64$ percent.

2. Assume sales are S. The current net revenue after costs will be the net sales after bad debts less the cost of goods sold.$= S(1 - 0.12) - 0.82S = 0.88S - 0.82S = 0.06S$

The net revenue less costs for the new policy $= 0.91S(1 - 0.05) - 0.82 \times 0.91S$
$$= 0.8645S - 0.7462S = 0.1183S$$

The new policy is better.

3. Prompt payers $= 2,000 \times 0.9 = 1,800$
   Slow payers $= 2,000 \times 0.1 = 200$

   (Prompt x probability) + (slow x probability) $= (1,800 \times 0.05) + (200 \times 0.22)$
   $$= 90 + 44 = 134$$

4. Expected profit $= 0.78(\$1,300 - \$1,100) - 0.22(\$1,100) = -\$86$

5. $0.78(REV - \$1,100) - 0 = \$242$
   $$REV = \$1,410$$

404

6. Expected payoff = (0.06 x $86) - $11 = -$5.84

7. 0.06X - $11 = 0; X = $183.33

8. Step 1: Expected profit on initial order = p_1 x PV(revenues - cost) - (1 - P_1) x PV(cost)

$$= (0.78 \times \$200) - (0.22 \times \$1,100) = -\$86$$

Step 2:

Next year's expected profit on repeat order = p_2 x PV(revenues - cost) - (1 - P_2) x PV(cost)

$$= (0.90 \times \$200) - (0.10 \times \$1,100)$$
$$= \$180 - \$110 = \$70$$

Step 3: Total expected profit = expected profit on initial order + probability of payment and repeat order x PV of next year's expected profit on repeat order

$$= 86 + \frac{0.78 \times \$70}{1.12} = -\$86 + \$49 = -\$37$$

It is still not worthwhile to extend credit to the slow payer.

33
Mergers

INTRODUCTION

The last two decades have seen a number of corporate mergers or unions. Mergers can be evaluated in the same way as any other investment. As long as the merged firms are worth more combined than when alone, the net present value of the fusion is profitable and shareholders are better off. Financial managers need to know under what conditions it is worthwhile to merge with another firm.

The chapter starts with reasons why companies merge. The motives for mergers include both those, which make sense, and those, which do not. This is followed by coverage of the benefits and costs of mergers and how these are evaluated. The chapter also provides summary coverage of the legal, tax, and accounting issues. A number of examples of recent merger activities are described with a discussion of defensive tactics adopted by companies opposed to being taken over. The last section discusses the benefits and costs of mergers to the economy in general and the effect of the threat of a takeover on corporate management.

Mergers can be the result of a hostile takeover or a friendly union. In either case, mergers typically result in a change of *ownership* and *control*. Even in the so-called mergers of equals, one can see that one company's management dominates the post-merger firm. Thus, merger activities are part of a broader market for corporate control. This market includes not only mergers, but also spin-offs and other restructuring activities, which change the structure of the corporation and provide the right incentives for managers. These and related issues are discussed in greater detail in the next chapter.

KEY CONCEPTS IN THE CHAPTER

Sensible Motives for Mergers: Most mergers are of one three categories: i) horizontal integration, in which two firms in the same line of business are merged, ii) vertical integration, in which firms which have supplier-customer linkage are combined, and iii) conglomerates, in which companies in unrelated businesses are combined. These are a number of possible reasons why two firms may be worth more together than apart. An acquisition adds value only if it generates additional economic rents - providing a further competitive edge that is not easily reproduced in the market in other ways. Here is a summary of motives, which make sense.

Economies of scale: Cost saving through operating economies of scale is among the most common reason for creation of value in horizontal mergers. Savings can come in a number of areas including production, marketing, distribution, administrative costs, and R and D.

<u>Economies of vertical integration</u>: Vertical integration can net costs savings through better coordination and administration, technological advantages, and synergy.

<u>Ability to surplus funds</u>: A firm in a mature industry with large cash surpluses can merge with a firm in a growth industry that is in need of cash for good investment projects can combine and effectively add through the internal cash transfer. The alternative to this would be external transfer, through stockholders. The latter course would be tax-inefficient.

<u>Combining complementary sources</u>: Mergers and combination involving companies, which have complimentary resources needed for full exploitation of each other's assets, can add value through the effective use of the assets. For example, a small firm may have the technology for a new product, but may lack the resources and skill to commercialize the know-how quickly. A merger with a large firm, which has the needed resources can, be mutually beneficial. Of course, there are alternatives (e.g. a strategic alliance) to a full-blown merger, but in some cases a merger may be the best approach.

<u>Eliminating inefficiencies</u>: Poor and inefficient management can be a problem in some companies and acquisition and changed and improved management can certainly add value by cutting the fat and inefficiencies.

These motives can make sense and can add value when the companies are combined. There may be difficulty in realizing many of the cost savings or other benefits because of the problems of coordinating activities across two different organizational "cultures," which are not used to working together.

Dubious Motives: While the above reasons for mergers can make sense, there are other professed motives, which do not. These include the following:

Diversification: It is often argued that by merging across different industries (conglomerate merger), the shareholders can enjoy the benefit of reduced risk. The shareholders get all the diversification they want at a much lower cost and more efficiently than by buying shares in the two companies separately.

Bootstrapping: When a company with a high price-earnings ratio (P/E) merges with a low P/E company, the combined firm can enjoy higher earnings per share. This looks like a neat trick, if you can pull it off. The problem is that the company with the lower P/E probably has a lower P/E because it has lower growth or less reliable earnings. The market will value the combined firm at a P/E lower than that of the high P/E firm, because the combined firm has lower growth or less reliable earnings. Unless, one believes in very inefficient markets and irrational investors, such mergers do not make sense.

Lower financing costs: The argument is that the combined firm can borrow at a lower rate. It is possible that the larger firm can enjoy economies of scale in terms of issue costs. It is also possible that the merging firms, by effectively guaranteeing each other's debt are lowering the risk of the lenders and thus, are transferring wealth from their stockholders to the bondholders. This is good for the bondholders, but not for the stockholders.

Benefits and Costs of Mergers: A merger adds value if the value of the combined firm is greater than the sum of the values of the individual firms. This will happen if the gain from the merger is more than the cost. We can write the gain from a merger of firms A and B as follows:

$$\text{Gain} = PV_{AB} - (PV_A + PV_B) = \Delta PV_{AB}$$

where PV represents the value of each firm and the combined firm. The cost of the merger is the price paid less the value of the firm. Assume that firm B is being bought by firm A and the price for B is paid in cash. Then the cost is:

$$\text{Cost} = \text{cash paid} - PV_B$$

The costs of cash deals are straightforward and the cost of a merger is the premium that the buying firm pays for the selling firm over the value of a selling firm's value as a separate entity.

The NPV of the merger will be:

$$\text{NPV} = \text{Gain} - \text{Cost} = \Delta PV_{AB} - (\text{cash paid} - PV_B)$$

This formulation of the NPV of the merger focuses attention on the gain and cost separately. The gain is given by the increase in value by the combination of the two firms. The cost represents the apportionment of the gain between the shareholders of the two companies. When the market anticipates the merger, the target firm's share price might have risen in anticipation. This overstates the true value of the firm. In other words, PV_B would be less than the market value. In such cases, you have to look at the intrinsic, or stand-alone, value of B. The actual cost to firm A will be higher and B's shareholders get more of the gains from the merger.

Cost of a Merger When Financed by Stock: When a merger is financed by stock, the cost of the merger depends on the value of the shares in the new company received by the stockholders of the target firm. If the sellers get N shares and each share is worth P_{AB} after the merger, then the cost is:

$$\text{Cost} = \text{Number of shares paid} \times \text{share price} - PV_B = N \times P_{AB} - PV_B$$

To get the true cost, you have to use the price after the merger.

The presence of *asymmetric information* between the acquiring firm's managers and the outside investors, including firm B's shareholders, may explain when the managers would choose stock or cash methods of payment. If the managers think that their stock is overvalued, then they are likely to use stock as the mode of payment for the merger. This explains why share prices fall when stock-financed mergers are announced.

409

The Mechanics of a Merger: Mergers are complicated affairs and involve complex legal, tax, and accounting issues. These are briefly discussed below.

Legal Aspects: Federal anti-trust laws can block well-laid plans for mergers. The government can act through the Justice Department by filing a civil suit in courts or the Federal Trade Commission can act under one of the several statutes, which regulate commerce and trade. The Clayton Act (1914), with later amendments and legislation, has the most important implications to merger activities. The law prohibits acquisition of any kind, which may lessen competition or tend to create a monopoly. The Act forbids even potential constraints and the Justice Department has used the Clayton Act as its main weapon to prevent corporate combinations, which, in its opinion, created a threat to competition in any industry or business. The Hart-Scott-Rodino Act (1976) requires that acquisitions of stocks over $15 million or 15 percent of a company's stock need to be reported to the federal agencies. This ensures that the federal government can monitor mergers and acquisition activities from the very early stage and take action if required. A number of potential mergers have been stopped or modified significantly by the actions of the Justice Department. Companies, which have significant business interests oversees do also need to be concerned with foreign laws and regulations regarding merger activities. The regulators of the European Union (union of 15 European countries) have acted in a number of mergers involving not only European companies, but American firms as well. The recent case of the blocked GE-Honeywell merger, which was killed by the European regulators after it was effectively approved by the US authorities, show that multinational firms should heed the European Union laws as well.

The Form of Acquisition: There are forms of acquisition normally used by corporations in the U.S. The first is to merge the two companies totally combining all assets and liabilities. The acquiring company assumes all the assets and all the liabilities of the seller. The second approach involves buying out the shares of the target firm in exchange for cash, shares, or other securities. In this approach, the buyer can deal directly with the shareholders and by-pass the managers of the seller firm. The last method involves buying some or all of the assets of the seller and the ownership of the assets are transferred to the buyer.

Accounting Issues: The main accounting issue is to decide the accounting treatment of the merger. Two alternatives are used. In the first approach is called the *purchase of assets*. This method shows any premium over the book value paid to the seller as goodwill. The fair value of the goodwill needs to be re-estimated each year and shown in the books. The alternative is to use the *pooling of interests*. The balance sheets of the two firms are simply added together; no goodwill is shown. In efficient capital markets, accounting treatments should make no difference, as there are no differences in the cash flows.

Tax Issues: Mergers can be *taxable* acquisitions, where the target firm's shareholders are viewed as having sold shares and taxed accordingly. The acquiring firm revalues the assets and starts with new depreciation schedules. In the alternative approach, the transaction is *tax-free* and

410

selling shareholders are seen as exchanging shares for new ones of like kind and quality; the firm is taxed as if two firms had always been together.

Merger Tactics: Many mergers are friendly transactions where the management of the two firms negotiates a mutually acceptable deal. But some acquisitions are *hostile takeovers,* where the target firm, or the management of the firm, is not keen on the merger. This leads to defensive tactics aimed at stopping the merger. What follows is often a battle of legal wits and firepower between the two firms. A colorful language has sprung up around takeover battles. Typically, the acquiring firm can go over the head of the unwilling target firm's management using *tender offers* inviting shareholders to sell shares directly to the acquiring firm. Once they have enough shares or shareholder support, the acquiring firm can start a *proxy* fight to get the needed support from the board of the target firm. Here are some other terms commonly used in the takeover jargon:

Arbitrageurs (or arbs): Speculators who buy the target firm's stocks in the expectation that it will rise quickly.

Golden parachutes: This describes a very liberal compensation package for managers who lose their jobs because of a takeover. The availability of the golden parachute will ensure that the managers will not have an incentive to fight any takeover of the company at the cost of the shareholders.

Greenmail: Buying out the raider's shares at an attractive price, without offering the same price to other stockholders.

Pacman defense: The target firm attempts the takeover of the raider and thus, hopes to takeover before being taken over.

Poison pill: Existing shareholders get rights, which are triggered when there is a significant purchase of the firm' shares, to buy the company's shares at a bargain price. This will make the raider's shares lose value.

Poison put: Bondholders get rights to sell the bonds back to the company, when there is a change of control as a result of a takeover.

Shark-repellent: Amendments to the corporate charter, which will make the firm very unattractive or difficult as a target. The amendments can include: restricted voting rights to new shareholders, requiring super-majority approvals for certain resolutions to be approved by the shareholders, and staggered change of the board of directors.

Many such tactics are challenged in the courts, and states tend to legislate in favor of the incumbent management. It is unclear whether an incumbent management wishes merely to perpetuate itself or act in the best long-run interest of shareholders when it fights a potential acquisition. Managers of target firms could be contesting takeover for protecting shareholders

411

interests and get as high a price as possible for the shareholders. It is also possible that they may be doing it because of the fear of losing their jobs.

Some companies do restructuring of the company's assets and liabilities to ward off the raiders. The restructuring often includes selling non-profitable businesses and increasing leverage, the kind of restructuring typically done by raiders. Firms become targets precisely because they are under-performing and their assets are worth less than they could be. Restructuring improves value and can act as the best long-term defense.

Mergers and the Economy: Mergers seem to come in waves, with the major merger activity occurring during periods of stock market buoyancy. Generally, it is also seen that most of the mergers during these merger booms seem to be concentrated in a few industries. This may be due to changing regulatory conditions as well as technology related factors specific to these industries. It is still not clear that these factors explain the merger waves of the past.

A more interesting and important question relates to the impact of mergers on the economy and society. Are mergers good for the economy? There are arguments, which suggest that they are. These include: mergers and acquisitions make firms more efficient; they get rid of inefficient management; and the fear of takeovers makes managers perform better. Others argue that: raiders take a short-term view, often use excessive leverage, and cut R&D and other expenses, which give long-term benefits. There is no general consensus among economists, though studies seem to show that merged firms have higher productivity and profits.

WORKED EXAMPLES

1. Major, Inc., plans to merge with Minor Corp. The capital market places a value on Major of $226 million and Minor is valued at $17 million, when they are evaluated separately. After the merger, economies of scale will result in additional cash flows, the present value of which is estimated at $9 million. Major will buy Minor for $21 million in cash. Major has 2.26 million shares outstanding, which are currently selling at a price of $100 each. What are the costs, gain, and NPV of the merger?

SOLUTION

$$\text{Cost} = \text{cash paid} - \text{PV}_{Minor}$$
$$= \$21 \text{ million} - \$17 \text{ million} = \$4 \text{ million}$$

$$\text{Gain} = (\$226 + \$17 + \$9) - (\$226 + \$17) = \$9 \text{ million}$$

$$\text{NPV} = \text{gain} - \text{cost}$$
$$= \$9 \text{ million} - \$4 \text{ million} = \$5 \text{ million}$$

2. How did the shareholders of Major and of Minor make out on the merger?

SOLUTION

To determine how shareholders make out from a merger, begin by recognizing that the cost of the merger is a gain to Minor's shareholders; they capture $4 million of the $9 million gain. The NPV calculated above is the gain to Major's shareholders. It works out this way:

Net gain to acquiring firm's shareholders   = overall gain to combination – gain captured by acquired firm's shareholders
= $9 million - $4 million = $5 million

3. Here is a bootstrapping merger. Regal Corp is considering the acquisition of Princes, Inc. The data for this deal are set forth in the table below. Assuming there are no economic gains from the merger, complete the final column of the table and comment on the merger.

	Regal Corp. (Pre-merger)	Princes, Inc.
A. Earnings per share	$6.00	$6.00
B. Price per share	$96.00	$48.00
C. Price-earnings ratio	16.00	8.00
D. Number of shares	500,000	500,000
E. Total earnings	$3,000,000	$3,000,000
F. Total market value	$48,000,000	$24,000,000
G. Current earnings per dollar invested in stock (A divided by B)	$0.0625	$0.125

SOLUTION

	Regal Corp (Post merger)
A. Earnings per share	$8.00
B. Price per share	$96.00
C. Price-earnings ratio	12.00
D. Number of shares	750,000
E. Total earnings	$6,000,000
F. Total market value	$72,000,000
G. Current earnings per dollar invested in stock (A divided by B)	$0.0833

The post-merger results are shown above. The share price of Regal Corp is twice that of Princes, Inc. Regal can, therefore, offer 1 share for every 2 of Princes. The final number of shares in the combined companies will be 750,000 (line D). The share price (line B) remains $96 and the total market value (line F) is the product of these ($72 million) and also the sum of the two individual market values, since there are no economic gains from the merger. Since the total earnings (line E) become $6,000,000, earnings per share (line A) increase to $8 and the price-earnings ratio (line C) becomes 12. Regal had been selling at a higher multiple of earnings per share than

413

Princes, and as a result, its earnings per share increase. The benefits of such "bootstrapping" is a myth and does not create value.

4. Refer to problem 1 above. Major, Inc., wishes to estimate the cost of a merger that entails an exchange of 210,000 shares, currently selling at $100/share, instead of $21 million in cash. What are the apparent and true costs of the merger?

SOLUTION

The apparent cost is straightforward:

$$\text{Apparent cost} = (\text{number of shares} \times \text{market price per share}) - PV_{Minor}$$
$$= (210,000 \times \$100) - \$17 \text{ million} = \$4 \text{ million}$$

This is the same as before. The true cost is determined by the amount of the new value the Minor shareholders obtain in the deal. We need to estimate the percent of the merged company's stock that will be held by Minor's shareholders. This equals:

$$x = \frac{\text{new shares issued to Minor's shareholders}}{\text{total shares outstanding after the merger}} = \frac{210,000}{2,260,000 + 210,000}$$
$$= 0.085 = 8.5 \text{ percent}$$

Major, Inc., gives up slightly more than 8.5 percent of its claim on the total value of the merged firm. Now, we proceed to determine the true cost of the merger in this way:

$$\text{True cost} = x \ (PV_{Major + Minor}) - PV_{Minor}$$
$$= 0.085(\$226 + \$17 + \$9) - \$17$$
$$= 0.085 \ (\$252) - \$17 = \$4.42 \text{ million}$$

This is about 10 percent more than the previous value.

SUMMARY

The chapter describes corporate mergers and the various issues involved. These include the benefits, motives, the mechanics, the tax and accounting issues and the defense tactics of firms, which do not want to merge or be taken over. Mergers have become quite common in the last two decades. A merger is a positive NPV activity if the value of the combined firm is more than the sum of the values of the combining firms. This gain can come from economies of scale, benefits of vertical integration, improved efficiency, use of tax shields and combination of complimentary resources. At least in some cases, companies merge for dubious reasons. Corporate diversification, for example, gives little benefit to shareholders, as the shareholders do it themselves far more efficiently and cheaply.

The chapter gave several examples of recent takeover "battles." There are some companies, or at least their management, which do not want to be taken over. The management use tough defense tactics and often succeed in preventing takeovers.

Whether mergers benefit the economy and the society is still being debated. Acquisitions and the fear of the same appear to make corporate management more efficient and responsive to shareholders. On the other hand, some people argue that corporate mergers result in leveraging of companies and trade-off long-term gains for short-term profits. These charges, while not quite proven, have a strong popular appeal. Courts and legislatures in many states appear to side with the incumbent management fighting to retain control over their firms.

LIST OF TERMS

Arbitrageur	Poison put
Bootstrapping	Pooling of interest accounting
Clayton Act (1914)	Purchase of asset accounting
General cash offer	Shark repellent
Golden parachute	Staggered board
Greenmail	Super majority
Hart-Scott-Rodino Act (1976)	Tender offer
Horizontal merger	Two-tier offer
Pac-man defense	Vertical merger
Poison pills	White knight

EXERCISES

Fill-in Questions

1. A(n) _____ is a friendly company, which steps in to prevent a hostile takeover.

2. Investors who speculate on the likely success of takeover bids are called _____.

3. When a firm, which is the target of a hostile takeover bid, mounts a takeover bid for the hostile raider, it is called the _____ defense.

4. The _____ Act of 1976 requires that the FTC and the Justice department be informed of acquisitions of shares worth $15 million or 15 percent of the company' stock, whichever is less.

5. The _____ Act focuses primarily on acts that tend to lessen competition substantially or create a monopoly.

6. _____ defense tactics include poison pills, super-majority requirements, and staggered board.

7. A(n) _____ merger is one that takes place between two firms in the same line of business; and a(n) _____ merger is one in which the buyer expands forward or backward to the ultimate consumer or the supplier of raw materials.

8. _____ mergers do not create any economic gains and involves two companies with different P/E ratios but similar earnings numbers.

9. _____ gives bondholders the right to sell the bonds back to the company if the management control changes on account of a takeover.

10. A(n) _____ is a general offer made directly to a firm's shareholders to buy their stock at a specified price.

11. When a merger takes place and two firms' separate balance sheets are added, this is called a(n) _____ from an accounting standpoint.

12. When the accounting technique used to give evidence to a merger gives rise to goodwill, it is safe to assume that a(n) _____ method of accounting was used.

13. A (an) _____ is a tender offer, which gives a higher price for shareholders who tender their shares earlier.

14. A _____ is a compensation arrangement, which gives a generous package for managers who have to leave the company because of a takeover.

15. _____ is the term used to describe various contractual and financial arrangements that make a firm a less attractive merger target.

16. When shares held by a raider are bought back by the company at a negotiated price above the current market price, it is called _____.

Problem

Use the data given below to answer questions 1 through 4 independent of the other questions.

1. What are the costs and net present value of the combination of Blue Mountain, Inc., and Red River, Inc., if, as a result of the merger, the gains expected are $400,000 and Blue Mountain, Inc., plans to pay $3 million in cash for Red River?

2. If Blue Mountain acquires Red River for $3 million in cash, how will the shareholders of each make out on the deal?

3. Calculate the apparent and true costs of the merger between Blue Mountain, Inc., and Red River, Inc., assuming expected economies of $400,000 and the shareholders of Red River receive one share of Blue Mountain for every two shares they hold.

4. Show the results of accounting for the merger between Blue Mountain, Inc., and Red River, Inc., using both pooling of assets and purchase of assets methods, where Red River is acquired for $3 million.

Data for problems 1, 2, 3 and 4

	Blue Mountain	Red River
Earnings per share	$4	$2
Price per share	$64	$28
Price-earnings ratio	16	14
Number of shares	200,000	100,000
Total earnings	$800,000	$200,000
Total market value	$12,800,000	$2,800,000

Book values:

	Blue Mountain	Red River
Net working capital	$1.1	$0.4
Net fixed assets	2.8	1.0
Total assets	3.9	1.4
Debt	2.0	0.7
Equity	1.9	0.7
Liabilities and equity	3.9	1.4

5. Data for Pink Ribbons Corp. and Green Valley, Inc. are given below:

	Pink Ribbons	Green Valley
Earnings per share	$4	$1.50
Price per share	$60	$15
Price-earnings ratio	15	10
Number of shares	300,000	300,000
Total earnings	$1,200,000	$450,000
Total market value	$18,000,000	$4,500,000

Pink Ribbons wants to acquire Green Valley for $4.5 million in stock. Green Valley shareholders will receive one share of Pink Ribbons for every 4 shares of Green Valley they hold. There are no economic gains from the merger. Show the bootstrapping effect of the merger.

Essay Questions

1. Explain why buying another company is just like any other investment decision that financial managers make.

2. What are some of the sensible motives for mergers and acquisitions?

417

3. What are the dubious reasons given for mergers?

4. Who gains more from a merger, the selling company or the acquiring one? Explain the reasons why you think one gains more than the other does. Is it possible that neither gains? Explain.

5. Management of some companies contest takeovers. Why do you think this is the case, and what techniques do they employ?

ANSWERS TO EXERCISES

Fill-in Questions

1. White knight
2. Arbitrageurs
3. Pac-man
4. Hart-Scott-Rodino Act
5. Clayton Act
6. Shark repellent
7. Horizontal; vertical
8. Bootstrapping

9. Poison put
10. Tender offer
11. Pooling of interests
12. Purchase of assets
13. Two-tier offer
14. Golden parachute
15. Poison pill
16. Greenmail

Problem

1. Cost = cost – $PV_{\text{Red River}}$
   = $3,000,000 - $2,800,000 = $200,000

   NPV = gain - cost
   = $[PV_{\text{BM+RR}} - (PV_{\text{BM}} + PV_{\text{RR}})]$ - (cash - PV_{RR})
   = $[(12.8 + 2.8 + 0.4) - (12.8 + 2.8)]$ - (3.0 - 2.8)
   = 16 - 15.6 - 0.2
   = 0.4 - 0.2 = 0.200 = $200,000

2. Net gain to acquiring firm = Gain to combination - gain captured by acquired firm
   Blue Mountain's gain = $400,000 - $200,000
   Red River's = $200,000

3. Apparent cost = (number of shares x market price per share) – $PV_{\text{Red River}}$
   = (50,000 X $64)- 2.8 = $3.2 million - $2.8 million
   = $400,000

True cost:

$$x = \frac{\text{new shares issued to Red River's shareholders}}{\text{total shares outstanding after the merger}} = \frac{50,000}{200,000 + 50,000} = 0.20$$

$$\text{True cost} = (x)(PV_{M+RR}) - PV_{Red River} = 0.2 \times 16.0 - 2.8 = 0.4$$
$$= \$400,000$$

4. Purchase of assets vs. Pooling of interest of Blue Mountain, Inc., and Red River, Inc.:

Initial Balance Sheets:

Blue Mountain, Inc

NWC	$1.1	D	$2.0
FA	2.8	E	1.9
	$3.9		$3.9

Red River, Inc.

NWC	$0.4	D	$0.7
FA	1.0	E	0.7
	$1.4		$1.4

Pooling Of Interest
Blue Mountain. Inc.

NWC	$1.5	D	$2.7
FA	3.8	E	2.6
	$5.3		$5.3

Purchase Of Assets
Blue Mountain. Inc.

NWC	$1.5	D	$2.7
FA	3.8		
Goodwill	2.3	E	4.9
	$7.6		$7.6

5. Number of shares used to buy Green Valley
   = value of Green Valley/market price per share of Pink Ribbons
   = $4,500,000/$60 = 75,000 shares

Total shares outstanding after merger = 300,000 + 75,000 = 375,000

Summary of bootstrapping effects of the merger between Blue Mountain, Inc. and Green Valley, Inc. is given below:

	Pink Ribbons (Pre-merger)	Green Valley	Pink Ribbons (Post-merger)
A. Earnings per share	$4.00	$1.50	$4.40
B Price per share	$60	$15.00	$60.00
C. Price-earnings ratio	15	10	13.64
D. Number of shares	300,000	300,000	375,000
E. Total earnings	$1,200,000	$450,000	$1,650,000
F. Total market value	$18,000,000	$4,500,000	$22,500,000
G. Current earnings/dollar	$0.067	$0.10	$0.073

34

Control, Governance, and Financial Architecture

INTRODUCTION

This chapter takes off from the last chapter and looks at issues broader than mergers. Mergers are part of a broader market for corporate control and governance as mergers and acquisitions cause change in corporate control. Corporate control and governance take on special meaning in the U.S. because professional managers of most large corporations are not dominant shareholders of the company. In other words, there is separation between ownership and control. What makes managers work in the best interest of the shareholders? What are the mechanisms, which will ensure that shareholder interests are heeded by the managers when they decide on important investment and financing decisions? How does the U.S. system differ from its counterparts in other industrialized countries? These are some of the questions raised and answered in this chapter.

The chapter starts with simple definitions of some commonly terms used in the discussion; *corporate control* denotes the power to make investment and financing decisions. *Corporate governance* stands for the broader oversight structure of a corporation including the role of board of directors and shareholders' actions to influence corporate decisions through the management. In essence, control is the day-to-day management and governance structure, which ensure that shareholders' interests are kept in mind by the management when it makes important decisions. *Financial architecture* is the financial organization of the whole business; it is partly corporate control and partly corporate governance.

The chapter has four sections. The first section two sections discuss leveraged buyouts (LBO), spin-offs, and other restructuring of corporations as attempts to change corporate control. The well-known RJR-Nabisco buyout of the eighties is described at length to bring out the main lessons from the tale. The following section describes conglomerates and the pros and cons of this corporate phenomenon, which appears to have differing degrees of success in different countries. While they are *not* considered particularly successful and appear headed for extinction in the U.S., they are alive and well in many other countries. The next section compares the governance structures in the U.S., Japan, and Germany and points out the striking differences across these three highly successful industrialized countries. It appears that the governance systems and financial architecture of large industrialized companies have evolved in somewhat different ways in these countries. Each country's history and the evolution and sophistication of its financial markets seem to drive its corporate ownership structure and funding sources. These in turn appear to be the key factors determining the corporate governance.

KEY CONCEPTS IN THE CHAPTER

LBOs, Spin-offs, and Restructuring: An LBO is the acquisition of a company financed by large amounts of debt. Typically, the company is taken private after the LBO. The group, which takes over the company, will usually be a partnership of investors. When the management of the company leads this group it is termed a management buyout (MBO). The chapter describes the RJR-Nabisco story in great detail, which is the largest LBO to date. The company was taken private by the partnership firm, Kohlberg, Kravis, and Roberts (KKR), after an initial bid by a group of managers led by the company's CEO. The RJR-Nabisco LBO is typical in some ways. Leverage was used to the hilt to finance the takeover. The shareholders of the pre-LBO company made huge gains in the market as their stock shot up from about $56 to $109 in just over a month. The new management cut back on waste and inefficiency and the company became lean and mean.

Was the LBO beneficial to all the stakeholders of RJR-Nabisco? The answer is no. Bondholders, in particular, lost as the value of their bonds declined sharply on account of the leveraging of the company. Thus part of the gain for the stockholders came from the loss of the bondholders. However, there were still gains of about $8 billion for the stockholders and most of this could have only come from improved operations and the value created by the LBO.

Leverage and Value: The prime driver of value in LBOs is the leverage. How does leverage create value? Part of the value comes from the tax deductions (see chapter 18). However, this appears to be a fairly small part. The main motive force is the incentives created by leverage. An LBO appears to make a company much more efficient and the managers and employees work harder, as they have to generate cash to service the debt. Typically, managers are also given incentives through ownership of the company. Empirical evidence supports the view that LBOs and MBOs make the companies more efficient and create value and not just transfer wealth from one group of stakeholders to another.

Leveraged Restructurings: The primary source of value in the LBO is leverage. Therefore, it is possible for companies to take on leverage without going through the buyout. The increased debt servicing requirements can make the company's managers strive harder. There are a couple of examples given in the text (Phillips Petroleum and Sealed Air). Leveraged restructuring appears to work well for some companies.

Financial Architecture of LBOs and Leveraged restructuring: As stated before, LBOs, MBOs, and leveraged restructurings are similar. The key components found in all LBOs (and MBOs) are:

- High leverage.
- Incentives for managers.
- Private ownership.

Leveraged restructuring has the first two elements; the restructured company remains a public corporation.

Fusion and Fission in Corporate Finance: Acquisitions and mergers are only one part of the restructuring story. Corporations sometimes go the other way and sell parts or turn them into independent companies or separate corporations with significant outside stock ownership. There are several ways this type of restructuring is done. Here is a brief summary of the main approaches used.

Spin-offs: A spin-off is a new company created out of some assets and operations of an existing company and the shares in the new company are distributed to the parent company's stockholders. A spin-off allows shareholders to invest in one or more parts of the original company without necessarily holding shares in all of the former company. Spin-offs can be tax-free to the shareholders of the parent company as long as the original shareholders are given at least 80 percent of the shares in the new company. Spin-offs can improve incentives for managers and allow them to focus better. If the businesses are independent, the investors can also value them better.

A *carve-out* is similar to a spin-off, but the shares are sold to the public. The parent company, typically, keeps control of the carved out company. A carve out still permits independent valuation and performance evaluation based on the stock market performance of the carved out firm. *Tracking stocks* are stocks tied to the performance of specific divisions. Essentially, this creates separate classes of stocks.

Asset Sales: The simplest way to divest an asset or division, which for some reasons is not performing well, is the outright of sale of the asset to another company interested in buying it. This form of divestiture is very common in manufacturing. Asset sales transfer assets to the firm, which is able to manage it better. Research has shown that asset sales are seen as positive news for the selling firm.

Privatization: There are many government owned companies engaged in all kinds of businesses around the world. This is true not just in the former socialist block countries, but even in the industrialized countries. Airlines and railroads have been government owned companies in many countries. It is generally accepted now that private corporations do the job better and therefore, privatization has become the very popular around the world. Essentially, privatization is the sale of a government owned company to private investors. The main benefits expected from privatization are:
- Increased efficiency.
- Share ownership and participation by employees and small investors.
- Revenue for the government.

The type of privatization varies from country to country. In some cases, the government owned companies are auctioned off to the highest bidders, and in other cases, only a part of the company is sold to investors in a public offering. While most privatizations are like carve-outs, there are also instances, where privatization is accomplished by something similar to a spin-off. This happened in some former Communist countries, where the citizens were given vouchers, which could be used to bid for shares of the privatized companies.

Conglomerates: Conglomerates are companies with many diversified businesses. They were very popular and were the rage in the sixties. This was the time when many American corporations rushed to acquire businesses to diversify and become larger and larger. Some companies had operations in 30 or more different industries. The eighties started seeing the decline and fall of the conglomerates and very few of them remain in the U.S.

The main benefits claimed for this form of corporate expansion are:

- Diversification and reduced risk,
- Better management, and
- Internal capital markets, which will enable channeling, funds to the divisions with best growth opportunities.

It is doubtful if any of these benefits add any real value to the firm. Diversification is of dubious benefit to the shareholder, who can get this at a lower cost directly in the market by buying shares of the companies in different industries. Better management is not the virtue of conglomerates only; in other words, a company can get better management without being part of a conglomerate. Also, internal capital markets are not likely to be better than the real (external) capital market in allocating capital efficiently. Thus, in a country like the U.S. with well functioning capital markets and a mobile pool of managers, the benefits of conglomerates are far less than the costs. The costs include the large bureaucracy, inefficiency, and internal politics. Most conglomerate shares sell at a discount compared to the value of their assets. The eighties and nineties saw the break up of many conglomerates and most of them have disappeared.

In order to be successful, the financial architecture of a conglomerate should be able achieve two managerial tasks. First it has to ensure superior divisional performance through the right incentives and rewards for divisional managers. Second, it should be able to measure performance and operate an efficient internal capital market, which is better than the external capital market in figuring out the right risk-return reward structure for capital allocation. Very few conglomerates have succeeded in getting this done right. The exceptions appear to be the *temporary conglomerates* such as KKR. They are private *limited partnerships*. The general partners manage the business and the limited partners invest most of the funds needed. The general partners look for companies to invest in and give incentives to the managers of individual businesses.

The partnership agreement runs for a limited term, typically ten years or less. The portfolio of companies must be sold and proceeds distributed. The fee structure of the partnership gives the general partners tremendous incentives to produce the best results. In terms of the businesses they buy, the general motto of the successful partnerships is *buy, fix, and sell*. They buy companies, which are poorly managed, fix them, and then sell them. On the other hand, the permanent conglomerates' policy appears to be *buy, manage, and keep.* The latter approach has not worked well.

While conglomerates are a dying breed in the U.S., they appear to have done well in Korea, India, and some Latin American countries. There are factors in these countries, which probably help in their success in these countries. These include:

- Small markets allowing little economies of scale or other advantages of size if the company is focused in one industry.
- Undeveloped capital markets imply that internal capital markets can be better.
- History and tradition.

Overall, it appears that conglomerates can succeed only in markets that are less developed or small. In industrialized countries with well-developed capital markets, they are not likely to have any significant advantage.

Governance Structure in Industrialized Countries: The broad corporate governance structure in the U.S. appears capable of tackling the agency problems and other conflicts of interests created by the separation of ownership and control commonly found in American companies. This governance structure of U.S. companies have evolved around the following key components:

- Right incentives for managers, such as compensation tied to stock price and performance.
- The legal, accounting, and other institutional structure.
- The threat of takeover.

The structures in Germany and Japan are very different, probably because of the very different ownership and institutional structures, which in turn are driven, at least in part, by each country's history and tradition might. The Brealey and Myers text gives examples of typical ownership structures in the two countries. Both countries have governance structures, which have significant internal control through corporate cross holding. The ownership structures are very complex in both countries with layered ownership and large block holding by banks, other financial institutions or corporate partners. The governance structures reflect the complex ownership structures. The outside minority investor does not appear to have a voice and this reflects the limited role for financial markets as a funding source. None of the three components, which are key to corporate performance in the U.S., (listed above) appears to be very important in either country. The Keiretsu structure in Japan, built around a major bank, internalizes all problems. While this may be good for companies, which are financially distressed, this can also keep inefficient operations going on forever.

The structure may be changing in Germany faster than it is in Japan. More and more German corporations are engaging in cross-border acquisitions and mergers and have started to use more external capital market funding. All of these can be expected to bring changes in the corporate control and governance structures.

SUMMARY

This chapter provided an overview of some of the issues relating to corporate control and governance. The LBOs and restructuring, along with mergers and acquisitions, are parts of the market for corporate control. The LBOs and leveraged restructuring often make the corporations more efficient and add value. While some LBOs may fail (and have failed) as part of the corporate process of governance and control, they add strength to the system. Shareholders get better value and the management pays attention to shareholders' interests.

The chapter also described the workings of conglomerates and why they have faded out of the American corporate scene. Conglomerates are being broken up by spin-offs, carve-outs, and restructurings with more incentives for managers. The notion of internal capital markets does not appear to work well for most conglomerates. While the American conglomerate is endangered specie, there are successful conglomerates operating in some countries. The stage of the economy and the capital markets in these countries appear to support the conglomerates better in these countries.

The financial architecture and governance structures in Germany and Japan differ significantly from that of the U.S. and most English speaking countries. The latter have systems based on well functioning financial markets with power to the stockholder, whereas in other countries, the system centers on banks and financial institutions. The international comparisons show different approaches to solving the problem of ensuring that shareholders' interests are taken care of. As cross-border mergers acquisitions increase and corporations seek more funding from capital markets, the systems are likely change rapidly.

LIST OF TERMS

Asset sales	Keiretsu
Carve-out	Leveraged buyout
Conglomerate	Leveraged restructuring
Corporate control	Management buyout
Corporate governance	Privatization
Financial architecture	Spin-off
Hostile takeover	Temporary conglomerate
Internal capital market	Tracking stock

EXERCISES

Fill-in Questions

1. _____ means the power to make investment and financing decisions of the firm.

2. The _____ of a firm is partly corporate control and partly corporate governance.

3. While many acquisitions are friendly mergers, there are also _____ where the target firm is unwilling to merge with the acquiring company.

4. In a _____, part of a company is separated into a new corporation and the shareholders of the parent company receive shares in the new company.

5. When the shares of a new company, created from an existing corporation, are sold to the public, it is usually referred to as a _____.

6. In a(n) _____, a company is acquired by a small group, taken private, and a large part of the acquisition price is debt financed. If this small group includes company's managers, then it is called a(n) _____.

7. _____ is a corporation with many businesses in different, unrelated industries.

8. In a typical conglomerate, the policy is buy, manage, and keep; _____ is characterized by the approach – buy, fix, and sell.

9. _____ is the Japanese network of companies loosely linked by cross holding of stock and usually organized around a major bank.

10. A _____ anticipates a takeover attempt and responds to that by restructuring the company with increased leverage.

11. Many countries around the world are attempting large-scale _____ in the hope of improving efficiency of former government owned companies.

12. Conglomerates often have _____, which seek to enforce the discipline of capital markets on their divisions.

13. Many companies issue a separate class of stock known as _____, which are entitled to earnings from only certain parts of their business.

14. _____ refers to the broad oversight of the corporate management, which ensures that the interests of the shareholders are heeded when important decisions are made.

ESSAY QUESTIONS

1. Explain the main differences in the governance and control structures among the U.S., Japanese, and German corporations. What would you expect to happen to the financial architecture of corporations in these countries over the next decade or so?

2. Are conglomerates successful in the U.S.? Why or Why not?

3. What are the differences between temporary conglomerates and conglomerates? Why are temporary conglomerates more successful?

4. Explain the following terms: i) leveraged restructuring, ii) leverage incentives, and iii) leveraged buyout.

5. Discuss the following statements:

    a. Good managers do not need leverage incentives or LBOs to make them do an excellent job.
    b. The Japanese Keiretsu is a better way of organizing large businesses. They reduce risk and allow managers to work without fear of being taken over by unscrupulous raiders.
    c. The main benefits from leverage in an LBO are the huge tax gains from interest deductions.

ANSWERS TO EXERCISES

Fill-in Questions

1. Corporate control
2. Financial architecture
3. Hostile takeovers
4. Spin-off
5. Carve-out
6. Leveraged buyout; management buyout
7. Conglomerate
8. Temporary conglomerate
9. Keiretsu
10. Leveraged restructuring
11. Privatizations
12. Internal capital markets
13. Tracking stock
14. Corporate governance

35

Conclusion: What We Do and Do Not Know about Finance

INTRODUCTION

This chapter summarizes the extent of our knowledge and the limitations of finance theory, as we know it now. The thirty-four chapters of the Brealey and Myers text and this guide covered the entire landscape of corporate financial management. The concluding chapter does two things: it highlights what we can claim with some certainty as things we know – the most important ideas and concepts of corporate finance; and it also points out the areas where we still are a long way from complete understanding.

We dispense with the format used so far in this guide and simply provide a brief annotated list of what we know and what we don't.

What We Know: The Seven Most Important Ideas in Finance

1. *Net Present Value* (NPV) is the most basic and valuable concept in finance and is the only proper way by which to evaluate assets. The NPV allows thousands of disparate shareholders to have a common corporate goal. This allows the managers to focus on maximizing the net present value without having to worry about individual stockholders' risk preferences or wealth levels.

2. The *Capital Asset Pricing Model* (CAPM) gives a simple, almost elegant way of thinking about risk and return. It tells us that assets have two kinds of risk: risks that you can diversify away and those that you cannot. Only the non-diversifiable or market risks count. Thus, an asset's return is a function of the market risk and the risk premiums are calculated as a direct function of the market risk measure, beta. The CAPM should not be judged by the strong assumptions, but by the results it produces and the ease of its application. We are probably going to see better theories in the future, but they will almost certainly separate risk into diversifiable and non-diversifiable risk. It is also unlikely that we will see a theory with a simpler intuition.

3. *Efficient Capital Markets* imply that security prices reflect information accurately. The three forms of market efficiency (the *weak form, the semi-strong form and the strong form*) give you degrees of efficiency. You will hear a lot of arguments and debates about how well the theory does or does not hold up. One can find any number of stories of investors making millions (or billions, if they are Warren Buffett or George Soros) by exploiting market inefficiencies, but it is good to remember that capital markets are, by and large, efficient.

Inefficiencies (as different from market imperfections, such as taxes and government controls) are the exception, not the rule. There are no money machines, no easy way of becoming the next Soros or Buffett. Competition in capital markets is very tough and financial managers will do well to remember the lessons of market efficiency. While empirical studies have a found a number of statistically significant market anomalies, few, if any, of these anomalies can be exploited to make easy money.

4. *Value Additivity and The Law of Conservation of Value* states the value of the whole is given by the sum of the parts. This implies that mergers and acquisitions do not add value unless the combined firm produces greater cash flows than the sum of what either firm produced when it was independent of the other.

5. *Capital Structure Theory* tells us (courtesy Modigliani and Miller) that in perfect markets, changes in capital structure do not affect value. This also comes from the value additivity principle. It is good to remember that the relevance and value of capital structure comes from deviations from the perfect market assumptions of MM. So, look for reasons why you think your firm has an optimal capital structure.

6. *Option Theory* provides us with a whole new way of thinking about many managerial situations and valuation problems. Remember that in finance, the term *option* refers narrowly to the opportunity to trade (or not to trade) in the future on *terms that are fixed today*. This is quite different from the everyday meaning of options as simply alternatives. Even where we can't justify using the Black-Scholes option valuation formula, the risk-neutral valuation approach may be applied.

7. *Agency Theory* helps us explain why complex contracts and arrangements are needed in many corporate transactions. A business corporation works because there are many men and women working for or with the corporation as managers, employees, lenders, shareholders, and customers. Agency theory gives you the framework to optimize contractual and working arrangements with minimal conflicts of interest among the individuals involved. The conflicts can never be eliminated, but an understanding of the conflicts can help us get the best working results.

These seven ideas are basic and fundamental to corporate finance. A financial manager, who understands these, can do her (his) job better. Of course, you do not get cook book solutions to every problem you are likely to face. Remember, that real life problems can be complex and difficult and solutions, which are simplistic are unlikely to work. The above ideas will certainly steer you in the right direction.

Now that we have listed things we know, we come to the list of things we don't. The list is longer, even though the list in the book does not include everything that belongs in this category.

What We Do Not Know: The 10 Unsolved Problems in Finance

1. *What Determines Project Risk and Net Present Value?* We know that NPV is the way to evaluate projects and that the cash flows should be discounted using risk adjusted discount rates. However, we do not know what makes some assets safer than others. We do not know why some companies earn economic rents and many others do not. We do not have a satisfactory general procedure for estimating project betas.

2. *Risk and Return - What Have We Missed?* CAPM, notwithstanding, our understanding of the risk-return trade-off is incomplete. CAPM is very hard to prove or disapprove, but it cannot explain many of the observed facts on risk and return. Firm size and book-to-market ratios, just to name two, appear to affect returns. Why? There are many other questions which cannot be answered by CAPM or, for that matter, any other theory we have at present.

3. *How Important Are the Exceptions to Efficient Market Theory?* The evidence is fairly convincing that the markets for financial assets, at the minimum, are fairly efficient, but a disquieting set of evidence has emerged in recent years that suggests that they may not be nearly as efficient as we once thought.

4. *Is Management an Off-Balance-Sheet Liability?* If the value added by the management team is less than the cost of maintaining them, then the answer to the question is yes! Many closed-end mutual funds, real estate companies, and even oil companies often sell at prices below what is justified by the assets they have. Also, a change of management often seems to be the tonic needed by some companies.

5. *How Can We Explain the Success of New Securities and New Markets?* An enormous number of new kinds of securities have been created in the last 20 years or so. What is the reason that some fail and some succeed? We do not have a clear idea what kind of financial innovations can succeed in the market.

6. *How Can We Solve the Controversy About Dividend Policy*: The theory and empirical research on dividends provide lots of insights and explanations for almost any position you like to adopt but no resolution of the controversy. More research is needed. But, we cannot be very optimistic that it will suddenly provide a single all-encompassing answer.

7. *What Risks Should A Firm Take?* We know much more about how to hedge than we do about which risks should be hedged and which should not be. Hedging makes sense when it adds to the value of the firm - but when is that?

8. *What Is the Value of Liquidity?* Corporate managers seem to prefer liquidity well above what can be reasonably explained by the current finance theories. We do not have a good theory of liquidity and cannot answer questions like: how much cash should a firm hold?

9. *How Can We Explain Merger Waves?* It is always possible to find reasons why a particular merger occurred, but we cannot explain the aggregate level of mergers or predict specific ones in advance. We do not have a general theory of mergers.

10. *How Can We Explain International Differences in Financial Architecture?* Chapter 34 described the important international differences in the way businesses are organized, fund their assets and generally set up their governance and control structures. Some systems see to work well in certain, but do not do well in others. While national history, tradition and the state of financial markets offer some explanations we do not have a complete understanding of the differences and the rationale for their success or failure under different conditions.

The End

Well, this is it! The end – something you probably have been looking forward to for some time! We are finished with covering corporate finance fairly exhaustively. But, to paraphrase an old cliché – end is beginning, your beginning. Now, go out there and practice what you learned, keeping in mind the ifs and buts. Good luck and all the best.

Complete List of Terms

435